JADE EMPIRE

PRIMA OFFICIAL GAME GUIDE

Prima Games
A Division of Random House, Inc.

3000 Lava Ridge Court
Roseville, CA 95661
(800) 733-3000
www.primagames.com

James Hogwood
David SJ Hodgson

Product Manager: Jill Hinckley
Editors: Kate Abbott, Rebecca Chastain
Copy Editor: Asha Johnson
Layout & Design: Jody Seltzer, Bryan Neff

ISBN: 0-7615-4720-7
Library of Congress Catalog Card Number: 2004107126
Printed in the United States of America

05 06 07 08 LL 10 9 8 7 6 5 4 3 2 1

CONTENTS

ACKNOWLEDGEMENTS

The Unsleeping Scribe would like thank:
At Prima:
David Hodgson the Immortal Strategist, Kate Abbott the Ever-Diligent, Rebecca Chastain the Mistress of Watchfulness, Jill Hinckley the Imperious Commander, Jody Seltzer the Eye of Heaven, Asha Johnson the Incisive Quill
At BioWare:
Guillaume Bourbonniére, Sheldon Carter, Mitchell Fujino, Iain Stevens-Guille, Luke Kristjanson, Bob McCabe, Shauna Perry, Chris Priestly, Jay Turner, Bruce Venne, Stan Woo, Georg Zoeller, Luke Kristjanson
At Microsoft:
William Hodge, Ryan Wilkerson, Chris Esaki, Michael McCormack, Carolyn Gold, Jared Doerr, David Moy, Matt Shimabuku, Jon Grande, Frank Klier, Michelle Lomba, Laura Hamilton, Ian Gantt
Last but not least, special thanks to:
Mischievous Kat, Dreaming Spyder, Thwomp the Slothful
If you love the world of the Jade Empire and would like to know more about the legends and folklore that inspired it, check out the following sources:
The Water Margin or *Outlaws of the Marsh*, translated by Pearl S. Buck
Three Kingdoms, Traditional
Bridge of Birds, by Barry Hugheart
Deer in the Cauldron, by Louis Cha

THE JADE EMPIRE

INTRODUCTION

Stretching from the quiet, rich lands of the Golden Delta to the bustling coastal trade cities of the Prosperous East, the Jade Empire has been a beacon of light and culture for centuries. A number of powerful dynasties have ruled since it was founded under the leadership of Emperor Sagacious Tien, and each has been more glorious than its predecessor. Not that the land is always peaceful, but the current ruler, Emperor Sun, has turned turmoil to harmony in the eyes of his people.

But now, in the idyllic Two Rivers School for the gifted martial arts practitioner, a new pupil's destiny is being written. Under the tutelage of the revered Master Li, this novice has bettered all students and seems ready to embark on a journey through lands of malice and dread. Still, that student is unaware of an epic path about to unfold.

Welcome to the lands of the Jade Empire.

HOW TO USE THIS BOOK

Inside these pages, you will receive enlightenment. Spoiler Alerts are placed before all information of a shocking and revealing nature, but be prepared for exhaustive descriptions of quests, critical choices, and character revelations. So that you can gain the maximum use of this tome, it has been separated into the following chapters:

INTRODUCTION: THE JADE EMPIRE

This is the section of the guide you are currently perusing.

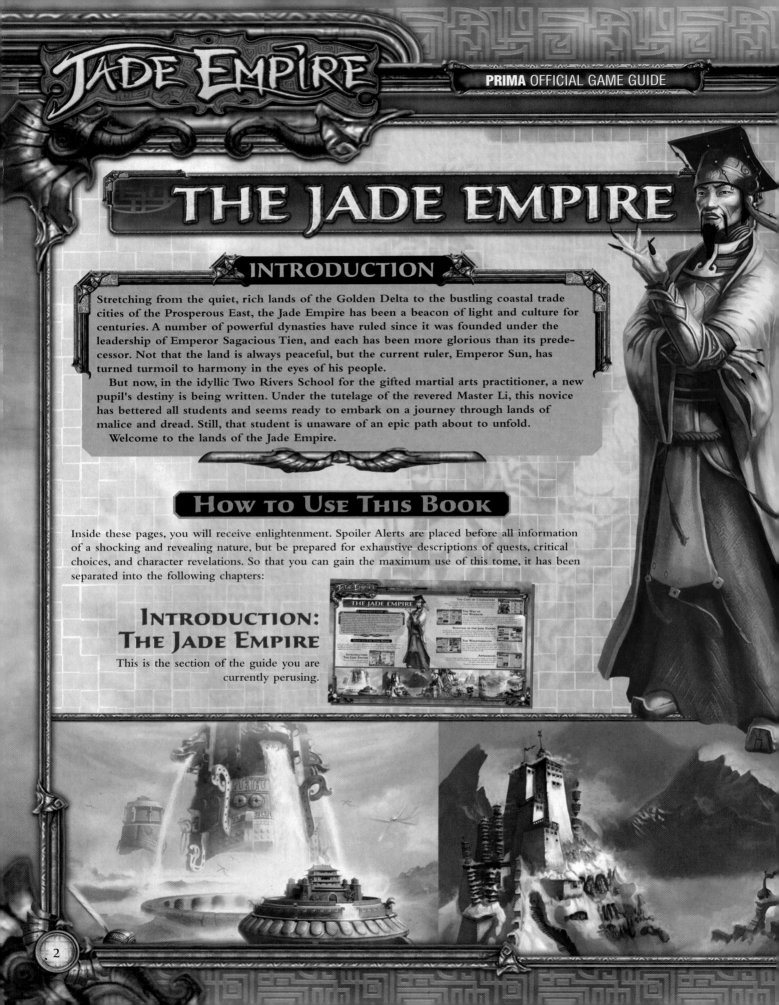

THE CAST OF CHARACTERS

This features information on the seven main characters and a dozen followers, detailing their differences, advantages, weaknesses, biographical information, and other unique facts. In addition, the locations of each of them are shown. Finally, a number of important entities are revealed as well as a Rogues' Gallery of the enemies you face in each chapter.

THE WAY OF THE WARRIOR

This section presents the different methods of defeating the many foes you'll face during the adventure. First, your combat maneuvers are detailed, as well as your avoidance tactics, then every single fighting style available to you is revealed, along with its strengths and weaknesses. The fabled Harmonic Combos are divulged, as are your Followers' options in combat, and fighting of a different kind: in the air, during minigames.

SURVIVAL IN THE JADE EMPIRE

General advice on surviving the wild lands, strange settlements, and odd characters that inhabit the less tranquil areas of the Jade Empire, can be found here. Discover how to receive Chi using your social charms, the Dragon Amulet, explorations, Techniques, and the two Paths open to you: The way of the Open Palm or the Closed Fist.

THE WALKTHROUGH

The bulk of this book concerns the multitude of quests available during your path to destiny. After a comprehensive overview of each area, with clearly labeled maps and an introduction to every single character, the critical path to take is revealed. After this, every side quest is shown, along with all methods of completing each task.

APPENDICES

The final chapter reveals a checklist of every gem, technique, and quest item contained in the lands of your adventure. Sensitive plot revelations concerning inter-party relationships are also revealed.

The path to enlightenment is now open to you....

Jade Empire

THE CAST OF CHARACTERS

THE GIFTED STUDENT

Your adventure begins by choosing one of seven character aspects. You can customize all of them to suit your play style, whether it is combat or Magic-based, molding any character look to any character type.

Lu the Prodigy

Character Type: Balanced
Starting Health: 140
Body: 4
Starting Chi: 130
Spirit: 3
Starting Focus: 130
Mind: 3
Starting Styles: Legendary Strike, Heavenly Wave
Description: While not the fastest or strongest of warriors, the balanced character is the most versatile. The balanced character excels at adapting to exploit his enemies' weaknesses.

Tiger Shen

Character Type: Strong
Starting Health: 150
Body: 5
Starting Chi: 120
Spirit: 2
Starting Focus: 130
Mind: 3
Starting Styles: White Demon, Heavenly Wave
Description: A strong character trades speed and magical aptitude for raw strength and power, enabling him to dish out and withstand much more damage than other warriors.

Wu the Lotus Blossom

Character Type: Balanced
Starting Health: 130
Body: 3
Starting Chi: 140
Spirit: 4
Starting Focus: 130
Mind: 3
Starting Styles: Legendary Strike, Heavenly Wave
Description: While not the fastest or strongest of warriors, the balanced character is the most versatile. The balanced character excels at adapting to exploit his enemies' weaknesses.

Radiant Jen Zi

Character Type: Fast
Starting Health: 120
Body: 2
Starting Chi: 130
Spirit: 3
Starting Focus: 150
Mind: 5
Starting Styles: Thousand Cuts, Heavenly Wave
Description: Fast characters may not be the strongest, but they can maintain Focus in battle longer than others, easily sidestepping strikes and delivering counterattacks with blinding speed.

Furious Ming

Character Type: Fast
Starting Health: 130
Body: 3
Starting Chi: 120
Spirit: 2
Starting Focus: 150
Mind: 5
Starting Styles: Thousand Cuts, Heavenly Wave
Description: Fast characters may not be the strongest, but they can maintain Focus in battle longer than others, easily sidestepping strikes and delivering counterattacks with blinding speed.

Scholar Ling

Character Type: Magic
Starting Health: 120
Body: 2
Starting Chi: 150
Spirit: 5
Starting Focus: 130
Mind: 3
Starting Styles: Leaping Tiger, Heavenly Wave
Description: Though not as physically strong as others, a magical character is the best at channeling their Chi to enhance their physical strikes and fuel powerful elemental magic.

Monk Zeng

Character Type: Magic

Starting Health: 130

Body: 3

Starting Chi: 150

Spirit: 5

Starting Focus: 120

Mind: 2

Starting Styles: Leaping Tiger, Heavenly Wave

Description: Though not as physically strong as others, a magical character is the best at channeling their Chi to enhance their physical strikes and fuel powerful elemental magic.

PARTY FOLLOWERS

Followers are bound to you through fear, affection, or a multitude of other reasons. Expect to encounter, and request the presence of, the following entities. They join your party and can be called upon to assist you in a variety of tasks. Their combat potential is revealed in The Way of the Warrior section. Their locations are shown in the Walkthrough section.

Dawn Star

Description: A demure, trusting, childhood friend. She is more closely tied to events than she realizes.

Age: 20

Gender: Female

Occupation: Student under Master Li. Your closest follower, and a "spirit touched" magically sensitive warrior.

Weight (lbs): 125

Past Traumas: She feels she was abandoned because of her spiritual sensitivities.

IQ: 130

Goals: To honor Master Li and support you, gaining a closeness to you.

Morals: She generally believes in always doing the right thing, but could be influenced into doing bad things for good reasons. A stronger moral counterpart to the princess, and one of the positive guiding influences on the party.

Poignant Memories: Being kidnapped by Gao the Lesser and rescued by you. Discovering the truth about Master Li.

Appearance: Fit and strong, but without a hard edge. Moves with quiet confidence.

Hobbies: Martial arts, magic

Dawn Star (cont'd)

Confidence: A bit unsure of the future, though she is very confident and definite when it comes to short-term goals.

Fears: That the destruction of Two Rivers is just the first of the loves she will lose. Losing you.

Health: Perfect health. Very fit.

Sense of humor: Ready to laugh, but not so ready to tell a joke. Warm.

Family: None she is aware of. Views you like family.

Flaws: Perhaps a bit unsure of her ability, especially when it comes to her magical prowess. Traditional roles are keeping her reserved.

Skills: Good organizational skills. A good diplomat. Powerfully attuned to magic.

Charisma: Likeable. Tries to adjudicate between people so everyone is content. Strong willed.

Speech patterns: A bit formal. She tends to be delicate, and less edgy than many of the other characters, though she is equally capable of taking care of herself. Her strength comes out when arguing.

Sagacious Zu

Description: A monk that has fallen from the correct path out of shame. Still skilled and healthy, but not as consistently trained as he once was. A man that does not want to confront his past.

Age: 40

Gender: Male

Occupation: Ex-Lotus Assassin

Weight (lbs): 170

Past Traumas: Abandoned the Lotus Assassins over innocent blood.

IQ: 125

Goals: To escape the past. He does not want to confront his own morals and prefers to avoid thinking of what the rulers of the Jade Empire have become. Their violation of the order of things troubles him greatly, despite the discord he otherwise embraces.

Morals: Inherently a bad but honorable man. Reluctant to confront the tyrants in power, because that will mean his trusted leaders are wrong and he will have to act.

Poignant Memories: Fighting the Lotus Assassins.

Appearance: Muscular, but not in shape like a disciplined fighter. Jaded and somewhat disheveled. He tries not to care about anything to avoid situations that would force his conscience to act. He is a monk without inner peace.

Sagacious Zu (cont'd)

Hobbies: Reading religious and philosophy texts. Meditation. Trying to come to terms with the past.

Confidence: Considerable self-doubt, but this is dwarfed by his doubt of the hierarchy of the Empire.

Fears: He fears confronting the past and the dishonorable leaders he once followed.

Health: Perfect health

Sense of humor: Gallow humor. Grim at times. No patience for fools.

Family: No family

Flaws: Evil but honorable, which causes a conflict with his masters and in his character. Afraid of admitting to his past.

Skills: Shrewd skeptic

Charisma: Bitter but pragmatic and clear-headed. It is difficult to earn his trust.

Speech patterns: Angry and dark. Suprising tenderness for those he cares for.

The Black Whirlwind

Description: A dim but quick-witted thug that lives to fight, preferably while drunk. He has no cares in the world except where the next battle will occur. He is not malevolent, just single-minded.

Age: 35

Gender: Male

Occupation: Brutish, stupid, drunken warrior

Weight (lbs): 300

Past Traumas: Was removed from the Imperial Army, mercenary groups, bandit group, thieves' guild, Assassin's guild, and martial schools for his drunkenness and violence. He was also a rising champion in the Imperial Arena, which he was expelled from for being a disgrace to the sport.

IQ: 90

Goals: To serve the player like a loyal, but stupid, dog.

Morals: Mean and stupid but loyal to the end. He doesn't care about anyone, including himself, except for the player.

Poignant Memories: Being bested, for the first time in his life, by you in combat. Discovering that he had killed his own brother (the likeable Raging Ox) in an incident that left him running from the Imperial City.

Appearance: Big, hugely muscular with some fat. Unkempt hair and beard, wide features, barbarian-like.

Hobbies: Drinking, swearing, drinking while swearing, and sharpening his axes while either drinking, swearing, or both.

The Black Whirlwind (cont'd)

Confidence: Thinks that he's unbeatable. May be too stupid to have self-doubt.

Fears: None

Health: Perfect health

Sense of humor: Very earthy, low-brow sense of humor. Not subtle; he likes physical comedy and mean/dirty jokes that belittle others. Typical bully sense of humor.

Family: Loves his dear old mother, whom he alternately fears and waxes poetic about. Doesn't talk about his brother, Raging Ox, who died a year ago in Whirlwind's arms.

Flaws: Stupid, drunken, filthy, and mean.

Skills: Very strong. Fearsome fighter.

Charisma: Has no friends other than you. He does, however, bond well with Sky, who enjoys Whirlwind's clarity of purpose and tendency to lose large amounts of silver.

Speech patterns: Loud, boisterous, and stupid, but not monosyllabic. Single-minded, always spoiling for a fight. Doesn't really care with who.

Zin Bu the Magic Abacus

Description: Zin Bu is a celestial bureaucrat charged with keeping track of how much chaos, damage, and destruction you inflict upon the world of the Jade Empire. He is flustered and beside himself...you have caused him a great deal of work. Now, he is leaving his post and taking a demotion to ply a trade in commerce.

Age: Ageless/Appears 50-60

ZIN BU'S MARKET

Zin Bu's "Market in your Pocket" stocks a number of interesting items, and he locates more throughout your adventure. Here's what he has on offer:

Item	Type	Cost	Available
The Path of the Warrior	Improvement	50,000	Chapter 6
The Path of the Monk	Improvement	50,000	Chapter 6
The Path of the Scholar	Improvement	50,000	Chapter 6
Flawless Scholar Gem	Gem	18,125	Chapter 6
Cyclone Gem	Gem	18,750	Chapter 5
Superior Warrior Gem	Gem	9,375	Chapter 5
Superior Monk Gem	Gem	9,375	Chapter 5
Superior Scholar Gem	Gem	9,375	Chapter 5
Warrior of the Unyielding Heart	Improvement	5,625	Chapter 4
Burning Essence	Gem	9,375	Chapter 4
White Demon	Style	12,500	Chapter 3

Zin Bu the Magic Abacus *(cont'd)*

After Completing either Executioner or Inquisitor plot			
Item	Type	Cost	Available
Gem of Unity	Gem	10,125	Chapter 3
The Gilded Tongue	Gem	10,000	Chapter 3
Heavenly Wave	Style	10,000	Chapter 3
Tiger Mantra	Improvement	4,375	Chapter 3
Lightning Gem	Gem	6,250	Chapter 3
Cow Bezoar	Plot Item	625	Chapter 3
Vial of Sulfurous Water	Plot Item	625	Chapter 3
Legendary Strike	Style	7,500	Chapter 2
After Leaving Heaven			
Item	Type	Cost	Available
Leaping Tiger	Style	10,000	Initial
Scholar Gem	Gem	4,750	Initial
Inferior Warrior Gem	Gem	1,875	Initial
Inferior Monk Gem	Gem	1,875	Initial
Inferior Scholar Gem	Gem	1,875	Initial

Henpecked Hou

Description: A cook who's life is ruled by his wife.

Age: 40

Gender: Male

Occupation: Ex-Arena fighter, Ex-drunk, and currently a bunmaster

Weight (lbs): 130

Past Traumas: Hen-pecking wife

IQ: 100

Goals: To keep his wife happy.

Morals: A simple, kind-hearted man. Simple-minded. As such, he acts on the live-and-let-live approach.

Poignant Memories: Marrying his wife

Appearance: Henpecked Hou is a thin-to-the-point-of-being-gangly, bald man with a carefully maintained mustache that shoots past the sides of his face. His normal attire is a cook's casual clothes and a slightly stained apron, coupled with a headwrap designed to keep the sweat from his eyes.

Hobbies: Making buns

Confidence: Confident in the quality of his wine, buns, and service. Never really thinks or talks about anything else.

Fears: Wife

Health: Perfect health

Sense of humor: Laughs at anything because he never wants to offend a customer.

Family: Loves and fears his wife.

Flaws: Wife

Henpecked Hou *(cont'd)*

Skills: Brews the best wine in the Empire.

Charisma: Likeable in a simple way.

Speech patterns: Friendly. A simple working man trying to operate outside of his element.

Wild Flower

Description: An oprhan killed in the flooding of Tien's Landing, Wildflower was resurrected to serve as a host for Chai Ka and Ya Zhen.

Age: 8

Gender: Female

Occupation: Host to celestial creatures

Weight (lbs): 85

Past Traumas: Dying. Rebirth.

IQ: Typical child

Goals: To serve as best she can the forces she doesn't really understand.

Morals: Strong toward duty

Poignant Memories: Learning that she was meant to play host to a celestial creature.

Appearance: Fit and strong, but without a hard edge. Pleasant young girl from a modest home.

Hobbies: None

Confidence: Sure of her purpose, although not sure of where that will take her.

Fears: Failing her purpose

Health: Good

Sense of humor: Endearing

Family: None

Flaws: Trusting

Skills: Host to celestial beings

Charisma: Charming child that does not annoy.

Speech patterns: Plain speech. She was from a simple but educated family.

Chai Ka the Heavenly Gate Guardian

Description: The guardian sent to aid the Spirit Monk meant to face the holder of the Water Dragon's power. Hosted by Wild Flower.

Age: Ageless

Gender: Genderless/Appears Male

Occupation: Guardian

Weight (lbs): Unknown

Past Traumas: Failing in his duty to protect the item he was guarding.

Chai Ka the Heavenly Gate Guardian (cont'd)

IQ: Off the human scale

Goals: To serve the player as is dictated by his role as a Guardian.

Morals: A conscience of sorts, but cannot refuse to do something despite the nature of it.

Poignant Memories: Unknown

Appearance: Towering twice as tall as a human, Chai Ka is a bestial demon who stands on two legs. His upper body is very strong and has long taloned arms. His face is bestial, almost lion-like in appearance, though his coloring is mostly white with darker accents.

Hobbies: Unknown

Confidence: Chai Ka is quietly confident. His comments are pronouncements of fact.

Fears: None

Health: Perfect health

Sense of humor: Virtually undetectable. Chai Ka is amusing once a millennia and he's still upset about the last time.

Family: Denizens of the heavens

Flaws: Unfailing loyalty

Skills: Unknown

Charisma: Imposingly powerful and good.

Speech patterns: Slow, deliberate, and carefully considered words slip from Chai Ka when he bothers to speak. The demon is also very formal.

Ya Zhen

Description: A malevolent demon balancing the good that Chai Ka represents. Always scheming, he cares little for the child he inhabits.

Age: Ageless

Gender: Genderless/ Appears Male

Occupation: Counterpart to Chai Ka

Weight (lbs): Unknown

Past Traumas: Being caged

IQ: Off the human scale

Goals: To achieve dominance within Wild Flower. He is willing to serve if you help him, because humans don't live very long anyway.

Morals: Evil. Conniving, scheming, sarcastic evil.

Ya Zhen (cont'd)

Poignant Memories: None

Appearance: Ya Zhen is a hulking toad demon. He stands twice the height of a human and is incredibly heavy and strong. His body is bipedal, but his head and body features are toad-like.

Hobbies: Scheming

Confidence: Ya Zhen is arrogantly confident. He acts as if he is at the zenith of all matters all the time.

Fears: Being trapped in service for forever, but doesn't believe in forever...so whatever.

Health: Perfect health

Sense of humor: Very, very dry and wry sense of humor. Is often funny because he's so very bluntly honest.

Family: Denizens of the heavens

Flaws: Ya Zhen is overconfident. He's smart but not quite as smart as he fancies himself.

Skills: Unknown

Charisma: Ya Zhen isn't likeable, but he's honest.

Speech patterns: Ya Zhen speaks down to people, and is almost always mildly condescending. He is also very blunt and unlike most demons, he speaks plainly as if he has nothing to hide. If he sounds coercive at all, it's usually because he's making fun of other demons' pathetic attempts to "tempt" humanity.

Sky

Description: Sky dresses in the latest in bandit clothing. Slim of build and athletic to the extreme, Sky is also extremely attractive, in a roguish sort of way.

Age: 25

Gender: Male

Occupation: Clever confidence man, thief

Weight (lbs): 145

Past Traumas: His young daughter was enslaved and murdered by a local merchant lord, and Sky is bent on revenge when you first meet him.

IQ: 120

Goals: To serve those who avenged his daughter. To be the number-one confidence man in the world. To make you fall in love with him.

Morals: Easy going, friendly, open liar. A con man, but one guided by morals. Loyal to you, to a point.

Poignant Memories: Finding and burying his murdered daughter's body. Leaving a trail of broken hearts and broken bodies as he sought revenge for her death.

Sky (cont'd)

Appearance: Short, lithe, happy, and friendly. Acrobatic.

Hobbies: Confidence schemes, fleecing novice gamblers, hitting on women.

Confidence: Rightfully believes himself to be a brilliant trickster. Is self-deprecating about any other subjects.

Fears: Sky is angry inside, and fears that one day his rage at Gao will break free.

Health: Perfect health

Sense of humor: Flippant, charming, and witty, like the classic swashbuckler whose tongue is as sharp as his sword.

Family: Dearly loved his daughter who is now dead. His wife is long gone, and he has made his peace regarding her.

Flaws: His flamboyant manner covers up his rage at losing his daughter. A simmering pot under the surface.

Skills: Schemer and fast talker. Very clever.

Charisma: Everyone likes him. It's why he's so good at ripping them off. It's important to note that most people refuse to believe that he was the thief.

Speech patterns: Friendly and slick, snappy. Charming. He is a roguish character but likable.

Kang the Mad: Local Eccentric/Inventor

Description: The inventor who created the Marvelous Dragonfly and other flying machines. Touched by madness, he is more than he seems.

Age: Unknown/Appears 40–60

Gender: Male

Occupation: Mad Scientist

Weight (lbs): 125

Past Traumas: Many, many explosions

IQ: Too erratic for standardized testing

Goals: To build clever devices with minimal loss of life.

Morals: No one's quite sure. "What, you want morals? I can build sixteen of those. If only I had the springs. Hmm, springs of pure water...bottled and sold for silver! Genius! Now I just need a pump...."

Poignant Memories: The thrill of discovery. Minute by minute.

Appearance: Weird by any standards

Kang the Mad: Local Eccentric/Inventor (cont'd)

Hobbies: Kang dabbles in the brewing and distilling of rotgut. "What? You want to drink that? Hoo-kay, but it's not easy on the stomach...or the legs, once it eats down that far...."

Confidence: He knows that he is the most clever inventor that has ever lived. It isn't bravado.

Fears: That he'll meet someone more clever than himself.

Health: Unknown, he seems fine

Sense of humor: Weird. People, however, find him extremely humorous.

Family: Unknown

Flaws: He seems barely aware of the level of danger his inventions cause to other people.

Skills: Incredible imagination that he can turn into reality.

Charisma: Most people find him weird and unsettling.

Speech patterns: Strange, excitable, mumbles to himself a lot. Steady stream of ideas. He will cut out of a line to clarify a thought for himself.

Princess Lian The Heavenly Lily (full name: Princess Sun Lian, also known as Silk Fox)

Description: Very proper when in her princess garb, but with a knowing wink. As Silk Fox she commands respect, but she will earn it if need be.

Age: 22

Gender: Female

Occupation: Elegant young princess, clandestine assassin

Weight (lbs): 110

Past Traumas: Her father is evil and, while at first she doesn't believe it, she is beginning to realize it.

IQ: 125

Goals: To spark romance. To stop her father's evil plans (even though she still loves him). To redeem her father.

Morals: The princess is ultimately a good person, but she is easily tempted. She is the more likely to understand your rationale when you perform an evil act (compared to Dawn Star), and eventually supporting such acts is more likely.

Poignant Memories: Taking on her alter ego, Silk Fox, and fighting in the wilds of the Empire. Helping you infiltrate the Lotus Assassin fortress in the Imperial City.

Appearance (Princess): Gorgeous, womanly, elegantly dressed. A radiant princess.

Appearance (Silk Fox): She is a black-garbed warrior. Still gorgeous, but with much more of an edge.

Hobbies: Shopping, manipulating the system, martial arts.

Confidence: Confident in her attractiveness and her skills. A sexy but strong female.

Princess Lian The Heavenly Lily (full name: Princess Sun Lian, also known as Silk Fox) *(cont'd)*

Fears: Death's Hand and his power over her father.

Health: Perfect health

Sense of humor: Mildly "naughty" humor. Teases people a lot.

Family: Known: Sun Hai, father. Unknown: Sun Kin/Death's Hand, uncle; Sun Li, uncle; possibly others.

Flaws: Her overconfidence leads her to think she can manipulate everyone she meets. Acts a bit brazen, but she is truly frightened inside.

Skills: Quick thinker, good at getting people to do what she wants.

Charisma: Most people are attracted to either her beauty or her strength.

Speech patterns: Well-educated but coy. More open and affectionate once she knows a person.

Abbot Song

Description: Abbot Song was once the head of the Spirit Monks. He was killed during the attack on the monastery 20 years earlier. Though he is extremely wise and benevolent, he has slowly been tiring in his spirit form. Twenty years of fighting the growing evil near Dirge, with no sign of a change, has taken its toll.

Age: 55 at time of death

Gender: Male

Occupation: Abbot

Weight (lbs): 155

Past Traumas: He was killed trying to rescue you during the attack on Dirge and the Spirit Monk.

IQ: 140

Goals: Restore Dirge and the Spirit Monks

Morals: Very high standards. Lives by the code of the Spirit Monks.

Poignant Memories: None

Appearance: Old, dead Spirit Monk

Hobbies: Unknown

Confidence: High, but a bit shaken

Fears: The corruption infesting Dirge.

Health: Dead

Sense of humor: Unknown

Family: None

Flaws: Crippling self-doubt after the fall of Dirge.

Skills: Unknown

Charisma: Somewhat likeable.

Speech patterns: Helpful but concerned. Grows more familiar and optimistic as you progress.

Death's Hand (or Prince Sun Kin the Hand of Heaven, also known as Prince Kin)

Description: A juggernaut of destruction. Calm, measured. Utterly unflappable. Authoritative. He is the enforcer of all the Emperor's desires.

Age: 50

Gender: Male

Occupation: The will of the Emperor

Weight (lbs): 180

Past Traumas: Formerly the impressionable Prince Sun Kin. A failed coup attempt during the fall of Dirge left him at the Emperor's mercy. Corrupted utterly by the Water Dragon's stolen power.

IQ: 150

Goals: To serve the Emperor's will and crush all opposition in the Empire. No personal goals, as he is completely a servant of the Emperor's will.

Morals: Corrupted by a pact with dark forces, more demon than man now. Completely sociopathic and lacking any qualms about killing anyone who stands in his way. Loyal only to the power behind the Emperor.

Poignant Memories: Being abandoned when the coup attempt failed. Being bound to the armor he now wears, trapped in his role as the will of the Emperor. Learning to revel in the destruction he causes.

Appearance: His corrupted flesh is forever hidden behind the battle armor he is bound to.

Hobbies: Enforcing the will of the Emperor. Controlling through fear with his Lotus Assassins.

Confidence: Never doubts anything that he does. His ego has been crushed beneath the stolen power of the Water Dragon for 20 years.

Fears: Nothing. He has no will beyond the influence of whoever holds the Water Dragon's power.

Health: Immeasurable. The power of a god sustains him.

Sense of humor: A twisted sense of humor: he gets his amusement in bullying and intimidating those weaker than he is; particularly messy executions where the victim suffers are also a source of amusement.

Family: While he was once Prince Sun Kin of the royal family, Death's Hand is so corrupted he is barely human anymore.

Flaws: Incapable of defying his master.

Skills: Unearthy martial artist, leader of the Lotus Assassins. Kills with ease.

Charisma: Unappealing to all. A dark threatening figure who uses fear to communicate.

Speech patterns: Cold, loud, commanding, evil.

Other Characters of Note and Trepidation

Whether to aid in harmony or discord, the following souls cross your path as you progress through the lands of the Jade Empire. Please note that these, and all other characters, are shown during the Walkthrough of this guide.

Hui the Brave (also known as Mistress Hui)

Description: A soldier that served with the greatest minds of the Imperial Army.

Age: 40

Gender: Female

Occupation: Loyal servant, tracker

Weight (lbs): 135

Past Traumas: The events at the fall of the Dirge.

IQ: 130

Goals: To protect the citizens and support you.

Morals: Strong, good woman who believes in protecting the innocent and punishing the wicked.

Poignant Memories: The fallout after the fall of the Dirge and the destruction of the Spirit Monks. The actions of the Emperor and how he has corrupted the Empire.

Appearance: Serious, experienced female warrior

Hobbies: Martial arts

Confidence: Unwavering, but growing weary.

Fears: Death's Hand

Health: Good

Sense of humor: She is like a loving but serious aunt and laughs only rarely.

Family: None

Flaws: She is very thoughtful but is blinded by loyalty and lost opportunity.

Skills: She imparts a very exotic and tactical fighting style.

Charisma: She is a good leader and a respectable woman.

Speech patterns: A bit motherly, quick to anger, and equally quick to calm back down.

Water Dragon

Description: The mournful victim, the eternal shepherd of the dead. A great creature suffering under the yoke of those who have stepped above their station.

Age: Eternal

Gender: Genderless/Appears Female

Water Dragon (cont'd)

Occupation: Keeper of the Gates of the Dead in the normal world. Shepherd of the Dead.

Weight (lbs): Unknown

Past Traumas: Was kidnapped and cut open by the Emperor to serve as an eternal source of pure water for the Empire. She has been in torment since.

IQ: Off the human scale

Goals: To free herself and get the cycle of life and death back on track.

Morals: A force of nature who exists only to bring balance to the world. Must be freed in order to do so.

Poignant Memories: Unknown

Appearance: Huge serpentine dragon with a wise, benevolent face. Occasionally appears as a human female, draped in light blue robes.

Hobbies: Unknown

Confidence: Worried for the future, but still certain that destiny will unfold as it should.

Fears: Fears for the fate of the Empire. No personal fears.

Health: Cannot die but in great pain at all times.

Sense of humor: Above such trivialities

Family: Denizens of the heavens

Flaws: Trusting in the order of things, certain that destiny can only unfold in the way it must.

Skills: Unknown

Charisma: Very charismatic, but disoriented from the pain, so she is somewhat confusing when you first meet her.

Speech patterns: Like a god, but caring and reaching for understanding. Above the concerns of others but knowing she must raise them up.

Inquisitor Lim (also known as Assassin Lim)

Description: Assassin Lim is a higher-up in the order of Lotus Assassins. A thoughtful, careful planner, Lim is tough and cold. He knows that failure equals death, but he is determined to win and will never stop fighting.

Age: 39

Gender: Male

Occupation: Senior Lotus Assassin

Weight (lbs): Unknown

Inquisitor Lim
(also known as Assassin Lim) (cont'd)

Past Traumas: Unknown

IQ: Unknown

Goals: Power. He wants to supplant Mistress Jia.

Morals: Strictly adheres to the tenets of the order of Lotus Assassins.

Poignant Memories: Unknown

Appearance: Lotus Assassin

Hobbies: Assassination

Confidence: Confident but careful

Fears: Unknown

Health: Reasonably healthy

Sense of humor: Unknown

Family: None

Flaws: Unknown

Skills: Unknown

Charisma: A little. He is a Lotus Assassin, so he is creepy and scary to those around him. You wouldn't invite him over for dinner, but when he speaks, you listen.

Speech patterns: Refined evil

Grand Inquisitor Jia
(also known as Mistress Jia)

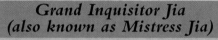

Description: Lotus Assassin Lieutenant. Vicious and cunning. She lies in wait for you in the Lotus Assassin fortress and was responsible for overseeing the attack on Two Rivers.

Age: 40–45

Gender: Female

Occupation: Assassin

Weight (lbs): 130

Past Traumas: Was reshaped from a peaceful monk into a heartless Assassin.

IQ: 150

Goals: To gain powerful influence in the new Empire under the god Emperor Sun. To serve Death's Hand's will.

Morals: Seduced by power, she obeys only the will of the Emperor through Death's Hand.

Poignant Memories: None

Appearance: Dignified assassin in Lotus Assassin robes. Harsh and severe looking.

Hobbies: Killing, oppression

Confidence: Very confident. She considers himself to be unequivocally on the winning team.

Grand Inquisitor Jia
(also known as Mistress Jia) (cont'd)

Fears: Fear of being perceived as weak or powerless

Health: Perfect

Sense of humor: None

Family: Unknown

Flaws: Egotistical and arrogant. She believes herself to be much smarter than everyone else and believes that serving Death's Hand will lead her to power.

Skills: Intimidating as the evil wizard

Charisma: Powerful and dominant voice

Speech patterns: Cold. Authoritative. She rules a feared group of Assassins that are devoutly loyal to Death's Hand.

Emperor Sun (full name: Emperor Sun Hai)

Description: His body is withered and worn, but he presents himself through an image of his younger self. Haughty, ruler of all he surveys. All others are to kneel before him.

Age: 75 but is immortal and looks 45

Gender: Male

Occupation: Emperor of the Jade Empire

Weight (lbs): 160

Past Traumas: Wasteful and arrogant as a youth, he threw away the kingdom's money on epic ego projects and made the evil decision to kidnap the Water Dragon to cure a drought. Been on the path of discord ever since.

IQ: 180

Goals: To become the immortal Emperor of the Middle Kingdom and to create an immortal army of golems infused with the enslaved spirits of the dead to crush all opposition. Rules with an iron fist and is immortal as long as he keeps the heart of the Water Dragon.

Morals: Has fallen completely to the path of discord. Arrogant, selfish, megalomaniacal. He will do anything to anyone, including killing his own brothers, to further his goals.

Poignant Memories: Cutting out the heart of the Water Dragon and becoming immortal. The treacherous action of his brother at the fall of Dirge after the destruction of the Spirit Monks.

Appearance: Larger than life, opulent, pure power. Huge crown/hat, golden clothes, looks much younger than his age due to being immortal.

Hobbies: Black magic

Confidence: Painfully arrogant

Fears: Losing his absolute grip on power.

Health: Perfect health

Emperor Sun
(full name: Emperor Sun Hai) *(cont'd)*

Sense of humor: None

Family: Princess Sun Lian, daughter; Death's Hand/Sun Kin, enslaved brother. He will speak the name of no other.

Flaws: Utter and complete arrogance.

Skills: Born leader, tightly controlled. Immortal.

Charisma: There is a cult of personality built around the Emperor. All those who crave power appreciate him.

Speech patterns: Callous, serpent-like. His power makes him arrogant. All others are beneath him.

Master Li (full name: Sun Li the Glorious Strategist)

Description: The current master of the Two Rivers School, he was once known as Sun Li the Glorious Strategist.

Age: 65

Gender: Male

Occupation: Martial Arts Master, formerly the Grand General of the Imperial Army

Weight (lbs): 160

Past Traumas: Failing to oppose his brother at the fall of Dirge.

IQ: 200

Goals: To raise and train you. You were orphaned by the actions of the army he commanded, and he sees you as key to circumventing the power of the Emperor. He plans for every possible known variable.

Morals: He will sacrifice anything for the glory of the Empire.

Poignant Memories: Fleeing the wrath of his brother. Finding you.

Appearance: Wise, well-lined face. Very fit for his age. Commanding.

Hobbies: Martial arts and study of philosophy. Military strategy.

Confidence: Very confident. A born leader.

Fears: The Empire falling to chaos.

Health: Perfect health for his age.

Sense of humor: Analytical of everything. Would acknowledge a joke to set people at ease, but it is a tool only.

Family: Emperor Sun Hai, brother; Sun Lian, niece; Death's Hand/Sun Kin, brother.

Flaws: His only flaw is that he considers his strategy absolute.

Skills: Flawless martial ability. Born leader and strategist.

Charisma: Everyone likes Master Li, but he is a strict master.

Speech patterns: Calm, serious, commanding. Always in control.

THE BESTIARY

In which the creatures, threatening entities, and animals of the Jade Empire are revealed, along with the chapter of your adventure that they inhabit. Entities you only face once, larger "boss" characters, and friendly or neutral characters, are revealed in the Walkthrough section. Non-human enemies can be grouped into four types: ogres, demons, spirits, and golems. Each type is completely immune to certain styles and attacks (except Transformation styles: no enemy can resist attacks in this category):

ENEMY IMMUNITES AND VULNERABILITIES

Enemy Type	Immunities	Vulnerabilities
Ogre	Support Styles, Tempest, Stone Immortal, Knock-back	Martial Styles, Weapon Styles, Dire Flame, Ice Shard, Transformation Styles
Demon	Support Styles, Magic Styles	Martial Styles, Weapon Styles, Transformation Styles
Spirit	Support Styles, Weapon Styles	Martial Styles, Magic Styles, Transformation Styles
Golem	Support Styles, Magic Styles, Martial Styles, Knock-back	Weapon Styles, Transformation Styles

Critters

Lapdog

Monkey

Pig

Goat

Small creatures are found throughout the Jade Empire. If you are pure Closed Fist, you can slay these animals; they often yield orbs.

Crane

CHAPTER ONE: ROGUES' GALLERY

Bandits & Outlaws

Most are untrained, but a few of them carry spears or swords. They are fought in Two Rivers and in the aptly named Bandit Swamp.

Mercenries

Mercenaries are bands of fighting men who sell their might to the highest bidder. As trained professionals, most mercenaries usually have at least a spear or other weapon style at their disposal.

Ogres

Unaffected by support styles, Tempest, or Stone Immortal. Too big to knock down with area attacks, they always carry massive iron clubs. Look for them in the Swamp Cave.

Toad Demon

The only one in this chapter has standard demon immunities and inflicts poisoning. He is very slow-moving and can't evade, so attack from his blind spot (in the back).

Ghosts

Ghosts use all types of styles (except transformations), including weapons, but commonly favor Ice Shard. These have the standard ghost immunities and are found in the Spirit Cave and on the beach at Two Rivers.

CHAPTER TWO: ROGUES' GALLERY

Pirates

Better equipped and trained than simple bandits, they usually carry weapons, and many of them use Storm Dragon. Their most common fighting styles are Iron Palm and White Demon. The pirate base swarms with them.

Imperial Soldiers

Found in the Ruins and Dam Site, they almost always carry weapons.

Lotus Assassins

Located in the Ruins and the Dam Site, they utilize magic and weaponry, but they suffer against Harmonic Combos.

Conscripts

Clad in tattered clothing and fighting under duress, Conscripts are encountered on the way to Tien's Landing. They are no match for you.

Guards and Thugs

There are a number of guards in Tien's Landing, usually around the Dockhouse. Crush them with Harmonic Combos.

Ogres

Aside from Zhong in the Tea House, a white-haired Ogre with a nasty club lumbers around the workshop area in the pirate base. Leap around, strike, then retreat.

Sailors

Without water deep enough for their boats to leave Tien's Landing, a number of sailors are up to no good in this area. Once again, Harmonic Combos deal with them.

Slavers

Despicable pirate slavers are moving their wares throughout the pirate base.

Teahouse Rowdies

These ne'erdowells are causing calamity in the previously serene tea rooms; if you're forced to deal with them, employ ham or table pieces for comedic, but brutal, effect.

Lost Spirits

These are floating masked spirits in tattered robes. They infest the Great Forest and have standard ghost immunities. They fire energy projectiles that arc slightly to home in on you and can even damage you in demon form. They can't be permanently destroyed; they reappear to attack again if you leave the area and return.

Lesser Cannibals

Once human, cannibals are deformed ghouls twisted by their demonic matron, the Mother. They have standard demon immunities. Small and weak, they attack in huge swarms. Found in Pilgrim's Rest and the Cannibal Caves. All lesser cannibals use simple claw attacks.

Greater Cannibals

More human-looking than the lesser cannibals, these use magic styles. Often accompany a swarm of lesser cannibals. They have standard demon immunities.

Rat Demons

Smallest of the infernal breed, they are fairly agile, but not powerful. Found in the Ruins, Pirate Base, and Cannibal Caves. They have standard demon immunities.

Horse Demons

A larger and much tougher form of demon. Found in the Pirate Base. Their flaming manes damage you when you touch them. They attack with trampling hooves and fireballs. Area attack causes spikes to thrust out of the ground. They have standard demon immunities.

Elephant Demons

Found guarding Gao's Treasury and as the Forest Shadow's bodyguard, they are slow but incredibly strong. They emit an area attack that resembles Stone Immortal. They have standard demon immunities. They cannot evade.

Fox Spirits

Found in Heaven, Fox Spirits use a fighting style that resembles Leaping Tiger: quick claw rakes with good range. They have standard demon immunities. They seem to all be female, and have a certain feral elegance. Their area attack resembles Hidden Fist.

Ghosts

The ghosts in the Great Forest tend to use Dire Flame more often than others. Otherwise, they are the same as above.

Toad Demons

Found in Heaven. See previous *Toad Demon* entry for complete information.

Golems

The only two golems in this chapter guard the Jade Heart of the Great Dam. You don't have to fight them if you know the password. They have standard golem immunities, so use weapons and transformations on them. All golems wield stone axes that inflict severe wounds. They move very slowly and cannot evade.

CHAPTER THREE: ROGUES' GALLERY

Mummies

Found in the Necropolis, mummies are slow and inflict Disease with every touch (similar to Poisoning). Unlike spirits and other undead, mummies have no immunities.

Ghosts

Found in Necropolis and Lotus Assassin fortress, many Necropolis ghosts are poor civilians with no combat training and are easy to disperse.

Lost Spirits

They constantly attack you as you explore the Necropolis. See previous *Lost Spirits* entry for complete information.

Lotus Assassins and Assassin Guild Members

Deadly masters of the martial arts, they often use Viper style, which poisons you (even if you're transformed), but they can use just about any style except transformations. Use Harmonic Combos to defeat them. Lotus Acolytes are similar, but they sometimes have nothing but Basic style to use.

Imperial Soldiers and Guards

These are similar to Lotus Assassins, but they are more likely to use weapons than Magic or Support styles. They are found in Scholar's Garden, and some arena combats feature them.

Black Leopard Students

Distinguished by their use of multiple styles, but they mainly focus on Hidden Fist. They seldom use weapons, and are found in Black Leopard School.

Ogres, Students, Lesser Cannibals, Greater Cannibals, Toad Demons, Elephant Demons

You fight them all during your battle to become champion of the arena.

Clay Golems and Jade Golems

Found in the Lotus Assassin fortress, where they are fairly numerous (it is a Golem Factory, after all). Jade Golems are bigger and much stronger; otherwise see previous *Golems* entry for complete information.

CHAPTER FOUR: ROGUES' GALLERY

Lotus Assassins

There are hordes of them here, and they are very tough to slay. Almost all use both Viper and Sword styles. See previous *Lotus Assassins* entry for complete information.

Imperial Soldiers and Guards

They also use Viper and Sword styles, while some in the Palace area use Twin Hammers, a rare style. See previous *Imperial Soldiers and Guards* entry for complete information.

CHAPTER FIVE: ROGUES' GALLERY

Lost Spirits

There are a number of these on the Spirit Plain and in Dirge itself. They often appear at a great distance here, making it tough to get close without being struck by their energy bolts. See previous *Lost Spirit* entry for complete information.

Rat Demons

These employ the same scratching techniques as the rat demons in the Ruins and Quarry, and you can deal with them in the same manner.

Horse Demons

Fearsome flaming manes and projectiles aside, horse demons only appear in ones and twos during this chapter; see previous entry for complete information.

Red Ministers

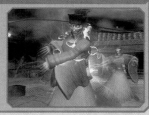

Two fearsome red ministers, and another guarding a gem, arrive to thwart your progress. Dispatch them, one at a time, usually from range or using a Transformation.

CHAPTER SIX: ROGUES' GALLERY

Horse Demons

These horse demons arrive in seemingly endless waves, but you can either destroy the Disturbances through which they appear or defeat their ancient leader to defeat them.

Imperial Soldier Ghosts

Apparitions of fallen warriors, they attempt to waylay you as you try to return to your team. Harmonic Combos work well here.

Imperial Soldiers

Available during the bridge battle, these warriors are cut down with Dawn Star and Silk Fox's blades.

Jade Golem

The Black Whirlwind must hack apart the towering jade golem before he can secure the courtyard. Well-timed axe strikes will do the trick.

Lotus Assassins and Acolytes

These Assassins back up the jade golem with their limitless numbers. Slay them with brutal axe strikes after the jade golem falls.

CHAPTER SEVEN: ROGUES' GALLERY

Lotus Assassins and Acolytes

Well versed in all manner of martial arts, but with added magical delivery courtesy of conjurers. Deal with those aiming ranged attacks at you first.

Constructs

Gigantic stone constructs of the demonic foes you've met on your travels. Defeat them as you would an elephant demon.

THE CREATION OF THE JADE EMPIRE

BioWare Corp. spent months crafting histories, backgrounds, organizations, rulers, and characters for this game. Notes regarding these game elements are presented over the next four pages, and give a glimpse at how the early Jade Empire was perceived to be.

CAUTION
SPOILER ALERT
The following information may not be accurate to the final world of the Jade Empire, and is presented as a "behind the scenes" look at the creative process of the game. However, some parts are still sensitive to plot revelations in the game.

JADE EMPIRE HISTORY

Blood Dynasty
The third dynasty; an age of battles and bitter wars that spanned centuries; the time in which the current boundaries of the Empire were set.

Dragon Dynasty
The first dynasty of the Jade Empire; an age of mythical heroes and wars with the animal spirits.

Hidden Dynasty
The second dynasty; a mysterious age in which demons ruled the land.

Lao Tsi
Ancient philosopher and scholar whose work serves as the foundation for Jade Empire culture and civilization.

Lotus Dynasty
The fifth (and current) dynasty; a time during which the power of the Empire was strengthened and consolidated.

Mad Emperor Zian
Insane emperor who sent the army after women and children to slake his bloodlust.

Sagacious Tien
The first emperor of the Jade Empire.

Star Dynasty
The fourth dynasty, a cultural renaissance during which much of today's technology and culture were created or refined.

LOCATIONS

Bandit Swamp

The swamp that leads to the cave to which Dawn Star flees; where you meet Sagacious Zu.

Dirge

Home of the Spirit Monks almost eliminated by the Emperor's attack 20 years ago.

Dirge Temple

Temple in Dirge where you face Death's Hand's spirit.

Emperor's Gate
The gate through the wall to the preserve of land around the palace.

Ghost Cities
Cities left deserted in the Great Desert when that land's water table dried up.

Glass Ocean
Eastern Ocean of the world of Jade Empire.

High Desert Plains
A snowcapped mountain range in the Great Desert that supports some farming and herding.

Kwan's Tea House

The teahouse in Tien's Landing.

Little Goat River
A great river in the Hills of the Six Holy Scrolls that flows from the snow-capped mountains to a frigid lake in the lowlands.

Lord Lao's Wondrous Furnace
A place in heaven where Lord Lao's mysterious contraption is kept.

Mysterious East
Land of barbarians known only through legends.

Ocean of Tempus
Western Ocean of the world of Jade Empire.

Phoenix Gate
Far-off trading center, viewed as the center of many odd customs.

Pilgrim's Rest Inn
Inn controlled by the cannibals in the forest.

Pirate Base

The lair of the pirates in Chapter Two.

Temple Peaks

The sites of temples in the Hills of the Six Holy Scrolls; Six of these house the writings of Lao Tsi, the father of Jade Empire civilization.

The Imperial Arena

The arena in the Imperial City.

The Artisans' Quarter

A noisy, busy neighborhood full of bustle and activity, where workshops stand in untidy rows on cramped, winding streets that surge with activity day and night.

The Barbarian Isles

In the Plain of Barren Hope, a land of subarctic climate where live barbarians with facial hair, light skin, and a guttural language.

The Cataclysm

The Western pole, a geyser of boiling water and poisonous gasses.

The Dam Site

The site of the dam that was opened, revealing the ruins of the old town of Tien's Landing.

The Dragon Font

A font of pure water in the Imperial plaza; powered by the heart of the Water Dragon.

The Great Southern Forest

The strange and foreboding world where the Cannibal Inn is located.

The Golden Delta

The rich heartland of the Jade Empire, and home to its poorest denizens.

The Grandfather River

One of the two large rivers in the Jade Kingdom.

The Great Desert

A blasted wasteland north of the Jade Empire, home only to hermits and a few nomadic tribes, and the astrologers who maintain the remote Star Sign Citadel.

The Heart of the Empire Tavern

Tavern in the Imperial City in which the arena is located.

The Heavenly Map

The inner district in the seat of heaven where the nobles' houses must maintain a miniature representation of the Empire as a whole.

The Hills of the Six Holy Scrolls

The spiritual heart of the Jade Empire, and the birthplace of its most precious ideals of life, death, duty, and civilization.

The Imperial Academy

School where officers in the Imperial military are trained.

The Imperial City

The center of the Emperor's power and of commerce within the Empire.

The Imperial Sky Bridge

An ambitious project begun by the Emperor, this bridge will eventually connect every notable settlement in the kingdom to every other.

The Wall

Structure that once surrounded the young Jade Empire. Each emperor has added to the wall in some way during his reign.

The Golden Way

The walled inner city is the provenance, headquarters, and exclusive playground of the aristocracy.

The Island of Enlightenment

An oasis of civilization on the high seas, and one of the few allies of the Jade Empire in the known world.

The Forest Shadow's Heaven

Home of the Forest Shadow.

The Land of Howling Spirits

An inhospitable region of sheer mountains and frigid lakes to the west of the Jade Empire.

The Lotus Assassin Fortress

Fortress of the Lotus Assassins in Chapter Three.

The Market District

The common district in the Imperial City.

The Mysterious East

The land far to the east of the Jade Empire, known only via myths and legends.

The Necropolis

The graveyard where the Lotus Assassin fortress is located.

The Northern Wastes

The northern region of the Plain of Barren Hope, where arable land disappears in red dust.

The Outer Wall Slums

The poorest and most chaotic section of the capital.

The Palace Catacombs

Catacombs beneath the Imperial Palace where lie the tombs of past emperors. One of the tombs has been carved out to make room for the Water Dragon's body.

The Palace of the Emperor

The Emperor's ornate and floating palace.

The Plain of Barren Hope

Vast grasslands that house the savage horse lords. Over the past few decades, this fierce warrior tribe has increasingly come into conflict with the Jade Empire along the latter's northern border.

The Prosperous East

The economic jewel of the kingdom: The center of both manufacturing and trade, and a beacon of ingenuity and invention in an age of ignorance.

The Quarry

The cave system overrun by ghosts of men drowned when the dam was closed.

The Realm of the Monkey King

A jungle-realm to the south of the Empire; home to a race of monkey people and the vine-covered ruins of an ancient civilization.

The Ruins

The ruins of old Tien's Landing, recently revealed by the opening of the dam.

The Scholars' Garden

District in the Imperial City where scholars gather to debate.

The Seat of Heaven

A district that makes up a third of the Empire; the seat of political power and the font of Imperial authority, as well as home to the Empire's noble families.

The Seven Auspicious Trees

Trees believed planted by Sagacious Tien himself; the oldest living things in the Empire.

The Silkworm River

One of the two large rivers in the Jade Kingdom.

The Spirit Cave

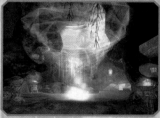

The cave where your first test is to occur.

The Star Sign Citadel

An observatory in the Great Desert known for its perfect placement; much astrological study is performed here.

The Undertow

The Eastern pole; a vast whirlpool that swirls around a frozen airless point.

Three Stone Bay

A safe harbor for the Phoenix Gate's merchant and fishing fleets.

Tien's Landing

A small trading town near the Great Southern Forest. Situated at the headwaters of the Silkworm River.

Two Rivers

A small town on the borderlands of the Jade Empire, where Master Li's Two Rivers School lies.

Two Rivers School

Master Li's martial arts school, where you are raised and trained.

JADE EMPIRE RELIGION

Mother of the Plough

Along with the Princess of Silk, one of the goddesses of agriculture.

Princess of Silk

Along with the Mother of the Plough, one of the goddesses of agriculture.

The Animal Princess

The spirits of the animals, serving under the Heavenly Sage.

The August Personage

The leader of the Celestial Bureaucracy; the moon is his exiled concubine; the August Personage of the First Origin.

The Celestial Bureaucracy

The pantheon of gods whom the people of the Jade Empire worship.

The Celestial Court

The court of the gods, the center of which is the sun.

The Celestial Dragon

The being who created the world in the beginning and set heaven and the planes in place before settling into his throne in the night sky.

The Five Elements

The elements of shamanism and one of the few ideas from shamanism to survive the rise of the worship of the Celestial Bureaucracy: wood, water, fire, metal, earth.

The Four Ministers

The ministers of the North, South, East, and West; assistants to the August Personage.

The Great Wheel

The mystical circle of reincarnation; The Fire Dragon controls where on the Golden Wheel each dead soul returns to life.

The Heavenly Sage

Assistant to the August Personage.

The Moon Concubine

The exiled concubine of the August Personage and the mother of the stars.

The Sixty Messengers

In shamanism, the will of the Three Forces made material.

The Star Daughters

The daughters of the moon concubine and the August Personage.

The Ten Thousand Spirits

In shamanism, the essences of all living things in the world.

The Three Auspicious Portents

Astrological omens (comets, eclipses, stars) taken seriously by scholars in the Jade Empire.

The Three Forces

In shamanism, the immaterial laws that govern the world.

JADE EMPIRE CULTURE

Council of Generals

Group of generals in the Imperial City that indirectly oversees remote army outposts.

Gongshi

An art form consisting of stone worked to be pleasing to the eye according to its shape, color, and significance.

Penjing

The art of breeding and growing miniature trees to create small landscapes; similar to Japanese bonsai.

Lotus Assassins

An order of monks twisted by Death's Hand into assassins.

Spirit Monks

Servants of the Water Dragon.

The Artisans' Guild

The guild of artisans, represented in the Imperial Court and exempt from many taxes.

The Guild

An organized group of criminals, thieves, assassins, and crime lords who hold sway over the seedier parts of the Empire. The Imperial Arena and the pirates' lair near Tien's Landing are connected to the Guild.

The Imperial Army

The fighting force of the Empire, run by the Minister of War, who is typically the eldest son of the Emperor.

The Imperial Court

The cluster of society centered around the Emperor and the Empire's noble families.

The Imperial Family

A family believed descended from the first man and from which the Emperor ascends.

The Ling Family

One of the two most powerful noble families in the Imperial Court; viewed as upstarts, the Ling family controls much of the silk and rice trades and has more money than the Imperial treasury.

The Nine Ministries

The ministries of War, Star Signs, Harmony, Treasury, Rice, Silk, Culture, Records, and Health; the only sources of authority outside the Emperor.

The Scholars' Guild

The guild of scholars, represented in the Imperial Court and exempt from many taxes.

The Shu Family

One of the two most powerful noble families in the Imperial Court; the mother of Princess Sun Lian is from the Shu family.

Jade Empire

THE WAY OF THE WARRIOR

Many inhabitants of the Jade Empire seek fulfillment in different ways, but none are more inscrutable than those choosing the way of the warrior. Practitioners of the martial arts and other more arcane styles of combat endure countless months of guidance and training (usually under a venerable master) and you are no different, although your skills are exemplary. This section reveals the many styles you can master, and discusses combat in general.

THE BASICS OF COMBAT

When you engage in combat, you must follow these two basic tenets: To switch moves within a style (vary your strikes), and to switch styles (flick between your styles).

The following buttons are used during combat. Where appropriate, the visual representations of the following moves are shown using Leaping Tiger style, although they are appropriate to almost every other combat type.

BASIC COMBAT MANEUVERS

Fast Attack

Button: Ⓐ
Button Type: Single press
(Chainable)
Speed: Fast
Damage: Medium
Effect: Push-back
Attack Arc: Forward
Blockable: Yes

Notes: The fast attack is both interruptible and blockable, and it's sometimes preferable to the combo if you aren't out to knock your enemy back or give him time to recover. Picking at a foe has its uses, but this move is easily blocked. Defend by blocking or dodging.

Fast Attack Combination

Button: Ⓐ, Ⓐ, Ⓐ
Button Type: Rapid press
Speed: Slow
Damage: Compounded
Effect: Push-back
Attack Arc: Forward
Blockable: Yes

Notes: Although a quick tap of Ⓐ three times results in a series of quick strikes, you should vary your hits to two or four taps depending on the style or proximity of the target. These are fast attacks, chained together. You can stop short of completing a combo, and catch an enemy with two quick hits, then repeat this in a series of pummels your foe cannot react to. With practice this becomes an impressive method of foe disposal. Unfortunately, if you are attempting a regular combo, these are interruptible and can be slow to recover from. Be sure you check your Magic styles, as even some of these have fast attack combinations!

Power Attack

Button: Ⓧ
Button Type: Single press
Speed: Slow
Damage: High
Effect: Knock back or special ability
Attack Arc: Forward
Blockable: No

Notes: Interruptible and unblockable, all the Harmonic Combos are completed using the power attack. With a slow charge time, this strike leaves you susceptible to all manner of attacks as your power builds to deliver it, so plan this move carefully or use Focus. If you are using a power attack with a Magic or Transformation Style, prepare for some unusual effects! Martial- and Weapon-style power attacks are more mundane, but they have the bonus of plowing through blocks and knocking a foe back (unless it is large). To defeat a power attack, interrupt it, dodge it, or transform into a creature immune from the hit.

Area Attack

Button: Ⓐ + Ⓧ
Button Type: Single press
Speed: Medium
Damage: Low
Effect: Knock back or group debilitation
Attack Arc: 360 degrees
Blockable: Yes

Notes: With the advantage of being uninterruptible (i.e., if you are struck, your area attack isn't spoiled), but blockable, this is still the finest method of dealing with multiple incoming enemies at once. When you are outnumbered or cornered, it gives you time to adjust. This affects all non-blocking enemies in the attack's range; which depends on your style. Weapon and Martial styles have a quick area attack that send enemies flying backward from the impact, but inflict almost no damage. Magic and Support area attacks are spectacular and usually incapacitate the enemy somewhat, but they're very slow. Beware of being overly evasive; if you are leaping about, area attacks will defeat you every time. Instead, patiently press Ⓑ and remain stationary. Area attacks are very entertaining to use against the swarming enemies with little health.

Block

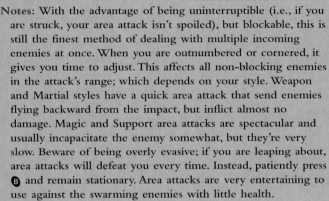

Button: Ⓑ
Button Type: Hold
Speed: Instant
Damage: None
Effect: Negates all attacks except power attacks
Attack Arc: 360 degrees
Blockable: N/A

Notes: Employ this defensive posture, and an amber shield appears to protect you in all directions. However, you cannot attack during this time. It blocks fast and area attacks but not power attacks. These are easy to spot coming, so react early and avoid them. One method is to "block bait." Wait for an enemy to begin a power attack in response to your block, then quickly evade to the side and pummel the foe (ideally with a three-hit Chi-charged combo, or a power attack with Focus mode on)! This is effective even against fast Magic-style attacks, not only Martial styles. Finally, you automatically face a targeted enemy when blocking, allowing you to spin around without moving the analog stick. This is especially useful when using a ponderous Transformation style such as Toad Demon or Jade Golem.

Evade (Forward)

Button: Ⓑ + ↑ or Forward
Button Type: Single press
Speed: N/A
Damage: None
Effect: Maneuver 4.5 meters long; staggers opponents in path
Attack Arc: Forward
Blockable: Yes, blocked evades cause evader to be staggered.

Evade (Back)

Button: Ⓑ + ↓ or Back
Button Type: Single press
Speed: N/A
Damage: None
Effect: Flip back 2 meters; staggers opponents in path
Attack Arc: Rear
Blockable: Yes, blocked evades cause evader to be staggered

Evade (Left)

Button: Ⓑ + ← or Left
Button Type: Single press
Speed: N/A
Damage: None
Effect: Rolls left 4 meters; staggers opponents in path
Attack Arc: Left
Blockable: Yes, blocked evades cause evader to be staggered

Evade (Right)

Button: Ⓑ + → or Right
Button Type: Single press
Speed: N/A
Damage: None
Effect: Rolls right 4 meters; staggers opponents in path
Attack Arc: Right
Blockable: Yes, blocked evades cause evader to be staggered

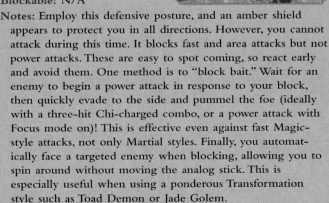

Evade (Right) *(cont'd)*

Notes: Evading (or dodging) with the analog stick and Ⓑ is uninterruptible and blockable. Use this when you want to leap, roll, or tumble; basically, moving while blocking. You can use these quick evades to interrupt a foe's attack, or to trip him up slightly, halting any attack. No damage is caused, however. This becomes incredibly useful when you realize you can leap over foes and attack them from behind; this is the easiest way to tackle demonic adversaries. This is the only defense against power attacks, but not area attacks, as they flatten you while you're darting about. Evasion moves are relative to the targeted enemy:

Toward an enemy = high leap over
Away from an enemy = short somersault back
Perpendicular to enemy = side roll

PUTTING IT ALL TOGETHER: COUNTER MEASURES

Study and learn the following diagram, as it shows you the fundamentals of combat in the lands of the Jade Empire. Revealed are the moves that counter other moves, and this is the core of the tactical relationships of battle.

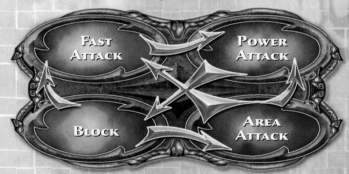

The following visuals illustrate the countering system in action:

The Fast Attack

This counters a power attack but is countered by an area attack and a block.

The Power Attack

This counters a block but is countered by a fast attack and an area attack.

The Area Attack

This counters a fast attack and a power attack but is countered by a block.

The Block

This counters a fast attack and an area attack but is countered by a power attack.

OTHER COMBAT TECHNIQUES

You should now have grasped the overall principles of basic fighting in Jade Empire. Now we shall endeavor to teach additional combat abilities.

Chi Strike

Button: Ⓑ🄻🄺
Button Type: Toggle
Effect: Player starts expending Chi for every move successfully executed to inflict extra damage. Individual effects are on a style-by-style basis.

Notes: Employ this concentration of Chi when you attack. Press Ⓑ🄻🄺 again to toggle it off and on. Your fists and limbs glow blue, and extra damage is added to each hit, whether the style is Martial, Support, Transformation, Weapon, or Magic. The Chi Strike upgrades for each style increase both the Chi cost and the additional damage done for each Chi-enhanced attack in that style.

TIP

*Start the Chi Strike as combat begins, and keep it running as you attack; you lose Chi only as you strike, and not when preparing to strike or moving around to a combat position. Also try Chi Strikes with quick Support attacks, such as Storm Dragon, to inflict far more impressive damage than normal; this is the **only** way to inflict direct damage with Support styles.*

Chi Heal

Button: ⊞ᵂᴴᵀ

Button Type: Hold

Effect: Player regains Health over time as Chi is expended over time.

Notes: You *must* learn how to Chi Heal to transfer energy from your Chi reserves into your Health. Chi Heal can be used both in and out of combat, but it's most useful during a fight, after you've been wounded. A white glow surrounds you as you Chi Heal, and you cannot attack or block during this process, so back or flip away from danger, or tap ⊞ᵂᴴᵀ quickly for small, fast increases that don't leave you exposed. Note that some Transformation styles that are immune to Magic (such as Toad Demon) do not let you heal while you are in the guise of a demon.

Targeting (Counterclockwise)

Button: Ⓛ

Button Type: Single press

Effect: Selects the next counterclockwise target within the targeting range of the style.

Targeting (Clockwise)

Button: Ⓡ

Button Type: Single press

Effect: Selects the next clockwise target within the targeting range of the style.

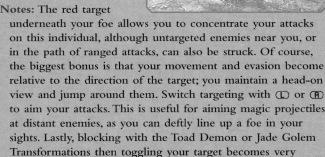

Notes: The red target underneath your foe allows you to concentrate your attacks on this individual, although untargeted enemies near you, or in the path of ranged attacks, can also be struck. Of course, the biggest bonus is that your movement and evasion become relative to the direction of the target; you maintain a head-on view and jump around them. Switch targeting with Ⓛ or Ⓡ to aim your attacks. This is useful for aiming magic projectiles at distant enemies, as you can deftly line up a foe in your sights. Lastly, blocking with the Toad Demon or Jade Golem Transformations then toggling your target becomes very useful, as the Demon instantly locates the foe rather than lumbering around.

Free Target

Button: Ⓛ + Ⓡ

Button Type: Toggle

Effect: Enters a combat mode where no target is selected. No automatic orientation occurs.

Notes: Pressing both buttons together removes the targeting reticle and allows you to freely maneuver in combat, as you would when not engaged in battle. You must manually aim your attacks for them to strike. This is useful for running circles around large or slow enemies, retreating completely out of combat, or moving to a vantage point without continuously looking at an enemy. Manually striking adversaries is more of a hit-or-miss affair (literally) than targeted striking, so only those with the required combat experience or skill should attempt such maneuvers. Free Target mode allows you to dismantle objects to trigger explosions and release orbs; this is one of the only ways to smash scenery you normally cannot aim at. You can also evade (block roll) into scenery and smash it while in targeting mode.

Focus Mode

Button: Ⓨ

Button Type: Toggle

Effect: Player enters Focus mode.

Focus mode (combat)

Focus mode (dashing)

Notes: Your powers of concentration are so in tune with your surroundings that you are able to process tactics at a far faster rate than normal, effectively slowing time. When you activate Focus mode, you gain additional speed. Focus drains away quickly (especially if you are using Weapon styles at the same time), so use it only in short bursts. Focus mode is incredibly useful, and it allows you to strike down bewildered enemies with amazing speed before they can react (and sometimes while they are finishing a strike against you!). Use Focus mode to help complete Harmonic Combos in combat and to run faster in Exploration mode.

TIP

Use Focus mode only when it is advantageous, and do not waste it! Use it to launch an attack or maneuver away from danger, but don't keep Focus mode employed after an attack has connected, or once you are in position. Short bursts are the preferred tactic here.

FIGHTING STYLES

Now that you've learned the basics of combat, it's time to move on to the specific styles themselves. Some styles are unique to the character you have chosen, while others are learned during your adventure. The styles available to you are located in the following areas:

STYLE LOCATIONS

The following information shows the earliest possible locations for each style. *Onward* indicates that the style is available from Zin Bu anytime after he becomes a Follower. *Specific area* indicates the exact location where you obtain the style.

MARTIAL ARTS STYLES

Drunken Master

LOCATION
Chapter Two (onward): Forest, learn from Follower Henpecked Hou.

Legendary Strike

LOCATION
Chapter One: starting.
Chapter Two (onward): from Zin Bu.

Chapter Two (specific area): Forest, from Spear Catches Leaf.

Thousand Cuts

LOCATION
Chapter One: starting.
Chapter Three (specific area):

Imperial Arena, from Sweet Poison Lyn.

Leaping Tiger

LOCATION
Chapter One: starting.
Chapter Two (onward): from Zin Bu.

Chapter Two (specific area): Darting Lynx, Tien's Landing.

White Demon

LOCATION
Chapter One: starting.
Chapter Three (onward):

Zin Bu, after Lotus Executioner quest complete.

SUPPORT STYLES

Storm Dragon

LOCATION
Chapter Two (specific area): Forest, Spear Catches Leaf.

Heavenly Wave

LOCATION
Chapter One: starting.
Chapter Three (onward).

Paralyzing Palm

LOCATION
Chapter Three (specific area): Black Lotus School, Master Radiant.

Hidden Fist

LOCATION
Chapter Three (specific area): Black Lotus School, Master Smiling Hawk.

Spirit Thief

LOCATION

Chapter Two (specific area): Hui the Brave, outside Tea House, Tien's Landing.

⚔ WEAPON STYLES

Longsword "Fortune's Favorite"

LOCATION

Chapter One (specific area): Gujin the weapon master.

Longsword "Dragon Sword" (Artifact)

LOCATION

Chapter Three (specific area): Faceless Blacksmith (Tseng).

Dual Axes "Tang's Vengeance"

LOCATION

Chapter Three (specific area): Imperial Arena, defeat the Ravager.

Double Saber "Crimson Tears" (Artifact)

LOCATION

Chapter Three (specific area): Imperial Arena, Crimson Khana (inform her of the poisoning plot, then defeat her).

Double Saber "Eyes of the Dragon"

LOCATION

Chapter Three (specific area): Defeat Crimson Khana.

Staff "Golden Star"

LOCATION

Chapter One (specific area): Gujin the weapon master.

Staff "Flawless" (Artifact)

LOCATION

Chapter Three (specific area): Faceless Blacksmith (Tseng).

Staff "Tien's Justice"

LOCATION

Chapter One (specific area): Gujin the weapon master (limited edition game only).

Mirabelle

LOCATION

Chapter Three (specific area): Scholars' Garden (Outlander side quest).

Improvised Ham

LOCATION

Chapter Two (specific area): Tea House, Tien's Landing.

Improvised Table Legs

LOCATION

Chapter Two (specific area): Tea House, Tien's Landing.

☯ MAGIC STYLES

Dire Flame

LOCATION

Chapter One (specific area): Spirit Cave, Water Dragon.

Chapter Three (specific area): Merchant Kia Jong, Lotus Assassin fortress.

Ice Shard

LOCATION
Chapter One (specific area): Spirit Cave, Water Dragon.

Chapter Three (specific area): Acolyte Trainer Guang, Lotus Assassin fortress.

Stone Immortal

LOCATION
Chapter Two (specific area): Tien's Landing, Mistress Vo, Open Palm only.

Tempest

LOCATION
Chapter Two (specific area): Tien's Landing, Master Jian the Iron Fist, Closed Fist only.

TRANSFORMATION STYLES

Toad Demon

LOCATION
Chapter One (specific area): Swamp Cave (after facing a toad demon).

Horse Demon

LOCATION
Chapter Two (specific area): Heaven, (after facing a horse demon).

Red Minister

LOCATION
Chapter Five (specific area): side quest (after defeating the Red Minister).

Jade Golem

LOCATION
Chapter Three (specific area): Lotus Assassin fortress (after defeating the Jade Golems).

MARTIAL STYLES

The crux of a warrior's repertoire, the Martial style allows the practitioner to inflict a series of channeled attacks using only the power of the body and the mind. Usually striking at close range, they do not need Chi to power them (indeed, martial arts are used when more Chi-sapping styles have depleted your energies), although you can do extra damage by applying Chi Strike. Martial styles are the most versatile, as they are effective against every enemy type except golems. Every character (whether following the Open Palm or Closed Fist) can learn all the Martial styles, with their trademark fast area attacks and ability to complete Harmonic Combos.

Drunken Master

Fast Attack: Drunken Rage

Damage: ~30 per hit

Power Attack: Collapse
Damage: 60

Area Attack: Scramble

Speed: Fast

Overview: Pick up Hou's wine jugs to activate the Drunken Master style. This series of moves mimics inebriation but its strikes are actually extremely powerful and meant to distract foes. This style does much more damage than other Martial styles, but it is available for only a short time once activated and is non-upgradeable. Picking up more wine jugs extends the duration of Drunken Master style.

Stance (Idle)

Additional: This style can complete a Harmonic Combo.

Advantages: The strongest Martial style. An area attack with a long duration.

Disadvantages: Not upgradeable. Only lasts for a short amount of time. Only occurring with Henpecked Hou as your Follower (meaning other Follower benefits are not available).

Swig down these casks to perfect Drunken Mastery.

Legendary Strike

Fast Attack: Three rapid kicks   **Damage:** ~10 per hit

Power Attack: Spin Kick   **Area Attack:**
Damage: 30   Foot Sweeps (2)

Speed: Fast

Overview: Many in the Jade Empire have heard of Legendary Strike, but few have actually seen it in action. Fewer still have mastered this Martial style, but those who have are to be feared—their blows rain down too fast to block, and their kicks can quickly put an opponent out for good.

Stance (Idle)

Additional: This style can complete a Harmonic Combo.

Advantages: This is the most balanced Martial style; it is reasonable in all circumstances and against most enemies. Single fast attacks, without employing a combo, can be more effective than the combo itself. Finish the three-hit combo and the enemy is pushed back. Tap Ⓐ without combo completion and the enemy remains close and you can still intercept his attacks most of the time. Should the enemy block, use the strong attack. A good one-on-one strategy.

Disadvantages: The least visually impressive of the Martial styles. Balanced, therefore not strong in any one area.

Thousand Cuts

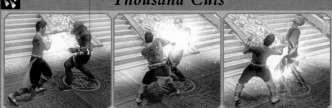

Fast Attack: Fast Arm Strikes (6)   **Damage:** ~7 per hit

Thousand Cuts (cont'd)

Power Attack: Flurry of Blows   **Area Attack:**
Damage: ~32   Foot Sweeps (2)

Speed: Fast

Overview: Thousand Cuts is aptly named, though the style does not involve blades. A master of this style relies on numerous light strikes in quick succession instead of singular punishing blows or thunderous kicks. Most opponents reel under such a relentless assault, unable to counter fast enough to find an opening for their own attacks.

Stance (Idle)

Additional: This style can complete a Harmonic Combo.

Advantages: It is the fastest of the Martial styles. Excellent for melee combat. When upgrading, maximize your Chi Strike level completely first; this adds considerably to the attack's effectiveness. You can strike an enemy four times with one combo. You can chain normal attacks after you finish a strong attack. Before you complete the strong attack, but after it is launched, keep pressing Ⓐ to land more strikes; you can hit the enemy before he has a chance to block. This works in most circumstances.

Disadvantages: It is also the weakest style and has very short range. The strong attack has a long delay. Harmonic Combos are difficult to complete due to this delay, unless you resort to Focus mode. It is unwise to use the strong attack in a one-on-one fight, as the delay leaves you open to attack. Instead, block and when the foe strikes, the fast attack is quick enough to interrupt him. Enemy demons or those carrying spears with large area attacks are deadly against a Thousand Cuts practitioner. It is dangerous to use Thousand Cuts against enemies with damage shields (such as horse demons and Grand Inquisitor Jia), because the strong attack consists of several fast, separate attacks, and thus you take damage when each attack hits.

Leaping Tiger

Fast Attack: Punches (2), Flip Kick   **Damage:** ~10 per hit

Leaping Tiger (cont'd)

Power Attack: Leaping Strike

Damage: 20

Area Attack:

Spin Kicks (2)

Speed: Fast

Stance (Idle)

Overview: With the vigor and speed of the animal for which this Martial style was named, Leaping Tiger dazzles onlookers even as it carves up opponents. Practitioners of this Martial style focus so completely on the strength and quickness of the tiger that razor-sharp claws seem to sprout from their fists. The style's quick, leaping techniques and punishing strikes create a flurry of death that can keep even armed opponents at bay.

Additional: This style can complete a Harmonic Combo.

Advantages: It's the Martial style with the longest reach, and it's quite fast. Single fast attacks, without employing a combo, can be more effective than the combo itself. Finish the three-hit combo and the enemy is pushed back. Tap Ⓐ without combo completion and the enemy remains close and you can still intercept his attacks most of the time. Should the enemy block, use the strong attack. It's a good one-on-one strategy, and preferred to other attacks where this exploit can be used, as you can trap an enemy in a cycle of interruptions if you time attacks correctly.

Disadvantages: There are no major disadvantages to employing this style.

White Demon

Fast Attack: Slow Kicks (3)   Damage: ~20 per hit

White Demon (cont'd)

Power Attack: Arm Strike

Damage: 30

Area Attack:

Single Arm Sweep

Speed: Slow

Stance (Idle)

Overview: Many martial artists criticize the White Demon style for being slow and ponderous, but in the hands of a true master it can be one of the deadliest Martial styles of all. While it lacks the crowd-pleasing panache of faster styles, White Demon's sheer power and intimidating techniques plow through opponents like an ogre in a tea house.

Additional: This style can complete a Harmonic Combo.

Advantages: It's the most damaging Martial style that can be upgraded. Speed up the strikes by spending Style Points or employing Focus mode. It's very strong and easy to use, and it defeats enemies quickly and very effectively. Many practitioners believe this to be the best of the Martial styles.

Disadvantages: It's slow and easily overlooked, as the techniques are not as crowd-pleasing to view as those of other styles—do not make that mistake!

SUPPORT STYLES

Support styles are named for the assistance they grant to fighters. Some see these styles as not incredibly useful, because many enemies are immune to support styles (for example, the poison a toad demon inflicts is more potent as it affects all types of enemies). The specific debilitating effects are wondrous to behold, but they cause no actual damage without Chi Strike support. Fast attacks have only slight effects, except when you combine them with Chi Strikes; this can lead to formidable damage. Execute a power attack in any of these styles to begin a Harmonic Combo. Area attacks are slow but devastating against groups, as the debilitation usually affects all within its blast radius. Use it as enemies close in on you. Every character (whether following the Open Palm or Closed Fist) can learn all Support styles with the exception of Hidden Fist and Paralyzing Palm, which are mutually exclusive.

Storm Dragon

Fast Attack: Slow Kicks (3)   Damage: Special (Shocked)

Power Attack:
Double Arm Strike
Damage: Special (Shocked)

Area Attack:
Electrocution

Speed: Slow

Overview: The forms and strikes of Storm Dragon enable the master to call upon the power of lightning to damage an opponent. While this style's attacks don't cause any direct damage, its motions summon forth electricity to course through its victim, doing small but constant damage over time. Storm Dragon will rarely win a fight on its own, but combined with other styles it can easily change the tide of a difficult battle.

Stance (Idle)

Additional: Does direct damage in Chi Strike mode. This style can initiate a Harmonic Combo that produces a Focus power-up, even when area attack is employed.

Advantages: This style lets you shock your enemies with electricity, making them vulnerable to attacks for a medium time and interrupting their moves.

Disadvantages: Slow, no real damage caused, and not always useful unless employed with Chi Strikes.

Heavenly Wave

Fast Attack: Punch Kick Mix   Damage: Special (Slowed)

Heavenly Wave (cont'd)

Power Attack:
Forward Cone Cast
Damage: Special (Slowed)

Area Attack:
Arms Out Cast

Speed: Slow

Overview: Fighters skilled in Heavenly Wave learn techniques that can slow their opponents to a crawl. While this Support style does no damage on its own, a master can manipulate the Chi in the area around opponents, rendering them sluggish and easily defeated. Even the most lightning-fast foes can be slowed to a turtle's pace with the skillful application of Heavenly Wave.

Stance (Idle)

Additional: Does direct damage in Chi Strike mode. This style can initiate a Harmonic Combo that produces a Health power-up.

Advantages: This style lets you slow your enemies down, making them vulnerable to attacks for a longer time. Combine this slowdown with your Focus mode to create a temporary situation where the enemies are almost stationary. The final strike in the fast attack combination lands low to the ground, making it useful to slow or damage prone enemies before they rise.

Disadvantages: Slow, no real damage caused, and not always useful unless employed with Chi Strikes.

Paralyzing Palm

Fast Attack: Slow Arm Strikes (3)   Damage: Special (Paralyzed)

Power Attack:
Slow Arm Strikes (2)
Damage: Special (Paralyzed)

Area Attack:
Arms Out Cast

Paralyzing Palm (cont'd)

Stance (Idle)

Speed: Very Slow

Overview: This esoteric style has a sinister reputation, but many more peaceful masters prefer it for its ability to render an opponent helpless without killing him. More unscrupulous masters take advantage of this style's paralyzing blows to weaken foes for the killing blow. It is designed around its magical palm strikes, which can stop a man in his tracks with a single hit.

Additional: Does direct damage in Chi Strike mode. This style can initiate a Harmonic Combo.

Advantages: This style lets you paralyze enemies, making them extremely vulnerable to attacks for a short time. The Harmonic Combos it sets up are also among the fastest to complete.

Disadvantages: Slow (even for a Support style), no real damage caused, and not very useful unless employed with Chi Strikes.

Hidden Fist

Fast Attack: Fast Arm Strikes (3)   **Damage:** Special (Disoriented)

Power Attack: Dust Cloud   **Area Attack:**
Damage: Special (Disoriented)   Earth Pound

Speed: Fast

Overview: Warriors willing to tread a darker path learn that a confused mind is a weakened one. This infamous Support style is a collection of techniques that render the practitioner's foe disoriented and unable to fight back. A master of Hidden Fist is not above using dirty tricks and forbidden strikes to serve the goal of total domination.

Stance (Idle)

Hidden Fist (cont'd)

Additional: Does direct damage in Chi Strike mode. This style can initiate a Harmonic Combo that produces a Chi power-up, even when area attack is employed.

Advantages: This style disorients enemies, essentially making them helpless against attacks. This is an ideal method of starting a Harmonic Combo, because it drops a Chi orb, arguably the most useful. The area attack is also reasonably quick.

Disadvantages: Slow (although not as slow as other Support styles), no real damage caused, and not as useful unless employed with Chi Strikes.

Spirit Thief

Fast Attack: Slow Arm Strikes (3)   **Damage:** Special (Chi gain)

Power Attack: Thievery Shards   **Area Attack:**
Damage: Arms Out Cast
Special (Immobilized, Chi gain)

Speed: Slow

Overview: Those most adept at manipulating Chi find that even the spiritual energy of others is within their grasp. The strikes and forms of the Spirit Thief style enable practitioners to tap an enemy's vital energies and refill their own reserves. While the techniques of this style do no physical damage to its victims without being charged with the user's Chi, those who face a Spirit Thief master find themselves without the resolve to put their hearts into the fight.

Stance (Idle)

Additional: Does direct damage in Chi Strike mode.

Advantages: Not strictly a Support style, this unique style allows you to steal Chi from enemies to replenish your own Chi. Arm strikes quicken the Chi appropriation. To use, attempt a strong attack and shoot your striking filament and you can siphon off the Chi from your enemies. This can be your only means of healing in long battles or against dangerous foes. Lengthy use against a single foe can render

THE WAY OF THE WARRIOR

Spirit Thief (cont'd)

them completely harmless (and Chi-less) if they are magicians. Invest your Style Points into increasing the speed of this style immediately, but don't waste them in any other upgrade; the cost isn't worth the reward.

Disadvantages: Fast attacks inflict no damage, except when imbued with Chi Strike. Power attacks do not benefit from Chi Strike. Enemies recover from this attack quickly, so back away while you are draining.

> ### TIP
> *An impressive use of Spirit Thief is to defeat all opponents but one, then place your Follower on Support mode so that you can drain Chi from your unvanquished foe at your leisure. This tactic works best with Sky, because he replenishes your Focus while you restore your Health and Chi. Use a Spirit Thief combo attack in Focus mode for a greater chance of uninterrupted Chi recovery.*

WEAPON STYLES

Crafted by the finest weaponsmiths in the empire, ornate weapons of four different types (the sword, the staff, the dual axe, and the dual swords) are yours to wield and seek the mastery of. Weapon styles generally have more range and do more damage than Martial styles, but this power comes at the cost of your Focus. Each successful hit drains your Focus, and when your Focus is gone, you cannot use Weapon styles. As weapons use Focus only when they strike, you can unsheathe them at any time during combat. Every weapon has another advantage: their extended reach (when employed at close range) can turn a three-hit combination strike into a four-hitter. Maneuver in close for extra damage. Weapons do not damage ghosts, but they are extremely effective against golems. Finally, each weapon has an "artifact" upgrade (see above for the location) that uses the same points you already spent in the corresponding basic Weapon style. For example, if you bought six dots in Fortune's Favorite, you'll have six dots in Dragon Sword when you buy that weapon.

> ### NOTE
> *Upgraded weapon styles use more Focus than the basic versions of those styles.*

Longsword "Fortune's Favorite"

Fast Attack: Wide Arc Swings (3)   **Damage:** ~20 per hit

Power Attack: Decapitating Swing
Damage: 20

Area Attack: 360 Degree Swings (2)

Stance (Idle)

Speed: Fast

Overview: This longsword bears the mark of Shining Fortune, the blacksmith of the gods. Shining Fortune's weapons were so finely crafted that the gods forbade him from creating weapons for anyone but them. When his son was enlisted to subdue the barbarians from the west, Shining Fortune forsook his oaths and forged this marvelous longsword for his son. The gods cursed Shining Fortune for breaking his oath, and he was never again able to produce weapons of any worth. Still, the blade he made for his son never experienced defeat. It is truly Fortune's Favorite.

Additional: Drains Focus

Advantages: It's the most balanced Weapon style, proficient at everything. Quick, with reasonably long range, the strong attack can even decapitate human enemies if they are struck with low (20 percent or less) health.

Disadvantages: Aside from Focus-sapping and a slightly smaller range than the staff, there are none.

Longsword "Dragon Sword" (Artifact)

Overview: Before his departure to the unknown, the Celestial Dragon crafted the first true warrior, Lu Fang. Though Lu Fang's fists were stronger and quicker than any blade, the Celestial Dragon forged the Dragon Sword to give the warrior a weapon worthy of his skill. Hard as dragon scales and sharp as a dragon's tooth, it is still one of the most formidable swords in the Empire.

Additional: Artifact weapon. Drains Focus, +25 percent damage over basic longsword style. Otherwise, all longsword information applies.

Dual Axes "Tang's Vengeance"

Fast Attack: Over-Arm Swings (3)   **Damage:** ~20 per hit

Power Attack:
Double Overhead Swing
Damage: 30

Area Attack:
Double Wide Arc Swing

Speed: Slow

Overview: When Emperor Fong died without an heir, the Empire became fractured and divided. After years of war, Tang the Merciless rose to be the forerunner in the battle for the contested throne of the Jade Empire. Tang's own father betrayed him into the hands of his enemies, fearing that his son's violent ways would ruin the Empire. Rumor has it that before he fled into exile, Tang the Merciless used these very axes to cut off his father's head. These devastating axes remain extremely sharp, even after hundreds of years of use.

Stance (Idle)

Additional: Drains Focus

Advantages: This is the most damaging Weapon style. Drains Focus while in use. Both the fast and strong attacks can decapitate human enemies if they are struck with low (20 percent or less) health.

Disadvantages: This is also the slowest of the Weapon styles. However, the damage makes up for this shortfall.

Double Sabers "Eyes of the Dragon"

Overview: Before his departure to the unknown, the Celestial Dragon crafted the first true warrior, Lu Fang. Though Lu Fang's fists were stronger and quicker than any blade, the Celestial Dragon forged the Dragon Sword to give the warrior a weapon worthy of his skill. Hard as dragon scales and sharp as a dragon's tooth, it is still one of the most formidable swords in the Empire.

Double Sabers "Eyes of the Dragon" (cont'd)

Additional: Artifact weapon. Drains Focus, +25 percent damage over basic longsword style. Otherwise, all longsword information applies.

Double Sabers "Crimson Tears" (Artifact)

Fast Attack: Spinning Attacks (3)   **Damage:** ~25 per hit

Power Attack:
Wide Arc Double Attack
Damage: 44

Area Attack:
Double Bladed Spin

Speed: Slow

Overview: The inscription on these unique swords is written in a long-forgotten dialect. The writing, deciphered by Scholar Shao Shen many years ago, reads, "The innocent are cut down with the guilty; the brave die beside the craven; the blades do not weep for the dead." Rumor has it that the Crimson Tears have ended more lives than the great drought itself. Despite centuries of use, these swords are as sharp and deadly as the day they were forged.

Stance (Idle)

Additional: Artifact weapon. Drains Focus.

Advantages: This is the preferred Weapon style for fighting groups of enemies and is one of the fastest of styles of all.

Disadvantages: This is still effective, but slightly less so, when facing single enemies.

Staff "Golden Star"

Fast Attack: Forward Moving Strikes   **Damage:** ~10 per hit

Power Attack:
Double Hand
Overhead Strike
Damage: 15

Area Attack:
Sweeping 360 Arc

Speed: Fast

Stance (Idle)

Overview: Forged under an auspicious comet, this staff was originally a gift for the Water Spirit of the Silkworm River. A young prince named Seng Lo sought to win the heart of the Water Spirit and had the staff created as a gift. He then convinced the Great Eastern Serpent to fly him to the heavens, where he dipped the staff in the golden comet. The light of the comet dimmed, but the staff became more powerful than any before it. To this day no one knows if Seng Lo won the Water Spirit's heart, but there is no questioning the magnificence of the staff he created.

Additional: Drains Focus

Advantages: This is the Weapon style with the longest reach. It also inflicts reasonably quick area attacks.

Disadvantages: The damage inflicted is very low, and you are susceptible to retaliatory strikes as you follow through your attack. Avoid Staff style unless you're looking for extra challenge.

Staff "Tien's Justice"

Fast Attack: Forward Moving Strikes   **Damage:** ~10 per hit

Staff "Tien's Justice" (cont'd)

Power Attack:
Double Hand
Overhead Strike
Damage: 15

Area Attack:
Sweeping 360 Arc

Speed: Fast

Stance (Idle)

Overview: This ceremonial staff was once displayed in Sagacious Tien's great hall. Many years after his reign, Emperor Yan Shun took up the staff to defend the palace from rebels. Once the infidels had been stopped, Yan Shun gathered his army and left the palace, vowing to rid the Empire of all dissidents before he returned. Emperor Yan Shun returned after 17 years. In that time, Yan Shun and Tien's ceremonial staff had become a symbol for justice in the Jade Empire.

Additional: Drains Focus

Advantages: This Weapon style has the longest reach. It also inflicts reasonably quick area attacks. Aside from aesthetic differences, this is identical to "Golden Star."

Disadvantages: The damage inflicted is very low, and you are susceptible to retaliatory strikes as you follow through your attack. Avoid Staff style unless you're looking for extra challenge.

Staff "Flawless" (Artifact)

Overview: The scrolls of Peng Qi contain the story of a monk who shaped a flawless staff using only swatches of silk. At first, the silk did nothing but polish the rough wood, but after 34 years the staff was perfectly smooth, straight, and flawless. After finishing the staff, the monk told his abbot he was going for a walk to test his new staff, and he never returned. An exiled warrior eventually discovered the staff and attached a sharp blade that is every bit as perfect as the staff itself. It has since been adorned with precious metals, but it remains as flawless as ever.

Additional: Artifact weapon. Drains Focus, +25 percent damage over basic staff style. Otherwise, all staff information applies.

Mirabelle

Fast Attack: Belching Fire   **Damage: 80 per hit**

Power Attack: Roaring Dragon
Damage: 125

Speed: Very slow

Stance (Idle)

Overview: A strange weapon from a strange culture, Mirabelle is made of wood and steel and emits thunder and fire. Loud and ungainly (like its previous owner), Mirabelle is nonetheless capable of doing real harm at medium range. Etched with undecipherable symbols from the Outlander's language, this weapon is a unique (and dangerous) trophy. The power of some enemies is such that fate itself turns away the cold, foreign steel Mirabelle projects.

Additional: Drains Focus

Advantages: The only weapon that inflicts ranged damage, it is ideal for slaying foes, no matter how fearsome, at range. It suffers from a far smaller reduction per Focus reduction level (3 percent compared to 20 percent of most weapons). Use Sagacious Zu in Support mode and activate Chi Strike, and Mirabelle becomes the ultimate weapon for big game such as golems. Remember to use Focus to increase your chance of a hit.

Disadvantages: Very slow, and no area attack. Do not employ in close combat. Use strong attacks sparingly, due to the damage they inflict (and the time they take to complete). The fast attack, although almost a contradiction in terms of speed, still fires fast enough to be more useful, and uses far less Focus. Compare the Focus use and damage chart below, and you should notice that while the damage is similar, you can aim six quick shots, which are likely to be more effective against foes.

Mirabelle (cont'd)

MIRABELLE DAMAGE (FAST OR STRONG)

Attack	Focus Cost (cumulative)	Damage (cumulative)
Fast (first)	100	80
Fast (second)	200	160
Fast (third)	300	240
Fast (fourth)	400	320
Fast (fifth)	500	400
Fast (six)	600	480
Strong (first)	150	125
Strong (second)	300	250
Strong (third)	450	375
Strong (fourth)	600	500

Improvised Ham

Fast Attack: Over-Arm Swings (3)   **Damage: ~15 per hit**

Power Attack:
Double Overhead Swing
Damage: 20

Area Attack:
Double Wide Arc Swing

Speed: Slow

Stance (Idle)

Overview: When engaged in an ugly fracas, the more unruly fighters, or those with less skill in styles, scramble to obtain any object to use in a threatening manner. Breakable tables and moist ham shanks cooking on a grill are available to the combatant with little other choice of styles, or those with skill who wish to embarrass the enemy by fashioning impromptu weaponry for the defeat of their foes. The only discernable difference between Ham and Wood, aside from the delicious aroma, is that the Ham three-hit combo only usually connects twice.

Additional: Does not drain Focus

Advantages: Weapon-like combat is available without the associated Focus loss.

Disadvantages: Broken tables and hamstands in the Tea House must be smashed before the weapons can be obtained. Limited use.

Improvised Table Legs

Fast Attack: Over-Arm Swings (3)   Damage: ~15 per hit

Power Attack:
Double Overhead Swing
Damage: 20

Area Attack:
Double Wide Arc Swing

Stance (Idle)

Speed: Slow

Overview: When engaged in an ugly fracas, the more unruly fighters, or those with less skill in styles, scramble to obtain any object to use in a threatening manner. Breakable tables and moist ham shanks cooking on a grill are available to the combatant with little other choice of styles, or those with skill who wish to embarrass the enemy by fashioning impromptu weaponry for the defeat of their foes. The wooden implements act like a pair of axes, but with less slicing power. However, it does tend to strike victims three times, instead of the greasy ham shanks' two hits.

Additional: Does not drain Focus

Advantages: Weapon-like combat is available without the associated Focus loss.

Disadvantages: Broken tables and hamstands in the Tea House must be smashed before the weapons can be obtained. Limited use.

Followers' Weaponry

While these are equipped and used automatically by your Followers, their blades have a rich and varied history, as we are about to uncover:

GUJIN'S FAVOR (DAWN STAR)

This blade is surprisingly keen and well-balanced considering its humble origins. A standard militia blade, it was carried from the abandoned town of Broken Path by Gujin, the guard who would become weapon master of Two Rivers. Since then the

Followers' Weaponry (cont'd)

blade has been carefully rebalanced, honed, and cared for like a treasured heirloom. While it is not inherently magical, the blade never seems to lose its edge. Dawn Star keeps it with her as a reminder of the only place she ever felt she could call home.

THORN AND SHINING CARP (DAWN STAR ADVANCED)

This blade is claimed by two legends, one from the Prosperous East and one from the Golden Delta. In the first, a flower girl was wronged by an official, and an outlaw incited revenge for his own purposes. Trapping the official, the woman beat him savagely with a bouquet of roses, the thorns raking eyes and skin. An observing fox spirit frowned on hatred abusing such beauty, and transformed the flowers into a sword. The official was killed, leaving the woman to ponder the hardening of her heart. In the second tale, the outlaw instead urged restraint and suggested asking the river for guidance. A golden carp answered the woman's plea and, as it swam by, the sun on its scales took the shape of a blade that fell in the shallows at her feet. She took up arms in the spirit of justice and order was restored. Stories—and people— change with the influence that others bring.

CAPTAIN'S BLADE (SILK FOX)

When a soldier becomes captain in the Imperial Army, he is awarded one of these masterwork blades. Carefully balanced and made of the keenest steel, these deadly badges of honor are borne only by the best soldiers in the Empire, all except this particular blade, of course. Purloined from her father's armory, this blade has been at Silk Fox's side for many years, and in her hands it moves with deadly precision.

BLADE OF THE BROKEN BOUGH (SILK FOX ADVANCED)

The story of the Broken Bough is a sad page in the history of the Jade Empire. When Emperor Zuwan, ninth emperor in the time of divisions, died suddenly with no heir, his wife, Seng Si, assumed the throne to prevent chaos. Though respected, she was seen as merely a ceremonial caretaker. When war erupted a decade later the Imperial Army would not follow her orders, so she took up a sword and asked instead that they follow her lead. Emperors led armies only in legends; Seng Si's commitment stunned her detractors, and her death shamed the nation. Seng Si the Broken Bough changed the face of the Imperial court, though the relics of her rule were never displayed.

Followers' Weaponry (cont'd)

THE TWINS (THE BLACK WHIRLWIND)

Like two old friends who happen to have razor sharp edges, Whirlwind's axes have been with him a long time. According to their engravings, they're called "Left" and "Right," though some suspect the names to be little more than a mnemonic. Whirlwind simply thinks of these axes as "The Twins," and considers them his most valuable—and possibly only—possessions. They may lack an epic history, but in Whirlwind's hands they're unquestionably deadly.

MAKER'S BANE AND PLACID GUIJU (THE BLACK WHIRLWIND ADVANCED)

Maker's Bane was forged from a falling star that tore from the heavens as the Celestial Dragon shaped the world. The loss of life resulting from its use is thoroughly predictable. Placid Guiju is a sepulcher for the God of Agricultural Poetry. Guiju of Words and Land transformed into a plowshare to aid the workers of the Golden Delta, but was trapped when the farmers remade their tools into weapons to repel invading Horselords. Pounding plowshare to sword might have held ironic appeal, but being an axe causes injury to Guiju's poetic sensibilities. The effectiveness of this blade is agony for his gentle spirit, an insult that will eventually destroy him and strip "field verse" from the Lexicon of the Ages. It also makes the wielder slightly giddy.

MAGIC STYLES

Used by those with enough Chi to thrill an enemy with impressive incantations before slaying them, Magic styles rely on your own Chi reserves to work; run out of Chi, and Magic is no longer available to you. Magic does not affect demons or golems, and Stone Immortal and Tempest do not affect ogres, but despite these shortfalls, Magic is an impressive style to master. Use your primary ranged attacks liberally; shoot bolts from your fists at targeted enemies. Magic also causes debilitating effects, similar to Support styles, but with actual damage inflicted. Area attack magical effects range wildly, from

the overly lengthy (Dire Flame) to the incredibly useful (Tempest). Some Magic attacks can initiate Harmonic Combos. Lastly, two Magic styles are mutually exclusive: You may either learn Stone Immortal *or* Tempest, but not both.

Dire Flame

Fast Attack: Small, Fast Fireball   **Damage:** 10 per hit

Power Attack: Large, Slow Fireball **Damage:** 30

Area Attack: Dragon Construct (Immolation)

Speed: Varies

Overview: Practitioners of Dire Flame can throw bolts of fire, project explosive fireballs, and even summon dragon-like burning constructs that immolate enemies with tongues of flame. Sometimes the sight of a fighter wielding the power of flame is enough to reduce the bravest of opponents to begging for mercy.

Stance (Idle)

Additional: Drains Chi. This style can initiate a Harmonic Combo that produces a Health power-up.

Advantages: This magic style has the most damaging strong attack and a very quick fast attack. Victims are Immolated (constantly burning), acting in a similar way as being Shocked.

Disadvantages: While the strong attack is incredibly useful and impressive, the spectacular but flawed area attack, which can take too long to launch and leave you exposed, negates these bonuses when compared to Ice Shard style. The Ice Shard also begins a Harmonic Combo producing a Chi orb power-up compared to the Health power-up with Dire Flame (Chi orbs are more versatile because they can bolster Health or Chi).

Ice Shard

Fast Attack: Slow Ice Dagger   **Damage:** 10 per hit

Power Attack: Ice Pillar
Damage: 0 (Frozen)

Area Attack:
Ice Storm

Speed: Varies

Stance (Idle)

Overview: While some warriors swear by the power of Dire Flame, others seek to master the powerful Ice Shard. By using Chi to summon forth the soul-chilling cold of the highest mountains, masters of Ice Shard can send daggers of ice flying toward enemies, call a freezing ice storm to slow their shivering foes, or even encase opponents in columns of ice before shattering them with a single blow. Few fighters have the courage to stand up to the cold stare of an Ice Shard master.

Additional: Drains Chi. This style can initiate a Harmonic Combo that produces a Chi power-up.

Advantages: This is the most balanced Magic style; offering favorable results with every type of strike. The strong attack encases an adversary in ice, which proves very useful. The Harmonic Combo results in a Chi power-up; the most useful to find.

Disadvantages: The area attack is still extremely slow and easy for the enemy to dodge.

Stone Immortal

Fast Attack: Slow, Small Stone   **Damage:** 15 per hit

Stone Immortal *(cont'd)*

Power Attack:
Petrifying Rock Channel
Damage: 40 (Petrified)

Area Attack:
Shockwave

Speed: Varies

Stance (Idle)

Overview: Fighters who study this style gain mastery over the ponderous element of earth, putting the mighty power of stone and crystal at their command. Masters of Stone Immortal can attack enemies with crystalline missiles, encase foes in stone, or even open the ground beneath an opponent's feet. To command the power of earth requires a mind centered on balance, stability, and order. Therefore, Stone Immortal is a favored style among Followers of the Way of the Open Palm.

Additional: Drains Chi. This style can initiate a Harmonic Combo.

Advantages: This style features a long-ranged paralyzing strong attack that encases an enemy in stone. It's extremely useful when you wish to immobilize a troublesome foe. This also begins a Harmonic Combo.

Disadvantages: Those seeking discord should not learn this style, as it primarily benefits those seeking the Way of the Open Palm. Does not effect ogres (unlike Dire Flame and Ice Shard).

Extras: Stone Immortal is an "Open Palm" style that shifts in power the more the player follows the way toward harmony. You also need to be four-fifths of the way toward pure Open Palm (consult the pointer on your character screen) to learn this style in Tien's Landing.

STONE IMMORTAL EFFECTIVENESS

Player Alignment	Damage Modifier
Very Open Palm	+60% total damage
Open Palm	+30% total damage
Slightly Open Palm	regular damage
Neutral	–30% total damage
Slightly Closed Fist	–30% total damage
Closed Fist	–60% total damage
Very Closed Fist	–60% total damage

Jade Empire
PRIMA OFFICIAL GAME GUIDE

Tempest

Fast Attack: Slow, Breath of Wind   Damage: 15 per hit

Power Attack: Whirlwind
Damage: 40 (Immobilized)

Area Attack:
Wind Storm

Speed: Varies

Stance (Idle)

Overview: Warriors proficient in Tempest have the winds at their beck and call. Fighters who have faced this style and survived tell tales of blasts of gale-force winds and of powerful whirlwinds that effortlessly sent them flying away from the Tempest master himself. Many practitioners of Tempest face entire gangs without ever taking a wound, as the mighty winds at their command keep their foes at bay. Warriors with the chill of the wind in their hearts find Tempest far easier to command, so it is a favored style of the Way of the Closed Fist.

Additional: Drains Chi. This style can initiate a Harmonic Combo that produces a Focus power-up.

Advantages: This Magic style has the most impressive area attack move. Many practitioners argue that this is the best Magic style to obtain. The area attack traps multiple enemies in whirlwinds and is extremely quick to launch. Use power attack to begin a Harmonic Combo that ends with a Focus power-up.

Disadvantages: Does not effect ogres (unlike Dire Flame and Ice Shard).

Extras: Tempest is a "Closed Fist" style, that shifts in power the more the player follows the way toward discord. You also need to be four-fifths of the way toward pure Closed Fist (consult the pointer on your character screen) to learn this Style in Tien's Landing.

Tempest *(cont'd)*

TEMPEST EFFECTIVENESS

Player Alignment	Damage Modifier
Very Open Palm	-60% total damage
Open Palm	-60% total damage
Slightly Open Palm	-30% total damage
Neutral	-30% total damage
Slightly Closed Fist	default damage
Closed Fist	+30% total damage
Very Closed Fist	+60% total damage

TRANSFORMATION STYLES

The most fearsome styles of all allow the user to alter his or her appearance for a short amount of time (until Chi runs out), and take on a frightening and usually demonic visage. Nothing is immune to Transformation styles; test this out by throwing a Horse Demon's fireball into the hide of a demon or golem (who are usually immune to magic). While active, Transformations drain Chi, and you cannot heal while transformed, so be aware of your Health while you fight in this style. Not only do you take on the countenance of a demon, but you are immune to Support and Magic attacks from foes as well. These are the strongest styles, but the most expensive to use. Transform only when you are about to strike a foe; do not waste Chi walking to a fight. All characters can learn all Transformation styles. Although of limited use when facing a group, Transformations are exceptional in one-on-one confrontations.

TIP
Transformation Tips
Transforming lights up the screen, making it difficult to see what is happening during this time. While this occurs, the Transformation does not sap Chi. Try one or two attacks (or take one or two hits), transform to a second form, repeat the attacks, and continue to transform again and again. The screen is entirely obscured (and you cannot block), but you can attack continuously without losing Chi. You can also switch between a Transformation and another style, and back again; even casting Magic without the associated Chi cost. Be sure your Health can survive this.

Some Transformation styles take longer to turn when changing targets. Try pressing B (Block); the demon instantly spins toward that direction.

Toad Demon

Fast Attack: Arm Slams (2) and Lick **Damage:** ~35 per hit

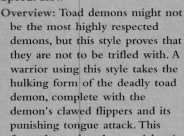

Power Attack: Belly Rush **Damage:** 55 (Poisoned)

Area Attack: Tongue Sweep

Speed: Slow

Overview: Toad demons might not be the most highly respected demons, but this style proves that they are not to be trifled with. A warrior using this style takes the hulking form of the deadly toad demon, complete with the demon's clawed flippers and its punishing tongue attack. This form also makes the martial artist immune to all Support styles, just like the toad demon itself.

Stance (Idle)

Additional: Drains Chi. Removes negative effects (such as slow or paralysis).

Advantages: This is the only style that lets you poison your enemies, and it makes the player immune to Support styles. The strong attack causes poisoning, which can affect every type of enemy. Be sure you upgrade this style's damage level to create a monstrous killing host that can crush even the most powerful enemy in seconds.

Disadvantages: Extremely slow and unable to evade, so run up to your enemies before transforming.

Horse Demon

Fast Attack: Arm Slams (2) **Damage:** ~50 per hit

Horse Demon *(cont'd)*

Power Attack: Fireball **Damage:** 60

Area Attack: Spiked Ground Wave (Immolation)

Speed: Slow

Overview: Powerful warriors can gain the power to take the form of the fearsome horse demon. This Transformation grants the horse demon's legendary ferocity, as well as its mastery of the element of fire and its immunity to the effects of Support styles. Faced with the immolating brutality of the horse demon, the target is helpless while beating out the flames.

Stance (Idle)

Additional: Drains Chi. Removes negative effects (such as slow or paralysis).

Advantages: This is the only style that causes fear in your enemies. It makes you immune to Support styles. The ranged fireball strike affects all enemies. The horse demon's flaming mane damages all enemies that strike you.

TIP
This game exploit allows you to defeat every enemy without expending any Chi. Transform into horse demon, and as the Transformation begins, repeatedly tap ⊗ until you begin to throw the fireball. Immediately select a non-Transformation style. The fireball continues and strikes its target, without you incurring a Chi cost. Repeat to defeat.

Red Minister

Fast Attack: Arm Strikes (3) **Damage:** Special (Chi & Health gain)

Red Minister (cont'd)

Power Attack: Forward Sweep

Damage:
Special (Chi & Health gain)

Area Attack:
Spin and Ground Wave

Speed: Slow

Stance (Idle)

Overview: When an eminent sage dies, its spirit sometimes returns as a ghostly red minister. Taking the form of a red minister grants a warrior the nefarious ability to feed on an opponent's life force and the incorporeal spirit's immunities to Weapon and Support styles. Few people in this troubled age have the resilience to withstand the spine-chilling touch of a red minister.

Additional: Drains Chi. Removes negative effects (such as slow or paralysis).

Advantages: This is the only style that lets you drain Health with every attack, and it makes you immune to Weapon styles. It also drains enemy Chi with every attack. As a ghost, you're immune to weapons. Power up enough, and you can use this continuously. It allows you to replenish a part of your Health and Chi with each hit. Fast attack steals 30 Health/Chi per attack, and strong attack steals 60 Health/Chi.

Disadvantages: Confusing and Chi-sapping at basic levels. Doesn't defeat enemies as quickly or spectacularly as other Transformation styles.

Jade Golem

Fast Attack: Single Swipe

Damage: ~60 per hit

Jade Golem (cont'd)

Power Attack:
Overhead Smash
Damage: 100

Area Attack:
Ground Pound

Speed: Slow

Overview: This style imbues the martial artist with the power and form of the towering Jade Golem. Powerful and terrifying, the Jade Golem mauls foes with brutal strikes and inhuman cunning, and the form's complete immunity to Magic and Martial styles makes it the perfect tactic when facing deadly sorcerers and certain demons.

Stance (Idle)

Additional: Drains Chi. Removes negative effects (such as slow or paralysis).

Advantages: This is the slowest but most damaging Transformation style, and it makes you immune to Magic styles. It can also stun opponents. It can slay regulation enemies with one hit, and more powerful entities in three or four slams. Simply jump behind your foe, transform, and hammer the ⊗ button until you swing, then transform back out and roll to safety. Being immune to everything except weapons makes this technique highly effective.

Disadvantages: Cumbersome and slow.

DAMAGE COMPARISON (PRIOR TO UPGRADES)

Fighting Style	Damage (Fast)	Damage (Strong)
Drunken Master	~30 per hit	60
Legendary Strike	~10 per hit	30
Thousand Cuts	~7 per hit	~32
Leaping Tiger	~10 per hit	20
White Demon	~20 per hit	30
Longsword	~20 per hit	20
Dual Axes	~20 per hit	30
Double Swords	~25 per hit	44
Staff	~10 per hit	15
Mirabelle	80 per hit	125

Fighting Style	Damage (Fast)	Damage (Strong)
Dire Flame	10 per hit	30
Ice Shard	10 per hit	0
Stone Immortal	15 per hit	40
Tempest	15 per hit	40
Jade Golem	~60 per hit	100
Horse Demon	~50 per hit	60
Red Minister	0	0
Toad Demon	~35 per hit	55

Chi damage starts at 5 per hit and is adjusted by +25 percent per level. Base weapons have a base of 5 Focus per hit. Upgraded weapons have a +100 percent to the Focus cost.

UPGRADING YOUR STYLES

Every time you gain a level, you receive a set number of points to spend upgrading the styles you know. Each upgrade category has five levels, requiring an increasing number of Style Points to be spent (1, 2, 4, 6, and 10 respectively).

To fully maximize your three upgrade paths on a single style, you need 69 Style Points. To put this into perspective, if you spent *every* Style Point on *one* style from the beginning of your adventure, you would reach Level 12 before you maximize your style potential.

With this in mind, take care to spend your Style Points wisely, on styles with the least number of disadvantages. There is no need to cram points into Heavenly Wave at the beginning of the game. Put Style Points into Jade Golem and Artifact Weapons later in the adventure for much more impressive combats.

UPGRADE CATEGORIES

CHI DAMAGE INCREASE (FOR ALL STYLES)
1. Advanced Chi Strikes
2. Enhanced Chi Strikes
3. Marvelous Chi Strikes
4. Deadly Chi Strikes
5. Ultimate Chi Strikes

DURATION INCREASE (FOR SUPPORT AND MAGIC)
1. Slight increase
2. Small increase
3. Moderate increase
4. Large increase
5. Drastic increase

SPEED INCREASE (FOR FAST ATTACKS IN WEAPON, MARTIAL, AND SUPPORT STYLES)
1. +5%   4. +20%
2. +10%   5. +25%
3. +15%

DAMAGE INCREASE (FOR ALL STYLES EXCEPT SUPPORT)
1. +25%   4. +100%
2. +50%   5. +125%
3. +75%

LOWER CHI COST (FOR MAGIC)
1. –5%   4. –20%
2. –10%   5. –25%
3. –15%

CHI COST REDUCTION (FOR TRANSFORMATIONS)
1. –10%   4. –40%
2. –20%   5. –50%
3. –30%

FOCUS COST REDUCTION (FOR WEAPONS)
1. Somewhat less Focus   4. Drastically less Focus
2. Moderately less Focus   5. Very little Focus
3. Much less Focus

Therefore, depending on the category of style, three different parameters are upgradeable:

MARTIAL:
Damage Increase	Chi Damage Increase	Speed Increase

SUPPORT (INCLUDING SPIRIT THIEF):
Chi Damage Increase	Duration Increase	Speed Increase

WEAPON:
Damage Increase	Focus Cost Reduction	Speed Increase

TRANSFORMATION:
Chi Cost Reduction	Damage Increase	Chi Damage Increase

MAGIC:
Lower Chi Cost	Damage Increase	Duration Increase

AN OPTIMAL CHARACTER

With limitless preferences, each adventurer is likely to enjoy a particular style that another does not. But you should heed some general methods of creating a powerful character. Foster *at least* the following styles:

- One Weapon style
- One Support style (duration only)
- All Transformations
- One Martial style
- Tempest or Stone Immortal
- Spirit Thief (speed only)

ADDITIONAL COMBAT INFORMATION

ENEMY RESISTANCES

The following entities you encounter on your travels are susceptible to certain forms of attack, and it is wise to learn which to use on them, and which they are immune to.

Spirits

Immune To	Damaged By	
Weapon Styles	Martial Style	
Support Styles	Magic	
—	Transformation	

Golems

Immune To	Damaged By
Magic	Martial Style
Support Styles	Transformation
—	Weapon Styles

Demons

Immune To	Damaged By
Support Styles	Martial Style
Magic★	Transformation
—	Weapon Styles

★(Large demons only, small demons are still hurt by magic)

Ogres

Immune To	Damaged By
Support Styles	Martial Style
Earth Magic	Transformation
Air Magic	Weapon Styles
—	Fire and Ice Magic

Cannibal Mother

Immune To	Damaged By
Everything	No Styles

ENEMY TRINKETS

All enemies except demons (including cannibals, fox spirits, etc.) and ghosts drop silver when they die, and this amount varies. For example, ogres drop about one and a half times the amount humans do. Golems, meanwhile, give out double the silver compared with humans. The average earning you can expect from each battle is shown in the battle tables throughout the Walkthrough section. The only exceptions are enemies in the Imperial City Arena, who never drop silver. However, when you are a ghost, enemies do not drop silver.

Some enemies (usually the more powerful beings you face) drop items or gems. Items are always carried by the same person and so are most gems, so when you replay the adventure, you know where powerful items are located. Some enemies have a small chance of dropping a gem, so you might receive a few random prizes, but this occurs rarely, and it's always a more common gem you could purchase or locate easily.

ENEMY TACTICS

Most tactics are explained during the Walkthrough section, but foes will attempt some common techniques:

Enemies use Chi to perform Magic attacks and other offensive posturing, just as you do. This means they can run out of Chi just like you. Some enemies also use Chi Strikes and Chi Heal.

Enemies get stronger, with more Hit Points, but also *smarter* the farther you progress in your adventure: they start blocking, leaping over you, sidestepping, and attempting other cunning maneuvers. They utilize Chi Strike and Chi Heal more often and command multiple styles, including martial arts you are unable to obtain, such as Viper or Monkey style.

Enemies can hit each other. If you are fighting two opponents, and one of them is a sorcerer who is attempting to strike you from a distance, while the other is a thug fighting in melee range, try sidestepping around the thug so that the sorcerer hits him instead of you. This takes a little agility but can turn the tide of a confrontation.

Difficulty settings, both in the main adventure and in minigames, can affect enemy interaction. Foes have less Health and Chi on Student difficulty and more on Grand Master difficulty. Enemy Experience Points rewards and silver piece allocations remain unchanged.

FOLLOWERS IN COMBAT

Each of your Followers brings his or her unique skill set to the combat zone, and you must make two important choices before each battle. First, choose the correct Follower for the task at hand. Second, choose to use them in either the Attack or Support function. For further information on your Followers, consult the "Cast of Characters" section.

> **TIP**
>
> *Use the stronger Followers to aid you in combat with multiple foes, or to "tag-team" on a single foe. Or leave your Follower to attack while you rest and save your energy. If your Follower is supporting you, look to his or her abilities and how best these serve your continuing survival. Usually, a constant increase in Chi is preferable.*

Follower	Attack Ability	Support Ability
Dawn Star	Longsword combat	Chi recovery
Sagacious Zu	Staff combat	You inflict extra damage when using Weapon styles
Chai Ka	Demon creature	Health
Ya Zhen	Demon creature	Health
The Black Whirlwind	Dual Axe combat	None
Henpecked Hou	None	Drunken Master style
Kang	None	None
Zin Bu	None	None
Silk Fox	Longsword combat	You inflict double damage when using Martial styles
Sky	Dual Sword combat	Focus recovery
Abbot Song	Spear combat	Health, Chi, Focus recovery
Death's Hand	Sword combat	None

USING FOLLOWERS

As you can see from the chart, the chosen tactic you give your Followers greatly changes your combat options. Support mode is for those who wish to crush all opposition themselves, and who are relying on their Follower to siphon energy to them. Attack mode is for defeating groups of enemies, bigger entities, or ganging up on a single enemy. For example, you can let your Follower take the brunt of combat while you stand back and shoot ranged attacks at the enemy.

Read through the descriptions of the styles to create combinations of weapons and Followers to tear through particular enemies. Synergistic combat is a step forward to enlightenment! The finest example of this is Sagacious Zu. Place him in a Support role, thus increasing your weapon potency, and wield a weapon—previously fearsome golems now crumble into dust in seconds!

Also note that weapons your Followers wield can harm spirits, whereas your weapons cannot, and that Followers never attack the enemy you are targeting, unless it's the only enemy left.

> ### TIP
> *A fight can change from impossible to effortless with simple adjustments. Are you outnumbered? Try using a Follower in Attack mode. Are you using up your Focus too quickly? Try setting a Follower who restores your Focus to Support mode. Are you being demolished by Magical attacks? Then check to see if one of your Followers is immune to Magic and use that Follower as a shield.*

POWER-UPS

During your adventure you can find five types of power-ups (also known as orbs):

Health *Chi* *Focus* *Unblockable* *Full Restore*

They sometimes appear as the ethereal mist of the recently slain leaves for the spirit world. They restore a random percentage of the given statistic (25 percent, 50 percent, or 100 percent). They never fade away unless you leave the map you are in, so you can save them for when you need them. You can also "create" orbs by finishing a Harmonic Combo with a particular style.

"Unblockable" power-ups make your attacks temporarily unblockable.

"Full restore" power-ups heal all your energy types to maximum.

The game difficulty influences when power-ups are awarded. The frequency is common for Student difficulty, and rare for Grand Master difficulty.

SWITCHING STYLES

Another tenet for successful command of your styles: Know which four styles to equip (on the D-pad icon in the screen's bottom left), and which series of styles flow to and from each other with appealing clarity. There are limitless possibilities, but remember two main points: keep different styles equipped (never have two different weapons assigned, or four martial arts, for example) and hold down a direction on the D-pad to pause and quick-change a style, even during combat. Switch styles often, to suit the occasion.

> **TIP**
>
> *Switch into another style faster by switching style in the middle of the animation. For example; create a Heavenly Wave power attack, and before the animation finishes, switch to Legendary Strike. You will be in the Legendary Strike pose as soon as the Heavenly Wave animation ends.*

HARMONIC COMBOS
HARMONIC COMBO STARTERS

Storm Dragon (Focus power-up)

Produces a flesh explosion

Heavenly Wave (Health power-up)

Produces a flesh explosion

Paralyzing Palm (No Orb)

Produces a petrifying and shattering

Hidden Fist (Chi power-up)

Produces an absorption

Dire Flame (Health power-up)

Produces a charred corpse

Ice Shard (Chi power-up)

Produces a shattering

Stone Immortal (No Orb)

Produces a shattering

Tempest (Focus power-up)

Produces a disappearance

HARMONIC COMBO FINISHERS

Drunken Master

Legendary Strike

Thousand Cuts

Leaping Tiger

White Demon

Harmonic Combos are incredibly proficient and spectacular methods of slaying human and ghostly foes. They also produce orb power-ups. Choose any starter (which influences the orb created) and pair it with any finisher. If you are low on energy, don't wait and hope for a power-up; create one with Harmonic Combos and refill your desired statistic while continuing the battle!

Using Focus mode allows a Harmonic Combo to be completed much more easily. This is an especially good tactic if you have Sky in Support mode.

The time it takes to switch styles in a Harmonic Combo is longer (almost twice as long) if you change styles when the Support/Magic style is finishing or has finished the Harmonic attack. If you change styles at the beginning or during the first attack in the combo, you can instantly pull off the power attack with the Martial style.

Paralyzing Palm combined with Leaping Tiger is the fastest Harmonic Combo pair; it takes 2.9 seconds to combine them both. The longest is Dire Flame with Thousand Cuts, which takes 9.3 seconds to perform. The fastest projectile-based Harmonic Combo is Stone Immortal or Ice Shard combined with Leaping Tiger (with Legendary Strike and White Demon at a close second).

MISCELLANEOUS MUSINGS

Teachers, style practitioners, and other learned scholars from the great northern tundra have granted the following information:

Use area attacks on large groups, and always single out an enemy (usually one that can hit with ranged attacks or has the most pestering style of combat) to defeat. Kill him before moving to the next. When confronted with large groups, evade to the edges of the group whenever possible. This allows you to concentrate on one or two opponents at a time.

Always react to your enemy, launching a power attack when he blocks, or a ranged attack if he is closing the gap between you.

When necessary, fight with your back to the wall. When an opponent knocks you down, you can regain your feet much more quickly than you would elsewhere.

After executing a combo, flip over your opponent and launch a power attack from behind.

After being poked once with a spear, sidestep to avoid a second spear poke.

After executing a combo, backflip to avoid potential counterattacks.

Lost spirits have attacks that home in on you; destroy them early.

Attack large, slow demons from behind whenever possible, and use Free Target mode to inflict a few hits, then retreat before they can react.

MINIGAMES
FLYING MISSIONS

When Kang the Mad joins your group in Chapter Two, he brings with him a flying machine he's dubbed the Marvelous Dragonfly. Powered by a blend of technology and magic, the Marvelous Dragonfly is one of the greatest achievements of the Jade Empire.

The skies are full of enemy aircraft: bandit planes, Imperial gunships, and mine-dropping dirigibles to name a few. The amount of punishment the Marvelous Dragonfly can withstand is represented by a red Health meter on the upper left; if you run out, Kang forces you to abort the mission. Make repairs by collecting red Health orbs.

Health orbs help keep you aloft.

Standard single-shot cannon

Grab a Weapon orb for double the firepower.

A second Weapon orb enables three-way shots.

Cloudburst

Consume Spirit

Your primary weapon (A) is a rapid-fire cannon that fires straight ahead. Yellow Weapon orbs dropped by your enemies grant increased firepower for the duration of the mission by enabling multiple shots.

NOTE

The double-shot weapon in the mini-game (the one you get from picking up just one weapon orb) allows auto-fire if you just hold down A. Single-shot and triple-shot require repeated button mashing.

Dragon's Wrath

Firestorm

FLYER UPGRADES

Flyer upgrades (X) channel your Chi to create potent offensive and defensive effects. Chi, represented by the blue meter, is replenished by destroying enemies; the more powerful the enemy, the more Chi is restored. Only three upgrades can be equipped at any time; if you own more than that, you're given a chance to select which ones to use before each mission. Installed upgrades are represented by icons in the lower left; cycle between them by pressing L or R. The types of upgrades available are summarized on the following table:

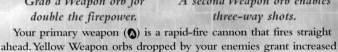

Mirage

Radiant Aura

FLYER UPGRADES

	Name	Effect	Chi Cost	Location
	Cloudburst	Inflicts moderate damage over time	Moderate	Complete Mission 4: Kang's First Mission
	Consume Spirit	Restore Health by absorbing from enemies	Moderate	Complete Mission 6: Spirit Journey
	Dragon's Wrath	Destroys all nearby enemies	Very High	Buy from Hin Goo (3,000 SP) after completing Mission 9: Rescue
	Firestorm	Inflicts severe damage over time	High	Buy from Hin Goo (3,000 SP) after completing Mission 9: Rescue
	Mirage	Enemies and their weapons pass harmlessly through you	Moderate	Complete Mission 5: Kang's Second Mission
	Radiant Aura	Creates protective shield, can be used to ram enemies	Moderate	Initial upgrade, obtained after Mission 1: Returning Home
	Reverse Tides	Causes all enemies to slow down for a short time	Moderate	Buy from Hin Goo (3,000 SP) after completing Mission 8: Escorting the Prefect
	Shrieking Fury	Launches a homing missile	Small	Obtained when you get the Marvelous Dragonfly
	Spirit's Calling	Stronger version of Radiant Aura	High	Complete Mission 11: Battle of Dirge
	Tremor	Causes moderate damage to all enemies	Moderate	Buy from Hin Goo (3,000 SP) after completing Mission 7: A Test for Hin Goo

Reverse Tides

Shrieking Fury

Spirit's Calling

Tremor

You can try 13 different flying missions during your adventure. The first two missions, Returning Home and Leaving Town, take place before you meet Kang; for these flights, you pilot a less-advanced flyer known as a Mosquito. The Mosquito missions are described in the Chapter One walkthrough. Three other missions are offered by Mechanic Hin Goo during Chapter Three; his missions are detailed in the Hin Goo side quest. The other eight missions are described below. All flying missions except the first are optional.

The XP received for completing each mission depends on your skill. The values shown below represent the maximum possible award. One quarter of this amount is automatically earned simply by completing the mission. How much of the remainder you get depends on how many enemies you shoot down.

Missions 11, 12, and 13 occur when you use the Marvelous Dragonfly to travel to or from Tien's Landing, the Imperial City, or the Imperial Palace. The first such jaunt offers a maximum award of 1,500 XP, but on successive missions this amount diminishes. After 10 trips, the XP award becomes zero.

> **TIP**
>
> The total XP award depends solely on the number of destroyed ships, not their size or strength. Maximize the award by concentrating on the smaller, more numerous targets.

> **TIP**
>
> It's a good idea to equip upgrades with widely different effects, thus allowing you to react flexibly to different situations. For example, Tremor (area attack), Shrieking Fury (homing missile), and Radiant Aura (shield) make an excellent combination.

The flying missions not covered in the walkthrough are described in the following sections. Details on Mission 1 and Mission 2 can be found in the Chapter One walkthrough.

	FLYER MISSIONS				
Mission Name	Chapter (Requirement)	# of Enemies	Max XP Award	Upgrade Award	Legendary High Score
1 Returning Home	Chapter One (rescue Dawn Star)	33	500	Radiant Aura	4,300
2 Leaving Town	Chapter One (end of chapter)	92	400	None	6,807
3 Leaving the Workshop	Chapter Two (defeat Gao the Greater)	41	1,100	Shrieking Fury	4,300
4 Kang's First Mission	Chapter Two, Three, or Four (talk to Kang)	30	0	Cloudburst	2,850
5 Kang's Second Mission	Chapter Two, Three, or Four (complete 3 Furnace Configurations)	45	0	Mirage	3,175
6 Spirit Journey	Chapter Two, Three, or Four (complete 3 Furnace Configurations)	50	0	Consume Spirit	5,380
7 A Test for Hin Goo	Chapter Three (Hin Goo side quest)	162	1,000	Tremor	8,650
8 Escorting the Prefect	Chapter Three (Hin Goo side quest)	79	2,000	Reverse Tides	4,450
9 Rescue Mission	Chapter Three (Hin Goo side quest)	78	2,500	Dragon's Wrath, Firestorm	3,900
10 Battle of Dirge	Chapter Six (before siege of Dirge)	112	6,000	None	5,500
11 Encounter in the Skies 1	Chapter Two, Three, or Four (travel)	90	1,500 or less	None	7,700
12 Encounter in the Skies 2	Chapter Two, Three, or Four (travel)	90	1,500 or less	None	3,700
13 Encounter in the Skies 3	Chapter Two, Three, or Four (travel)	90	1,500 or less	None	3,650

Mission 3: Leaving the Workshop

This easy mission is actually a tutorial on using your Marvelous Dragonfly's upgrades. Stay low and fire continually to destroy the weak enemies that weave back and forth across your path. This is a great chance to get a feel for the effectiveness of Shrieking Fury; note that each missile you launch can blast through several ships before exhausting itself. The second half of the mission features heavier planes that fly in wide arcs from left to right; avoid them and target the two accompanying balloons to release Weapon orbs. Once you have three-way shots, stay as far back as possible in the center to stay safe from the remaining formations; don't swoop from side to side and instead just let the enemies cross right into your stream of fire.

Mission 4: Kang's First Mission

This mission opens with erratically moving waves of enemies that descend from the left and right. Choose a side and line up your guns with their point of entry while using upgrades to destroy the planes on the other side. A wing of three flying schooners inaugurates the second half of the mission. One of them flies in from directly behind you, so move forward to let it pass or destroy it with an upgrade such as Tremor. The final enemy is a large gunship; if you shoot fast enough you can destroy it before it has a chance to return fire.

Mission 5: Kang's Second Mission

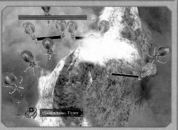

A plague of balloons swarms across the sky in this mission. Stay in the center, as the balloons come toward you from every direction. Solid barriers suspended from stationary pairs of balloons block your path; blast a hole through them to create an opening. Save your Chi for a floating box of dynamite that drifts in from the right. During a break in the action, your Marvelous Dragonfly speeds up for the home stretch. This gives you less time to smash the barriers, but if you picked up a Weapon orb or two, they should pose little problem. Avoid hanging back, as balloons continually drift up from behind.

Mission 6: Spirit Journey

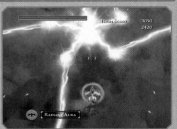

In this unique mission, your flyer ventures into the shadowy storms of the spirit world to tackle ghostly aircraft; be sure to equip Radiant Aura for this. Stay low and maintain a high rate of fire, sweeping back and forth to destroy the many small, weak enemies that appear. Be especially watchful for the small pink and blue sparks; these entities dive toward you quickly and attempt to ram you. When the larger purple flyers appear, move into the center so you're not struck by them as they circle around behind you. Avoid using upgrades and save all your Chi for the final battle against a massive cloud of energy. Five smaller vortices orbit it, acting as shield and point defense. For maximum points, destroy these before taking out the core. Concentrate on evasion and activate Radiant Aura to protect yourself. The enemy's strongest attack is a stream of lightning; observe the small orbs carefully to see which way the bolts will go, then find a safe place to wait out the storm.

Mission 7, Mission 8, and Mission 9 are described in the Hin Goo side quest in the Chapter Three walkthrough.

Mission 10: Battle of Dirge

Equip Tremor or some other area attack upgrade for this mission. This is one of the more difficult missions, though it starts off mildly with a few quick but very weak enemies. Shoot them to grab a Weapon orb or two before the real onslaught begins. A row of schooners arcs slowly across your path, leaving behind a trail of mines. Concentrate on destroying or avoiding the fast ships that dive toward you, and clear away the mines with your chosen area attack upgrade. After they pass by, move to the center and stay there; more large ships slowly circle you, dropping mines and taking potshots at you. Concentrate on evasion while firing continually; try to build up as much Chi as possible for the massive mothership that appears at the end of the mission. This colossal aircraft fires triple spreads of bullets that, thankfully, move quite slowly. Reverse Tide makes evasion much easier. Thread your way between the gaps, firing away at all times, and use your upgrades to take care of the homing missiles launched at you. This ship has a *lot* of Health, so place a priority on evasion to minimize damage so you can outlast it to victory.

Mission 11: Encounter in the Skies 1

This is by far the most difficult of the three recurring travel missions. Tremor can save your life here, and you should always take it with you when flying from place to place. The first wave of enemies zig-zags quickly across the screen, but they whither under a steady barrage from your guns. As they switch direction, stay out of the center until the wave passes. Two mine-laying schooners and a large gunship appear next; wait until the last possible moment before using Tremor to destroy the greatest number of enemies (and their mines) in one blast. During a lull in the attack, reposition yourself as far back as possible. Twin rows of light planes swoop across from left to right; fire continually to restore your Chi before their big brother arrives. The heavy biplane that appears at the end may not seem imposing, but this flyer can take a great deal of punishment. Fortunately, the twin streams of planes passing by act as a shield, protecting you from incoming flak. Your guns can't destroy the biplane's homing missiles, but upgrades with an area effect can. Save your Chi for missile defense and fire relentlessly to complete the mission.

Mission 12: Encounter in the Skies 2

This short mission can be tricky without the right tactics. Two schooners weave forward on either side, laying clusters of mines. They're trying to herd you toward the center, where smaller, faster ships swoop in and try to ram you. A nonstop stream of bullets up the aisle between the mines can destroy most of these before they get close. Save your upgrades for the ones that slip through. The mission ends after the large mine-dropping schooners finish their pass.

Mission 13: Encounter in the Skies 3

Several streams of medium flyers swoop around the screen in a circle, forcing you to stay in the center. As they orbit you, smaller and weaker aircrafts try to collide with you. Hold your ground and blast them as they close in, grabbing any Weapon orbs left behind. Stay in the center and keep firing until the onslaught relents, then move back to prepare for the second wave, which consists of a dozen mine-laying schooners. Sweep back and forth, painting the sky with flak to destroy them before they cross your path.

LORD LAO'S FURNACE

MAP LEGEND

- ● Container
- ○ Scrollstand
- 1 Cranking Cauldron
- 2 Clapper Chimney
- 3 Conductor
- 4 Water Wheel
- 5 Whirling Cogs
- 6 Fuel Hopper
- 7 Dragon Button
- 8 Tiger Button

Cranking Cauldron

Clapper Chimney

Conductor

Water Wheel

Whirling Cogs

Fuel Hopper

Dragon Button

Tiger Button

The Celestial Order, Vol. 3: This document tells how sacred spirits can fall from their appointed duties and become demons.

After you complete Kang's First Mission, you arrive at a corner of the celestial realm known as Lord Lao's Furnace, an assemblage of magical contraptions that can refine commom substances into rare goods.

To use the furnace, you need two things: the fuel, which is usually a mundane item found during your adventures, and a configuration, which tells you which apparatuses must be activated to perform the refinement. After you've visited the furnace once, speak with Kang repeatedly to receive hints on where more fuels and configurations can be found. Once you have a configuration, throw the levers that correspond to the devices listed; they are scattered around the yard in front of the furnace and are all clearly labeled. Next, enter the building and examine the fuel tank to load it with the specified raw material. Finally, activate the furnace using either the Dragon switch or the Tiger switch.

The furnace resets after each use in preparation for another run, but implementing the Configurations of the Goat or Rat permanently wrecks the furnace. Performing refinements leads to new flying missions from Kang. Mission Five: Kang's Second Mission unlocks after you make three items, while Mission Six: Spirit Journey unlocks after you make six items. Purchase any needed flyer upgrades before trying the Spirit Journey; if you accept the challenge, then give up before completing it, Kang never mentions the mission again.

The eight configurations you can implement are detailed in the table here:

LORD LAO'S FURNACE

Configuration	Fuel	Fuel Location	Kang's Notes	Configuration Location	Combination	Button	Reward
Configuration of the Ox	A Vial of Sulfurous Water	Chest in the Pirate Workshop	None	Ceramic Urn in Lord Lao's Furnace	Clapper Chimney, Water Wheel	Dragon	Gem: **Spirit of the Master** (Magic style damage +25%)
Configuration of the Tiger	A Bar of Nickeled Iron	Purchase from Blacksmith in the Market District	Transcribed Gear Etchings	Given by Jinlin, in the Necropolis, for helping her on her quest	Conductor, Whirling Cogs	Dragon	Technique: **The Quieted Mind** (Focus +30)
Configuration of the Rabbit	Cow Bezoar	Ceramic Urn in Lord Lao's Furnace	Interpreted Furnace Movement	Scrollstand in Lotus Assassin fortress	Conductor, Clapper Chimney, Whirling Cogs	Dragon	Gem: **Heaven's Blessing Gem** (Wind shield, Open Palm only)
Configuration of the Dragon	A Vial of Sulfurous Water	Given by Kang upon completion of the first flyer mission	Scrap Paper Note or Transcribed Leaf Note	Bamboo Cask in the Market District	Clanking Cauldron, Whirling Cogs	Tiger	Technique: **A Mountain Within** (Body +5)
Configuration of the Snake	A Bar of Nickeled Iron	Chest in Tien's Landing	Transcribed Post Carving	Scrollstand in Scholars' Garden	Conductor, Clapper Chimney, Cranking Cauldron	Tiger	Technique: **Calm as the Morning Breeze** (Mind +5)
Configuration of the Horse	Cow Bezoar	Given by the Ghost of Merchant Bai, in the Necropolis	Scrap Paper Note or Transcribed Leaf Note	Scrollstand in the Pirate Workshop	Conductor, Clapper Chimney, Cranking Cauldron, Water Wheel	Tiger	Technique: **The Song of the Spirit** (Spirit +5)
Configuration of the Goat	Eyes of the Void	Given by Kang	None	Given by Kang	Conductor, Whirling Cogs, Water Wheel	Tiger	Technique: **Harmony and Balance** (Body +3, Spirit +3, Mind +3)
Configuration of the Rat	Eyes of the Void	Given by Kang	None	Given by Kang	Clapper Chimney, Cranking Cauldron, Whirling Cogs, Water Wheel	Dragon	Gem: **Strength of the Bull** (Martial style damage +25%)

NOTE

Once you can reach Lord Lao's furnace, you can get extra experience and see some fun effects by messing with the machine without configurations. For a chuckle, try activating the Water Wheel, Cranking Cauldron, and Clapper Chimney and then pressing the Tiger button to start the machine. This combination causes you to briefly change into a member of the opposite gender, much to the amusement of your Followers.

NOTE

You are also able to buy Cow Bezoar or Sulfurous Water from Zin Bu. This is a requirement to completing all configurations if you took the evil path and destroyed Bai, or forgot to loot the Pirate chest before leaving.

SURVIVAL IN THE JADE EMPIRE

BODY, MIND, AND SPIRIT

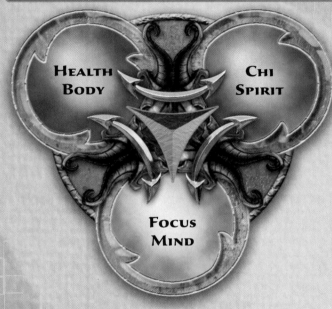

The Wheel of the Soul: Your abilities flow from, and between, these three characteristics.

Surviving and thriving in the Jade Empire involves a full commitment to learning the nuances of your being: your Body, Mind, and Spirit. During your adventuring, your Body's energy levels are measured using the Health meter, the red line. Your Spirit, known as Chi, is the blue line. Your Mind, or Focus, is the golden line.

Your Health shows how physically unscathed you are. The lower your Health, the weaker, or more wounded you become. Lose all your Health, and you drop dead.

Your Chi allows your inner Spirit to react and manipulate situations. It's responsible for magical incantations of all kinds, as well as an inner healing power you can apply to your Health.

Your Focus, and years of training, allows you to concentrate on a battle and slow the pace of it so that your actions become precise and devastating. You also wield weapons using this innate ability.

Comprehensive methods for using your abilities are detailed in the previous chapter.

ABILITY MANAGEMENT

When you gain enough experience to move up a level, you receive three Ability Points to spend. The following formula uses your Body, Mind, or Spirit to calculate your total Health, Chi, or Focus:

Ability Total = 100 Starting Ability Points + (Ability Points x 10)

Therefore, increasing a statistic by one Ability Point (of which you receive three per level) adds 10 actual points to your total. For example, if you place all three points into Chi when you level up, you receive:

3 AP x 10 = 30 Chi Points

> ### TIP
> *Although a sturdy frame and a healthy physique are a must, a large reserve of Chi is more useful, as it allows you to heal yourself and employ Magic. This versatility usually allows you to survive for longer.*

Whether you wish to concentrate on your Health, Chi, or Focus is up to you. However, your victory pose after each battle reflects which ability has the highest statistics.

Health poses

Chi poses

Focus poses

STAYING IN SHAPE

To continue your adventuring, you must replenish your abilities. You may use the following methods:

A Focus Shrine (restores Focus)

A Spirit Font (restores Chi, also fills Health)

Chi healing (restores Health)

Spirit Thief style (restores Chi)

Red Minister style (restores Health and Chi)

Harmonic combos (an orb of a differing ability appears after your foe is dispatched)

Placing Abbot Song, Wild Flower, Dawn Star, or Sky in Support mode (restores Health, Chi, or Focus)

Entering an area, such as returning to Tien's Landing or between Arena battles (restores Health, Chi, or Focus)

The rate at which power-up orbs appear is random, but it's also based on the Difficulty level you chose, as the following table demonstrates:

ORB APPEARANCE PERCENTAGES

Difficulty	Percentage Chance of Orb Appearance
Easy	66
Normal (Chapter One)	45
Normal (rest of adventure)	33
Hard	20

Additionally, the chance for power-ups to appear decreases by two percent per chapter after Chapter One.

The type of orb you gather from the remains of the recently slain is revealed in the following table:

ORB APPEARANCE TYPE

Health		Chi	
	Percentage Chance of Orb Appearance 40		Percentage Chance of Orb Appearance 30
Focus		**Unblockable/Full Restore**	
Percentage Chance of Orb Appearance 20		Percentage Chance of Orb Appearance 10	

The last opponent in any combat always has an increased chance of generating a power-up.

Each orb, gathered by running into it, replenishes your ability to the maximum. The unblockable orb allows even your fast attacks to penetrate your opponents' shields.

THE GENTLE ART OF PERSUASION

Mindless violence is not appreciated in certain quarters of the Jade Empire, where effective verbiage is more powerful than the martial art. Three emotional traits can influence a conversation: Charm, Intuition, and Intimidation. Each skill is based on a blend of two different abilities; its value is equal to the average of these abilities, plus any modifiers applied by gems or Techniques.

CONVERSATION SKILLS

Skill	Base Abilities
Charm	Body, Mind
Intuition	Mind, Spirit
Intimidation	Body, Spirit

Charm: Use your witticisms and charisma to sweet talk your way out of a situation.

Intuition: Use innate quick-thinking to react knowingly to a problem.

When these appear during dialog, employ them to manipulate others into doing what you want. The game compares your conversation skill, plus a small random amount, to a target number that depends on how strong-willed or determined the person you're talking to is. Gems that enhance conversation skills are often critical to successfully influencing others; place them in your amulet before opening a dialogue.

Intimidation: Use posturing to appear menacing or important to win a discussion.

If you fail in your attempt, you can sometimes attempt again (or simply save your game before the conversation, and restart that way), but not in every instance. Thankfully, the Walkthrough informs you of every occasion.

THE DRAGON AMULET

The Dragon Amulet allows the use of essence gems. It is a key item during your early adventures, though your character will eventually progress beyond the need for it. You can use three (later five, ultimately seven) essence gems at a time, gaining abilities that range from the mundane to the almost omnipotent.

Gain your first piece of the amulet in the Spirit Cave.

Gain your second piece of the amulet by defeating Inquisitor Lim in Chapter Two.

Essence gems have a range of benefits. Some affect your abilities and conversation skills. Some affect damage from traps, enhance your evasion, and raise the frequency of obtaining power-ups. Three gems change you character's appearance by cloaking you in damage shields that surround you in powerful whirlwinds.

TIP

- *Don't use gems that raise the frequency of obtaining power-ups, as they penalize your abilities. If you are hoping for a particular orb to appear, use a Harmonic Combo.*
- *Don't purchase gems from merchants during Chapters One, Two, or Three. The same gems can be obtained, for free, in chests or by defeating enemies.*
- *If you're holding onto gems you never use, or have a more potent version of them, sell them!*
- *Don't equip gems with abilities that cancel each other out.*

The Heaven's Blessing Gem, Gem of Storm's Rage, and Cyclone Gem each wreathe you in whirlwinds.

TECHNIQUES

Techniques are objects that have special powers imbued in them. As soon as you obtain one, its effects are permanent. They almost always have beneficial aspects, but they're not as powerful as gems. Techniques can affect your Health, Chi, and Focus directly, as well as conversational skills. Some rare and highly potent Techniques boost Body, Mind, or Spirit, as much as gems do. Other than that, they have no additional effect.

TIP

When perusing a merchant's wares, always buy Techniques first, unless otherwise instructed in the Walkthrough.

Techniques: Reasonably priced, and guaranteed to increase your prowess

THE TWO PATHS

"The teachings of Sagacious Tien are very simple, but the implications are astoundingly complex. At the heart of the teachings are the concepts of harmony and discord.

"Also referred to as the Way of the Open Palm and the Way of the Closed Fist, one cannot exist without the other, but neither can they co-exist in one person.

"Harmony *with* the world comes from understanding your place *in* the world. An ant that believes it is a tiger will never achieve harmony.

"In other words, accepting your place in the world and using your skills accordingly is the optimal way of following the path of harmony.

"Discord is the other side of the coin. People who choose the path of discord seek their own advancement over everything else.

"These people will ignore the world and use whatever means necessary to raise themselves above their station.

"Sagacious Tien taught both harmony and discord to his students, for one cannot be fully known without the other. However, he himself followed the way of harmony."

—The teachings of Sagacious Tien (excerpt), as explained by Philosopher Jiao, Scholars' Garden, Imperial City.

The path of harmony or discord is open to you, and all the moral choices you make occur during dialog with others. It is wise to choose a path and stick to it as additional styles and gameplay elements become available, and the strength of certain styles increases as you align yourself with either the Open Palm (harmony) or Closed Fist (discord). Your Followers slowly gravitate to your chosen alignment, and when you make a particular dialog choice, your character's face reflects the alignment of the response you've chosen, too.

This idling character has yet to decide on a path.

The character's stance in your menu also reflects your chosen path.

THE WAY OF THE OPEN PALM

Choose harmony. Choose to help rather than hinder, to give rather than take, and to respect rather than insult.

Those following the Open Palm path can use the Magic style Stone Immortal and receive powerful bonuses the farther along the path they travel. Your character's appearance reflects your choice, and a blue halo forms around your head.

Stone Immortal style

Open Palm

Pure Open Palm

THE WAY OF THE CLOSED FIST

Choose discord. Choose deviousness rather than honesty, to show strength rather than weakness, and to focus on yourself, ignoring others.

Those following the Closed Fist path can use the Magic style Tempest and receive powerful bonuses the farther along the path they travel. Your character's appearance reflects your choice, as a red glow begins to swirl around you, and your shadow becomes twisted.

Tempest style

Closed Fist: Note the writhing shadow (left)

Pure Closed Fist

Pure Closed Fist practitioners can kick monkeys and lapdogs into another dimension, or employ some Followers to do the same. Health orbs often adorn the aftermath.

EXPLORING THE EMPIRE
CONTAINERS

The lands of the Jade Empire are scattered with relics, booty, and long-forgotten treasures that are ripe for the picking. Although many appear as wooden chests, containers also can be vases, cabinets, the interior of a dead body, or a cask. The current environment may hinder your treasure hunting; long grass makes containers particularly difficult to spot.

Casks   *Chests (small)*

Chests (medium)   *Chests (large)*

Urns (with a hinged lid)   *Cabinets*

Stalagmites   *Headstones (type I)*

Headstones (type II)

Vases

Jars

Scrollstands

Solve the problem of overlooking a well-hidden container by using your Targeting Cursor: it automatically locates hidden objects for you. Examine all areas your cursor shows as potentially interesting.

Now you don't see it...

...Now you do. Thanks to the Targeting Cursor.

Containers usually award you with a fixed number of silver pieces. If the container has a gem stored inside, its appearance is often random. Other containers seem to have been looted previously and have nothing inside, although there is a chance you can earn a free gem. Items can also be found in containers, and plot-specific ones are called out in the Walkthrough. Sometimes you find containers that cannot be targeted at all; do not ignore these, but smash them open in Free Target mode. Free Target mode, however, can only occur while you are in combat.

Your path also affects how you open containers. Those following Open Palm tend to gently cajole a container to unlock. Those following Closed Fist tend to kick or smash them.

TRAPPED CONTAINERS

Those storing their valuables sometimes lay a snare inside treasure containers to wound you as you open them. These containers look identical to regular ones—unless you are equipped with the Gem of Thief's Sense, which forewarns you of traps. The maps in this guide's Walkthroughs show you every trapped container, for your convenience.

Trapped containers still contain treasure, however, in the form of silver pieces. The following table shows how much to expect:

TRAPPED CONTAINER SP CONTENTS			
Chapter	Amount	Chapter	Amount
One	25–50	Five	125–250
Two	50–100	Six	150–300
Three	75–150	Seven	175–350
Four	100–200		

In addition to your possible SP prize, every trapped chest grants you a random gem 25 percent of the time.

Adventurers such as yourself, with skill and guile, soon learn to "Focus evade" a trap. This is based on how high your Focus is compared with your other statistics. If your character is balanced (i.e., your Health, Chi, and Focus are all the same amount), then without gems to boost your statistics, your chance to evade a trap is 75 percent. Naturally, if your character has a higher Focus, and the bar is full (i.e., your Focus bar is 120 percent compared to your Health and Chi), expect that chance to increase. Focus evade is triggered automatically and costs five percent of your total Focus.

Avoid an unpleasant surprise with lithe athleticism and a mind sharper than Gujin's ceremonial blades.

TRAP KNOWLEDGE

The Gem of Thief's Sense shows a dark red aura.

This general information regarding traps should aid your progress:

- The Gem of Thief's Sense allows you to see red vapor dissipating from a trapped chest.
- Gems can affect (reduce or negate) the damage you receive from traps.
- Gems can affect your chance to Focus evade traps.
- Gems can remove the Focus evade cost.
- Trapped containers always appear in the same place.
- A trap will almost never kill you, but it can reduce your statistics significantly, so beware of combat occurring just afterward.

There are three types of traps: fire traps (removing Health), gas traps (also removing Health), and magic traps (removing Chi). The following table shows the type of damage they can deal:

The fire trap

The gas trap

The magic trap

TRAP DAMAGE TABLE	
Type of Trap	Damage
Fire Trap (Chapter One, Two, Three, Four)	Between one-sixth and one-third of current Health
Fire Trap (Chapter Five, Six, Seven)	Between one-quarter and one-half of current Health
Gas Trap (Chapter One, Two, Three)	Between one-eighth and one-quarter of current Health
Gas Trap (Chapter Four, Five, Six, Seven)	Between one-sixth and one-third of current Health
Magic Trap (Chapter One, Two, Three, Four)	Between one-sixth and one-third of current Chi
Magic Trap (Chapter Five, Six, Seven)	Between one-quarter and one-half of current Chi

SCROLLSTANDS

Imparting wisdom to those patient enough to read the knowledge contained on the reed paper, scrollstands dot the Jade Empire landscape. Voracious readers should be pleased to know that there are additional benefits from studying the insight inked on these scrolls (aside from background knowledge and sometimes humorous comments on the neighborhood you are visiting). You receive one percent of your total XP each time you review a scrollstand (from Chapter Three onward,

this drops to three-quarters of a percent). In addition, be sure to look out for "sets" of scrollstands; reading them all grants you a "literary technique." Fortunately, you need not look far; all the scrollstands are shown on the maps and in the Walkthrough.

> **TIP**
>
> To squeeze the maximum number of Experience Points from each scrollstand, put off reading them as long as possible.

LET THE EXPLORATION BEGIN!

Your training is at an end. The tranquil backwaters of the Two Rivers School awaits you. The remainder of this guide enlightens your path. Good luck in your adventuring.

WALKTHROUGH INTRODUCTION

Your epic adventure through the Jade Empire unfolds over the course of seven chapters. The walkthrough is divided correspondingly, with all the information for each chapter grouped into three main sections: Area Overview, Critical Path, and Side Quests.

OVERVIEW

The Overview is a detailed travel guide to every location visited during that chapter. Maps are labeled with markers that pinpoint landmarks, treasure, and notable persons, as shown:

DAM SITE

to Ruins

Crash Site

Drawbridge

Jade Heart

Great Dam

to Ruins

Imperial Watch Tower

Ruins Gate

to Tien's Landing

MAP LEGEND

	Container
	Trapped Container
	Focus Shrine
	Scrollstand
	Spirit Font
1	Silk Fox
2	Chen Yi
3	Water Dragon's Spirit
4	Wild Flower/ Chai Ka

Following the map, key sites are featured in greater detail with information on local history, population, hazards, and events.

The Benefits of Being Well-Read: Every scrollstand in an area is shown, with the title referenced. Read them all to gain XP and learn literary techniques.

Character Portrait

The Jade Empire is full of notable characters from all walks of life, and not all of them are human. Each are noted on the map with a number that corresponds to their description in the chapter. These brief portrait/bios give information on quests and items associated with each person. If the character is a merchant or otherwise sells items, his or her inventory is shown.

CRITICAL PATH

The second section of each walkthrough chapter follows the events that *must* be triggered to pursue the story to its conclusion. It's broken into sections that correspond roughly to the entries in your Quest Journal.

If you purchased the version of this guide that includes Prima's exclusive DVD strategy, you'll see a DVD symbol throughout the walkthrough that lets you know there's a corresponding menu available on the companion DVD.

Innumerable foes lie between you and the completion of your quest. Each confrontation is accompanied by a table providing details on who (or what) you're up against. Most XP and SP awards are variable; in this case an average is shown, as indicated by a "~" in this example:

BANDIT BATTLE: ~40 XP, ~30 SP			
Enemy	Style	Health	Chi
Bandit	Basic	25	25
Bandit	Legendary Strike	25	25

During your adventure, you're given many opportunities to make a moral gesture by choosing from several courses of action. When this happens, the potential outcomes are broken down into choices as shown below:

Choice 1 👐 Actions that show a masterful understanding of the Way of the Open Palm are listed with a double icon.

Choice 2 🤚 Deeds of lesser Open Palm merit are listed next, with a single icon.

Choice 3 ✊ This icon signals consequences that carry the force of the Closed Fist.

Choice 4 ✊✊ A double icon is reserved for the Closed Fist's greatest expressions.

Choice 5 Neutral outcomes usually carry the least reward. Any unfavorable, unusual, or miscellaneous outcomes are grouped at the end.

NOTE

Note boxes contain supplemental information such as a reminder that a merchant has new inventory or as a pointer to hard-to-spot containers.

TIP

Tips contain practical strategies that can make your adventure easier, such as how to earn a discount from a merchant or useful tactics that apply to specific enemies or battles.

CAUTION

Caution boxes point out the deadliest pitfalls that lie in your path and how to avoid them. The information found here could very well save your life.

SIDE QUEST

For the intrepid adventurer, opportunities for side quests abound. Deeds and exploits that lie off the beaten path are heralded in a box such as this, which refers you to the appropriate heading at the end of the chapter.

SIDE QUESTS

Side quests are optional events. They aren't required for completion of the game but are still important parts of the overall tale. Many of the Empire's greatest rewards lie down these paths. Each side quest is listed under a separate heading that corresponds to a boxed reference in the critical path. The side quests comprise the third section of each walkthrough chapter except the last three, which feature few or no side quests.

QUEST SUMMARY

NOTE

The following list summarizes all the quests exactly as they appear in your Quest Journal during the game. For simplicity some of these quests have been consolidated or reassigned to other headings in our walkthrough, but fear not: nothing has been omitted. This list is provided as a reference for those who wish to ensure that their Quest Journal is complete.

CHAPTER ONE CRITICAL PATH

A Master's Teachings: Use the skills and knowledge you learned from Master Li to fight bandits, save the town, and complete your lessons in the spirit cave.

The Search for Dawn Star: Follow Gao's trail through the swamps north of Two Rivers and save Dawn Star.

The Burning Town: Search for survivors in the burning wreckage of Two Rivers.

CHAPTER ONE SIDE QUESTS

The Flower of the Fields: Help Merchant Hing find his beloved Fen.

An Unfortunate Debt: A man in Two Rivers owes money to Gao the Greater. Help him out, one way or another.

The Lions of Two Rivers: A lion statue in Master Li's home has a few lessons to teach you.

Kia Min: Help heal Kia Min so she can join in as you challenge her record and fight for Smiling Mountain's prize.

CHAPTER TWO CRITICAL PATH

Picking up the Pieces: You crash landed near the town of Tien's Landing. You must find a way to get back on the route to the Imperial City.

A Woman in Black: You meet a mysterious woman named Silk Fox, who seems to be on your side.

Hui the Brave: Hui the Brave, an old friend of Master Li's, tells you that a piece of your Dragon Amulet is in the ruins of old Tien's Landing. Go find it.

Find a New Flyer: Head out to the pirates' lair downriver to look into acquiring one of their flyers.

The Sickened Forest: Lord Yun will give you a wind map if you can help cure the sickened Great Southern Forest.

Speak with Kang: Speak with Kang the Mad to leave for the Imperial City.

CHAPTER TWO SIDE QUESTS

The Beaten Baker: Baker Bei gets beaten up daily by a gang of thugs. Find out why.

The Promise: Baker Bei's attackers are on Ai Ling's payroll. It seems he promised her that he would marry her. Something's just not right here.

Matchmaker: You've broken up Ai Ling and Baker Bei, but now you must find Ai Ling a husband. Good luck.

The Zither of Discord: Scholar Six Heavens wants you to find the pieces of the Zither of Discord, an ancient Closed Fist artifact.

The Test of the Closed Fist: Bladed Thesis tests you to see if you are a true follower of the Way of the Closed Fist. Answer him with the correct Closed Fist philosophy.

Stranded Orphan Girl: The ghost of a young girl is stranded in the caves below the ruins of old Tien's Landing. Help her get out.

The Great Dam: Minister Sheng asks you to go close the Great Dam and bring prosperity to Tien's Landing once more. Merchant Jiang asks you to sabotage the dam so he can continue to sell wine at high prices.

Trapped: A ship and its sailors are trapped in Tien's Landing and are causing problems. Close the Great Dam to see them on their way.

Old Mother Kwan: Three Sheets Dutong took the Tien's Landing Tea House from the previous owner, Old Mother Kwan. Dutong's documents don't seem to be entirely in order, however.

An Ancient Game: Two masters, Jian the Iron Fist and Mistress Vo, play a mental game of strategy in Tien's Landing. They have both offered to train you if you can prove to one of them that you are following that one's path faithfully enough.

The Drowned Orphans: Bin and Miao, ghosts of two drowned orphans, want rest and revenge, respectively. Go find Kindly Yushan and help them find satisfaction.

Yifong and Fuyao: Yifong and Fuyao were captured by pirates on their way out of town. You can choose to free them or sell them into slavery, and you can poison young Fuyao's mind in the process.

Gems in the Quarry: A rat demon told you about some gems hidden in the quarry. This quest is sure to have an explosive solution.

Zhong the Ox Carrier: A giant, grief-stricken ogre refuses to leave the Tea House. Maybe you can reason with him.

The Stolen Memento: A sailor named Tong stole a figurine from Merchant Cheung. Go get it back.

Fox Hunt: While you're in the forest, some nice inn patrons ask you to take out the mean fox spirit that keeps attacking the people in the forest.

Cannibals in the Inn: While you're in the forest, those nice inn patrons turn out to be evil cannibals. Kill them and their Mother.

Chapter Three Critical Path

The Emperor and the Assassins: Silk Fox shows up and challenges you to find evidence that Death's Hand is working against her father, the Emperor. To do that, you must infiltrate the Lotus Assassin fortress.

The Executioners: To impress the Lotus Assassin Executioner recruiter, advance to the Silver Division championship in the Imperial Arena.

The Inquisitors: To impress the Lotus Assassin Inquisitor recruiter, prevent Minister Sheng from delivering his testimony to Judge Fang.

Infiltrate the Lotus Assassin fortress: Enter the Lotus Assassin fortress and find the evidence Silk Fox needs.

Kill Master Shin: Master Gang asks you to kill his superior, Master Shin.

Create a Spirit Shard: Master Gang asks you to prepare a spirit shard with which to create a Jade Golem. Sagacious Zu has some ideas about how best to do this.

Chapter Three Side Quests

The Outlander: An unruly Outlander is making waves in the Scholars' Garden. Go shut him up.

The Play's the Thing: Take the role of an actor in a play and either play it straight or sow controversy.

Mechanic Hin Goo: Mechanic Hin Goo has a number of missions for you to undertake in your flyer.

The Gambler's Favor: Gambler Daoshen asks you to deliver his fees to the Guild so he can raise the stakes on his betting game in the arena tavern.

The Imperial Arena: The Imperial Arena is a great place for a fighter to show off his or her skills. This is also part of the Executioners' plot in the critical path.

A Bronzed Opportunity: Lucky Cho offers you a deal: For a small sum of silver, he will have Crimson Khana poisoned, giving you an easy match for the Bronze Division title in the arena.

Soldier's Offer: Iron Soldier offers to throw the Silver Division championship bout if you take care of an old enemy of his, General Stone Kao.

Fading Moon's Bounty: Captain Sen has two bounties for you. One is the nefarious arsonist, Fading Moon.

Creative Yukong's Bounty: Captain Sen has two bounties for you. One is the cunning con man, Creative Yukong.

Aishi the Mournful Blade: An old man fills you in on a third available bounty once you finish the other two. Aishi the Mournful Blade is a deadly criminal, and the reward will be great if you can bring her in.

The Slavers: Prefect Jitong needs help solving a mystery involving slave traders. He has two suspects, and he asks you to figure out which one is truly guilty.

The Black Leopard School: The Black Leopard School suffers from having two masters with radically opposed philosophies. Maybe you can help sort things out.

Jinlin: Jinlin needs to find an item deep in an ancient tomb in the Necropolis.

The First Gravedigger: Gravedigger Shen has a number of jobs for you, seeing as his graveyard is overrun with ghosts.

A Mournful Ghost: The ghost of Miss Chan grieves for her missing son. To put her to rest, you have to convince her that she and her son are both dead.

A Fearful Ghost: The ghost of Merchant Bai fears further torment from the ghosts of the men who killed him. Help him find peace.

A Vengeful Ghost: The ghost of Mister Ren seeks revenge on his wife for killing him. Find some way to bring him peace.

The Tanners Fong: The "ghost" of the Elder Tanner Fong seems to have risen and left to visit his son. Find out what lies beneath the surface.

The Scientist: Mad Wen needs to perform a liver transplant on his dying daughter. Either find him another liver or get him in touch with someone who can help.

Sagacious Zu's Hidden Past: Sagacious Zu's secrets will come out just before his last breath.

Chapter Four Critical Path

The Height of Power: With the proof against the Emperor in hand, go to the Imperial Palace and confront him about his misdeeds.

Chapter Four Side Quests

None

Chapter Five Critical Path

The Land of Spirits: You are dead. The Water Dragon can restore your life, but you must restore her corrupted fountains, the source of her power, first.

Chapter Five Side Quests

Gem of Power: A powerful gem is hidden somewhere in Dirge. Find it.

Chapter Six Critical Path

The Return to Dirge: You have returned to life, but the armies of Master Li are not far behind. You and your Followers must protect the temple and drive back the army.

Chapter Six Side Quests

None

These entries are added to your Quest Journal during Chapter Six and they only appear while you are playing that particular character during the siege.

The Black Whirlwind's Journal

Daily Reminder: A reminder of tasks the Black Whirlwind must do daily.

Protect Spear Catches Leaf: A note to himself to protect Spear Catches Leaf from when he was in Lord Yun's employ.

Conquer the Southern Continent: A reminder of the Black Whirlwind's journeys in the south.

Defend Dirge from Sun Li's Troops: A reminder to the Black Whirlwind to help defend Dirge from the oncoming troops of Master Li.

Dawn Star's Journal

Capital Aspirations: Dawn Star wants to visit the Imperial City.

Silk Fox: Dawn Star is not sure of the intentions of this Silk Fox, but she must band with her to save Dirge.

Protect Kang: Dawn Star must protect Kang the Mad as he places explosives during the siege.

Prince Sun Kin's Journal

One Chance: Prince Kin's spirit has one chance to free itself from the yoke of the Water Dragon's power by defeating Death's Hand.

Silk Fox's Journal

An Unlikely Ally: Silk Fox keeps a journal of meeting the player and joining up with him or her.

The Lotus Assassin Fortress: Silk Fox must find proof of the treachery of Death's Hand.

Dawn Star: Silk Fox must lead the naïve farm girl to protect the temple of Dirge.

Flight to Dirge: Silk Fox and Dawn Star must protect Kang the Mad as he places explosives during the siege.

Chapter Seven Critical Path

A Master's Fate: Face Master Li and defeat him once and for all. Decide the fate of the Jade Empire.

Chapter Seven Side Quests

None

BEGIN YOUR ADVENTURE...

The gender you select is reflected in most conversations.

To start a new game, you must first select an appearance and gender for your character. Gender is the only aspect of this choice that has any bearing later on. After making your choices, you can accept the default profile shown, or you can customize the profile to your liking. By customizing, you can turn Tiger Shen into a lithe Magic specialist or evolve Radiant Jen Zi into a close-combat juggernaut.

When making a custom character, your abilities each start off with a minimum score of two. You're given four points to distribute in addition to the minimum. Avoid assigning all four points to a single ability, as your undeveloped areas can prove a weakness in earlier chapters. Spirit and Mind are the two best choices to specialize in, depending on whether you favor Magic or Weapon styles respectively. The choice is yours; for an interesting challenge you could put all your points in Body and expect to weather some tough storms. As you increase a stat, your character strikes a pose that reflects the change.

Mind specialist pose

Next, choose one of the four martial styles to start out with: Thousand Cuts, Leaping Tiger, White Demon, or Legendary Strike. Leaping Tiger's range and White Demon's power make these the two strongest choices. While Thousand Cuts and Legendary Strike can be deadly in the right hands, they are more difficult to master.

Body specialist pose

Spirit specialist pose

Choose a name for yourself as the final touch. With that, your character customization is complete and the mythical epic of the Jade Empire begins....

CHAPTER ONE

OVERVIEW

The people are scared... I do not have all the answers, but I know you will become very important to the fates of many. You will be called to face a great evil.

If he is truly better than me, let him prove it. I challenge him.

Master, student, farmer... whatever I was, I should be dust. Instead, I am pulled to nowhere. Frustration!

Wherein a Master foretells of doom,   *A rival challenges for station,*   *And the past haunts the present.*

Your training nears its completion in the idyllic setting of Two Rivers. Master Li promises that soon you will know more about how you came here and where your future will lead. All the while, strange tales begin to spread of ghosts that will not rest and shadowy assassins that heed no law.

Two Rivers School

Old Master's Tomb

Master Li's Quarters

Sparring Ring

Sparring Arena

Dawn Star's Garden

to Two Rivers Village

MAP LEGEND

⚪	*Focus Shrine*
⚪	*Scrollstand*
⚫	*Spirit Font*
1	*Master Li*
2	*Smiling Mountain*
3	*Dawn Star*
4	*Gao the Lesser*
5	*Student Jing Woo*
6	*Student Kia Min*
7	*Student Lin*
8	*Student Wen*
9	*Student Si Pat*

Two Rivers School is the only home you have ever known, though how you came here is a mystery that Master Li has never explained. An organic complex of training grounds, winding garden paths, and solemn shrines, the school is ideally suited for contemplative study.

Sparring ring

The heart of Two Rivers School is the sparring ring, a fenced circle of beaten dirt open to the sky. Its central location forces students to hone themselves under the scrutinizing eyes of their peers and Master Li.

Auspicious Portents: This bookstand northwest of the sparring ring explains the import of comets, eclipses, and meteors.

The Old Tongue, Vol. 1: Found north of the sparring ring, this tome relates the origin of Tho Fan.

Master Li's quarters

Largest of all buildings in Two Rivers, Master Li's quarters border the sparring ring on the northeast. In accord with the simplicity and frugality taught at the school, the interior is sparsely furnished. The only exception is a massive lion statue in the back room that conceals a clever puzzle designed by the school's founder.

The Long Drought: Learn of Emperor Sun's triumph over the forces of nature by reading the documents on Master Li's porch.

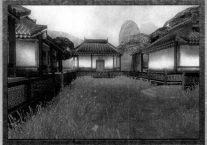

Sparring arena

Less formal than the sparring ring, the sparring arena is a simple lawn between a group of buildings on the school's south side. Smiling Mountain oversees a training competition that takes place here.

Old Master's Tomb

In the northeast corner of the grounds, behind Master Li's Quarters, is a humble tomb. It's the resting place of the Old Master, founder of the Two Rivers School. A clue to the lion statue puzzle in Master Li's quarters can be found here.

Across the southeast bridge that leads to the village lies a beautiful garden where Dawn Star, your childhood friend and another top student at Two Rivers School, lives. A Spirit Font, Focus Shrine, and the school's main gate are also here.

Dawn Star's garden

The Inner Self: A lesson for those seeking to understand the mystery of life and death. Look for it by Dawn Star's home.

CHARACTERS

Master Li

As the head of Two Rivers School, Master Li is the wisest and strongest warrior in the area. He's the only guardian that you've ever known, and the entire village looks to him for guidance and protection. His mysterious past conceals many surprising secrets....

Smiling Mountain

The assistant instructor, known affectionately as Smiling Mountain, supplements Master Li's teachings by arranging training bouts for the students in the sparring arena. If you have enough SP, you can also purchase some gems and techniques from him.

SMILING MOUNTAIN'S STORE

Item (Number Available)	Cost (SP)
Flawed Warrior Gem (1)	200
Flawed Monk Gem (1)	200
Flawed Scholar Gem (1)	200
Belly of Iron (1)	400
Heart of Gold (1)	400
Mind of Steel (1)	400

NOTE

You can buy Smiling Mountain's gems only after you've obtained the Dragon Amulet. Even then you shouldn't worry about it; you find many flawed gems in the course of your adventure.

Dawn Star

Dawn Star is one of Master Li's top students, and her sensitivity to the spirit realm has taken her down the path of sorcery. She grew up with you at Two Rivers School and is your oldest friend; this naturally leads her to become your first Follower.

Gao the Lesser

Son of Gao the Greater, Gao the Lesser arrogantly believes he deserves special treatment because of his family's wealth. His obsessive jealousy over your close relationships with Master Li and Dawn Star eventually leads to his downfall.

Student Jing Woo

Jing Woo is your sparring partner in the tutorial battle that begins your quest. He's a serious student who doesn't waste a lot of time with idle chatter, so you won't get much information from him.

Student Kia Min

Kia Min is renowned for holding the record in Smiling Mountain's training tournament. After you've helped treat the injuries she receives during the bandit raid, you can challenge her record.

Student Lin

Lin's family sent her to Two Rivers a few years ago to help her learn discipline and self-control. She's proud and ambitious, but not unfriendly; if you want to hear all the latest gossip about Two Rivers, she's the one to talk to. Student Lin is willing to spar if you have time; she puts up a respectable fight but has no defense against the blinding speed of your Focus mode.

TUTORIAL BATTLE: 40 XP, 0 SP

Enemy	Style	Health	Chi
Student Lin	Staff	100	100

Student Wen

A newcomer from the Imperial City, Wen feels a little homesick and isn't sure that Two Rivers is the right place for him. He can give you a general sense of the anxiety settling over those who live near the heart of the Empire. If you want to spar with Student Wen, simply ask!

STUDENT WEN (SPARRING MATCH): 32 XP, 0 SP

Enemy	Style	Health	Chi
Student Wen	Thousand Cuts	40	40

Student Si Pat

As one of the newest students, Si Pat is eager to make a good impression. He's been assigned the job of keeping watch at the school gate. His innocence and enthusiasm make his terrible fate all the more tragic.

TWO RIVERS VILLAGE

to Bandit Swamp

Town Gate

5

2

Beach

Gujin's Weapon Shop

6   3

1

to Two Rivers School

4

Village Square

MAP LEGEND

- Container
- Focus Shrine
- Scrollstand
- Spirit Font
- 1 Gujin the Weapon Master
- 2 Ni Joh
- 3 Old Ming
- 4 Merchant Fen Do
- 5 Guard Yung
- 6 Mrs. Jong

The residents of Two Rivers Village live in peaceful self-reliance, thanks to Master Li's protection and to their remoteness from the Imperial City. The river to the south serves as a moat and connects the town with the rest of the Empire. A stout wall stands along the northern border against the wild swamps beyond.

Village square

The south side of Two Rivers features a paved market square where villagers gather for trade; Merchant Fen Do can usually be found here. The gate to Two Rivers School opens to the west, while a wide stone stairway leads uphill to the north side of town.

Gujin's Weapon Shop

The Martial Arts: The scrollstand in the weapon shop describes the spiritual benefits of rigorous physical discipline.

The north side is dominated by Gujin's Weapon Shop, where you obtain your first weapons. Across the street is a small group of residential buildings.

The town gate is the only way through the north wall. Under the watchful eye of Guard Yung, the gate is left open during the day. The path beyond leads north to the Bandit Swamp.

Town gate

There are no docks, so river traffic must stop at a gentle beach southeast of the village. It's too shallow for large ships, but rafts and canoes can easily come aground here. Keep an eye out for the hidden cave south of the path leading back into town.

Beach

CHARACTERS

Gujin the Weapon Master

1 The old weapon master keeps a forge and shop on the north side of town. He has two weapon styles for you, but you can only choose one or the other. Fortunately, you can come back anytime to exchange weapons if you like.

Ni Joh

2 Ni Joh is the son of a local farmer. When bandits raid the village, Ni Joh is not skilled enough to fight, though, to his credit, he refuses to flee. Look for him near the beach.

Old Ming

3 An elder resident of Two Rivers, Old Ming knows a great deal of history. He's also an expert on healing salves; seek him out when you're trying to treat Kia Min's wounds. He can usually be found by Emperor Sun's statue, near the beach.

Merchant Fen Do

4 Fen Do keeps shop in the village square. He boasts that he's never been outside of Two Rivers Village, which explains why his selection is so poor. Deal cautiously with Fen Do; he won't hesitate to exploit you for maximum profit if he can.

MERCHANT FEN DO

Item (Number Available)	Cost (SP)
Flawed Monk Gem (1)	200
Flawed Scholar Gem (1)	200
Inferior Charm Gem (1)	150
Inferior Intimidation Gem (1)	150
Inferior Intuition Gem (1)	150

> **NOTE**
> You can find all of the gems Fen Do has for sale in various treasure chests and other hidden places. Don't waste your silver on them.

Guard Yung

5 The massive gate in the north wall is watched during the day by Guard Yung. The Two Rivers area is usually peaceful, leading Yung to think of his job as strictly ceremonial. When real crisis strikes, he proves unreliable.

Mrs. Jong

6 When her son died in a fishing accident, Mrs. Jong was haunted by ghostly visions. Dawn Star's unique sensitivity to the spirit realm helps her lay the troubled spirit to rest... temporarily.

SPIRIT CAVE

Old Master's Burial Chamber

Portal ①

Dragon Amulet

②

Entrance

MAP LEGEND

- ⬤ Container
- ⚪ Scrollstand
- ⬤ Spirit Font
- ① Old Master
- ② Water Dragon's Spirit

Over the ages, the hills of Two Rivers School have been hollowed by erosion to form a series of natural chambers known as the Spirit Cave. Past generations have used it as a tomb; the Old Master is among those laid to rest here.

The misty southern chamber of the Spirit Cave is lit by twin rows of braziers and an eerie phosphorescence. Master Li hid your Dragon Amulet here when he brought you to Two Rivers School.

Dragon Amulet's Cave

Old Master's burial chamber

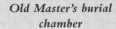

Jade Empire Bestiary, Vol. 3: Buried with the Old Master are documents warning that weapon styles have no effect on spirits.

At the back of the Spirit Cave is a rough cavern where the Old Master, founder of Two Rivers School, was buried. If you cleanse the cave of spirits, a magic portal appears here.

The Nature of the Spirit, Vol. 1: Also buried here is an explanation of various means by which a spirit may become unable to move on to the next world.

CHARACTERS

Old Master

1 The Old Master's ghost haunts the dark places beneath Two Rivers School. Although he was wise and kindly in life, now tainted by the corruption of undeath, he now only desires to slay everything that lives.

Water Dragon's Spirit

2 Your first of many encounters with the enigmatic Water Dragon occurs here. Later on she plays a critical role in your destiny, but for now she appears only long enough to bestow your first magic style.

BANDIT SWAMP

to Swamp Cave

Mosquito

Swamp Bridge

Standing Stones

Ruined Gazebo

to Two Rivers Village

MAP LEGEND

- ⬤ Container
- ⬤ Scrollstand
- ⬤ Spirit Font
- ⬤ Trapped Container
- **1** Sagacious Zu
- **2** Merchant Hing the Shunned
- **3** Sing Wa

A treacherous swamp sprawls to the north of Two Rivers Village. Sensible folk shun this area—outlaws roam everywhere in the dank and overgrown marsh, and ogres and demons make their lairs in the nearby caves.

Ruined gazebo

Standing stones

Several ruined buildings still stand here and there, remnants of a time when the swamp was more habitable. The gazebo near Two Rivers Village seems about to tilt over, but for now it still holds a usable Spirit Font.

Jade Empire Bestiary, Vol. 1: This document found among the broken pillars recommends using fire or ice magic against ogres.

More ruins dot the large clearing at the center of the swamp. These bits of shelter attract outlaws; fortunately your new Follower, Sagacious Zu, has already taken care of them for you.

While it's barely high enough to keep your feet dry, this collapsed bridge is the only safe path along the swamp's western edge.

Swamp bridge

Seldom seen in the borderlands, the Mosquito is one of the many types of flying machines invented for Gao the Greater by his pet inventor, Kang the Mad. This one is parked by the swamp cave. You can fly the Mosquito yourself after you defeat Gao the Lesser.

Mosquito

CHARACTERS

Sagacious Zu

1 Your second Follower, Sagacious Zu, is a jaded, disheveled fighter who ekes out a living on the fringe of civilization. His cynical indifference conceals a hidden conscience; when those he cares for are in trouble, he'll risk his life to save them.

Merchant Hing the Shunned

2 Merchant Hing ventured into the swamp when bandits kidnapped his precious "Flower of the Fields." The hapless merchant doesn't stand a chance unless you help him out.

Sing Wa

3 Wife of Merchant Hing the Shunned, Sing Wa was also kidnapped by bandits. She is indignant that her husband is more concerned with rescuing the family's water buffalo.

SWAMP CAVE

North Cavern

Central Cavern

South Cavern

to Bandit Swamp

MAP LEGEND

- ○ Container
- ○ Focus Shrine
- ○ Trapped Container

This lofty cavern, decorated with countless glowing mushrooms, would make a pleasant hideaway if it weren't for the prowling ogres and toad demons. You must fight through this cave to confront Gao the Lesser after he kidnaps Dawn Star.

The south cavern, nearest the entrance, consists of two parts. Monsters prowl to the west, while two chests await to the east. A path crosses from south to north through the cavern, leading deeper into the cave.

South cavern

North cavern

Your ultimate destination, the north cavern is where you reunite with Dawn Star and have your ultimate showdown with Gao the Lesser. There are also several treasure chests and a Focus Shrine here.

CRITICAL PATH

A MASTER'S TEACHINGS

SPEAK WITH MASTER LI

The story begins in Two Rivers School, where your martial arts training under Master Li is nearly complete. A junior student, Jing Woo, challenges you to a friendly training match in the sparring ring. This tutorial battle introduces the basics of combat. Follow the instructions that pop up during the battle; Jing Woo heals himself after each successful demonstration.

> ### NOTE
> *The tutorial is mandatory only if this is your first time playing* Jade Empire. *On subsequent new games, you can skip it.*

Tutorial Battle: 0 XP, 0 SP			
Enemy	Style	Health	Chi
Jing Woo	Basic	30	30

After the fight, you are told to seek out Master Li. Before you do, take time to explore the Two Rivers School and speak with your fellow students. Student Lin and Student Wen in particular have plenty to say. Gao the Lesser, your bitter rival, also gives you an earful, but the conversation is less pleasant. After looking around, head into Master Li's quarters.

Jing Woo delivers a summons from Master Li.

> ### TIP
> *Earn your first XP by reading the scrollstands scattered around the school grounds and by challenging Students Lin and Wen to sparring matches.*

Master Li prepares to complete your training by revealing your destiny.

Master Li begins to explain the great destiny that is set before you, but the conversation is interrupted. Si Pat barges in to announce that bandits have sailed up the river and invaded the village. You are instructed to seek out Dawn Star, the other top student at Two Rivers School, and take her into the village to get some weapons from Weapon Master Gujin.

> ### SIDE QUEST
> *You can now solve the riddle of the lion statue in Master Li's quarters. See* The Lion of Two Rivers *side quest for the full solution.*

FIND DAWN STAR

Gao takes advantage of the chaos to make a move on Dawn Star.

As you enter the garden on the school's east side, Dawn Star and Gao the Lesser are involved in a heated argument. Gao storms off in disgust when you interrupt the exchange. After he's gone, tell Dawn Star of Master Li's orders. She agrees to help and becomes your first Follower.

Dawn Star Profile

Attack Style: Long Sword
Support Ability: Recover Chi
Health: 130
Chi: 50

ACQUIRE YOUR WEAPONS

Go through the school gate to find a pair of bandits; you're just in time to watch as they kill a helpless villager. This is your first taste of real battle. One of the bandits uses the fast Legendary Strike style; nullify his speed by slowing him with Heavenly Wave or entering Focus mode.

BANDIT BATTLE: ~40 XP, ~30 SP			
Enemy	Style	Health	Chi
Bandit	Basic	25	25
Bandit	Legendary Strike	25	25

Arm yourself at the weapon shop before confronting the rest of the bandits.

Head south from the village square to find 25 SP in a barrel. Then ascend the main stairs and enter Gujin the weapon master's shop (50 XP). The old weapon master offers you a choice of two weapons: Fortune's Favorite, a sword, or Golden Star, a staff. The sword is a little faster, but the staff has longer reach. You can choose only one weapon, but if you return to Gujin anytime later, you can exchange it.

NOTE

If you're playing the Limited Edition release of Jade Empire, Gujin offers you Tien's Justice in place of Golden Star. Also known as a "monk's spade," Tien's Justice is a unique staff fitted at each end with a crescent blade.

TIP

The scrollstand in Gujin's shop forms a set with two others in Two Rivers School (Auspicious Portents and Inner Self). Reading all three (10 XP) earns a bonus technique: the Legacy of Master Li (Focus +7).

STOP THE BANDIT ATTACK

Si Pat interrupts your conversation with Gujin to announce that bandit reinforcements have just landed at the beach. This is the perfect chance to break in your new weapon! Exit the shop to find two of the invaders waiting for you—show them no mercy.

BANDIT BATTLE: ~40 XP, ~40 SP			
Enemy	Style	Health	Chi
Bandit	Basic	25	25
Bandit	Spear	25	25

Descend the stairs to find a quartet of burglars ganging up on Farmer Ni. You can try to save the hapless villager, but you have to act fast. This battle has two possible outcomes:

Choice 1 Save Farmer Ni by fighting aggressively. Use area attacks (Ⓐ+Ⓧ) to knock the enemies away whenever they get close to him, and make sure Dawn Star is in Attack mode to help distract the bandits. Farmer Ni can only withstand a few blows, so you must immediately target any enemy that approaches him. Use Focus mode to give yourself plenty of reaction time. Rescuing Farmer Ni has benefits even if you follow the Closed Fist, so do your best to keep him safe.

Choice 2 If Farmer Ni dies you still earn full XP for this battle.

SAVING FARMER NI: ~100 XP, ~85 SP			
Enemy	Style	Health	Chi
Bandit x3	Basic	25	25
Bandit	Spear	100	100

To find more bandits, go to the south side of town to stop a robbery in progress. Use your new weapon to quickly defeat the four invaders. The lieutenant's long sword can inflict big damage; if you're hit, back away and use Chi Heal to restore yourself.

BANDIT BATTLE: ~104 XP, ~90 SP			
Enemy	Style	Health	Chi
Bandit	Basic	25	25
Bandit	Basic	30	30
Bandit	Spear	25	25
Bandit Lieutenant	Long Sword	100	100

After the battle you find a chest left behind by the fleeing villagers. Go ahead and take the 200 SP from inside; you'll get the chance to return the money to its rightful owner later.

The hidden tunnel conceals a pair of barrels.

The village beach has become a war zone.

After taking care of business in the village, head east toward the beach to face the bandits at their landing site. Along the way, duck into the concealed tunnel on the right to find two barrels containing the bandits' loot; empty both to gain 117 SP. A scene of carnage awaits you on the beach as the bandit leader pelts the villagers with cannon fire from the safety of his ship. When you arrive, he commands his men to attack.

CAUTION

The cannonade doesn't let up as you fight bandits. Whenever you hear the sound of the ship's guns, take evasive action! If you move fast, you can escape the impact...but your enemies aren't so lucky. The beach's east side is out of the cannon's reach, too.

BANDIT BATTLE: ~138 XP, ~125 SP

Enemy	Style	Health	Chi	
Bandit x2	Basic	25	25	
Bandit x2	Basic	30	30	
Bandit	Spear	125	125	

When the first wave of bandits is defeated, a second group storms ashore. One of them uses a new martial style, Leaping Tiger. Use Chi Strikes to finish him quickly, but try to conserve your Focus for the next battle.

BANDIT BATTLE: ~158 XP, ~200 SP

Enemy	Style	Health	Chi	
Bandit	Basic	30	30	
Bandit	Spear	30	30	
Bandit	Basic	50	50	
Bandit Leader	Leaping Tiger	175	175	

The bandit leader recognizes you as a serious threat and unleashes stronger foes: summoned ghosts. These enemies might not have as much health as the bandits, but they can pelt you with shards of ice from long range. Close the distance quickly with evasive leaps, and continually change position between your attacks to avoid being targeted. If you saved your Focus during the previous battles, use it now.

TIP

Weapon and support styles have no effect on ghosts. Switch to your chosen martial style for this fight.

GHOST BATTLE: ~71 XP, 0 SP

Enemy	Style	Health	Chi
Summoned Ghost	Ice Shard	25	25
Summoned Ghost	Ice Shard	30	30
Summoned Ghost	Spear	50	50

One blow from Master Li causes the bandit ship to explode.

When the ghosts are defeated, the bandit leader finally decides to take you on personally. Master Li arrives just in the nick of time, however, and with a single strike destroys the bandit ship. He reveals that the bandit leader is actually a Lotus Assassin, a deadly killer and much stronger foe than you are prepared to face. Master Li then returns to the school and asks you to meet with him again after you have explored the village.

MEET WITH MASTER LI AGAIN

Before leaving the beach, head over to the statue of Emperor Sun to meet Old Ming. He has a lot of information about the history of Two Rivers Village and the Jade Empire, and he's happy for the chance to discuss these subjects at length.

Next, speak with Ni Joh. He asks about his father, Farmer Ni, whom you had the chance to rescue back in the village square. There are four possible outcomes:

Old Ming is a walking encyclopedia of history.

Choice 1 You saved Farmer Ni. Tell Ni Joh, "There is no more reason to be concerned."

Choice 2 You saved Farmer Ni. Tell Ni Joh that his father is "Alive and useless, like the rest of you."

Choice 3 Farmer Ni died. Tell Ni Joh, "The weak fall as they should."

Choice 4 Farmer Ni died. Tell Ni Joh, "I couldn't save him." There is no alignment shift with this outcome.

SIDE QUEST

*There is still more to do on the beach! Trigger the **Unfortunate Debt** side quest by talking to the villager by the lower tunnel opening.*

Mrs. Jong is lucky her encounter with spirits wasn't more dangerous.

Mrs. Jong, a villager who lost her son in a recent accident, approaches you when you leave the beach. When she saw her son's ghost, she thought Dawn Star's sorcery was to blame—but now she's realized her mistake and has come to apologize. Talk with her and Dawn Star to learn more about the unrest that plagues the spirit world, then head back into Two Rivers Village to check out the aftermath of the bandit raid.

Stop by Gujin's if you want to swap your weapons, then visit with Guard Yung. When he admits his cowardice, either seize the Closed Fist by extorting a few silver from him with this knowledge (20 XP, 50 SP) or just let him off the hook. Next, venture to the south side of town, and drunken soldiers loyal to Gao the Lesser attack you.

SOLDIER BATTLE: ~80 XP, ~40 SP			
Enemy	Style	Health	Chi
Drunken Soldier x2	Basic	25	25
Drunken Soldier	Spear	100	100

As you head through the grounds of Two Rivers School, chat with your fellow students to learn more about what happened during the bandit raid (and bask in their praise). Many are amazed at the power Master Li displayed when he destroyed the bandits' ship.

Take part in Smiling Mountain's training tournament.

SIDE QUEST

*Smiling Mountain now offers a series of training battles that pit you against an increasing number of opponents. By surviving the gauntlet and taking on a record five students at once, you'll gain XP and a new technique. Take advantage of the opportunity now; you can't train under Smiling Mountain after you return from the Spirit Cave. For all the details, see the **Kia Min** side quest.*

ANSWER GAO'S CHALLENGE

Your peaceful life in Two Rivers is coming to an end.

In light of the recent attack, Master Li decides to accelerate your training by sending you to the Spirit Cave. When Gao the Lesser overhears this, he erupts in an envious rage and challenges you to a duel for the right to explore the cave. Master Li approves of the match, but he warns Gao to use no sorcery or other tricks.

Your rival uses a variety of styles, but you can beat him by staying very close and interrupting his moves with your fastest attacks. This is easier to do if you slow him down first with Heavenly Wave.

DUEL WITH GAO: ~370 XP, 0 SP			
Enemy	Style	Health	Chi
Gao the Lesser	Iron Palm, White Demon, Heavenly Wave	500	500

After you defeat Gao, he struggles to his feet in a defiant final attack. He launches a deadly fireball at you, but Master Li deflects it. Completely beaten and humiliated, Gao the Lesser is cast out from Two Rivers School.

LEARN MORE FROM MASTER LI

I was known as Sun Li the Glorious Strategist. I am the brother of Emperor Sun Hai.

Master Li reveals that he is the Emperor's brother.

Return to Master Li's quarters when you are ready to continue your quest. Your old teacher, who has kept your past secret for so long, finally tells you the story of how he came to adopt you and bring you to Two Rivers. To take hold of your destiny, you must venture into the Spirit Cave, where Master Li has hidden a powerful relic called the Dragon Amulet.

EXPLORE THE SPIRIT CAVE

Read the tablets to break the seal on each gate.

Master Li moves a wall panel in his quarters, revealing the entrance to the Spirit Cave. When you enter, he locks the door behind you. Head down the path to the gate sealed by a stone tablet. Read the message Master Li carved on the stone; this causes it to crumble and opens the gate.

Enter the chamber and find the Dragon Amulet resting on a niche (100 XP). This potent heirloom of your lost people confers powerful benefits, but it acts as a magnet for wandering spirits. No sooner have you donned it when a trio of ghosts attacks. Avoid the braziers while fighting; if you bump into one you might catch fire.

[Essence gems are used by healers and upstart sorcerers and are common enough to be wasted on ornamentation. But with this amulet you can tap their true potential.]

The Dragon Amulet, relic of your lost family, is finally yours.

DRAGON AMULET BATTLE: ~110 XP, 0 SP			
Enemy	Style	Health	Chi
Restless Spirit x2	Basic	30	30
Restless Spirit	Spear	100	100

Shatter jars to find valuable treasure.

After the battle, search the area for a couple of breakable vases; gain 100 SP if you smash both. Your Dragon Amulet allows you to pass through the next two sealed gates and enter the Old Master's burial chamber. Though he may have once been wise and kindly, the pain of undeath has corrupted the Old Master's spirit, causing him to hate all life. You have the chance to ask him a few questions, then the battle begins. Concentrate attacks on the Old Master first so you can fight the other two spirits without getting pelted by ice shards.

THE OLD MASTER BATTLE: ~142 XP, 0 SP			
Enemy	Style	Health	Chi
Restless Spirit	Basic	25	25
Restless Spirit	Basic	30	30
Old Master	Ice Shard	175	175

After the battle a mysterious female spirit appears; her strange talon-like fingers and aura of power reveal that she's not quite human. Unlike the other spirits you've met, she doesn't attack. Instead, she bestows your first magic style; you can choose either Dire Flame or Ice Shard.

A powerful spirit grants you the ability to use magic.

> **NOTE**
>
> *The enigmatic spirit is actually an incarnation of the powerful Water Dragon. She plays a central role in your quest, and you can learn much more about her the next time you meet, when she has the time and strength to answer your questions.*

Exit the Spirit Cave

This portal leads out of the Spirit Cave.

After you've chosen a magic style, the spirit disappears and a huge swirling portal materializes. Before you enter it, explore the cavern. Open the chest in the deepest corner of the cave to find 5 SP, a minor gem, and the **Structured Body** technique (Health +3, Intimidation +1). A skeletal corpse with 100 SP and a couple of scrollstands are also found nearby. When you're ready, step into the portal to exit the Spirit Cave.

The Search for Dawn Star

For a price, Smiling Mountain teaches you his array of custom Techniques.

Master Li is surprised that you have returned from the Spirit Cave so quickly. After you describe your experiences, Jing Woo enters to report that Dawn Star has disappeared. Master Li seems almost pleased with this development; he sees it as the first real test of your abilities. After giving you an order to seek out Dawn Star, Master Li gives you 250 SP and sends you on your way.

> **TIP**
>
> *If you've taken every opportunity to earn silver pieces, you should have enough to buy all three techniques from Smiling Mountain: **Belly of Iron, Heart of Gold and Mind of Steel**. Don't hesitate to sell any gems you've found if needed; after you rescue Dawn Star, you won't have another chance to buy from Smiling Mountain.*

If you ask around the school, the students tell you that Dawn Star disappeared around the same time that Gao the Lesser left. Coincidence? To learn more, head into Two Rivers Village and ask around.

Student Si Pat is the first victim of Gao's murderous rampage.

Villagers gather around a charred corpse in the village square. It's Si Pat, Two Rivers' newest student; he tried to challenge Gao when the latter stormed out of the village. Tragically, Si Pat's bravery cost him his life. Talk to the bystanders to learn that Gao the Lesser fled north, into the swamp.

If you rescued the villager from the south of town during the bandit raid, he approaches you at the top of the stone stairs and asks about the chest of silver he abandoned then. You have options:

This villager has questions about his missing silver.

Choice 1 👊 Return *all* of the villager's silver, even the reward he offers you for your honesty (75 XP). If you spent the money, you can't opt for this outcome.

Choice 2 🖐 Offer to return the silver, or, if you already spent it, promise to pay it back. The villager gratefully lets you keep half as a reward (25 XP).

Choice 3 🗡 Refuse to return the silver. The villager knows he's not a match for you and won't try to recover his treasure by force, but he's not afraid to say he thinks you're even worse than the bandits. And he is right to say it.

At the town gate, two soldiers sent by Gao wait for you. You can reply to their taunts with Intimidation and send them running in cowardice (80 XP), or you can just fight them. Even though you are greatly outnumbered, your new magic style gives you a tremendous advantage.

Gao's mercenaries are sure of victory.

SIDE QUEST

If you told the unnamed villager from the Unfortunate Debt side quest to fend for himself, you discover that he's taken your advice by working for Gao. He replaces one of the usual mercenaries in this battle.

MERCENARY BATTLE:
~194 XP (OR ~282 XP WITH VILLAGER), ~175 SP

Enemy	Style	Health	Chi
Gao's Mercenary x2	Basic or Spear	30	30
Gao's Mercenary x2	Basic or Spear	40	40
Gao's Mercenary	Spear	40	40
Gao's Mercenary	Long Sword	125	125

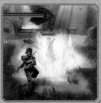

PURSUIT INTO THE MARSHES

After the battle, head north into the Bandit Swamp. Follow the path until you arrive at a clearing where Merchant Hing the Shunned is fighting a group of bandits.

OUTLAW BATTLE: ~96 XP, ~90 SP

Enemy	Style	Health	Chi
Outlaw x2	Basic	40	40
Outlaw	Spear	40	40

After you slay the bandits, talk to Hing. He came into the Bandit Swamp in search of Fen, his precious "Flower of the

Fields," after the bandits kidnapped her. He asks you to search for and rescue Fen on his behalf.

SIDE QUEST

For more details on how to help Merchant Hing, see The Flower of the Fields side quest at the end of this chapter.

Sagacious Zu makes a strong first impression.

Continue north into another open area. Here you find a lone outlaw fighting a group of Gao's mercenaries. Even though he's outnumbered, the warrior defeats all four of his enemies effortlessly. When you approach, he introduces himself as Sagacious Zu. If you ask about Gao's whereabouts, Zu offers little help until you mention Dawn Star's name. Overcome with a sudden change of heart, the scarred veteran joins you as a new Follower. He suggests you head deeper into the swamp, where Gao's men have set up a small camp.

Sagacious Zu Profile

Attack Style: Staff
Support Ability: Increased weapon-style damage
Health: ~228
Chi: ~228

A CAMP TO THE NORTH

Search around the clearing to find 32 SP among a pile of bones. Two paths lead north to the bandit camp; earn maximum rewards by exploring both. First, take the east road to rescue Merchant Hing's beloved Fen and complete **The Flower of the Fields** side quest. Then come back to the

The targeting icon points out concealed treasures.

clearing where you met Sagacious Zu and follow the west road over a pair of narrow bridges. Two groups of enemies ambush you at the same time here. Take down the mercenaries ahead of you first, then go back and mop up the outlaws.

SWAMP BRIDGE AMBUSH: ~64 XP, ~60 SP

Enemy	Style	Health	Chi
Gao's Mercenary x2	Basic	40	40

SWAMP BRIDGE AMBUSH: ~52 XP, ~45 SP

Enemy	Style	Health	Chi
Outlaw	Basic	25	25
Outlaw	Basic	40	40

Follow the path to the final clearing, where four more mercenaries await. After the battle, one of the enemies pleads for mercy and confesses everything he knows about the kidnapping. The mercenary's fate is in your hands:

Will you be his savior or his executioner?

Choice 1 Spare the mercenary's life. He flees, promising never to commit another violent act (250 XP).

Choice 2 There can be no mercy for those who try and take your life. The only way to make sure he never does it again is to kill him (270 XP).

MERCENARY CAMP BATTLE: ~136 XP, ~130 SP

Enemy	Style	Health	Chi
Gao's Mercenary x3	Basic	40	40
Gao's Mercenary	Legendary Strike	100	100

Focus evade allows you to automatically dodge traps.

CAUTION
You can earn about 50 SP and one or two gems by opening the barrels here, but the one on the right is trapped. Conserve or replenish your Focus before opening it to avoid taking damage.

RESCUE DAWN STAR FROM GAO

When you enter the Swamp Cave, Gao the Lesser is locked in combat with an ogre. Gao unleashes Dire Flame, which slays the ogre but also causes part of the cave to collapse. You must fight through the remaining beasts to reach him. Head for the

south cavern to find your first ogre. Heavenly Wave has no effect, so use weapons, magic, or martial styles for this fight. Time your strikes between the ogre's attacks and make every effort to avoid getting flattened by his massive club. Two blows can easily kill you, so back off and heal if you get hurt.

SWAMP CAVE, SOUTHWEST CAVERN BATTLE: ~40 XP, ~30 SP

Enemy	Style	Health	Chi
Ogre	—	100	100

After the battle, make your way to the east side of the cavern to find two more ogres. Defeat them, using magic attacks to soften them from a distance, then open the two chests they were guarding. The one on the left is trapped, while the one on the right holds 110 SP and, if you're lucky, a gem.

SWAMP CAVE, SOUTHEAST CAVERN BATTLE: ~80 XP, ~70 SP

Enemy	Style	Health	Chi
Ogre x2	—	100	100

With treasure in hand, take the north path leading deeper into the cave. A new type of enemy awaits you here: the toad demon. Like the ogres, this brute is slow and powerful; your greater speed and maneuverability are key to winning. Keep attacking the demon from behind with Chi-charged weapon strikes and it will go down in no time.

SWAMP CAVE, CENTRAL CAVERN
BATTLE: ~45 XP, 0 SP

Enemy	Style	Health	Chi
Toad Demon	—	100	100

After the battle, you automatically learn the **Toad Demon** transformation style. Using this style drains Chi, but also grants you the toad demon's immunities to magic and support styles. In addition, the Toad Demon's attacks can poison your enemies. All of these abilities will be useful in your next battle, so take time to equip the new style now. After locating a bone pile containing 82 SP (and possibly a gem), head north into the final chamber of the cave.

Dawn Star and Gao the Lesser are here; after a barrage of frustrated threats, Gao attacks. He makes free use of the Dire Flame style in this battle, but you can choose Dawn Star or Sagacious Zu to fight alongside you. Transform into a toad demon to make yourself completely immune to Gao's Dire Flame and Heavenly Wave, then switch to a martial style when he runs out of Chi.

GAO THE LESSER'S LAST STAND:
~300 XP, ~415 SP

Enemy	Style	Health	Chi
Gao the Lesser	Dire Flame,	500	500
	Heavenly Wave,		
	Iron Palm,		
	White Demon		

RETURN TO TWO RIVERS

The trapped chest poses less danger if your Focus is full.

With Dawn Star rescued (150 XP), it's time to head back to Two Rivers. Before you go, replenish your Focus at the shrine and empty the three chests at the back of the cave. The left chest contains **Viper's Wit** (Focus +2, Charm +1), the right chest holds 250 SP, and the center one is trapped. There's nothing left in the cave, so hike back to the entrance.

As you exit the cave, a squadron of Gao the Greater's flying machines passes overhead. Loaded with explosives and elite soldiers, these aircraft are headed for your village! Your only hope of catching them is to climb aboard the Mosquito and take to the air yourself.

Returning Home

Despite being compared to a "swimming ox," the Mosquito is actually very maneuverable and easy to control. Stay at the bottom center of the screen and blast away at the enemy aircraft that swoops in from the flanks. After the first wave, grab the Health orb that appears. Stay in the center to avoid being rammed by the massive bombers that enter from the sides. The bombers pull away before you have a chance to destroy them, so ignore them and concentrate on the smaller ships.

A Weapon orb appears next. Grab it and return to the safety of the bottom-center part of the screen. Keep firing at all times to destroy the next wave of ships that comes at you from dead ahead. There's a brief lull in the action as the Two Rivers Sparring Ring passes below you; you're almost home! The bombers that escaped you earlier now return. Take down the one on the left first by firing as rapidly as possible, then swoop over and take out the one on the right. If you shoot fast enough, you can destroy both bombers before you reach the end of the flight.

Returning Home (cont'd)
TIP

The Mosquito comes equipped with a single upgrade, Radiant Aura. Press ✗ to activate it. Upgrades require Chi (indicated, as usual, by a blue meter in the upper left). While Radiant Aura is active, you're protected from collisions with smaller enemies; ram them while the shield lasts to replenish your Chi. Bombers, however, can still ground you in no time if you collide with them. You can keep Radiant Aura for use in future flying missions you choose to try; all missions after the first are optional.

THE BURNING TOWN

LOOK FOR SURVIVORS

Do what you can together. We will meet in the heart of your school.

The Mosquito lands on the beach amid a scene of terrible devastation. Gao's machines are certainly efficient; the entire Two Rivers area is on fire! Could anyone have survived? Look by the statue of Emperor Sun to find poor Old Ming's body (20 SP), then head uphill into the village square to find and slay a pair of Gao's mercenaries.

MERCENARY BATTLE: ~40 XP, ~30 SP				
Enemy	Style	Health	Chi	
Gao's Mercenary	Basic	25	25	
Gao's Mercenary	Spear	25	25	

Continue to Two Rivers School. After passing through Dawn Star's garden, you encounter another group of mercenaries. There are a few different scenarios here that depend on choices you made earlier:

Choice 1 👊 If you treated Kia Min with red silk grass, she arrives and slays the mercenaries for you.

Choice 2 🐉 If you gave Kia Min bearded tongue grass and then challenge her for her title, she tries to fight the mercenaries but is struck down. You must then fight them yourself.

Choice 3 If you didn't beat Kia Min's training record, she doesn't appear at all. You fight the mercenaries as in Choice 2 above.

MERCENARY BATTLE: ~48 XP, ~30 SP				
Enemy	Style	Health	Chi	
Gao's Mercenary x2	Basic	30	30	

Veer left at the crossroads and stop by the sparring arena. Three more mercenaries await their doom; finish them off and search the bone pile for 78 SP and possibly a gem.

MERCENARY BATTLE: ~80 XP, ~60 SP				
Enemy	Style	Health	Chi	
Gao's Mercenary x2	Basic	30	30	
Gao's Mercenary	Basic	40	40	

Return to the crossroads and pass through the school gate. The last group of mercenaries has gathered in the sparring ring. With Master Li nowhere to be found, it's up to you to end the attack. This battle consists of two waves of enemies. The first wave consist of eight mercenaries, but no more than four attack at once. Note the pair of barrels on the left side of the ring; kick them in Free mode (Ⓛ+Ⓡ) to trigger an explosion that damages your enemies but leaves you unharmed. Try to save your Chi and Focus for the final wave.

MERCENARY BATTLE: ~256 XP, ~200 SP				
Enemy	Style	Health	Chi	
Gao's Mercenary x8	Basic	40	40	

The mercenary leader takes you on last. He's the strongest of the group by far, and he's backed up by two tough bodyguards with spears. Now is the time to spend the Chi and Focus you've saved through the first two waves. Try to eliminate the leader first, before he can shock you with Storm Dragon. Keep an eye on the bodyguards, as they will try to flank you while you battle the lieutenant. Keep moving and use area attacks to avoid being surrounded.

MERCENARY LIEUTENANT BATTLE: ~240 XP, ~200 SP

Enemy	Style	Health	Chi
Gao's Mercenary x2	Spear	100	100
Gao's Lieutenant	Leaping Tiger, Long Sword, Storm Dragon	350	350

I tried... I tried so hard. I'm sorry.

Master Li was taken when it began. He went without a fight, giving them what they wanted, but afterwards the students... they were killed anyway.

Gao the Greater was behind this attack, but I suspect there is someone else behind him. You will find your answers in the Imperial City.

When the final battle is over, Jing Woo staggers into the ring. With his dying breath, he tells about merciless warriors led by a mysterious figure in black armor. They took Master Li away and killed everyone else. Sagacious Zu, revealing a glimpse of his shady past, recognizes the armored figure as Death's Hand, leader of the Lotus Assassins. With allies like these, Gao the Greater was able to accomplish his goal of destroying Two Rivers. But why? To pursue the invaders and rescue Master Li, Zu suggests you take to the skies once again and fly toward the Imperial City (500 XP).

Leaving the Town

Your enemies are stronger and more numerous in this flying mission. Use Radiant Aura to protect yourself. The first wave enters from the left; fire rapidly and try to destroy as many as possible before they loop around and dive straight toward you. Repeat this process with the next wave, which comes in from the right. Watch for slightly larger ships that come from straight ahead; they drop Weapon and Health orbs when destroyed.

Leaving the Town (cont'd)

Floating mines appear in your path. They are difficult to destroy, but you should be able to take down enough to widen the gap and fly through.

After passing the mines, a colossal gunship appears. Concentrate on avoiding incoming flak while firing your own guns as fast as possible. Keep an eye out for small ships that fly in occasionally from the flanks. A second gunship arrives after you destroy the first one; shoot down both to complete the mission.

SIDE QUESTS

THE LION OF TWO RIVERS

Long ago, the Old Master of Two Rivers School installed a special lion shrine in his quarters. It's more than an altar; the shrine is also a puzzle used to test some of the more abstract principles taught at the school. There are several ways to solve the puzzle, each resulting in a different reward. For the best solution, four items are required.

AN ANCIENT TEST

Three of the items, the **Blue, Red, and Yellow Lion Figurines,** can be found within the chest by the lion statue. To get the fourth item, climb the hill behind Master Li's quarters. A pair of students challenges you to a sparring match. You can decline if you're in a hurry, but it's best to accept the challenge for XP and safe combat practice.

Find three lion figurines in a chest next to the lion statue.

Two Students Battle: ~44 XP, 0 SP			
Enemy	Style	Health	Chi
Student	Basic	25	25
Student	Staff	30	30

Make on offering of silver at the Old Master's Tomb to get the Lion Head Token.

After defeating the students, investigate the Old Master's memorial. Drop a silver piece into the offering bowl to release the **Lion Head Token** (10 XP). If you haven't left the school, then you won't have any cash yet. There are two options: either head into the village and defeat some bandits to earn silver, or return to Master Li's quarters and use the Lion Figurines to elicit a silver piece from the lion statue's altar (see the Note at the end of this side quest.)

Playing by New Rules

With all four items collected, approach the statue and insert the Lion Head Token into its mouth (25 XP). This causes the orb in the lion's paw to turn green. Place the Blue and Yellow Lion Figurines on the altar (because blue and yellow combined yield green). The orb turns from green to orange, so remove the Blue Lion

Greater rewards await those who take the more investigative path.

Figurine and replace it with the Red Lion Figurine. Finally, the orb turns purple; take back the Yellow Lion Figurine and set down the blue one to complete the puzzle. The **Gaze of the Lion** is your reward, which grants +2 Health and +2 Focus (50 XP).

> ### NOTE
> *There are other ways to deal with the lion statue. You can smash open the altar with brute force, earning 25 SP but also destroying the puzzle. If you don't have the Lion Head Token, you can still place the Lion Figurines on the altar in this order: blue, red, yellow. Doing so nets one silver piece, and doesn't deactivate the puzzle.*

An Unfortunate Debt

After ending the bandit raid, return to the beach and locate the lone villager on the west side. He borrowed 20 SP from Gao the Greater, and he can't afford to pay it back. He asks for your advice, leading to several outcomes:

The villager appears only after you return to Two Rivers School.

Choice 1 🖐 The villager's pride causes him to resist any offer of charity. It may take several attempts, but you can convince him to accept 20 SP from you to repay the debt (30 XP).

Choice 2 ✊ Tell the villager to find his own solution to the problem. He leaves with an oath to clear the debt somehow. When you fight Gao's mercenaries later, you'll discover that the villager repaid his debt by joining with the enemy.

> ### NOTE
> *If you choose the Closed Fist option, your alignment doesn't shift until you meet the villager in battle.*

Kia Min

Talk to Smiling Mountain and ask him to arrange a training battle for you. At first you can choose to fight up to four students at once. These aren't life-or-death battles; if your Health drops to zero, the battle ends and your Health is restored. You can try each battle as many times as you want (but you only get the XP award once.)

Smiling Mountain's Training, Level 1: ~10 XP, 0 SP			
Enemy	Style	Health	Chi
Student	Basic	25	25

Smiling Mountain's Training, Level 2: ~20 XP, 0 SP			
Enemy	Style	Health	Chi
Student	Basic	25	25
Student	Staff	25	25

SMILING MOUNTAIN'S TRAINING, LEVEL 3: ~30 XP, 0 SP			
Enemy	Style	Health	Chi
Student	Basic	25	25
Student x2	Staff	25	25

SMILING MOUNTAIN'S TRAINING, LEVEL 4: ~75 XP, 0 SP			
Enemy	Style	Health	Chi
Student	Basic	50	25
Student x3	Staff	50	25

NOTE

If you successfully win all four training matches, you earn a new technique: Lessons of the Forge (Health +2).

In order to battle five opponents at once and set a new school record, you need to get another student to join the fight against you. That student is Kia Min, who set the current record at four opponents, and who would love to defend her title. Unfortunately, she was seriously wounded during the bandit raid and is in no state for combat.

Kia Min's training record can't be challenged until her injuries have healed.

Ask Kia Min about Healing

You can find Kia Min just inside the school gate, near the sparring ring. Talk to her and offer to track down a remedy for her wounds. She recommends asking a town elder such as Old Ming for advice.

Kia Min refers you to Old Ming for help.

See if Old Ming Remembers a Curative Herb

Old Ming recommends an ancient remedy for Kia Min.

Go to the beach to find Old Ming. He tells you of two grasses with restorative properties (10 XP). Red silk grass, though expensive, is a true curative and can mend Kia Min's wounds. Bearded tongue grass is much cheaper, but only deadens pain without promoting healing.

Acquire and Deliver a Poultice

Fen Do hopes to profit from others' misfortune.

Both types of herbal poultice are sold by Merchant Fen Do in the village square. Talk to him and make your choice (10 XP):

Choice 1 Insist on red silk grass (50 SP).

Choice 2 Settle for bearded tongue grass (25 SP).

> ### TIP
> *Select replies corresponding to your strongest conversation skill to persuade Fen Do into giving you a 20 percent discount.*

Face Smiling Mountain's Challenge

Deliver your purchase to Kia Min (75 XP). When she offers to repay you, you have another chance to make a moral gesture:

Choice 1 Generously decline Kia Min's repayment and declare the poultice to be a gift.

Choice 2 If you went with bearded tongue grass, tell her it cost you 50 SP. Kia Min unquestioningly pays whatever you demand.

Choice 3 All other choices have no effect on your alignment.

Next, talk to Smiling Mountain and try his final training challenge. Use Focus, Chi, and a weapon to eliminate the opposition quickly. After the fight, Smiling Mountain rewards you with a secret technique: **Alloyed Body** (Health +5, Focus +5).

SMILING MOUNTAIN'S TRAINING, LEVEL 5: ~75 XP, ~100 SP

Enemy	Style	Health	Chi
Student	Basic	25	25
Student x3	Staff	25	25
Kia Min	Staff	100	100

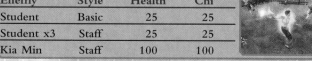

The Flower of the Fields

Find Merchant Hing the Shunned inside the swamp. Outlaws have kidnapped his beloved Fen (who he lovingly refers to as "The Flower of the Fields"). He begs you to look for her as you venture through the marshes. Your reply affects your alignment as follows:

Merchant Hing is overcome with concern for his precious Fen.

Choice 1 Reassure Merchant Hing and promise to keep an eye out for the Flower of the Fields.

Choice 2 Tell Merchant Hing you're not interested in his "petty concerns."

After meeting Sagacious Zu, go northeast from the standing stones to find Sing Wa, Merchant Hing's wife. Defeat a trio of mercenaries to rescue her and earn Open Palm points.

BATTLE FEN'S KIDNAPPERS: ~72 XP, ~75 SP

Enemy	Style	Health	Chi
Gao's Mercenary	Basic	30	30
Gao's Mercenary x2	Staff	30	30

Sing Wa's happiness at being rescued quickly turns to anger when she learns that Hing sent you in search of Fen—who turns out to be a water buffalo. With the happy family reunited (125 XP), they depart, leaving you with 250 SP as a reward.

When Merchant Hing spoke of his Flower of the Fields, he wasn't talking about his wife.

> ### NOTE
> *Before you leave, look carefully around the south end of the huge rock to find a concealed skeleton and 95 SP.*

CHAPTER TWO

OVERVIEW

Li told me about the slaughter of the Spirit Monks and how his brother entered their sacred temple. It was madness... the Emperor killed the Water Dragon itself!

Wherein the fall of Dirge is detailed,

Death's Hand went too far in ordering its destruction, and Gao the Greater sought to profit from it. My retribution will end with them, but it will begin with you.

The woman in black speaks of Death's Hand,

Of course, Gao. I was just waiting for the perfect time to tell you. I received a report from the destruction of Two Rivers. Your son, Gao the Lesser, is dead.

And Gao the Greater learns the fate of his son.

Two Rivers is in ruins, and Master Li has been taken captive. It is clear that this attack was carefully orchestrated and that shadowy forces have taken an interest in you and those around you. Leaving your home of twenty years, you set out after Death's Hand and his Lotus Assassins, intent on discovering the reasons behind this assault.

DAM SITE

to Ruins

Crash Site

Drawbridge

Jade Heart

Covered Bridge

Imperial Watch Tower

to Ruins

Ruins Gate

to Tien's Landing

MAP LEGEND

●	Container
●	Trapped Container
○	Focus Shrine
○	Scrollstand
●	Spirit Font
①	Silk Fox
②	Chen Yi
③	Water Dragon's Spirit
④	Wild Flower/ Chai Ka

Chapter Two is set within and around Tien's Landing, a modest waypoint on one of the Empire's main trade routes. The town lies on the edge of an artificial lake created by a dam built downstream. At least, it used to: Imperial soldiers have recently opened the dam, draining the lake and revealing the ruins of Old Tien's Landing, which was flooded when the lake first formed. You'll explore these areas, as well as infiltrate Gao the Greater's hidden fortress and lift the curse from a haunted forest, all in order to continue your pursuit of Death's Hand and Master Li.

The main feature of this area on the western outskirts of Tien's Landing is the famous dam. Two paths lead from here to the ruins of Old Tien's Landing, but they're both inaccessible when you first arrive: one is sealed behind a locked gate, while the other lies on the far side of a raised drawbridge. A third path leads to Tien's Landing.

The Mosquito you commandeered from Two Rivers crashes on the area's north side amid a jumble of ruins. Until the dam was opened, this area was completely submerged. With the water drained, the ghosts of those who drowned when the lake was formed have surfaced.

Crash site

Drawbridge

This wooden span leads to the dam's control structure. It can be folded and raised to prevent outsiders (such as you) from accessing the dam. You can lower the bridge later to create a useful shortcut, but for now it's an impassable barrier.

Tragedy in Tien's Landing: These documents found near the drawbridge control lever tell the story of the Great Dam.

Jade Heart

The Jade Heart is the mystical power source for the machinery that opens and closes the Great Dam. You can activate or destroy it as part of the **Great Dam** side quest, but you must get past a pair of Inquisitor Lim's golems first.

Covered Bridge

This Covered Bridge is your only path across the river for now. If you need Chi or Health restored, look for a Spirit Font by the north end.

Imperial soldiers are stationed at a watch tower that overlooks the only path leading to the newly exposed ruins. The soldiers have orders from Death's Hand to kill anyone who trespasses here.

Imperial watch tower

If the soldiers don't stop you from entering the ruins, this locked gate will. Minister Sheng, the governor of Tien's Landing, has the key.

Ruins Gate

CHARACTERS

Silk Fox

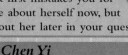
1 Mysterious and deadly, Silk Fox fights a lone vigilante war against Death's Hand and the Lotus Assassins. She makes her first appearance soon after you crash, and at first mistakes you for her enemy. She reveals little about herself now, but you'll learn much more about her later in your quest.

Chen Yi

2 A simple peasant from the small town of One Stone, Chen Yi was conscripted into the army by Death's Hand himself. Now stationed at the Imperial watch tower, he has no desire to fight and only wants to go home to his farm.

Water Dragon's Spirit

3 Mysterious and beautiful, the Water Dragon's Spirit makes her second appearance as you begin exploring the Dam Site. She drops a few hints about where you can find more pieces of your Dragon Amulet.

Wild Flower/Chai Ka

4 This little girl has an amazing secret: she's actually the host body for a powerful demon named Chai Ka. This unlikely duo joins you as a Follower after you've explored the ruins.

TIEN'S LANDING

- 9
- 10
- 11 to Forest
- 1
- Merchant Area
- 4
- Tea House
- 12
- 6
- Camp Site
- 5
- 3
- 2
- 18
- 19
- Beggar's Pier
- 14
- 15
- 13
- 16
- 8
- 7
- to Dam Area
- Boat House
- 17
- Ru's Barge

MAP LEGEND

- ⬤ Container
- ⚪ Scrollstand
- ⬤ Trapped Container
- 1 Minister Sheng
- 2 Yifong and Fuyao
- 3 Hui the Brave
- 4 Cook Teh and Dishwasher Wong
- 5 Gufu the Sweet
- 6 Seamstress Lan
- 7 Chumin
- 8 Lishun
- 9 Old Wei
- 10 Merchant Chiu
- 11 Merchant Cheung
- 12 Jian the Iron Fist and Mistress Vo
- 13 Big Tian
- 14 Baker Bei
- 15 Merchant Jiang and Merchant Shipeng
- 16 Darting Lynx
- 17 Captain Ing
- 18 Tong
- 19 Scholar Six Heavens

Named after Sagacious Tien, founder of the Jade Empire, Tien's Landing has changed a lot over the years. When Emperor Sun rose to power and built the nearby dam, most of the original town (known as "Old Tien's Landing") was submerged under the lake that formed. Since then, the surviving residents have adapted to their new life, rebuilding the village as it stands today.

An unused courtyard on the west side of town makes a perfect base camp. Return here any time to talk with your Followers.

Base camp

The Tea House, formerly owned by Old Mother Kwan, is now in the process of being turned into a tavern. This is just another symptom of the decay that's settled on Tien's Landing since the dam was opened.

Tea House

The Shadow in the Trees: These documents hint at the presence of a powerful spirit that watches over the Great Forest.

Bookstand

The town's reliance on the artificial lake is reflected in the Boat House, the largest building in Tien's Landing. It used to serve a vital role as the hub of waterborne trade; now it's a hideout for a gang of thugs.

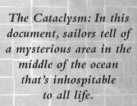
Boat House

The Cataclysm: In this document, sailors tell of a mysterious area in the middle of the ocean that's inhospitable to all life.

Scrollstand

The Airing of Grievances: Minister Sheng's list of complaints against the people of Tien's Landing is conspicuously placed outside his smoldering office.

Scrollstand

The Merchant Area is the heart of Tien's Landing. The jail and Minister Sheng's office, which once stood on the east side, now lie in a smoking ruin, the work of an unknown arsonist. Along the north side are several merchant stalls and a gate leading to the Forest. Paths from the Merchant Area lead west to the Tea House, or south to the Boat House.

Merchant Area

The southeast side of town, known as Beggar's Pier, is the seedy district. Courtesans, drunken sailors, street urchins, and thugs all can be found here, as well as the town's less reputable merchants.

Beggar's Pier

Two vessels are tied on the docks that jut from Beggar's Pier. Captain Ing's magnificent sailing ship, *Lucky Night*, is trapped in the mud at the end of the farthest dock. Next to it lies Ru's barge, a rickety scow small and light enough to still be usable.

The Lucky Night

The Undertow: The scrolls aboard Ing's ship relate a myth of evil sea monsters.

CHARACTERS

Minister Sheng

1 Minister Sheng is a pompous, arrogant weakling. Under normal circumstances, he is an official in the Jade Empire's Ministry of Harmony, which oversees both taxation and executions. When the Lotus Assassins came to town, he passively gave in to all their demands under threat of death. He has the key you need to unlock the Ruins Gate.

Yifong

2 Fed up with the crime and turmoil run rampant in Tien's Landing, Yifong thinks she has nothing to lose by fleeing into the wilderness with her daughter Fuyao. The two exiles hope to find better fortune in a new home.

Fuyao

2 Fuyao follows her mother out of town, but she doesn't seem confident that braving the wilderness is safer than staying home. Tales of kidnappings and ghosts have planted sensible doubts that are validated when Fuyao and her mother are captured by slave traders. You'll meet both of them again later on, when you're exploring Gao the Greater's hideout.

Hui the Brave

3 Hui, one of Master Li's most loyal friends, has been entrusted with keeping watch over the Dragon Amulet piece that's hidden in the nearby ruins. She's kept her vigil and her secret for 15 years, waiting for the day when you would finally come forward to claim your destiny.

Cook Teh

4 Cook Teh is the head chef at the Tea House. He proudly believes that his skill is beyond reproach…though his customers might not agree. He's got a reputation for cooking complex dishes that, according to Dishwasher Wong, "take some getting used to."

Dishwasher Wong

4 Serving as Cook Teh's apprentice isn't a pleasant life, but Dishwasher Wong has great ambition to become a master chef someday. Tedious kitchen chores are part of his training.

Gufu the Sweet

5 Gufu the Sweet is a fishwife who hangs around the entrance to the Tea House. She can tell you all about the troubles plaguing the town.

Seamstress Lan

6 This sorrowful seamstress can be found near the Tea House. Lan's fiancé, Baker Bei, suffers daily beatings from a group of thugs. You can help them both out as part of the **Beaten Baker** side quest.

Chumin

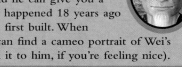

7 A gentle carpenter, Chumin has fallen on hard times because he can't bring himself to enforce the debts owed by his customers. He's not interested in charity, but if you get involved in the **Matchmaker** side quest, you can eventually find a good business partner for him.

Lishun

8 Also known as Lishun the Talkative, this poor basket maker maintains an almost baffling level of optimism, despite the town's problems. His nickname is well-earned; he's happy to discuss at length everything he knows about the town and its prominent residents.

Old Wei

9 Old Wei may be wrinkled and feeble, but his mind is still sharp. He's lived in Tien's Landing his whole life, and he can give you a firsthand account of what happened 18 years ago when the Great Dam was first built. When exploring the ruins, you can find a cameo portrait of Wei's departed wife (and return it to him, if you're feeling nice).

Merchant Chiu

10 Merchant Chiu specializes in mundane goods such as clothing, baskets, and soap. He doesn't sell anything you need. You can ply him for gossip, however; for instance, he's heard tales that Death's Hand is collecting and destroying all wind maps so that nobody else can navigate the skies except his Lotus Assassins.

Merchant Cheung

11 When drunken sailors can freely stumble out of your shop without paying, it's hard to run a profitable business. But Merchant Cheung has nobler motivations than mere profit: He's a simple, honest man trying to make a fair living. He has inventory to sell only if you close the Great Dam. You can earn a 15 percent discount by completing the **Stolen Memento** side quest.

MERCHANT CHEUNG

Item (Number Available)	Cost (SP)
Flawed Warrior Gem (1)	200
Inferior Warrior Gem (1)	1,500

Merchant Cheung (cont'd)

MERCHANT CHEUNG

Item (Number Available)	Cost (SP)
Flawed Monk Gem (1)	200
Flawed Scholar Gem (2)	200
Inferior Charm Gem (2)	150
Inferior Intuition Gem (1)	150
Storm Dragon Style (1)	4,500

Jian the Iron Fist

12 Jian the Iron Fist, an aging and bad-tempered warrior, knows the powerful Tempest style. He only teaches it to those who are strongly bound to the Way of the Closed Fist, as part of the **Ancient Game** side quest.

Mistress Vo

12 A former student of Jian the Iron Fist, Mistress Vo still keeps ties with her old teacher. Unlike him, she advocates the Way of the Open Palm. She teaches the Stone Immortal style to those who share her philosophy. The **Ancient Game** side quest has complete details.

Big Tian

13 Big Tian, a simple farmer from the countryside, has come to the "big city" to search for a wife. He may be friendly and hard-working, but any potential spouse will have to overlook his incredible stupidity to accept him as a husband.

Baker Bei

14 Baker Bei is engaged to Seamstress Lan, but his jealous childhood friend Ai Ling doesn't approve of the match. Undertake the **Beaten Baker** side quest to help him sort out his woes.

Merchant Jiang

15 For Merchant Jiang, wine seller, these are boom times. He plans to wring every last silver piece from the stranded sailors by restricting supply and charging outrageous prices. He wants the Great Dam to stay open, and he offers to share his profits if you help him make sure it does.

Merchant Shipeng

15 You can buy from Shipeng at the end of the **Great Dam** side quest. This odd little man has two very rare items for sale: the legendary staff known as **Flawless** (an Artifact Weapon, 25 percent stronger

Merchant Shipeng (cont'd)

than the staff Gujin had), and a **Cow Bezoar** (used in the **Lord Lao's Furnace** side quest).

MERCHANT SHIPENG

Item (Number Available)	Cost (SP)
Flawed Scholar Gem (1)	200
Inferior Scholar Gem (1)	1,500
Inferior Intimidation Gem (1)	150
Intimidation Gem (1)	900
Inferior Intuition Gem (1)	150
Flawless (1)	7,500
Cow Bezoar (1)	500

Darting Lynx

16 Darting Lynx, a traveling acrobat, earned her nickname by virtue of her grace and speed. For a modest fee, she teaches you some of the tricks of her trade. She also sells a few minor gems. Find her on Beggar's Pier.

DARTING LYNX

Item (Number Available)	Cost (SP)
Flawed Warrior Gem (2)	200
Inferior Intimidation Gem (2)	150
Leaping Tiger Style (1)	8,000
Balance of Nature (1)	4,250
Hawk's Elegance (1)	800
Conditioning of the Body (1)	800
Swallow's Grace (1)	600

Captain Ing

17 When the Great Dam was opened, Captain Ing and his ship *Lucky Night* became stranded in Tien's Landing. Now he's way behind schedule and, even worse, his restless crew has been causing trouble all over town. He rewards you handsomely if you decide to close the Great Dam.

Tong

18 Tong is one of Captain Ing's men. A combination of boredom and drunkenness has led him to commit a few minor crimes. He's the guilty shoplifter in the **Stolen Memento** side quest.

Scholar Six Heavens

19 Beggar's Pier is an unusual place to find a scholar. He desires an artifact known as the Zither of Discord, and he wants to recruit a ruthless warrior to go find it for him. He offers the job only to those who follow the Way of the Closed Fist.

TEA HOUSE

MAP LEGEND

1. Old Mother Kwan
2. Three Sheets Dutong
3. Steeper Yanru
4. Waitress Yanwan
5. Ru the Boatswain
6. Chai Jin
7. Kindly Yushan
8. Zhong the Ox Carrier
9. Dong Ping
10. Yaoru

It's unusual for a town the size of Tien's Landing to support such a large Tea House. The restaurant's success was due to Old Mother Kwan, who owned it until recently. It's now run by a drunken crook named Three Sheets Dutong, who's decided to transform the tranquil Tea House into a bawdy tavern.

Most Tea House employees can be found on the ground floor, which is set with tables and chairs. A massive staircase on the north side leads up to the balcony.

Ground floor

Balcony

A balcony runs the entire circumference of the Tea House. Sailors and other patrons who desire privacy loiter here. The south side, opposite the staircase, is the most secluded, and it's favored by the town's most reclusive residents.

CHARACTERS

Old Mother Kwan

1. Old Mother Kwan used to own the Tea House, but now that Three Sheets Dutong is in charge she's been reduced to pouring wine. You can help her get her Tea House back in the **Old Mother Kwan** side quest.

Kindly Yushan

7 You can find Kindly Yushan sulking in a corner of the Tea House balcony. He used to run the orphanage that was submerged when the Great Dam was built. He talks to you only if you're on the **Drowned Orphans** side quest.

Three Sheets Dutong

2 Dutong got his nickname from his constant drunkenness. He's a con artist who is trying to turn the Tea House into a tavern so he can indulge his drinking habit and make profit off the stranded sailors.

Zhong the Ox Carrier

8 Not all ogres are evil. Zhong used to work as a farmhand, but he caused a terrible accident that he can't forgive himself for. You can try to convince him to go back to work in the **Zhong the Ox Carrier** side quest.

Steeper Yanru

3 Before Dutong came around, Steeper Yanru was Old Mother Kwan's apprentice. Now he's a bartender trying to get the hang of dispensing vague advice to drunken patrons.

STEEPER YANRU'S ADVICE

- Every bureaucrat knows a tree grows toward the light—but a rock grows not at all.
- The wise man will remember that falling leaves spiral downward, but only until they rest on the earth.
- If you drop a rock in a well, you'll hear a splash—but if you drop a feather in a fire, you'll hear something very different.
- If you must sleep on the same bed, at least try to dream different dreams.
- When one's foot knows what one's hand is doing, one is dangerous; but if the belly button has not been consulted, havoc will ensue.

Dong Ping

9 Dong Ping is a farmer and Zhong's employer. Without the big ogre to help with the manual chores on his farm, Dong Ping will be ruined. He hasn't had any luck convincing Zhong to leave the Tea House and come home.

Yaoru

10 Yaoru is sometimes called "The Sailor" in jest by the other villagers because of his terrible seasickness. He's a pompous egotist in search of a submissive wife; you can hook him up with Ai Ling in the **Matchmaker** side quest, but it takes some work and at least normal intuition or a charm.

Waitress Yanwan

4 Waitress Yanwan works at the Tea House, and she's at her wit's end. The crowds of rude sailors and Dutong's horrible misman-agement are almost enough to make her quit her job.

Ru the Boatswain

5 Ru plans to close the Great Dam, saving the town and becoming a hero. He's quite brave but also incredibly drunk. He may never become a hero, but he's the only person foolhardy enough to give you passage to Gao the Greater's hideout.

Chai Jin

6 Chai Jin is a master cook from Shangdang county. He's in search of someone who can stomach his exotic delicacies. If you accept his challenge and survive a complete four-course meal, you'll be well rewarded. For full information, see the **Chai Jin** side quest.

Boat House

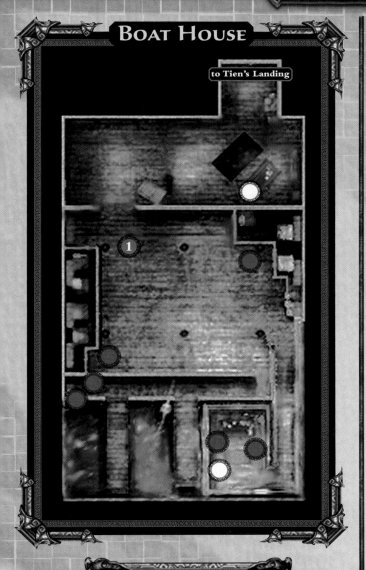

to Tien's Landing

1

MAP LEGEND

- ● Container
- ○ Scrollstand
- ① Ai Ling

The Boat House, largest building in Tien's Landing, has been taken over by a gang since the Great Dam was opened. Only those who have business with Ai Ling, the gang's leader, are allowed inside.

Lower level

The lower level is a large, open warehouse that's now mostly empty since shipping has stopped. A loading crane and catwalks stand at the building's south end. Ai Ling and her gang gather here, and they immediately confront all who enter.

Horselord Tactics: These tomes explain why infantry armies are completely helpless against well-trained cavalry opposition.

A small office built over the loading area gives the Boat House overseer a commanding view of the entire building. It's reached by a short flight of stairs with a locked gate at the bottom. The gate's key is hidden inside a big vase on the lower level.

Upper level

The Land of Howling Spirits: This document refers to your lost people, the Spirit Monks.

Characters

Ai Ling

① Ai Ling is the leader of the gang that's made the Boat House into their private hideout. From here she orchestrates the daily beatings administered to her former friend, Baker Bei. She plays a key role in both the **Beaten Baker** and **Matchmaker** side quests.

RUINS

to Dam Site

Lotus Assassins' Camp

to Quarry

Quarry Entrance

Abandoned Orphanage

1

2

Drawbridge

to Dam Site

MAP LEGEND

- ○ Containers
- ○ Trapped Containers
- ○ Spirit Font
- 1 Bin and Miao
- 2 Stabber Yuxi

The ruins of old Tien's Landing lie exposed now that the Great Dam is open. This area is extremely dangerous: Assassins and their rat demon slaves prowl everywhere, and the ghosts of those drowned when the lake was formed attack all living things.

Lotus Assassins' camp

The Lotus Assassins have encamped in a wide clearing at the north and safest end of the ruins. The Assassins have also stored some dragon powder here in a chest by the south gate. A path leads east from their bonfire to a Spirit Font on the cliff's edge.

The abandoned orphanage looms in the center of the ruins. Sadly, the children who used to live here drowned when the lake rose. These innocent souls now linger as vengeful ghosts. You can help two of them, Bin and Miao, find some peace by completing the **Drowned Orphans** side quest.

Abandoned orphanage

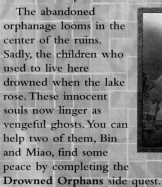

Quarry entrance

An old quarry lies on the ruins' east side. It's sealed behind a masonry wall, but with dragon powder you can blast through. The quarry was used as a prison before Old Tien's Landing was flooded, and the ghosts of drowned prisoners ruthlessly attack anyone who enters.

Drawbridge

Similar to the drawbridge in the Dam Site, this folding span can be retracted to prevent unauthorized persons from accessing the dam controls. Lower it using the nearby crane.

CHARACTERS

Bin

1 Bin was one of the children who died when the Great Dam was first built, and the wounding of the Water Dragon has left him unable to move on to the next world. Unlike most ghosts, Bin hasn't yet been corrupted by the pain of undeath. You can meet him in the abandoned orphanage.

Miao

1 Bin's friend Miao also died as the lake waters rose. In contrast to Bin, she has been changed by her condition into a creature of malevolence and hatred. Help these children by undertaking the **Drowned Orphans** side quest.

Stabber Yuxi

2 Stabber Yuxi is another ghostly resident of Old Tien's Landing. When the town flooded, the prisoners were left to drown along with the orphans. He was a violent criminal in life; death hasn't improved his mood.

QUARRY

MAP LEGEND

- Containers
- **1** Strangler Jizu
- **2** Turnkey Shiji

Valuable ore was once mined in this quarry, but when the vein was exhausted, the cave was converted to a prison. When the waters rose over Old Tien's Landing, evacuating the inmates was not a priority. Their angry ghosts are still here, waiting for prey.

The south cavern is also the largest. You battle a few convict ghosts here, and a decomposing skeleton in the southwest corner has some coins.

South cavern

The small pool in the middle of this cavern is barely deeper than your ankles, but for the ghost of a small child who drowned here, it's a terrifying obstacle. You can help her in the **Stranded Orphan** side quest.

Central cavern

North cavern

Hundreds of silver pieces and several potent gems lie in the deepest chamber of the quarry. To claim them, you must first exorcise the area of ghosts. Led by Strangler Jizu, the spirits of the dead convicts won't give up their treasure without a fight.

CHARACTERS

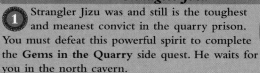

Strangler Jizu

1 Strangler Jizu was and still is the toughest and meanest convict in the quarry prison. You must defeat this powerful spirit to complete the **Gems in the Quarry** side quest. He waits for you in the north cavern.

Turnkey Shiji

2 Shiji was a jailer at the quarry prison. When the dam was first closed he tried to save the prisoners, but Jizu strangled him. He's now trapped here along with his former wards, imprisoned in the same spiritual limbo. If you defeat Jizu, Shiji rewards you with a potent gem.

LOWER PIRATE BASE

to Workshop

Warehouse

Slave Breaker

5

Slave Pens

3

2

Kang's Workshop

1

Dock

4

to Tien's Landing

MAP LEGEND

●	*Containers*
○	*Focus Shrine*
○	*Scrollstand*
●	*Spirit Font*
●	*Trapped Container*
1	*Pirate Cheung*
2	*Sky*
3	*Yifong*
4	*Kang the Mad*
5	*Fuyao and Lun*

Warehouse

The History of Flight, Vol. 1: Tells of the first disastrous attempt at flight using a crude rocket chair.

This soaring natural cave is filled with stocks, iron cages, and other instruments of torture. Slaves are kept in cells on the lower level. The upper exit is locked by a mechanism that requires two people to operate it; fortunately, Sky is there to help you.

Slave pen

Featuring numberless gadgets, tools, and assorted mysterious implements, the workshop is a laboratory provided for Kang the Mad by his master Gao. Not surprisingly, you meet Kang the Mad here.

Kang's workshop

Captured slaves are taken to a small cavern above Kang's workshop to be "broken," or trained for a life of servitude.

Slave breaker

CHARACTERS

Pirate Cheung

1 Cheung was once the captain of this band of pirates, and he led his men on merry raids and high sea adventures. Then Gao the Greater came along with his Lotus Assassins and took over the operation. If you get rid of Gao, then Cheung can happily take back command of his men.

Sky

2 This rogue has snuck into the pirate base for reasons of his own. You meet him in the slave pen during his attempt to free the pirates' captives. A temporary alliance leads him to later join you as a Follower.

Yifong

3 Your second meeting with Yifong takes place in the slave pen. You met her and her daughter Fuyao when you first arrived in Tien's Landing as they were heading out to try their luck in the wilderness. Now they're held captive by pirates, and it seems their luck has almost run out.

Kang the Mad

4 "Eccentric" is an understatement when applied to Kang the Mad. This inventor is the genius behind the flying machines used by Gao's men. He doesn't work for Gao willingly. Kang becomes your Follower after you've slain Gao.

Fuyao

5 Fuyao was captured after she fled Tien's Landing with her mother. You meet her in the slave breaker's cave and can either rescue her, sell her, or help her find the strength to fend for herself.

Lun
5 Lun came to pirate island to buy a slave. He's got his eye on Fuyao, but the spirited young girl would never submit to him. You find him and the slave breaker attempting to "train" Fuyao into subservience.

WORKSHOP

Gao's Room — **1**

Dragonfly
Release Switch

Hangar

to Pirate Base

2

Treasure Vault

MAP LEGEND

- *Container*
- *Focus Shrine*
- *Scrollstand*
- *Trapped Container*
- **1** *Gao the Greater*
- **2** *Xianshi*

At the peak of the pirate's island, Gao has built a magnificent workshop where Kang the Mad constructs his flying machines. Gao's private quarters are also found here.

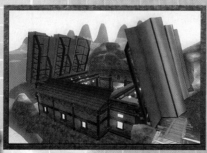

The hangar shelters Kang's masterpiece, the Marvelous Dragonfly, and features a hinged roof that can open to let the flyer take off. Gao summons several demons to protect the Marvelous Dragonfly, and they await you here.

Hangar

The History of Flight, Vol. 2: These documents continue the story of man's obsession with mastering the air.

Gao stashes most of his wealth in a locked vault, but you can blast it open with the Marevelous Dragonfly's guns. Xianshi, an elephant demon, provides a second line of defense.

Treasure vault

Jade Empire Bestiary, Vol. 4: This document prescribes martial and weapon attacks when fighting demons.

Gao built his private quarters on the highest peak of the island, allowing him a commanding view of the entire base. Your final showdown with the crime lord takes place here.

Gao's room

The History of Flight, Vol. 3: The story of Kang the Mad's ornithopter innovations is told in these records.

CHARACTERS

Gao the Greater

 Gao the Greater is as evil as he is rich. When you meet him at the peak of the pirate's island, you can finally exact revenge for the destruction of Two Rivers.

Xianshi

 Xianshi is an elephant demon Gao summoned to guard his treasure vault. He doesn't want to fight you, but the power of Gao's magic compels him to slay anyone who enters the vault.

GREAT FOREST

to Heaven · Red Crystal · to Pilgrim's Rest · Furnaces · Blue Crystal · Forest Shadow's Temple · Crossroads · Bridge · Lord Yun's Camp · to Tien's Landing

MAP LEGEND

- Containers
- Focus Shrine
- Scrollstand
- Spirit Font
- 1 Lord Yun
- 2 Spear Catches Leaf
- 3 The Black Whirlwind
- 4 Bladed Thesis

The Great Forest stretches for a distance north of Tien's Landing. It's the only land route connecting the town with the rest of the Empire, but because of the ghosts it's no longer safe for travelers.

Lord Yun, forced to flee to the fringe of the forest, sets up camp as close to Tien's Landing as possible. He waits for you here after you agree to help him solve the riddle of the forest's curse.

Lord Yun's Camp

A stone bridge arches over the rapids that tumble through the forest. Your first battle with the Forest Shadow happens here.

Bridge

Forest Shadow's Temple

A temple to the Forest Shadow has been maintained by Lord Yun's family for generations. Once you get the Temple Crystal from the innkeeper at Pilgrim's Rest, you can use the temple's furnaces to open a gateway to Heaven.

Temple Records: A collection of notes from Yun's family, this document gives a hint on how to activate the portal to Heaven.

CHARACTERS

Lord Yun

1 Lord Yun manages the Great Forest, but he has been helpless to do anything about the curse that fills it with ghosts. He also possesses a rare wind map. You can have it if you return the forest to normal.

Spear Catches Leaf

2 One of Lord Yun's premiere hunters, Spear Catches Leaf was trying to solve the riddle of the sickened forest but hasn't made any headway. He's got some useful techniques, gems, and the **Legendary Strike** style for sale. You meet him at the Forest Shadow's temple.

SPEAR CATCHES LEAF

Item (Number Available)	Cost (SP)
Flawed Warrior Gem (1)	200
Flawed Monk Gem (2)	200
Slick Gem (1)	500
Legendary Strike (1)	6,000
Hunter's Spirit (1)	4,250
Boar's Strength (1)	1,250
Tracking Eye (1)	1,250
Predatory Intuition (1)	1,000

The Black Whirlwind

3 The Black Whirlwind is a coarse and crude mercenary who lives for the thrill of battle. What he lacks in manners and subtlety he makes up for in strength and courage. He will join you after Spear Catches Leaf leaves and you have the crystal.

Bladed Thesis

4 The Way of the Closed Fist started with this man, who was the first person to codify its ideals into a rigorous philosophy. He also created the Zither of Discord. He only appears if you found the zither's strings and case for Scholar Six Heavens.

CHAPTER TWO

PILGRIM'S REST

- to Great Forest
- Common Room
- 1
- Back Room
- 2
- to Cannibal Caves

MAP LEGEND

- ⬤ Containers
- ⚪ Scrollstand
- ⬤ Trapped Containers
- 1 The Innkeeper
- 2 Henpecked Hou

Deep within the Great Forest is an inn that serves merchants and other travelers to Tien's Landing. But something's not right here....

Common room

Most patrons loiter in the common room, waiting for more victims to stroll in. The place is a ruin, barely fit for human habitation. You meet the Innkeeper here.

Back room

Henpecked Hou hides out in the kitchens in the back of Pilgrim's Rest. A secret door here leads to the cannibal caves, but it only opens after you've met with the Forest Shadow.

The Tricksters: Explains the wily nature of fox spirits.

Characters

The Innkeeper

1 The Innkeeper tries his best to fool you into believing that Pilgrim's Rest is just a humble inn and that the Forest Shadow is an evil spirit. Don't fall for it! He's actually a blood-thirsty cannibal.

Henpecked Hou

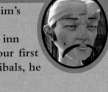

2 Henpecked Hou is the cook at Pilgrim's Rest. If he seems thin for a chef, it's because he's not a cannibal like the other inn patrons. You can buy gems from him at your first meeting. After you've dealt with the cannibals, he becomes your Follower.

HENPECKED HOU

Item (Number Available)	Cost (SP)
Flawed Scholar Gem (1)	200
Inferior Scholar Gem (1)	1,500
Intuition Gem (1)	900

Cannibal Caves

to Pilgrim's Rest

MAP LEGEND

- ○ Containers
- **1** The Mother

The eerie feeling you get at Pilgrim's Rest Inn is due to the fact that it's built over a series of caves inhabited by ghoulish cannibals. Filled with rotting corpses and gruesome human trophies, these caves are the lair for a powerful demon known as the Mother.

Characters

The Mother

1 The queen of the cannibals, known affectionately as "the Mother," resides in the heart of the Cannibal Caves. Only her death can lift the curse from the Great Forest.

Heaven

to Great
Forest

1

3 **2**

Forest
Shadow's Temple

MAP LEGEND

- Containers
- Focus Shrine
- Scrollstand
- Spirit Font
- Trapped Containers
- **1** Zin Bu the Magic Abacus
- **2** Shining Tusk
- **3** Forest Shadow

Forest Shadow's Temple

The Celestial Order, Vol. 1: Chaos and order combine to create the endless variety in the world, according to this file.

Characters

Zin Bu the Magic Abacus

1 There are many heavenly spirits assigned the task of monitoring balance in the world. Zin Bu is one of these spirits. It reflects on the importance of your destiny that you are the sole person Zin Bu must keep track of. This is easier for him to do as your Follower, which he becomes after you've met the Forest Shadow.

Shining Tusk

2 Forest Shadow's personal bodyguard is an elephant demon named Shining Tusk. He's very distrustful of you, and if you show the slightest aggression toward the Forest Shadow, he'll make you regret it.

JADE EMPIRE

Forest Shadow

3 The Great Forest is watched over by a fox spirit known as the Forest Shadow. She needs your help to defeat the cannibal Mother and lift the curse from the forest.

CRITICAL PATH
PICKING UP THE PIECES

The Mosquito makes a crash landing, but no one is hurt. Zu explains that navigating to the Imperial City is impossible without a wind map, but even if you had one now it would do no good because your flyer is scrap. Thankfully the town of Tien's Landing is nearby. Choose a Follower (it doesn't matter which) and head out to explore the area.

Sagacious Zu has a plan.

Three ghosts attack as you pass through the ruins. Your Follower can damage ghosts, so switch him or her to Attack mode, then take out the ghosts one at a time.

CONVICT GHOST BATTLE: ~168 XP, 0 SP			
Enemy	Style	Health	Chi
Convict Ghost x2	Staff	60	60
Convict Ghost	Ice Shard	60	60

After you defeat the ghosts, the Water Dragon's spirit appears to you in a vision. She drops a few hints about the Dragon Amulet. Other pieces of it are scattered throughout the world, and one of them lies here in Tien's Landing.

The Water Dragon's spirit offers more clues about the Dragon Amulet.

As you pass along the river's edge, keep an eye out for a headstone concealed in the tall grass. When you examine it, the headstone crumbles to dust and you're suddenly in the middle of a spectral ambush! All three ghosts use Ice Shard; immediately enter Focus mode and take evasive action, then divide and conquer.

Destroying this headstone summons angry ghosts.

CONVICT GHOST BATTLE: ~168 XP, 0 SP			
Enemy	Style	Health	Chi
Convict Ghost x3	Ice Shard	60	60

The raised drawbridge is unusable for now, so cross the river on the back of the Great Dam. Three Imperial conscripts try to stop you; they can take a fair amount of punishment, but without weapons or martial training they pose little threat.

Look for a concealed skeleton (5 SP) on the path to the drawbridge.

BATTLE ON THE DAM: ~102 XP, ~120 SP			
Enemy	Style	Health	Chi
Conscript x3	Basic	200	200

A WOMAN IN BLACK

With the soldiers defeated, cross the dam and look for a concealed barrel on the right (28 SP). As you continue along the path, a masked figure suddenly leaps down from the cliffs. She is Silk Fox, a deadly huntress in pursuit of Death's Hand and his

Lotus Assassins. Because you came from Two Rivers, she believes you were one of its destroyers. She wields the Long Sword with deadly swiftness; use Heavenly Wave and Focus mode to slow her to a crawl. Magic use is also an effective option.

SILK FOX BATTLE: ~125 XP, 0 SP				
Enemy	Style	Health	Chi	
Silk Fox	Long Sword	258	228	

After taking a few hits, Silk Fox senses there is something different about you and breaks off the attack. She promises that you will meet again, and departs with a warning: all who oppose Death's Hand meet the same fate as the people of Two Rivers.

You can count on plenty of run-ins with Silk Fox.

IMPERIAL WATCH TOWER

At a fork in the road ahead, the sign of the leaping carp points right, to Tien's Landing. Before you go there, explore the left path to fight the soldiers at the Imperial watch tower. The leader uses Storm Dragon, a support style that enervates victims with a surge of electricity, causing Health to slowly drain over time. Don't let this happen to you! Speed up with Focus mode, leap behind the leader, and take him out quickly.

IMPERIAL WATCH TOWER BATTLE: ~156 XP, ~165 SP				
Enemy	Style	Health	Chi	
Imperial Soldier x2	Spear	80	80	
Imperial Soldier	Storm Dragon	50	50	

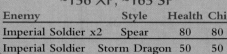

You can let Chen Yi go, or force him to stay and fight.

Chen Yi, a fourth soldier, emerges from hiding after the battle. He's a frightened, unwilling draftee who only wants to go in peace, and he offers to tell everything he knows about the ruins (not much) in exchange for his life. Will you accept his plea?

Choice 1 Chen Yi seems genuinely horrified by war and never raised his weapon against you. Allow him to escape.

Choice 2 Chen Yi claims he was just following orders, but his comrades might have said the same thing. It's not an acceptable excuse; by joining with your enemies, Chen Yi has forfeited his life.

CHEN YI BATTLE: ~61 XP, ~65 SP				
Enemy	Style	Health	Chi	
Chen Yi	Spear	80	80	

After dealing with the Imperial guards, scrounge 2 SP from a roadside barrel and then enter the watch tower to find the *real* treasure: a Focus Shrine and three chests. The chest on the left is trapped, so make sure your Focus is full before opening it. The chest next to it contains 22 SP and the Silk Strings for the **Zither of Discord** quest. The final chest holds 422 SP and a guaranteed gem.

Your Followers rest in the base camp when they're not traveling with you.

The Ruins Gate is locked, so your only option is returning past the carp stone to Tien's Landing. Whomever you left behind at the crash site is already waiting at the base camp, and he or she greets you with a **Gem of Good Fortune** (Intuition +5, Spirit +1, Mind +1). Choose a Follower to accompany you and head out to explore the town.

Look for a chest near your base camp to make a quick 100 SP.

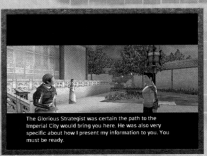

Hui fills in many details of Master Li's past.

After the fight, Hui reveals that she is a friend of both Master Li and Sagacious Zu. She knows of the siege at Dirge that wiped out your people, but she adds a new detail: Emperor Sun Hai slew the Water Dragon and used her power to end the drought, but without her governance over the Wheel of Life, departed souls can't move on to the next world. This means the recent hauntings and the end of the drought are connected.

TIP

Keep a close bond with your Followers by talking to them often, especially after significant events. They often have new concerns, insights, or revelations to share.

There are a *lot* of people to meet here. Your first encounter takes place as you cross a small bridge leading into town. Yifong, an old peasant woman, and her daughter Fuyao have decided to leave Tien's Landing because of the recent troubles. Nothing you can say deters them, and they head out to try their luck in the wilderness. You'll be seeing them again soon.

I am Yifong, a simple villager. I have lived all my life here in Tien's Landing, but now I must take my daughter and venture out to the wilderness.

Yifong has nothing to lose by facing the wilderness.

HUI THE BRAVE

SPEAK WITH HUI

In front of the Tea House, three rowdy sailors are picking a fight with a woman named Hui the Brave. The sailors won't back down, so you and Hui have no choice but to teach them a lesson.

Magic and weapons tire you. Draw on them too much and you could be left defenseless. Spirit Thief restores your chi and focus, prolonging your ability to fight or ignore wounds.

Hui also teaches you the secrets of **Spirit Thief**. This unique style will revolutionize the way you handle combat because it gives you the power to replenish your Chi during battle by draining it from your enemies.

Raid the Tea House kitchen for silver and gems.

SAILOR BATTLE: ~183 XP, ~180 SP				
Enemy	Style	Health	Chi	
Sailor	Basic	80	80	
Sailor x2	Spear	80	80	

Sailor

BAMBOO CASK

Nickeled iron can later be refined into a useful item.

Before you follow her, make an exploratory loop around the Tea House yard. Read the scrollstand by the entrance, then look along the back porch to find a barrel with 4 SP and a chest with 263 SP; one or both containers possibly bestow gems as well. While you're there, introduce yourself to Chef Teh and Dishwasher Wong, two Tea House employees. Next, look in the clearing northwest of the Tea House to find two more casks; the left holds a **Bar of Nickeled Iron**. This item is needed for **Lord Lao's Furnace**, a later side quest. The right cask is trapped. Finally, a box behind the northeast wall has 32 SP.

SIDE QUEST

To activate the **Beaten Baker** side quest, talk to Seamstress Lan; find her sobbing beneath a tree outside the Tea House. After taking care of the beaten baker, you can then immediately move on to the **Matchmaker** side quest.

THE TEA HOUSE

The sailors won't give up until you've thrashed them for good.

Enter the Tea House to continue your talk with Hui the Brave. The conversation is cut short when the sailors you thrashed earlier storm in. They want a rematch, and they've brought reinforcements: Sailors crash through the windows and drop from the rafters, completely surrounding you.

Grab two hunks of meat and start hamming it up!

You can use two special combat styles in this unique battle by smashing the Tea House furnishings and using the debris as improvised weapons. The first style utilizes a pair of gigantic hams like two cumbersome but powerful clubs. Obtain them by demolishing ham stands.

Shattered furniture also makes a good weapon.

Gain another style by splintering a wooden table or chair and wielding a pair of thick planks. Both improvised weapon styles are stronger than your usual weapons, and the best part is that they don't require any Focus.

NOTE

The red meter that appears when using improvised weapons represents how much damage the weapon can take before it breaks. When the meter is gone, so is your weapon. Both types can make about 15 strikes before wearing out.

TEA HOUSE BRAWL: ~490 XP, ~515 SP			
Enemy	Style	Health	Chi
Sailor x3	Basic	80	80
Sailor x3	Spear	80	80
Tea House Rowdy x3	Basic	80	80

Remember: Go to the ruins and claim the amulet before the Lotus Assassins do. You will need it to survive the trials that lie ahead.

When the fight is over, Hui finally finishes her tale. According to her, the Lotus Assassins have drained the lake because a piece of your Dragon Amulet was buried in the ruins of Old Tien's Landing, and she fears they may have already found it.

You now have three main objectives: exploring the ruins, obtaining a new flyer, and finding a wind map. The walkthrough follows them in this sequence, but you can complete them in any order you like. No matter where you go first, you won't get the Dragon Amulet piece until you've done everything else (Hui was right: the Assassins already have the amulet).

SIDE QUEST

*Before you leave the Tea House, take time to wander around and chat with the patrons and employees. You can undertake three side quests: **Old Mother Kwan**, **Zhong the Ox Carrier**, and **Chai Jin**.*

MINISTER SHENG

To get into the ruins, you must unlock the gates that block the path (you saw this gate earlier, by the Imperial watch tower). Minister Sheng, the official administrator of Tien's Landing, is said to have a key. Leave the Tea House and head east into the Merchant Area to find him.

Locate Minister Sheng in front of the smoldering ruin that used to be his official residence. As you approach, a drunken sailor is caught blatantly stealing from Merchant Cheung. Minister Sheng, irritated, wanders over to scold the thief. The sailor drops his stolen sword and staggers off unpunished while the minister complains of his inability to maintain law and order.

Minister Sheng seems to have stopped caring about what happens to Tien's Landing.

When you talk to Minister Sheng, he doesn't hesitate to flood you with a torrent of complaints. Pirates and ghosts are bad enough, but his main concern is getting the dam closed so that both the Lotus Assassins and the stranded pirates will leave Tien's Landing. Whether you offer to help or not, he slips the **Ruins Key** into your pocket in the hope that you'll solve his problems for him (500 XP).

> ### NOTE
> *For a real insight into just how whiny Minister Sheng is, check the official "List of Grievances" on the scrollstand by the charred ruins of his house.*

> ### SIDE QUEST
> *Not everyone wants the dam to be closed, however. Merchant Jiang, a wine seller, approaches you with a counteroffer as you leave the Merchant's Area. For full details, see the **Great Dam** side quest later in this chapter.*

EXPLORE TIEN'S LANDING
THE MERCHANT'S AREA

A chest in the Merchant's Area holds abandoned silver.

You can head for the ruins at any time, but you should completely explore the rest of Tien's Landing before you go. You can talk to the residents, find hidden containers, and activate many side quests. In the Merchant's Area, where you met with Minister Sheng, look for a chest along the stalls to the northwest (32 SP). The path leading northeast to the Forest is open, and you're free to explore it if you like, but it's best to wait until you've taken care of other loose ends first.

> ### NOTE
> *Talk to Merchant Cheung, who was being robbed when you first entered the Merchant's Area, to trigger the **Stolen Memento** side quest.*

THE BOAT HOUSE

Next, head south to explore the town's coastline. At the far western end, beyond a small open field, is a well-hidden barrel. Shatter it to reveal a minor gem.

From there, head east along the shore to the Boat House. The guard at the door refuses to let you in unless you're involved with the **Beaten Baker** side quest. On the east side of the building are a scrollstand and chest containing a **Gem of Thief's Sense**; with this gem equipped, trapped containers announce themselves with a sinister red glow.

Claim the Gem of Thief's Sense from a chest next to the Boat House.

Dawn Star

From the Boat House area, two paths lead east to Beggar's Pier. Check behind the house on the left path for a barrel with 22 SP. Then take the right path to enter Beggar's Pier.

BEGGAR'S PIER

Darting Lynx

Look left after passing through the gate into Beggar's Pier to spy a small jar with 18 SP inside. Proceed east and talk to the acrobat Darting Lynx.

Chest

Vase

Finish your tour of Tien's Landing by exploring the east and north sides of Beggar's Pier. Board the *Lucky Night*, moored on the easternmost dock, to find a chest with 1,200 SP and a scrollstand. On the north side, you can find a barrel on the east with 9 SP and a jar on the west with 14 SP.

EXPLORING THE RUINS

Ruins

Ruins Key has been used up.

After you explore the town and complete side quests, it's finally time to leave and search for the next amulet piece. Exit Tien's Landing to the west and use the Ruins Key that Minister Sheng gave you to open the gate by the Imperial watch tower.

As you proceed into the ruins, you see a Lotus Assassin giving orders to a group of rat demons. The Assassin and the rats depart, leaving behind a trio of Imperial soldiers to deal with you. Head forward and confront them. The lieutenant tries to poison

Lieutenant, you are in charge while I go up to the Great Dam and check on the sentry golems. If anyone tries to enter these ruins, kill them.

you with the Viper style; deal cautiously with this foe, attacking from the rear whenever possible. If you get poisoned, switching to Toad Demon style is the best cure. After the lieutenant goes down, turn your attention to the remaining soldiers.

IMPERIAL SOLDIER BATTLE: ~135 XP, ~147 SP			
Enemy	Style	Health	Chi
Imperial Soldier x2	Long Sword	60	60
Lieutenant	Viper	50	50

After the battle you receive a another Gem of Thief's Sense. Before moving on, explore the camp to find several stashes of loot. The ceramic urn by the pillar is trapped; open it, then look near the campfire for a pair of skeletons. One contains 95 SP, the other 121 SP—each might hold a gem as well. Finally, open the chest by the southern gate and take the dragon powder (100 XP), which you need shortly.

Pass through the gate to encounter your first rat demon. These creatures are small and slow, so you should have no problem defeating just one. Remember that Support and Magic styles have no effect on demons.

Claim the dragon powder from this chest south of the assassin's camp.

RAT DEMON BATTLE: ~54 XP, 0 SP

Enemy	Style	Health	Chi
Rat Demon	Rat Demon	60	60

After defeating the rat demon, the miserable creature begs you to spare its life in exchange for information. He hints at a potent treasure that can be accessed only by blasting open a wall deeper within the ruins. Fortunately, you already have the dragon powder needed for this task. After hearing this, you have two choices:

Choice 1 Keep your end of the bargain and let the rat demon escape (100 XP).

Choice 2 Break your word and kill the rat demon anyway.

More rat demons await inside this old house.

Look next to the gate you just passed through for a barrel with 7 SP, then enter the mostly intact building on the right to face two more rat demons. Show the vermin no mercy, then open the ceramic urn they were guarding to claim 256 SP.

RAT DEMON BATTLE: ~108 XP, 0 SP

Enemy	Style	Health	Chi
Rat Demon x2	Rat Demon	120	60

Salvage an exquisite cameo portrait from this skeleton.

After emptying the building, look behind it to find a skeleton. Search the bones to get the **Cameo Portrait**; closer inspection reveals that it's engraved with the name "Wei." When you return to Tien's Landing, show it to Old Wei in the Merchant's Area. He recognizes the cameo: it depicts his departed wife. You have a few options here:

Choice 1 Give the cameo to Wei, free of charge (800 XP).

Choice 2 Demand that Old Wei pay you for the cameo. Reluctantly, he hands over 450 SP (600 XP).

Choice 3 Extort 450 SP from Old Wei as in Choice 2, then treacherously keep the cameo anyway (600 XP).

BLOW UP THE WALL

Use the rockets to destroy both the wall and the soldiers guarding it.

Continue deeper into the ruins to find a set of rockets aimed at a crumbling wall; this is the place the rat demon told you about earlier. Three Imperial soldiers guard the area; you can fight them, or blow them to smithereens by using your dragon powder to ignite the rockets (500 XP). If you choose to fight, keep a close eye on your Health. All three soldiers wield swords and can deal a lot of damage in short order.

IMPERIAL SOLDIER BATTLE: ~144 XP, ~140 SP

Enemy	Style	Health	Chi
Imperial Soldier x3	Long Sword	60	60

SIDE QUEST

After blowing up the wall, you can explore the area beyond in search of gems. This is completely optional, and is detailed in the Gems in the Quarry and Stranded Orphan side quests. Another side quest, Drowned Orphans, is triggered by entering the abandoned orphanage.

Look for a gravestone in an alcove across the yard from the orphanage (988 SP), then search the area behind the orphanage. Slay the lone rat demon here, then open the cask to find 65 SP.

RAT DEMON BATTLE: ~56 XP, 0 SP

Enemy	Style	Health	Chi
Rat Demon	Rat Demon	60	60

Go south to finish your sweep of the ruins. An Assassin and an Imperial Soldier on the road ahead discuss the command word ("Shao Hua") needed to safely pass the golems ahead. After letting this vital information slip, the Assassin flees while the soldier charges to attack. He tries to shock you with Storm Dragon, but without allies for support he's easily defeated.

IMPERIAL SOLDIER BATTLE: ~50 XP, ~45 SP

Enemy	Style	Health	Chi
Imperial Soldier	Storm Dragon	60	60

When you approach the drawbridge ahead, the Assassin who fled earlier raises it to deter your pursuit. Go right and operate the crane lever; this causes the crane to swing around and nudge the drawbridge controls, lowering the bridge.

The Gem of Thief's Sense makes trapped containers easy to spot.

With the bridge lowered, cross over and open the pair of casks on the other side. One is trapped, while the other has a mere 5 SP (though you might also get a gem, if you're lucky).

As you approach the gate leading back to the dam site, you suddenly have another vision of the Water Dragon. Her mysterious advice seems to hint at other forces manipulating your destiny. Before she can elaborate, the Water Dragon grows weaker and the vision fades. After coming back to your senses, you can finally move on to the next area.

More enigmatic hints from the Water Dragon.

WILD FLOWER

You find yourself back at the dam site, but now you're on the other side of the raised drawbridge you saw when you first arrived. A small girl is here, standing over the dead body of the Assassin that fled from you in the ruins. If you ask her what happened, she makes a few ominous hints about a "Guardian" and runs away. A moment later, the Guardian, a gigantic bestial demon named Chai Ka, appears.

Like most demons, Chai Ka is immune to both Magic and Support styles. You must rely on Weapon and Martial styles to win. If you've invested heavily boosting your Spirit, you can still use your Chi with Chi Strikes. Chai Ka is very strong; keep moving and strike from the rear or while the demon is recovering from his own attacks. Monitor your Health closely and use Chi Heal when needed. Also note that blocking can stop Chai Ka's damaging clear attack.

When Chai Ka has lost about one quarter of his Health, he makes a few defiant comments about slaying all Lotus Assassins. It seems he's mistaken you for one of them! Nothing you can say convinces him otherwise, and the battle continues.

CHAI KA BATTLE: ~250 XP, 0 SP			
Enemy	Style	Health	Chi
Chai Ka	Chai Ka	700	700

After the battle, Chai Ka speaks to you. Finally convinced you're not a Lotus Assassin, he tells you that he was summoned by some greater power to guard the Dragon Amulet until the day you came to claim it. Unfortunately, the Assassins got here first and took the Dragon Amulet from Chai Ka through trickery.

I am sworn to serve you, great one. My entire purpose in the mortal realm is to help you fulfill your destiny. I will do everything in my power to aid you.

Don't be fooled by appearances. Chai Ka is actually your ally.

Despite his failure to guard the amulet, Chai Ka is determined to fulfill the second part of his duty: becoming your Follower. He explains that the girl you met earlier, Wild Flower, is his anchor to the mortal realm. She harbors the demon within her, transforming into Chai Ka when danger threatens.

She is an anchor binding me to the mortal realm. I could not exist in your realm without her. I protect Wild Flower from danger, and she allows me to fulfill my duties.

Chai Ka Profile

Attack Style: Chai Ka

Support Ability: Recover Health

Health: ~348

Chi: ~294

After answering your questions as best he can, Chai Ka reverts to Wild Flower. The girl gives you two items: the **Inscrutable Power Source** (which you need to get a flyer operating later on), and a random gem. You can take Wild Flower with you, or send her back to the base camp.

Now enter the gazebo ahead and use the lever to lower the drawbridge, allowing you to return to Tien's Landing.

> ### SIDE QUEST
> *Before you head back to town, you can follow up on two side quests. See **The Zither of Discord** and **The Great Dam** headings at the end of this chapter.*

Lord Yun governs much of the Great Southern Forest. He petitioned the Lotus Assassins for a wind map so he could settle a trade disruption.

As you pass the carp stone, Silk Fox makes another appearance. She claims to be on your side, against Death's Hand, and advises that if you want to reach the Imperial City, you'll need to get a wind map from Lord Yun in the Great Forest (500 XP).

THE PIRATE LAIR

TALK TO RU THE BOATSWAIN

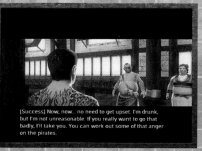

[Success] Now, now... no need to get upset. I'm drunk, but I'm not unreasonable. If you really want to go that badly, I'll take you. You can work out some of that anger on the pirates.

Ru is willing to sail you into danger after a nip of liquid courage.

With the first of your three main tasks completed, it's time to move on to the next: finding a flyer. Go to the Tea House and head upstairs to find Ru the Boatswain. Eager for a chance to do something adventurous, Ru agrees to ferry you to Gao the Greater's pirate base (1,000 XP). Meet him at Begger's Pier when you're ready to go.

Board Ru's barge at Beggar's Pier.

PIRATE CHEUNG

After Ru drops you off at the pirate base, head inland to witness a gang of Gao's men bullying one of the sailors. The victim limps away to find shelter under a tree. The man is Pirate Cheung, and he used to run this outfit until Gao the Greater came along and forced the pirates into the slave trade. He plans on getting revenge against the bullies by untying the rope that suspends a massive cannon over their heads. There's only one problem: if the cannon falls, it will also hit an innocent servant boy. What will you do?

Trip me? Make me crawl like a dog? This'll teach 'em a lesson they won't forget! Come on... stupid rope! Come on... Make them sorry they ever... huh?

Choice 1 Innocent bystanders are of no concern. Cut the rope and let the cannon fall (1,000 XP).

Choice 2 There is no alignment shift if you simply fight the pirates the old-fashioned way. There are only three of them, but the cramped boardwalk is an awkward battlefield. Use plenty of area attacks to keep yourself from being overwhelmed. Above all, watch out for the Hidden Fist style used by one of the pirates. Hidden Fist is a Support style that causes no damage on its own, but it can leave you disoriented and unable to attack.

PIRATE BATTLE: ~210 XP, ~195 SP

Enemy	Style	Health	Chi
Pirate x2	Long Sword	80	80
Pirate	Hidden Fist	80	80

Up near the top, you'll find the airships and Gao himself. Maybe Inquisitor Lim, too. He's so cold he could scare a spirit back to life, then scare him dead all over again.

Afterward, Pirate Cheung has words with you. You can ask him about his past and about the pirate base, then leave him and head inland to begin battling your way to Gao. There are *tons* of pirates everywhere, so expect frequent battles against numerous foes. Fortunately, pirates aren't immune to any of your styles. Slow them with Heavenly Wave, summon a fire dragon with Dire Flame, or transform into a Toad Demon.

Move on to the warehouse to face the next group of pirates. Keep an eye out for the leader, who not only uses Storm Dragon style but also has more than three times as much Health as the others. With so many opponents, keep your Follower in Attack mode to divide their attention. After thrashing them, smash a jar by the Focus Shrine in the corner for 200 SP.

PIRATE BATTLE: ~530 XP, ~500 SP

Enemy	Style	Health	Chi
Pirate x3	Basic	80	80
Pirate x2	Long Sword	80	80
Pirate	Spear	80	80
Pirate	Storm Dragon, Tempest	250	250

SKY

You're not the only intruder in the pirate base.

From the warehouse, follow a narrow, winding staircase deeper into the base until you arrive at a large natural cavern: the slave pen. As you enter, a dashing stranger clad in blue dives from a high balcony and smashes open the slaves' cell. As pirate reinforcements arrive and boast of their overwhelming numbers, the stranger also claims to have brought backup: you!

With that, the battle begins. With both the stranger and your Follower on your side, it's an even battle. Concentrate your attacks on the pirate who uses Storm Dragon while your allies keep the other pirates busy. When you've taken your man down, mop up the rest.

PIRATE BATTLE: ~320 XP, ~300 SP

Enemy	Style	Health	Chi
Pirate x3	Long Sword	80	80
Pirate	Storm Dragon Tempest	250	250

Speaking of which, there's a very secure and equally intimidating gate blocking the way. If we work together, though, it will be simple to crack.

Cooperation is the only way to open the sealed gate.

When the battle's over, the stranger (who you'll later learn is named Sky) pauses to speak with you. Sky doesn't reveal anything about himself or why he's here, but he seems to be against the pirates. He tells you about a door at the top of the cavern that's unlocked by holding a lever forward, but because the door and lever are on opposite sides of the room, you need his help to get through. He promises to lend a hand, and departs.

SIDE QUEST

Before you go, one of the slaves that Sky released calls out to you. It's Yifong, the woman you met when you first arrived in Tien's Landing. You can help rescue her and her daughter from the pirate base. See the Yifong and Fuyao side quest at the end of the chapter for full information.

DAWN STAR

Before you move on, look near the central pillar to find 45 SP on an old skeleton. Then climb the stairs to find the sealed door Sky told you about. True to his word, he releases the lock so you can open it and go through. Four more pirates await on the other side. This time you have to fight them without Sky's help.

PIRATE BATTLE: ~320 XP, ~300 SP

Enemy	Style	Health	Chi
Pirate x3	Long Sword	80	80
Pirate	Storm Dragon, Tempest	250	250

KANG THE MAD

I... I want to be alone. I... I must grieve for my son. No one is to disturb me! No one!

Continue up the stairs until you come to a large building. As you walk around the perimeter, you get the first chance to spy on your adversaries: Gao the Greater, his pet inventor Kang the Mad, and Inquisitor Lim. After their conversation, in which Gao learns that his son was killed in Two Rivers, they leave. Keep following the path to the entrance of the building and go in.

When you enter, four pirates move in to attack. As they stalk toward you, a sudden explosion (courtesy of Kang the Mad) detonates in their midst. Take advantage of the confusion to finish them off quickly.

PIRATE BATTLE: ~320 XP, ~300 SP

Enemy	Style	Health	Chi
Pirate x3	Long Sword	80	80
Pirate	Storm Dragon, Tempest	250	250

Kang the Mad approaches you after the fight. He's not a willing servant of Gao's and he offers to help you in whatever way he can, though he's no good at fighting. If you free him from his slavery to Gao, he offers to become your Follower and let you use his latest flying machine, the Marvelous Dragonfly.

If you stage a combat-related accident for Gao, like falling down a flight of punches, I'll replace the inductor on the Dragonfly and we can fly away! What do you say?

Grab 175 SP from a chest in the corner of Kang's workshop, then head up to the second floor and exit the building. Continue along the path to do battle with another knot of pirates. Like most of the battles you've had in the pirate base, look for and target the leader, who uses Storm Dragon, and eliminate that enemy first.

CHEST

PIRATE BATTLE: ~320 XP, ~300 SP			
Enemy	Style	Health	Chi
Pirate x3	Long Sword	80	80
Pirate	Storm Dragon, Tempest	250	250

SIDE QUEST

If you want to complete the Yifong and Fuyao side quest, head northwest into the cave. Otherwise, continue northeast to the next level of the pirate base.

AN AUDIENCE WITH GAO THE GREATER

You've waded through an army of pirates, but now you're finally near the top of the island. Ascend into the workshop area and head for the gigantic hangar. Gao has left a few demons here to slow you down. If you've been to the ruins, you'll recognize the rat demons. Horse demons, however, are something new. They can use both melee and magic attacks. Their flaming manes sear you whenever you strike them, even if you're using weapons, so watch your Health very closely. Worse still, horse demons explode when defeated, causing significant damage. Using Dawn Star in Support mode replenishes your Chi, which you will need for Chi Heal. Use Chai Ka in Support mode to have him increase your Health.

HANGAR BATTLE: ~394 XP, 0 SP			
Enemy	Style	Health	Chi
Rat Demon x2	Rat Demon	50	50
Horse Demon x2	Horse Demon	80	80

When you defeat the demons, more enemies arrive before you can catch your breath. This time the pirates have brought an ogre with them. Setting your Follower to Attack mode can distract the enemy, allowing you time to recharge with Spirit Thief before you join the battle. The pirates' spears give them a little extra reach, but you can reach even farther with magic styles. Use area attacks to scatter the enemies, allowing

you to take them out one by one with Harmonic Combos. Save the ogre for last, keeping your distance from the slow beast until you're ready to fight him.

PIRATE BATTLE: ~348 XP, ~325 SP			
Enemy	Style	Health	Chi
Pirate x5	Spear	50	50
Ogre Guard		300	300	300

GAO'S TREASURY

You're now free to explore the hangar and collect items. Examine the scrollstand in the northeast corner to obtain a strange document: **The Configuration of the Horse**. You'll need this for Lord Lao's furnace in a later chapter. A cask in the same corner holds 500 SP and a gem. You can also find a scrollstand against the west wall and a chest by the south door with 750 SP and a gem.

Gao is a wealthy man, and his treasury is bursting with riches. Plundering it is optional, but you don't want to miss this opportunity. To get there, you need to unlock the south door. Examine the Marvelous Dragonfly's control panel; this causes the flyer, which is suspended from the ceiling, to drop and fire its guns, blasting the door open (500 XP).

The Marvelous Dragonfly boasts some serious firepower.

Enter the treasury and meet Xianshi, an elephant demon placed here by Gao to guard the vault. You must defeat him before you can start looting. Weapon and Martial styles are effective, and since the beast is so ponderously slow, you

can dance circles around him between your attacks (especially in Focus mode). What Xianshi lacks in speed he makes up for in power, so avoiding his mighty fists is your highest priority.

Another option is to assume demon form yourself; if you've invested style points in Toad Demon you can destroy the beast in just a few blows.

XIANSHI BATTLE: ~177 XP, 0 SP

Enemy	Style	Health	Chi
Xianshi	Elephant Demon	550	550

With the guardian defeated (500 XP), you can help yourself to all of Gao's ill-gotten wealth. There are three chests here: the small one closest to the door is trapped, another small chest holds 971 SP and a gem, and the larger one next to it has 250 SP, a gem, and a **Vial of Sulphurous Water** needed for Lord Lao's furnace later. Open the large cabinet for another gem and 550 SP. There's also a breakable vase that yields 550 SP. Finally, gain a few more XP by reading the scrollstand near the door.

GAO THE GREATER

Now only Gao the Greater himself remains to be dealt with. Ascend the final staircase to his chamber at the island's peak. Before you go in, circle around the back to find a bonsai tree yielding 29 SP and a gem.

When you enter Gao the Greater's room, he attacks without hesitation. He's backed up by three pirates; slay these men first so you can concentrate on Gao without interruptions. Gao is a tough warrior who uses multiple styles. Because he uses

evasive leaps and the quick Thousand Cuts style, slow styles like Toad Demon and White Demon are not very effective against

him unless you impede him with Heavenly Wave first. Know how to react to him: If he's leaping around, use an Area attack to floor him; if he starts winding up a strong attack, jump over and hit him from behind; if he's blocking, use a strong attack of your own. Gao also uses Dire Flame. When he summons a fire dragon, you have the perfect opportunity to drain away his Chi with Spirit Thief. If you just run in with fists flying, expect to be slaughtered. Study his movements and fight reactively to ensure victory.

GAO THE GREATER BATTLE: ~2,326 XP, ~2,400 SP

Enemy	Style	Health	Chi
Pirate x3	Long Sword	80	80
Gao the Greater	Dire Flame, Thousand Cuts	700	700

CAUTION

If the pirate base is the last area you choose to visit during Chapter Two, you must fight Inquisitor Lim and Gao the Greater at the same time. This makes the battle much harder. You can find more info about Inquisitor Lim at the end of the Great Forest section of the walkthrough.

Sky and Kang the Mad show up when the battle is over. Slavers took Sky's daughter Pinmei, and he's upset that he didn't get to exact personal vengeance against Gao. Your crusade against Death's Hand and the Lotus Assassins, who supported Gao's operation, prompts Sky to become your Follower.

I wanted nothing more than to watch this man die.

Sky arrives too late to take his personal revenge on Gao the Greater.

Sky Profile

Attack Style: Twin Saber
Support Ability: Recover Focus
Health: ~408
Chi: ~328

Gao keeps almost all his wealth safely locked away in the treasure vault downstairs, so you won't find anything in his room except the third volume on the History of Flight. If you read the first two volumes on your way through the pirate base, you get a new technique: **Strength of Wood** (Health +2) (100 XP).

Go back to the hangar, where Kang the Mad has opened the roof so you can get the Marvelous Dragonfly out. Pirate Cheung meets you there and thanks you for getting rid of Gao the Greater. After he's gone, Kang offers to fly you back to Tien's Landing. Without

The Marvelous Dragonfly is now yours.

an Inscrutable Power Source, however, you won't get any further than that. If you've already obtained this item from Wild Flower, you can give it to him now (1,500 XP).

THE SICKENED FOREST

The Great Southern Forest, which lies north of this village, suffers from a terrible disease.

Your second main task is complete! Now only one thing remains: to find a wind map. Silk Fox told you earlier that you could get one from Lord Yun in the Great Forest north of Tien's Landing. This is your next destination.

LORD YUN

The forest is suffering from a powerful curse that has caused aggressive spirits to swarm everywhere. Several of them attack the moment you enter the forest. The lost spirit, clad in a mask and a tattered black robe, appears many times in the forest. They like to attack from a

The forest's sickness manifests as bloodthirsty ghosts.

distance with blasts of energy similar to Dire Flame, and they can also teleport.

SPIRIT BATTLE: ~168 XP, 0 SP			
Enemy	Style	Health	Chi
Ghost x2	Legendary Strike	80	80
Lost Spirit	Lost Spirit	80	80

Perhaps you could get something done for me. If so, I might be persuaded to foolishly risk the Lotus Assassins' wrath by making a copy of one of their precious maps.

Lord Yun arrives after the battle. The forest is his land, and he's been unable to find out why it's grown evil. If you can get to the bottom of this for him, he'll give you a copy of his wind map. He suspects the sickness might have something to do with the Forest Shadow, a fox spirit that watches over and protects the forest. His advice: head into the forest and look for a temple to the Forest Shadow. You should be able to contact her there.

EXPLORE THE FOREST

Climb the stone steps to reach the next clearing. Three ghosts materialize and attack. To make this battle much easier, switch to Free Targeting and run over to the shrine across the clearing. It reacts to your presence and emits waves of positive energy that form pools all over the area. Any ghosts touching these pools are heavily damaged, while you can pass through them unharmed. When the pools fade, approach the shrine again to re-activate them.

SPIRIT BATTLE: ~168 XP, 0 SP			
Enemy	Style	Health	Chi
Ghost	Leaping Tiger	80	80
Lost Spirit x2	Lost Spirit	80	80

Rely on your targeting icon to find concealed skeletons.

On the eastern path, which leads to a Spirit Font, you can find a skeleton holding 50 SP. Use the Font to recharge, then return to the clearing and take the western path. Follow it until you see the river, then search the bank for another skeleton (80 SP). As you cross the bridge, a man comes running toward you from the other side with two lost spirits in pursuit.

BRIDGE BATTLE: ~134 XP, 0 SP			
Enemy	Style	Health	Chi
Lost Spirit x2	Lost Spirit	80	80

The trees obey the will of the Forest Shadow.

The man explains that he came from Pilgrim's Rest, an inn deep in the forest. He was trying to reach Tien's Landing to get help (or so he claims). After witnessing your skills, he implores you to follow him back to the inn. As he runs off, the Forest Shadow appears. She causes the trees to entangle the man and turns him to stone, then she turns on you. She notices something different about you, though, so instead of destorying you, she disappears back into the forest (150 XP).

After the fox spirit attacks you, she realizes you are not a cannibal and leaves you alone.

TIP

Don't be fooled by appearances! The patrons of Pilgrim's Rest are actually cannibals. They don't want help, they want victims. And the Forest Shadow isn't evil, she's benevolent. She attacks you to make sure you track her down, and prompt a Water Dragon vision.

Cross the bridge and smash two headstones, netting 102 SP. Follow the winding path, keeping an eye out for another headstone on the left (4 SP). Any of these containers might also hold a gem.

Ghosts and lost spirits stalk the path ahead. Your first priority is to disperse the lost spirits, which tend to hang back and fling energy bolts at you. A shrine to the left works exactly like the one you saw earlier, flooding the area with energy pools when you approach. Use this to help eliminate the rest of the ghosts.

CROSSROADS BATTLE: ~168 XP, 0 SP

Enemy	Style	Health	Chi
Lost Spirit x2	Lost Spirit	80	80
Ghost x2	White Demon	80	80

The two headstones in front of the shrine don't give up any SP, but might contain gems. Then take the right path, which leads to Pilgrim's Rest. More ghosts appear when you enter the wide lawn in front of the inn. There is another shrine here you can use to help defeat the ghosts. Fortunately, the enemies materialize in waves of two or three instead of attacking all at once.

SPIRIT BATTLE: ~588 XP, 0 SP

Enemy	Style	Health	Chi
Ghost x5	Legendary Strike	80	80
Ghost	Dire Flame	80	80
Lost Spirit x2	Lost Spirit	80	80

PILGRIM'S REST

Climb the steps to reach Pilgrim's Rest. Three more lost spirits appear and try to keep you from going inside. They're widely spaced around you, placing you in a deadly crossfire. Use Focus mode to escape from their midst and quickly defeat one of the spirits. Then you can take care of the other two. Keep moving to avoid being blasted and pelt them with magic from a distance.

SPIRIT BATTLE: ~191 XP, 0 SP

Enemy	Style	Health	Chi
Lost Spirit x3	Lost Spirit	80	80

Before entering the inn, look in the east corner of the yard for a trapped cask, then check the west corner for a breakable rock yielding 84 SP. Then head inside for a chat with the innkeeper.

The innkeeper divulges little during your first conversation, except to express his hatred of the Forest Shadow. Look in the back room for a few smashable vases. The two in the east corner only have 1 SP each, but might hold gems. The vase by the kitchen is trapped.

Next, talk to Henpecked Hou, the chef. He's not a cannibal, but he's afraid to speak openly about the innkeeper's dark secret. Use Conversation skills to coax him into dropping a hint about the "Mother" (20 XP).

The secret of Pilgrim's Rest is revealed.

Talk to the innkeeper again and tell him what Hou said. He dispels his disguise, revealing himself and the inn's patrons to be horribly deformed ghouls. He asks you to destroy the Forest Spirit, leading to two options:

Rend her flesh! Her screams should echo in the town below!

Choice 1  There's no way you're going to side up with a bunch of evil, demonic freaks. The innkeeper won't let you escape now that you know his secret, and orders everyone in the inn to attack (1,000 XP). Cannibals are immune to magic, like most demons, but support styles affect them. This is a good thing, because you'll need everything you've got to outlast their overwhelming numbers. Fortunately, they are very slow and awkward. Set your follower to Attack mode to keep the cannibals busy while you concentrate on the innkeeper. Area attacks with support styles work wonders here. Toad Demon style is also very potent, as its sweeping attack arc can strike many enemies at once.

PILGRIM'S REST BATTLE: ~1,551 XP, ~900 SP			
Enemy	Style	Health	Chi
Cannibal x8	Cannibal	80	80
Innkeeper	Cannibal, Ice Shard	550	550

After defeating all enemies, another wave of cannibals storm the inn. Deal with them in the same way as the first group.

PILGRIM'S REST BATTLE: ~300 XP, ~200 SP			
Enemy	Style	Health	Chi
Cannibal x6	Cannibal	60	60

Our offer stands firm. Go swiftly, and there may be even more than silver awaiting you.

It's unclear if the Innkeeper is promising you an extra reward or making a threat.

Choice 2  Agree to help the cannibals. You can renege on this promise later on, but it lets you avoid a tough battle for the time being (60 XP).

Whichever choice you make, the **Temple Crystal** is yours afterward. This item is needed to activate a portal in the Forest Shadow's temple.

HENPECKED HOU

After you slay the innkeeper and his cannibals (whether now or after you meet the Forest Shadow), Henpecked Hou becomes a new Follower. He can be brought into battle only in Support mode, which causes jugs of wine to appear while you fight. Picking these up enables Drunken Master style, but like the improvised weapons you used in the Tea House, it only lasts for a limited time. To show you how it works, Hou arranges a tutorial battle for you (100 XP).

But, you'd be surprised what tricks an old bun master might know. Have you ever heard of Drunken Master style?

Henpecked Hou teaches you how to use Drunken Master style.

For this fight, the ghost doesn't have enough Chi to use ranged attacks. Grab a jug of wine and try out your new style!

DRUNKEN MASTER TUTORIAL: ~86 XP, 0 SP			
Enemy	Style	Health	Chi
Ghost	Ghost	300	10

Henpecked Hou Profile

Attack Style: Basic
Support Ability: Drunken Master Style
Health: ~276
Chi: ~360

THE BLACK WHIRLWIND

Bones

With the Temple Crystal in hand, leave Pilgrim's Rest and follow the west path, which leads to the Forest Temple. Keep an eye out for a skeleton on the right (140 SP). When you arrive at the temple, you're attacked by a mighty hunter who wields two axes. He's the Black Whirlwind, and he's the type who attacks first and asks questions later. Mistaking you for a ghost, he charges into battle.

THE BLACK WHIRLWIND BATTLE: ~86 XP, 0 SP			
Enemy	Style	Health	Chi
The Black Whirlwind	Twin Axes	200	200
Ghost	Basic	200	200

After the fight, the warrior and his companion, Spear Catches Leaf, introduce themselves. They were employed by Lord Yun to look into the forest's sickness before you came along and Whirlwind mistook you for a ghost. Like the Forest Shadow, they mistook you for cannibals. Realizing their mistake, and learning that you have the Temple Crystal, they ally with you (200 XP).

The Black Whirlwind Profile

Attack Style: Twin Axes

Support Ability: None

Health: ~432

Chi: ~204

THE FOREST SHADOW'S TEMPLE

Item Lost: Temple Crystal

Pedestal: [You place the once-missing crystal into the pedestal. The crystal clicks into place, and the pedestal begins to move.]

Close

Examine the pedestal at the top of the stairs and insert the Temple Crystal you got from the Innkeeper. This reveals a crystal in the roof of the temple and removes the locks from the two furnaces further down the hill.

Switch

Switch

Red switch

Blue switch

Turn on both furnaces to activate a pair of light rays. Follow them to find some crystals attached to ropes. Your goal is create a purple light, matching the banners and flags hung everywhere. Do this using the red crystal and blue crystal. The pedestal where you inserted the Temple Crystal rises back out of the ground. Examine it to open a portal to Heaven in the back of the Forest Temple and go through (1,000 XP).

ASCENSION TO HEAVEN

The Black Whirlwind

(Sigh) You have no idea what I'm talking about, do you? I am Zin Bu, the Magic Abacus. I was assigned to record, tabulate, and itemize the destruction that you cause.

Head forward and open the urn for 210 SP and a gem. Continue on to meet Zin Bu the Magic Abacus, a celestial accountant who keeps track of your deeds. He becomes your Follower, but you can't use him in battle. Instead, he sells you rare gems and techniques that you can't get anywhere else. See his profile in this guide's Cast of Characters section for complete details.

The demons come again! Human, if you value your life, help us against these fiends!

Further down the road is another urn with 20 SP and a gem. Atop the next hill, a trio of fox spirits are ambushed by two toad demons. Join the fight and help them defeat the demons to earn the right to approach the Forest Shadow.

DEMON BATTLE: ~154 XP, 0 SP

Enemy	Style	Health	Chi
Toad Demon	Toad Demon	80	80

Keep going past the Focus Shrine to interrupt another battle between demons and fox spirits. The toad demon here is puny for one of his type, but the horse demon is very strong. With three fox spirits and your Follower helping out, you should

They will attack you, as well. My sisters will try to protect you, but we need your help as much as you need ours. You must reach my mistress quickly.

be able to defeat him handily. Remember that magic and support styles have no effect on demons, so you must rely on martial or weapon strikes.

DEMON BATTLE: ~326 XP, 0 SP

Enemy	Style	Health	Chi
Horse Demon	Horse Demon	500	500
Toad Demon	Toad Demon	80	80

After the battle, you obtain a new transformation style: **Horse Demon**. This grants the same support and magic immunities that Toad Demon style does. This form isn't as strong as the Toad Demon, but it's much faster and includes a ranged fire attack.

DEMON BATTLE: ~326 XP, 0 SP

Enemy	Style	Health	Chi
Horse Demon	Horse Demon	500	500
Toad Demon	Toad Demon	80	80

Check the edge of the clearing to find a trapped urn, then resume your climb up the path. Cross a long covered bridge to find another demon battle in progress. This is a good chance to try out your new style!

DEMON BATTLE: ~403 XP, 0 SP

Enemy	Style	Health	Chi
Horse Demon	Horse Demon	500	500
Toad Demon x2	Toad Demon	80	80

A nearby urn holds 180 SP and a possible gem. Climb the final flight of stairs to meet Forest Shadow and her guardian, an elephant demon known as Shining Tusk. The Forest Shadow talks about the Mother, the demon who rules the cannibals at Pilgrim's Rest. Now you must choose your path:

CERAMIC URN

I am the Forest Shadow - I will help you understand the significance of what happens in my forest. And then I shall be most intrigued to see which fork you choose to take.

Your decision to fight the Forest Shadow or Mother is strictly your moral preference; Lord Yun is satisfied either way.

Choice 1 The Mother must be destroyed. Forest Shadow opens a secret door for you in the back room of Pilgrim's Rest that leads to the cannibal's hidden caves (1,000 XP). The Forest Shadow then transports you back to the entrance to Heaven.

Choice 2 The Forest Shadow must be destroyed. Her bodyguard, Shining Tusk, won't let you near her unless you can get past him first. With a trio of fox spirits helping him out, he attacks.

SHINING TUSK BATTLE: ~377 XP, ~190 SP

Enemy	Style	Health	Chi
Fox Spirit	Fox Spirit	80	80
Shining Tusk	Elephant Demon	350	350

If you try to attack the Forest Shadow, all the fox spirits left in Heaven turn hostile. Six of them are waiting for you in small groups as you make your way back through Heaven.

FOX SPIRIT BATTLE: ~340 XP, ~50 SP

Enemy	Style	Health	Chi
Fox Spirit x6	Fox Spirit	80	80

After battling your way through the lesser fox spirits, the Forest Shadow herself challenges you. She is far stronger and faster than the others you've met; Focus mode will help you move faster still.

FOREST SHADOW BATTLE: ~377 XP, ~188 SP

Enemy	Style	Health	Chi
Forest Shadow	Fox Spirit	550	550

The Forest Shadow defeated, you are automatically transported back to Pilgrim's Rest (3,000 XP). In addition, you receive the **Gem of Earth Power**. From here, you can still enter the cannibal caves and fight the Mother. Accept the reward offered by the cannibals (2,500 XP) and the **Mother's Touch** technique.

> ### NOTE
> For a balanced outcome, you can kill both the Mother and the Forest Shadow. Doing so will add the Mother quest to your journal.

COMBATING THE CANNIBALS

THE BUTCHER BATTLE: ~765 XP, ~730 SP

Enemy	Style	Health	Chi
Butcher	Cannibal	550	550
Cannibal x10	Cannibal	60	60

When the butcher and his minions are defeated, one of their captives comes forward. He's already begun the transformation into a ghoul and begs for the release of death. You have two options:

They...ungh...they're capturing people, changing some and eating the rest. By the spirits, you have to help me!

Choice 1 👊 Concede to his request and kill him.

I can't... No! Argh!

If you don't grant this prisoner the release of death, he transforms into a cannibal before your eyes.

Choice 2 🔵 Allow him to live on and complete his transformation. Note: If you have Zu with you, and refuse to kill the cannibal, Zu will do it for you.

There are a number of small chambers around the circumference of the chamber. All of them are empty except the northern one. Examine the chest and pile of corpses there to net 300 SP and, possibly, two gems.

Head into the next chamber. Several rat demons are penned here, but when you enter, the handler opens the gate and commands the beasts to attack.

DEMON BATTLE: ~641 XP, ~85 SP

Enemy	Style	Health	Chi
Rat Demon x7	Rat Demon	80	80
Handler	Cannibal	200	200

Now you can scour the room for items. Two skeletons against the south wall yield 51 SP between them; each might hold a gem as well. Poke around the demon's pen to find another skeleton, earning 300 SP (and possibly a gem).

Take the west tunnel to advance further into the caves. After crossing a narrow bridge, a horde of cannibals awaits you. Carve a swath through them.

DEMON BATTLE: ~641 XP, ~570 SP

Enemy	Style	Health	Chi
Cannibal x14	Cannibal	60	60

When the dust settles, the Black Whirlwind and Henpecked Hou arrive (if you haven't brought one of them already). They've both got a personal grudge against the Mother and want to be present when you fight her. Behind a screen to the south you can find a cask with 250 SP and, if you're lucky, a gem. When you're ready, take the northwest tunnel to confront the Mother.

There's no way you're going down there without us. I came here to help you deal with this... "Mother" thing. Spear Catches Leaf told me to look after you, so here I am.

The Mother draws her power from the cannibals who worship her, and can't be defeated using normal tactics. Instead of targeting her, look for the three huge pillars that support the cavern's roof. Direct your attacks against these stone columns while keeping an eye on the Mother. If she gets too close, abandon your position and move on to another pillar. Keep circling the cavern, whittling away at the stone, until the ceiling finally collapses, burying the Mother under an avalanche of boulders.

THE MOTHER BATTLE: ~2,000 XP, ~1,500 SP			
Enemy	Style	Health	Chi
The Mother	Cannibal	1,000	1,000
Cannibal x15	Cannibal	50	50

ESCAPING TIEN'S LANDING

I am tired of seeing our carefully laid plans fall to your thuggish fists. The operations in the ruins and Gao's factory were my responsibility. Their destruction is my shame.

After you've finished all three tasks, Inquisitor Lim finally decides to confront you personally. If you've followed our walkthrough, this happens in the Great Forest, but you could meet him at the Dam Site or in Gao the Greater's room depending on which task you complete last. If you fight Lim in Gao the Greater's quarters in the pirates' lair, he will fight alongside Gao instead of with the Lotus Assassins he normally fights with. You must defeat Lim and his assassins to reclaim the second piece of your Dragon Amulet. Defend against Dire Flame by assuming demon form with either Toad Demon or Horse Demon style. Watch Lim's movements closely and activate Focus mode as he attacks. Step out of his way, switch Focus mode off, and unleash a combo on his exposed backside. Support styles and Magic style effects (such as freezing) are very effective against these enemies.

INQUISITOR LIM BATTLE: ~147 XP, ~150 SP			
Enemy	Style	Health	Chi
Lotus Assassin	Dire Flame	200	200
Inquisitor Lim	Viper	200	200

Whether you've slain the Forest Shadow, the Cannibal Mother, or both, Lord Yun lives up to his end of the deal and gives you a copy of his **Wind Map** when you return to his camp by Tien's Landing. At last you have everything you need to move on to the Imperial City! Return to your base camp and talk to Kang the Mad to board the Dragonfly and continue your quest.

Here is the wind map you wanted. The copy is near perfect, and I assure you that the Assassins will never know you have it.

SIDE QUESTS

THE BEATEN BAKER

INVESTIGATE BAKER BEI

It's my fiancé, Baker Bei. Every day a group of thugs attacks him and beats him up. He tries to avoid them, but they find him wherever he goes.

This side quest begins after you talk to Seamstress Lan outside the Tea House. She explains that her fiancé, Baker Bei, is beaten every day by a mysterious gang of thugs. Tell Lan that you'll look into the situation.

You're a little too interested in our business, friend. Looks like we gotta teach you to back off when Ai Ling's boys are working.

When you first enter Beggar's Pier, you're just in time to rescue Baker Bei from his attackers. These thugs are used to picking on helpless villagers, but this time they're in for a painful surprise.

RESCUE BAKER BEI BATTLE: ~135 XP, ~120 SP			
Enemy	Style	Health	Chi
Thug x3	Spear	60	60

After you deal with the thugs, Baker Bei explains that they were sent by Ai Ling, a local gang leader, but he protests that there's no reason at all why they should target him. It looks like you'll have to get to the bottom of this yourself, so agree to help him (350 XP). Bei tells you that Ai Ling can be found in the Boat House.

TALK TO AI LING

Mention Ai Ling's name to the guard at the Boat House door.

Go to the Boat House and talk to the guard by the door. Tell him you've come to see Ai Ling about Baker Bei, and the guard willingly ushers you in. Ai Ling strikes up a conversation when you enter; she explains that Baker Bei promised to marry *her* instead of Seamstress Lan, and she intends to enforce that promise. Several options now lie before you:

The gang leader explains her relationship to Baker Bei.

Romance aside, it's not reasonable to expect someone to live up to a childhood promise.

Busting into the gang's hideout and issuing threats has predictable results.

Choice 1 👊👊 It's possible to resolve the situation without bloodshed. First, offer to set up a meeting between Ai Ling, Baker Bei, and Seamstress Lan. Bei reveals that he did, indeed, promise to marry Ai Ling—when he was *six* years old! With this revelation, it's easy to convince Ai Ling to relinquish her claim on the baker (1,000 XP). Bei is now free to get married in peace; in gratitude, Seamstress Lan offers to give you her dowry (250 SP).

Choice 2 ✋ To achieve a more straightforward solution, subtract Ai Ling from the picture. Greet her with threats when you enter the Boat House. She doesn't tolerate insolence, and orders her gang to attack (950 XP). She comes at you with Leaping Tiger style while her four guards surround and distract you. Use area attacks to give yourself room to concentrate on Ai Ling and take her out first, then mop up the underlings.

BOAT HOUSE BATTLE: ~333 XP, ~325 SP

Enemy	Style	Health	Chi
Ai Ling	Leaping Tiger	200	100
Guard x5	Basic	80	80

Convince Lan that her fiancé has been unfaithful and she'll give you her dowry.

After the battle, return to the Tea House and talk to Seamstress Lan. Don't tell her anything about Bei's childhood promise to marry Ai Ling, just let her know that you've ended the attacks on her fiancé (1,000 XP). In joyous gratitude, she offers to give you her dowry (250 SP). Earn further Open Palm prestige by telling Lan to keep her money.

Choice 3 ✊ Enter the Boat House and goad Ai Ling into attacking you as in Choice 2 above (950 XP). Then go to the Tea House and tell Lan that Bei promised to marry Ai Ling (300 XP). Lan renounces her engagement and, with no use for her dowry, gives it to you (250 SP). You can achieve the same outcome without fighting Ai Ling, but you miss out on the XP and SP gained from the battle.

Ai Ling's violent nature leads to disaster.

Choice 4 The situation can rapidly devolve into tragedy under your influence. Set up a meeting between the three villagers as in Choice 1. Insist that Lan and Ai Ling fight each other for the right to marry Bei. The outcome is a scene of carnage in which Ai Ling kills both Lan and Baker Bei (250 XP). Stricken with remorse, Ai Ling then turns her talons on you, and you must fight her as in Choice 2.

SIDE QUEST

Of the various outcomes to Baker Bei's conundrum, Choice 1 is the only option that allows you to follow up with the Matchmaker side quest. If Ai Ling is killed or Bei's wedding is cancelled, the Matchmaker quest is not available.

Demolish this beautiful vase to claim the Dock House Key.

However you deal with Ai Ling, you can search the Boat House afterward for her gang's ill-gotten treasure. A chest in the southwest corner holds 41 SP and a minor gem, while the vase in the opposite corner holds the **Dock House Key** needed to unlock the upstairs office. Before you go up there, check the walkway by the loading crane for two barrels containing 23 SP total.

Using the Dock House Key, unlock the office gate and go upstairs to find more loot. Besides a scrollstand, there's a chest with 750 SP (200 XP) and a vase holding 5 SP and, if you're lucky, a gem.

MATCHMAKER

If the **Beaten Baker** side quest ended happily for Bei and Lan, you can ice the cake by finding another suitor for Ai Ling. She even offers you a cash reward if you can locate an acceptable match. Her high standards and gruff attitude make this a tall order. She skeptically gives you the names of the town's most eligible bachelors; one of these men is perfect for the tough gang leader.

Ai Ling needs a new object for her "affection."

Chumin's kind nature is the perfect foil for Ai Ling's fiery spirit.

Of all the candidates, Chumin the Carpenter is the most suitable choice. He's gentle and patient, and Ai Ling's determination is just what he needs to manage the cash side of his business. Chumin knows Ai Ling's reputation, but reluctantly agrees to give her a chance (50 XP). When the two meet, they hit it off, and Ai Ling, in surprised gratitude, hands over the 500 SP she promised (1,000 XP).

Prosperous times lie ahead for this happy couple.

NOTE

While Chumin is the most fit candidate, you can persuade Ai Ling to accept other suitors. Yaoru (in the Tea House), with his overbearing arrogance, is accepted if you use conversation skills. Ai Ling even agrees to give Big Tian (outside the Boathouse) a chance if your conversation skills are very high.

OLD MOTHER KWAN

INVESTIGATE DUTONG'S WRIT

Talk to Old Mother Kwan to hear the tale of how she lost ownership of the Tea House to Three Sheets Dutong. He showed up with an Imperial Writ proclaiming the property was his, but his story sounds suspicious. It seems nobody ever looked closely at Dutong's documents.

Yes, yes. I owned the teahouse for many, many years. At least, I thought I did. But then Master Dutong came to town with that Imperial Writ. Oh my, wasn't that a shock!

GET DUTONG DRUNK

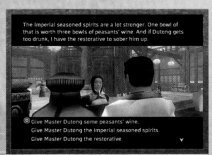

The Imperial seasoned spirits are a lot stronger. One bowl of that is worth three bowls of peasants' wine. And if Dutong gets too drunk, I have the restorative to sober him up.

Give Master Dutong some peasants' wine.
Give Master Dutong the Imperial seasoned spirits.
Give Master Dutong the restorative.

Dutong is too crafty to simply turn over the Imperial Writ to you, but you can trick him into revealing his deception by using his one weakness: wine. Steeper Yanru, who serves the drinks, explains that Dutong has three stages of increasing drunkenness: friendly, sorrowful, and paranoid. In the friendly and paranoid stages, Dutong reveals nothing. Your object is to get Dutong into his sorrowful mode: drunk enough, but not too drunk. First, send him a restorative to get him completely sober. Follow up with two bowls of Imperial seasoned spirits, then one drink of peasant's wine, until he staggers up from his desk.

When Dutong is at the right level of drunkenness, talk to him and mention the Imperial Writ. Now you can use conversation skills to squeeze a confession out of him. If your attempt at persuasion fails, keep trying until it works.

Oh, I'm a deshpicable pershon! A bad, bad man. The writ... it'sh a fake! A forgery. I made it all up!

Dutong finally admits that his Imperial Writ is a forgery (20 XP), but after his guard sobers him with restorative he offers you a bribe to keep his secret:

You've given me back the only thing I ever cared about... and you've done a service for this town, too. I'm going to turn this place back into a respectable, quality teahouse!

Reveal Dutong's deception...

Choice 1 🖐 How could you even consider selling out Old Mother Kwan? Refuse the bribe and tell Kwan the good news: The Tea House is hers again (1,000 XP).

...or accept his bribe.

I will give you a great deal of silver to keep this little secret from getting out. Lots of silver for both of you, if you keep quiet about this.

Choice 2 ✊ The sound of silver coins is all you needed to hear. You have to split the bribe with Steeper Yanru, but you still get 1,000 SP (380 XP).

ZHONG THE OX CARRIER

Locate the ogre Zhong and his employer Dong Ping on the Tea House balcony. After he accidentally killed one of the oxen, Zhong fled Dong Ping's farm in remorse and shame. He refuses to go home, and his frightful presence is scaring away Tea House patrons. You can handle the situation in two different ways:

Zhong! You can't stay up here forever. This isn't your home! You need to come back with me to the farm.

With some coaxing, Zhong can be persuaded to leave peacefully.

Zhong kill ox. Zhong too strong, too rough with ox. Zhong not want to hurt ox, Zhong only playing. Now Zhong cries for ox.

Choice 1 ✋ Approach the ogre and choose the kindest replies as he tells his story. You then have a chance to use conversation skills; avoid Intimidation and keep trying Charm or Intuition until the ogre agrees to leave peacefully (400 XP).

Noooo! Zhong won't let you hurt ox!

Any mention of ox-killing causes Zhong to snap.

Choice 2 ✊ The most direct solution: Zhong must die. Talk to him and choose the most aggressive replies; the ogre finally snaps when you threaten the other oxen (250 XP). Zhong is very strong, even for an ogre; Chi Strikes and Focus mode give you a vital advantage! Using your fastest attack style, you can easily dance circles around the slow beast, scoring repeated combos. Avoid knocking him into the corner so you can easily leap over his head and keep attacking from the rear. You've killed an innocent ogre, impoverished Dong Ping, and gotten paid to do it: nice work!

ZHONG BATTLE: ~238 XP, ~230 SP

Enemy	Style	Health	Chi
Zhong	Ogre	550	550

Three Sheets Dutong (or Old Mother Kwan, depending on how you resolved her side quest) thanks you for clearing up the disturbance with a reward of 300 SP.

AN IRON STOMACH

Chai Jin has set up a small kitchen on the Tea House balcony. He serves exotic dishes that are mildly poisonous; for 300 SP you can try a three-course dinner consisting of some very questionable dishes. (For an additional 300 SP, you can opt for a four-course dinner.) If you manage to keep everything down, Chai Jin promises a hefty reward.

Give me 300 silver, to cover my expenses. If you can eat all three dishes in a row... and survive, I'll give you back your money, and a little bit more besides.

Excellent. Now, if you can, try to describe the taste to me, and what it does to you... and remember, this is for posterity, so please... be honest.

As you wish.

For the first three courses, you must select from an array of three dishes that affect your Body, Mind, or Spirit as shown in the following table. Each course gets progressively more poisonous. Check your abilities before you dig in, and choose the meal corresponding to your lowest ability for the first course, your next strongest ability for the second course, and reserve your highest ability for the third course. The key is to spread the toxins out so that your stats are fairly balanced afterward.

This new dish has no name yet, or at least none that I can pronounce. I learned it from a loud, annoying foreign man I met in the Imperial City.

If you're still standing after all three courses, Chai Jin offers you a final, untested dish for an extra 300 SP. Accept this offer only if you made it through without suffering any side effects; if you felt ill at all, take your original 300 SP back and try again. The final course affects all three of your abilities, so a balanced approach to the first three courses gives you the best chance.

CHAI JIN'S EXOTIC DISHES

Course (Toxicity)	Name	Affected Ability
First (Mild)	Roasted bear heart	Body
First (Mild)	Monkey brain stew	Mind
First (Mild)	Shark spleen stew	Spirit
Second (Moderate)	Haunch of deer	Body
Second (Moderate)	Eagle eye soup	Mind

CHAI JIN'S EXOTIC DISHES (CONT'D)		
Course (Toxicity)	Name	Affected Ability
Second (Moderate)	Jellied eels	Spirit
Third (Severe)	Boiled ox testicles	Body
Third (Severe)	Curdled porcupine bladder	Mind
Third (Severe)	Raw alligator eggs	Spirit
Fourth (Deadly)	Unknown	All

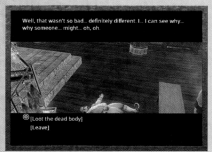

If you survive the final dish, Chai Jin excitedly asks how it made you feel. Now is your chance to turn the tables on the chef:

Choice 1 Lie to Chai Jin and tell him it wasn't poisonous at all. He takes one bite and falls over dead (250 XP).

Chai Jin can now unleash his culinary experiments on an unsuspecting world.

Choice 2 Simply telling the truth in this case doesn't shift your alignment (500 XP).

Whichever choice you make, you get back all your silver afterward, as well as a gem: **The Bronze Tongue** (Charm +4, Intimidation +4, Intuition +4).

THE GREAT DAM

Most residents of Tien's Landing would like to see the Great Dam closed. With the lake drained, trade has ground to a halt and stranded sailors have been getting into trouble all over town. However, some are making a killing off of the situation....

MERCHANT JIANG

Merchant Jiang, wine seller, has been making unbelievable profits while the sailors are stuck in Tien's Landing. He approaches you with a proposition: sabotage the dam for good so that it can never be closed. If you bring him proof of the deed, he offers to give you 20 percent of his profits to date—no small sum! Naturally, sabotaging the dam dooms most of the town's residents and is a strong expression of the Closed Fist.

TRAPPED

For a completely opposite point of view, locate Captain Ing at the foot of the dock where his ship *Lucky Night* is moored. He's stranded in Tien's Landing and at his wit's end. He pleads with you to close the Great Dam so he can sail on to

other ports, and he offers a substantial reward of silver if you do.

NOTE

You don't have to choose between sabotage or salvation until you get to the dam's control structure. If you close it, be prepared to fight Merchant Jiang when you get back to Tien's Landing.

THE JADE HEART

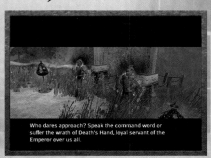

After meeting Wild Flower, you can finally access the dam's control device, the Jade Heart, and either activate or destroy it. The Lotus Assassins have left two powerful sentinel golems to guard the path leading there. When you approach, they ask for a password. You heard the enemy discussing this back in the ruins; the password is "Shao Hua" (500 XP).

You can fight the golems if you want, but you should prepare yourself before the battle. They are immune to Magic, Support, and Martial styles, so your best bet is to rely on weapons. Bring Sagacious Zu with you in Support mode, giving you a boost to all weapon damage, and equip your Dragon Amulet with gems that enhance your Body and Mind. When you're ready, approach the golems and give the wrong password. Concentrate on eliminating one statue at a time. The statues are ponderously slow, giving you plenty of chances to leap over their heads and attack from behind.

SENTRY STATUES BATTLE: ~384 XP, ~400 SP

Enemy	Style	Health	Chi
Sentry Statue x2	Clay Golem	350	350

Follow the path beyond the statues to reach the Jade Heart. Now you must decide which path to follow:

Choice 1 Close the Great Dam (3,000 XP). If you do this, you'll never be able to go back to the ruins, so make sure you've tied up any loose ends (such as the **Drowned Orphans** side quest) beforehand.

Once you remove the Jade Heart, the Great Dam remains stuck open forever.

Choice 2 Destroy the control mechanism by taking the **Jade Heart** (4,000 XP).

When you return to where the golem sentries were, a squad of Imperial troops awaits. They intend to slay you for tampering with the dam (even though they tampered with it first). Use area attacks to give yourself room, then take down the soldiers one by one.

GREAT DAM BATTLE: ~353 XP, ~315 SP

Enemy	Style	Health	Chi
Imperial Soldier x2	Spear	80	80
Sergeant	Long Sword	200	200
Lotus Apprentice	Long Sword	300	300

CONSEQUENCES

When you get back to Tien's Landing, the consequences of your choice become apparent:

Choice 1 If you closed the Great Dam, Captain Ing sends a runner to deliver the reward he promised you: 2,300 SP (500 XP). Merchant Jiang, who asked you to sabotage the dam, is waiting for you by the Tea House. He's angry about having his best customers sail away—angry enough to attack. After dealing with him, go talk to Minister Sheng and let him know his dam problems are over (1,500 XP).

MERCHANT JIANG BATTLE: ~222 XP, ~225 SP

Enemy	Style	Health	Chi
Thug	Basic	80	80
Thug	Staff	200	200
Merchant Jiang	White Demon	200	200

Captain Ing decides to join his men in drunken oblivion.

Choice 2 If you took the Jade Heart, head for Beggar's Pier to find Merchant Jiang happily selling bowl after bowl of wine to the crew of the *Lucky Night*—including Captain Ing. Talk to the merchant to claim your reward: 2,600 SP and a **Gem of Purpose** (Body +1, Mind +1, Spirit +1; 1,000 XP).

<table>
</table>

TONG BATTLE: ~48 XP, ~50 SP			
Enemy	Style	Health	Chi
Tong	White Demon	80	80
Sailor	Spear	60	60
Sailor	Basic	200	200

TIP

After talking to Jiang, there is a final chance to incite violence and earn further Closed Fist prestige. Talk to Captain Ing and, using Conversation Skills, persuade him to kill Merchant Jiang for putting him in this situation. He's not easy to convince, and you'll need to equip appropriate Charm- or Intuition-boosting gems in your Dragon Amulet to pull this off (1,020 XP).

With the **Clay Figurine** in hand, return to Merchant Cheung and deliver it to him. He can't offer a reward, but promises to give you a discount on his wares later. Unfortunately, he doesn't have anything in stock right now.

NOTE

Returning the figurine is an Open Palm gesture. If you're adamant about adhering to the Closed Fist, then either keep the figurine for yourself or avoid this side quest altogether.

THE STOLEN MEMENTO

Merchant Cheung, found in the Merchant's Area, is resigned to the petty thefts he suffers at the hand of restless sailors. There's one item, however, which he'd love to get back: a clay figurine given to him by his mother. It was taken by Tong, a sailor who hangs out on Beggar's Pier.

The only thing I'm really upset about is a clay figurine. Yesterday, Tong, one of the sailors, took it. There was nothing I could do to stop him.

AN ANCIENT GAME

I will make you an offer. Show me that you understand every nuance of the Way of the Closed Fist, and I will teach you how to bend the storms to your will through Tempest.

He would like nothing more than to have you as a student, but show me that you walk the Way of the Open Palm, and I will teach you the mysteries of Stone Immortal.

Mistress Vo and Jian the Iron Fist manage to get along well, despite following opposite philosophies. You can find them outside the Boat House, playing a complex strategy game known as "Yi"—without using a board or pieces. They are martial arts masters, and each one can teach you a new Magic style. However, you must first prove your worthiness by showing devotion to either the Open Palm or the Closed Fist.

My ma used to have figurines like that. I ain't seen her in a long time. I really missh her. I jusht borrowed the figurine to remind me of her.

Locate Tong and confront him about the stolen figurine. There are two ways to get it back:

Choice 1 Use conversation skills to convince Tong to relinquish the figurine (50 XP).

Choice 2 Taking the figurine by force doesn't affect your alignment. Ignore the other sailors and concentrate your attacks on Tong. Tong gives up when he runs out of Health and sulks off, leaving you with the figurine.

NOTE

The alignment requirement is fairly strict. Enter the menu and look at your character record. If your alignment meter is closer to either end than to the center, you qualify. If you're still nearer the middle, then come back and talk to Vo and Jian later, after you've increased your devotion. If you've completed all the other side quests in Tein's Landing and strongly adhered to your chosen path, you can qualify before you leave town.

Choice 1  If you satisfy Mistress Vo that you understand the Open Palm, then she agrees to teach you the **Stone Immortal** style. But first, you must face the style in battle. Keep your distance from Mistress Vo, and wait for her to make the first move. If she uses an area attack, stay away and wait for it to lapse, or answer with ranged Magic attacks of your own. When she launches stone missiles, leap behind her and take advantage of the opening. You can also assume Toad Demon form to make yourself immune to Vo's magic. Make liberal use of Focus mode and Chi Strikes to end the battle quickly.

MISTRESS VO'S TEST: 0 XP, 0 SP			
Enemy	Style	Health	Chi
Mistress Vo	Stone Immortal	400	400

Choice 2 Jian the Iron Fist teaches the **Tempest** style, but only if he feels you understand the Closed Fist. As in Choice 1, you must test yourself against the new style in battle first. Use evasive moves to stay behind Jian, striking him between his attacks. Your Toad Demon form is immune to magic and is the best defense against the whirlwinds of Jian's Tempest. Add Chi Strikes and Focus mode into the mix and Jian's defeat is assured.

JIAN'S TEST: 0 XP, 0 SP			
Enemy	Style	Health	Chi
Jian the Iron Fist	Tempest	400	400

After you've learned either Stone Immortal or Tempest style, Mistress Vo and Jian the Iron Fist conclude their game of Yi and depart for good.

THE ZITHER OF DISCORD

Scholar Six Heavens explains the significance of the Zither of Discord.

This side quest is available only if you have begun to follow the Way of the Closed Fist. Scholar Six Heavens, found in the north side of Beggar's Pier, is himself a devotee of the Closed Fist, and he's searching for an artifact called the Zither of Discord. Specifically, he needs you to find two pieces of the instrument: the silk strings and the case.

FIND THE STRINGS

You find the **Silk Strings** before you enter Tien's Landing. Look in a chest in the guard house near the gate to the ruins (100 XP).

FIND THE CASE

The **Zither Case** is in Gao the Greater's private room at the pirate base.

THE TEST OF THE CLOSED FIST

Scholar Six Heavens needs one more piece to assemble the Zither of Discord: the instrument's bridge. It's said that Bladed Thesis hid it somewhere in the Great Forest and enchanted it so that only those who understand the Way of the Closed Fist could find it.

If we can recover the last part of this zither, the bridge that would lift the strings off the case, then I will double the silver I was going to give you.

After you talk to Six Heavens, locate Bladed Thesis by a Spirit Font in the south part of the Great Forest. He agrees to give you the bridge, and confides that Six Heavens will die if he assembles the Zither of Discord. You now have a choice:

Choice 1  Even though this quest is only offered to those on the Way of the Closed Fist, it is possible to complete it with an Open Palm shift. Speak with Bladed Thesis and correctly answer his question, learning that he means to kill Scholar Six Heavens. Then, refuse to go along with the plan, as in Choice 2. When you return to Scholar Six Heavens with the Zither Bridge, tell him that you killed Bladed Thesis because "someone has to protect the weak". The scholar rethinks his philosophy and embarks on a new path.

Choice 2  Refuse to be a part of Bladed Thesis' plan, which prompts the spirit to attack. Bladed Thesis uses a powerful technique that lets him drain your Health and Chi (much like Spirit Thief) with every touch. Close with him quickly, battling aggressively and using Focus mode and evasive moves to get behind the ghost and pelt him with combos from behind.

After the ghost is dispersed, take the **Zither Bridge** back to Scholar Six Heavens to claim your reward (500 SP, 500 XP).

BLADED THESIS BATTLE: ~300 XP, 0 SP			
Enemy	Style	Health	Chi
Bladed Thesis	Red Minister	350	350

Choice 3 He gives you the bridge only if you correctly answer his riddle, "Who deserves to die?" Choose the second answer that tells of the man who wasted his strength on a vain display. Scholar Six Heavens suddenly steps out of hiding; it turns out he secretly follows you into the forest. When you hand over the bridge, Bladed Thesis appears and absorbs the Scholar's soul (500 XP, 500 SP). The spirit then departs, leaving you with a final lesson in the form of a new Technique: **Chaotic Strains** (Health +5, Chi +5).

GEMS IN THE QUARRY

After blowing up the wall across from the orphanage, head through the gap to confront a trio of convict ghosts.

GHOST BATTLE: ~183 XP, 0 SP			
Enemy	Style	Health	Chi
Convict Ghost x3	Ice Shard	60	60

With the three ghosts defeated, take time to explore. **The Soft Petal** (Charm +5, Body +1, Mind +1) is hidden within a headstone on the south. Another headstone on the clearing's opposite side is trapped.

Examine headstones to find silver and gems.

STABBER YUXI

You have to get by Stabber Yuxi before you can enter the quarry.

As you head into the quarry, more ghosts appear, led by Stabber Yuxi. Like many ghosts, he attacks with Ice Shard. With your Follower in Attack mode to help distract the weaker ghosts, concentrate all your attacks on Yuxi. This

ghost has far more Health than any you've met so far. Chi Strikes and Magic attacks are your best offensive options. Don't forget that you can use Spirit Thief style to replenish your Chi if you run out; it's technically not a Support style and ghosts have no immunity to it.

STABBER YUXI BATTLE: ~434 XP, 0 SP			
Enemy	Style	Health	Chi
Convict Ghost x4	Basic	60	60
Stabber Yuxi	Ice Shard, Spear	350	350

THE QUARRY

After defeating Yuxi, head into the quarry. When you enter the first big cavern, four ghosts materialize and ambush you. You know what to do! If you need a recharge during this battle, switch to Free Targeting mode and kick the stalagmites to reveal Health, Chi, or Focus orbs.

GHOST BATTLE: ~244 XP, 0 SP			
Enemy	Style	Health	Chi
Convict Ghost x3	Basic	60	60
Convict Ghost	Ice Shard	60	60

With the ghosts dispersed, look for a skeleton in the southwest corner (50 SP) that sometimes holds a gem. Continue into the next cavern and locate an unusual stalagmite formation in an alcove on the right. Demolish it for 180 SP, then head into the quarry's final chamber.

STRANGLER JIZU

Your most difficult battle yet awaits in the north cavern. During life Strangler Jizu was a dangerous psychopath. Now that he's a ghost, Jizu is meaner and deadlier than ever. To make things worse, he's got a horde of convict ghosts backing him up.

Jizu can fully restore himself by absorbing one of these ghosts, so your first priority is to destroy them all. Only then can you finish off Jizu for good. As you fight the weaker enemies, keep moving at all times to avoid being targeted by Jizu's Dire Flame. Remember that Spirit Thief is effective against ghosts, so use it to recharge if you need to. Keep your Follower in Attack mode to give yourself a little breathing room.

STRANGLER JIZU BATTLE: ~824 XP, 0 SP			
Enemy	Style	Health	Chi
Convict Ghost x9	Basic	60	60
Strangler Jizu	Dire Flame	500	500

When Jizu has been eliminated, the ghost of Turnkey Shiji appears and tells his story. After he's spoken, you have a few replies to choose from:

Turnkey Shiji tried to save the prisoners, but he paid for his kindness with his life.

Choice 1 "There must be something more I can do to help you."

Choice 2 "Jizu didn't know how to finish the job and disperse you properly. I do."

Choice 3 "Goodbye, ghost."

Shiji departs, leaving you with a new gem: **The Wanderer's Jewel** (Body +3, Spirit +3, Mind -5). If you like to use Weapon styles, this gem isn't for you; but if you rely on Magic attacks, then equip it right away. Shiji might also leave behind a **Thick Skin Gem** (Body +1, Trap Damage -50%), but this doesn't always happen.

Before you leave, scour the cavern for more treasure. Along the north wall are a jar (251 SP), a chest (159 SP), and a skeleton (61 SP). In addition to silver, the jar also contains a random gem. After taking everything, return to the ruins.

The quarry is still a profitable source of silver and gems.

SIDE QUEST

A small side quest, The Stranded Orphan, is triggered as you leave the quarry. See the next section for details.

STRANDED ORPHAN GIRL

When you return through the quarry after defeating Strangler Jizu, an orphan's ghost is waiting for you in the central cavern. Her traumatic death under the lake has left her in utter terror of water; even the small pool in the cave is too frightening for her to wade through. She begs for your help; what will you do?

Choice 1 Create a dry walkway by knocking down the three posts that hold up the scaffolding (350 XP). Now the girl can escape the caves.

Choice 2 Refuse to help. The only thing keeping the girl from leaving is her own fear. She must conquer it on her own, or not at all.

DROWNED ORPHANS

Enter the abandoned orphanage, where a lone rat demon lurks. He mutters something about "strange children," then attacks. You should have no trouble defeating him.

RAT DEMON BATTLE: ~44 XP, 0 SP			
Enemy	Style	Health	Chi
Rat Demon	Rat Demon	50	50

Miao has learned to enjoy inflicting pain on others.

With the demon slain, two orphan ghosts appear. They are Bin and Miao, and they tell the story of how the orphan-master, Kindly Yushan, left them to drown when the lake waters rose. Bin has maintained his sanity, but Miao is clearly becoming twisted and evil by her ghostly existence. Both spirits are extremely weary, and they ask you for help. Bin wants you to find Yushan and bring him back to the orphanage so he can bury their bones, giving them a little peace. Miao, on the other hand, is hateful and wants you to bring back Yushan's head.

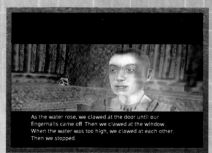

Bin paints a haunting image of his last living moments.

You might remember seeing Kindly Yushan back in the Tea House. Go back there and look for him on the balcony, near Chai Jin's kitchen. Ask him about the orphanage, and he tells you the whole miserable tale. You now have a few options:

Choice 1 🖐 Tell Yushan to return with you to the orphanage and bury the orphans' bones. The ghosts vanish and Kindly Yushan rids himself of some of the guilt he's been carrying around (1,750 XP).

Choice 2 ✊ Tell Yushan that you're here to kill him. He's lost the will to live and doesn't put up a fight. Take **Yushan's Head** back to the orphanage and give it to the children (1,750 XP). Bin is saddened that more lives were lost, but Miao enjoys playing with her new toy.

Choice 3 ✊ ✊ Bring Yushan back to the orphanage as in Choice 1 and turn him over to Miao (1,750 XP). She gleefully leads him away to a eternity of torment.

YIFONG AND FUYAO

You might remember meeting Yifong and her daughter Fuyao when you first arrived at Tien's Landing. The two women were fleeing the troubles of the town, but they didn't get far before being snatched by pirates. When you rescue Yifong from the slave pen, she begs you to search for Fuyao, who was taken upstairs by the slave breaker.

You find the slave breaker, his assistants, and a slave-buying customer named Lordling Lun in a cave above Kang's workshop, just in time to stop them from torturing Fuyao. All three enemies favor the Leaping Tiger style. Take them down from a distance with Magic attacks, or use Focus mode to slow down the action and pepper the slave breaker with combos.

PIRATE BATTLE: ~192 XP, ~150 SP			
Enemy	Style	Health	Chi
Guard	Leaping Tiger	60	60
Slave Breaker	Leaping Tiger	200	200

After the fight, Lordling Lun demands that you honor his agreement with Gao to purchase the girl. You have several choices of replies:

Choice 1 🖐 Tell him the girl is not for sale (1,000 XP).

Choice 2 ✊ Give the girl a chance to earn her freedom by killing Lordling Lun. She summons the strength to go through with it, and takes her own first steps down the Way of the Closed Fist (1,200 XP).

Choice 3 ✊ ✊ You rescued the slave girl, so she's now your property. You can sell her for 2,500 SP (800 XP).

CHAPTER THREE

OVERVIEW

As the Heavenly Lily I am above suspicion, but I am restrained by fawning servants. Silk Fox can go anywhere, and people are not shy about their reactions.

◎ [Enter the Lotus Assassin Fortress.]
[Leave.]

Wherein the Imperial City is revealed,   *Silk Fox reveals her station,*   *And the Lotus Assassins are infiltrated.*

The Marvelous Dragonfly bears you away from Tien's Landing toward the Imperial City. The fall of Gao the Greater and Assassin Lim will have far-reaching consequences, and your enemy will not let your actions go unanswered. Terrible forces gather ahead, and as you draw close, they will leave their mark as surely as you have left yours.

MARKET DISTRICT

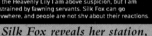

Base Camp

City Gate

to Imperial Arena

Market Square

to Black Leopard School

to Golden Way

MAP LEGEND

●	Container
○	Scrollstand
1	Bai the Outcrier
2	Captain Sen
3	Lina and Junda
4	Blacksmith
5	Lotus Inquisitor
6	Mechanic Hin Goo
7	Prefect Jitong, Chandler Ling, and Scholar Songtao
8	General Stone Kao
9	Jinlin
10	Ren Feng
11	Younger Tanner Fong and Elder Tanner Fong

The Market District is the bustling heart of the Imperial City, where merchants, commoners, Lotus Assassins, and nobles all come into uneasy contact.

A plaza on the northeast side of town serves as a landing site for airships arriving at the Imperial City. Scaffolds allow passengers to climb down from their vehicle while leaving the craft anchored in the air. Any Followers you aren't traveling with wait for you here.

Base camp

To the east lie the massive city gates. Captain Sen, who offers you a few bounty-hunting contracts, can be found here. A bridge south of the gates leads to an entrance to the Golden Way.

City gates

Shoppers with silver to burn should stop by the blacksmith's shop here, where you can purchase upgraded weapons. The Black Leopard School lies to the south, while across a bridge to the north towers the Imperial Arena.

Merchants' Square

The History of Flight, Vol. 4: These scrolls explain the importance of the Inscrutable Power Source, a fuel cell that makes flight possible.

CHARACTERS

Bai the Outcrier

1 Visitors to the Imperial City are greeted by Bai the Outcrier, who can tell you about the city's prominent landmarks. He's honored to speak with someone as obviously important as yourself.

Captain Sen

2 Captain Sen customarily hires mercenaries to track down wanted criminals, giving him time to concentrate on his other duties. Talk to him if you want to earn extra silver by moonlighting as a bounty hunter. Find him at his post by the city gates.

Lina

3 Lina is a juggler from a local circus, but she supplements her income by selling buns in the Merchant's Square. She can share plenty of gossip about the main districts of the city.

Junda

3 Lina's husband Junda performs in the circus as a fire-eater, but he also earns a mundane living selling buns with his wife. Like Lina, he's willing to tell you about the city's hot spots.

The Blacksmith

4 The blacksmith on the district's southwestern side sells some potent weapon upgrades. Make him one of your first stops when you arrive in the Imperial City.

BLACKSMITH

Item (Number Available)	Cost (SP)
Storm Dragon Style (1)	4,500
Dragon Sword (1)	10,000
Flawless (1)	7,500
Bar of Nickeled Iron (1)	500
Craftsman's Litany (1)	1,600

Lotus Inquisitor

5 The Lotus Inquisitor appears at your base camp after you've met Silk Fox and spoken to Scholar Dongow. You gain access to the Lotus Assassin fortress if the inquisitor is sufficiently impressed with your skills.

Mechanic Hin Goo

6 Hin Goo can supply you with upgrades for the Marvelous Dragonfly if you complete some flying missions for him. Look for him in your base camp.

Prefect Jitong

7 Prefect Jitong is responsible for judging and sentencing criminal cases. He's holding two men, Chandler Ling and Scholar Songtao, on suspicion of slave trading, but he doesn't have definitive evidence to support his hunch that Songtao is innocent. You can help solve the mystery in the **Slavers** side quest.

Chandler Ling

7 Chandler Ling is a convicted slave trader, but his powerful friends have pulled some strings to get him acquitted of the crime by falsifying evidence. You can help set him free (and doom Scholar Songtao), or reveal the truth and watch him get what he deserves.

Scholar Songtao

7 Scholar Songtao is as poor as he is kind. This makes him vulnerable to exploitation by a corrupt legal system. He's been falsely accused of slave trading, and unless you find exculpatory evidence he will be sent to the Wall for a crime he did not commit. You can buy his gems only if you exonerate him.

SCHOLAR SONGTAO

Item (Number Available)	Cost (SP)
Inferior Scholar Gem (1)	1,500
Scholar Gem (1)	3,800
Inferior Charm Gem (1)	150
Charm Gem (1)	900
Superior Charm Gem (1)	2,500
Inferior Intuition Gem (1)	150
Superior Intuition Gem (1)	2,500

General Stone Kao

8 General Stone Kao appears in the Market District only if you've agreed to kill him for Iron Soldier as part of deal to rig the Silver Division championship.

Jinlin

9 Jinlin is just a little girl, but she's burdened with the dangerous job of heading into the Necropolis to recover a special artifact from the Emperor's tomb. You can help her out in the **Jinlin** side quest.

Ren Feng

10 Ren Feng appears only if you've met the ghost of her husband, Mister Ren, in the Necropolis. She can help you dissipate the ghost and complete the **Vengeful Ghost** side quest.

Younger Tanner Fong

11 When his father died, the Younger Fong inherited the family home and settled in as the head of the household. After it's revealed that the Elder Fong wasn't quite dead after all, Younger Tanner Fong is tempted to kill his father and thereby keep his inheritance.

Elder Tanner Fong

11 Elder Tanner Fong was mistakenly declared dead and buried alive. He's quite upset that his family wasn't happy to see him come back home.

THE GOLDEN WAY

to Market District

to Ministry Hotel

2

to Necropolis

1

3

Theatre Pavillion

to Scholar's Garden

MAP LEGEND

- ⬤ Containers
- ⚪ Scrollstand
- ① Beggar Song
- ② Incisive Chorus
- ③ Thespian Phong

The Golden Way is the Imperial City's upper-class district. There's a theater on the east side, near the entrance to the Scholars' Garden. On the west side, gates lead to the Market District and the Necropolis.

Theatre pavilion

Theatre is an important part of life in the Jade Empire, and the works of famous playwrights are frequently staged here. You can tackle a role in one of these dramas in a side quest, **The Play's the Thing.**

Music and the Arts: The importance of fostering cultural pursuits is explained in these documents.

CHARACTERS

Beggar Song

① Song is from a noble family, and he's voluntarily chosen to live as a beggar for a while so that, according to him, he can have time to ponder. In reality, it's just an excuse to avoid responsibility.

Incisive Chorus

2 Incisive Chorus the Playwright needs your help to ensure that his latest work is a success. He offers you one of the lead roles in the play, Lady Fourteen Flowers, if you agree to his offer.

Thespian Phong

3 First Degree Thespian Phong is a master of his art. He helps you prepare for the role you take in Incisive Chorus's latest play.

SCHOLARS' GARDEN

Entrance

to Golden Way

Debating Ground

MAP LEGEND

- ● Container
- ○ Focus Shrine
- ○ Scrollstand
- ● Spirit Font
- **1** Silk Fox / Princess Sun Lian
- **2** The Outlander / Sir Roderick and Percival
- **3** The Minister of Culture
- **4** Scholar Heng
- **5** Scholar Zou
- **6** Scholar Cai
- **7** Scholar Gu
- **8** Scholar Dongow
- **9** Scholar Zenyu
- **10** Scholar Kongyu / Creative Yukong
- **11** Philosopher Shendao
- **12** Philosopher Jiao
- **13** Tong Wei
- **14** Servant Ji

Scholars, philosophers, and students all gather in this beautiful garden to study and teach. It's a serene retreat where rival schools of thought can co-exist in mutual respect, but this calm has been perturbed by the belligerent arrogance of the Outlander, Sir Roderick, a recent arrival.

Entrance

Even philosophers must have food and other basic supplies, which are all stored here. Silk Fox joins you when you first enter this area. Your duel with the Outlander takes place here as well.

The garden itself, watered by a tranquil stream, is laced with gently winding paths that connect the most idyllic spots. Some of the Empire's brightest minds have recorded their thoughts on the many scrollstands that dot the area.

Garden

The Physical Universe—A Rebuttal: Many philosophers believe spiritual forces to be the main cause of worldly events.

The Physical Universe—The Scholar's Hypothesis: Some maintain that the laws of nature trump even the powers of the heavens.

The Physical Universe— The Philosopher's Viewpoint: This contends that without spiritual guidance, research is futile.

The Physical Universe—A Final Word: Scholar Dongow's studies lead him to conclude that natural phenomena are ultimately quantifiable.

The Long Drought: These records tell of the devastation caused by 10 years of scorching heat and little rain.

The Sprightly Stones

These magical boulders levitate due to some mysterious inner power, and they were used to construct the floating Imperial Palace. Several raw stones are chained in the garden; the largest one has been carved into a bust of Sagacious Tien, the first Emperor.

When ideas clash, leading thinkers gather in the debating ground to judge their merits. The Outlander, harshly critical of the Empire, lingers here as the reigning champion. Test your oratorical skills by challenging him to a formal debate.

Debating ground

The Mysterious East: This reference set offers speculation about the mysterious tribes that live on the far side of the Glass Ocean.

Characters

Silk Fox / Princess Sun Lian

1 Silk Fox finally reveals herself to be Princess Sun Lian, daughter of Emperor Sun Hai. She blames Death's Hand for the evil turn her father's rulership has taken and has vowed to undo the Assassin leader's influence over the Emperor. She becomes your Follower when you meet her in the Scholars' Garden.

The Outlander / Sir Roderick

2 Sir Roderick Ponce von Fontlebottom the Magnificent Bastard, known as the Outlander for short, has come from a distant land to visit the Jade Empire. His blustery vehemence has caused a stir, but you can earn his respect by besting him in the **Outlander** side quest.

Percival

2 Percival is Sir Roderick's squire. He's not afraid to tell you what he thinks of his uncouth master.

The Minister of Culture

3 The Minister of Culture is responsible for supporting the arts and philosophies that make the Jade Empire unique. He asks you to help defend the Empire's way of life against Sir Roderick's harsh criticism. He's the first of five judges in your debate with the Outlander.

Scholar Heng

4 Scholar Heng, the second of the five debate judges, admits that the Outlander makes some compelling arguments. She only wishes that his bad manners weren't so disruptive to the garden.

Scholar Zou

5 Scholar Zou is the third debate judge. He's never presided over a formal debate and is excited for this chance. He believes that what you say isn't as important as how you say it.

Scholar Cai

6 The fourth debate judge, Scholar Cai, is utterly disgusted by the Outlander and can't wait for the debate to be over with so he might leave them all in peace.

Scholar Gu

7 Scholar Gu rounds out the debate panel as the fifth judge. The Outlander's condescending attitude upsets him, and he hopes that you can bring convincing arguments that will win the debate where all others have failed.

Scholar Dongow

8 Known for his brilliant theory of cloud formation, Scholar Dongow can be found in the halls north of the garden. He arranges a meeting with the Lotus Assassin recruiter for you.

Scholar Zenyu

9 Zenyu is one of the newer elites to join the Scholars' Garden. He's full of enthusiastic ideas and can fill you in on the most interesting places to visit around the Imperial City.

Scholar Kongyu / Creative Yukong

10 Kongyu is no scholar; he's actually Creative Yukong, a fugitive with a bounty on his head. He appears here only if you've talked to Captain Sen about him in the Market District.

Philosopher Shendao

11 It can sometimes be hard to tell if Shendao, the eldest philosopher in the garden, is speaking in riddles or merely senile. If you have the patience to sift his words, you can gain some insight into the Imperial City's current troubles.

Philosopher Jiao

12 Jiao has an expert's knowledge of the teachings of Sagacious Tien, founder of the Jade Empire. He talks with you at length about the moral gulf that separates the Ways of the Open Palm and the Closed Fist.

Tong Wei

13 The Master Excavator Tong Wei oversees the work in the Valley of Sprightly Stones, where the floating rocks that decorate the garden are quarried.

Servant Ji

14 Overlooked by the scholars and philosophers, Servant Ji actually can provide some good advice on what sorts of arguments easily sway the debate judges.

MINISTRY HOSTEL

to Golden Way

MAP LEGEND

| ● | *Container* |
| **1** | *Minister Sheng* |

Sheng's room

The Ministry Hostel is a building set aside for visiting ministers to use. Unfortunately for Minister Sheng, its only occupant, the building hasn't yet been converted from its old function as a rundown warehouse. You can enter only if you've taken an assignment for the Lotus Inquisitor.

CHARACTERS

Minister Sheng

1 You met Minister of Harmony Sheng back in Tien's Landing. He's come to the Imperial City to report on the events you (and the Lotus Assassins) set in motion. Find him here after you've talked to the Lotus Inquisitor.

Jade Empire

IMPERIAL ARENA

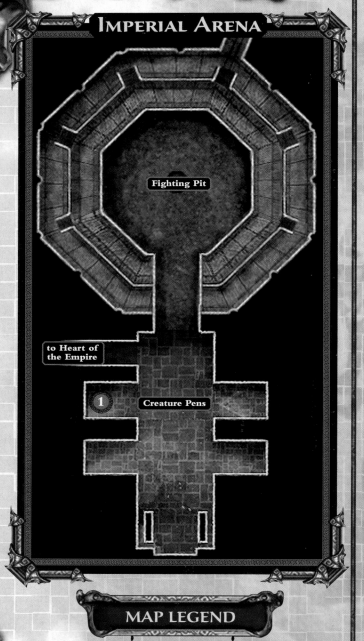

Fighting Pit

to Heart of the Empire

1

Creature Pens

MAP LEGEND

1 *Cao Zeng*

Qualifying Division, Bronze Division, Silver Division, and Gold Division. You can earn silver, gain a powerful reputation, and earn admission into the Lotus Assassin fortress by battling your way through the ranks and becoming a new champion.

You'll become very familiar with the fighting pit as you battle through the arena tournaments. It's rigged with numerous traps that add spice to some matches.

Fighting pit

Creature pens

The arena's beasts, demons, and other wild creatures are kept behind massive wooden gates until it's time for them to fight. Your fight with Lucky Cho takes place down here.

CHARACTERS

Cao Zeng

1 Cao Zeng is one of the big players in the Imperial City's criminal underground. He's a slave trader, and he asks you to help get one of his agents, Chandler Ling, released from Imperial custody during the **Slavers** side quest.

"The Trials of the Seven Gladiatorial Schools of Beneficent Light," or the arena (as it's usually called), is where the strong, the brave, and the foolhardy meet to test their physical might in honorable combat. There are four levels of competition:

THE HEART OF THE EMPIRE TAVERN

to Market District

Betting Floor

13

9

Tavern

14

2

12

16

17

5

6

4

1

7

Fight Office

10

15

11

to Imperial Arena

3

8

MAP LEGEND

●	Container
○	Focus Shrine
○	Scrollstand
●	Trapped Container
1	Qui the Promoter
2	Lotus Executioner
3	Kai Lan the Serpent
4	Hapless Han
5	Crimson Khana
6	Iron Soldier and Pretty Li-Li
7	Sung Sui, Sung Bo, and Sung Bu
8	The Ravager
9	Lustful Lao
10	Lucky Cho
11	Sweet Poison Lyn
12	Gambler Doshen
13	Thunderous Taoran
14	Zi Bao
15	Dr. An
16	Judge Fang
17	Gentle Breezes

The Heart of the Empire tavern is just one part of the large ring of buildings that surrounds the arena. It's a busy place that provides all the services that visiting spectators could want.

Betting floor

The arena tournaments draw gamblers from all over the Empire, and the betting floor sees heavy traffic daily. You can't get in on the action, unfortunately, because fighters are prohibited from placing wagers.

Imperial Champions: The scrolls here record the names of some of the arena's greatest fighters. The scrollstand that lists the arena champions changes to list your name once you have beaten the arena.

Tavern

The tavern upstairs is fairly empty, perhaps because patrons such as Lustful Lao and the Lotus Executioner make other customers uneasy. Food for both visitors and the fighters who live at the arena is prepared in the large kitchen.

Cookbook, Vol. 1: This gruesome recipe was placed here by the staff to deter nosy customers.

Many of the arena's fighters are gathered in the fight office, where they await the cue for their next battle from Qui the Promoter. A staircase leads down from the office to the creature pens in the basement.

Fight office

CHARACTERS

Qui the Promoter

1 Qui the Promoter manages the arena. He's always looking for strong new fighters; talk to him when you're ready to test yourself against some of the Empire's toughest warriors.

Lotus Executioner

2 The Lotus Executioner, a recruiter for the Lotus Assassins, follows the arena tournaments closely in his search for promising candidates. You can catch his eye and earn an invitation to join the Lotus Assassins by winning the Silver Division championship.

Kai Lan the Serpent

3 Kai Lan is a former Imperial Champion who now heads the Guild's operations in the arena. He's made a vast fortune by fixing fights and reaping huge windfalls on the betting floor.

Hapless Han

4 Han may be the top fighter in the Qualifying Division, but he's hardly a champion. Even so, his optimism is invincible. You must beat him to earn a shot at a bigger title.

Crimson Khana

5 Crimson Khana is the current champion of the Bronze Division. She's an accomplished sword fighter from the Prosperous East who's come to the arena to try her skills against the best. She can teach you the secrets of the Crimson Tears, an advanced double saber style.

Iron Soldier

6 Iron Soldier, a blunt veteran who relishes battle above everything else, is the top fighter in the Silver Division. If you wrest the title away from him, you can get an invitation to join the Lotus Assassins.

Pretty Li-Li

6 Li-Li is drawn to strength, which led her to fall in with Iron Soldier. She serves him as a personal assistant and trainer.

Sung Sui

7 Sui is the eldest and most learned of the three Sung brothers. Steeped in the Empire's mystic lore, he relies on his spiritual powers in battle more than his younger siblings do. He's one of your opponents in the Gold Division tournament.

Sung Bo

7 The middle Sung brother is renowned for his speed in combat. He's the most approachable of the three, and he's willing to talk about even such delicate subjects as Kai Lan and the Guild. He fights alongside his brothers in the Gold Division tournament.

Sung Bu

7 The youngest Sung brother is also the most physically powerful. He's not very talkative and usually just follows the lead of the elder two Sungs. Like them, he fights you during the Gold Division Tournament.

The Ravager

8 The reigning Imperial Champion, the Ravager, is a masked warrior of unrivalled power. Only by defeating him in the Gold Division title match can you reveal his true identity.

Lustful Lao

9 You can find this lecherous pervert in the tavern, but he has little to offer you besides lewd invitations and crude innuendos. There is literally nothing else on his mind.

Lucky Cho

10 Lucky Cho is one of Kai Lan's chief enforcers. Despite his nickname, he doesn't like leaving things to chance. When you battle the Bronze Division champion, he offers to help you cheat by poisoning your opponent before the match.

Sweet Poison Lyn

11 Lyn earned her venomous nickname by supplying poisons to the guild, which uses them to rig critical bouts. She also sells a few gems and can teach you Thousand Cuts style.

SWEET POISON LYN

Item (Number Available)	Cost (SP)
Inferior Warrior Gem (1)	1,650
Warrior Gem (1)	4,180
Charm Gem (1)	990
Inferior Intimidation Gem (1)	165
Superior Intimidation Gem (1)	2,750
Thousand Cuts Style (1)	13,200

Gambler Doshen

12 Gambler Doshen may be used to getting by on luck, but he takes a big risk when he starts taking bets in the Heart of the Empire without cutting in the Guild on a share of the profits. He asks you to help him buy their protection in the **Gambler's Favor** side quest.

Thunderous Taoran

13 Taoran sells souvenirs to spectators from his booth on the betting floor. He hasn't got any inventory you'd be interested in, but he can supply some gossip about the major personalities in the arena.

Zi Bao

14 Zi Bao helps you contact the highly secretive slave traders operating in the Imperial City, but only if the price is right.

Dr. An

15 Qui the Promoter needs to keep his fighters in top condition, so he hired Dr. An, a blind acupuncturist, to serve as their personal physician. She sells Intuition Gems and Techniques that enhance your Health and Focus. She can also help you perform a liver transplant in the **Mad Wen** side quest.

DR. AN

Item (Number Available)	Cost (SP)
Inferior Intuition Gem	150
Intuition Gem	900
Superior Intuition Gem	2,500
Cleansed Body and Mind	5,000
Vigorous Body	2,500
Clear Mind	2,500
Porcelain Skin	2,000

Judge Fang

16 There are few things in the Empire more twisted than Judge Fang, the most infamous degenerate in the Imperial City. Rich and powerful, he spends his days at the arena, cheering on the fighters to new heights of savagery. You can force him to resign in disgrace during your quest to get recruited by the Lotus Inquisitor.

Gentle Breezes

17 Gentle Breezes is Judge Fang's favorite courtesan. Even though she's very well paid, she despises Fang's sadistic brutality and helps you arrange his downfall.

BLACK LEOPARD SCHOOL

Training Ground

to Market District

Dining Hall

MAP LEGEND

- ⬤ **Container**
- ⚪ **Scrollstand**
- **1** *Master Smiling Hawk*
- **2** *Master Radiant*
- **3** *First Brother Kai*
- **4** *Third Brother Renshan*
- **5** *Fourth Brother Yu*
- **6** *Fifth Brother Shangjin*
- **7** *Sixth Brother Gaoshan*
- **8** *Novice Bo and Novice Feng*
- **9** *Novice Shen and Novice Han To*
- **10** *Whispering Willow*
- **11** *Aishi the Mournful Blade*

The Black Leopard School is an academy that trains students in the martial arts. Its leadership is split between two rival masters, a situation that can only lead to violent conflict.

A large training ground outside the school gives students room to spar and practice. Most of your battles with the school's students take place here.

Training ground

Black Leopard Style: These scrolls tell how Zou How created his own unique fighting style from scratch.

When they're not busy training, students gather in the dining hall even though Whispering Willow, the school cook, is one of the harshest shrews you could meet.

Dining hall

Master Black Leopard: Zou How changed his name to Master Black Leopard when he founded this school.

CHARACTERS

Master Smiling Hawk

1 Master Smiling Hawk is an exemplar of the Closed Fist, and with no overt resistance from Master Radiant, he has taken charge of the Black Leopard School. He asks you help him make his position secure by finishing off his rival, Master Radiant.

Master Radiant

2 Master Radiant follows the Open Palm and would love nothing more than to wrest control of school back from Master Smiling Hawk. However, the curse of undeath confines him helplessly to his room. He teaches you the Paralyzing Palm style if you help him.

First Brother Kai

3 First Brother Kai is the only student brave enough to remain outwardly loyal to Master Radiant. After seeing your fighting skills, he invites you to join the school in the hope that you'll ally with him in ousting Master Shining Hawk.

Third Brother Renshan

4 Third Brother Renshan is Master Smiling Hawk's most promising pupil, and he gives every sign of turning out to be as ruthless and evil as his teacher. If Renshan's not careful, Smiling Hawk will teach him that the Closed Fist can work against him if he shows any weakness.

Fourth Brother Yu

5 When the Second Brother disappeared, Yu sent the novices into town to look for him. They came back empty-handed, and Yu is beginning to suspect foul play.

Fifth Brother Shangjin

6 Shangjin doesn't seem to prefer either of the school's masters; he only wishes that there weren't two of them. He rightly considers divided leadership to be a detriment to his studies.

Sixth Brother Gaoshan

7 Fanatically devoted to Master Smiling Hawk, Sixth Brother Gaoshan has eagerly taken his first steps down the Way of the Closed Fist. He's motivated more by selfishness rather than by philosophical convictions.

Novice Bo

8 Leaping Tiger is the style favored by Novice Bo. He may be a novice, but he's still more skilled than many other less humble warriors you've met.

Novice Feng

8 Novice Feng is learning the Iron Palm style. He's a serious student who will go far if he keeps up his training.

Novice Shen

9 Like his fellow student Bo, Novice Shen is a disciple of Leaping Tiger style. He is impudent when you first meet him, but later on he realizes his error and offers an apology.

Novice Han To

9 Novice Han To is another devotee of the Iron Palm. Like the other novices, he can usually be found in the school's dining hall.

Whispering Willow

10 Whispering Willow used to be an opera singer before a freak costume accident ruined her singing voice and left her an angry, bitter woman. Her shouting voice is still strong, and as headmistress of the school she has lots of chances to use it.

Aishi the Mournful Blade

11 Aishi the Mournful Blade lingers sorrowfully in the garden of Black Leopard School. She is the third bounty offered by Captain Sen, but she appears only if you've collected Sen's first two bounties.

NECROPOLIS

Tomb of the Dignified Collector

to Lotus Assassin Fortress

The Pagoda

Tomb of Ji Xin

6

Unfinished Tomb

to Golden Way

5

2

7

4

3

1

Gravedigger Shen's House

Tomb of the Forgotten Scholar

Tomb of the Masses

MAP LEGEND

⬤	Container
⬤	Focus Shrine
⬤	Scrollstand
⬤	Spirit Font
⬤	Trapped Containers
1	Gravedigger Shen
2	Miss Chan
3	Merchant Bai
4	Mister Ren
5	Wen Zhi
6	Ji Xin
7	Fading Moon

The Necropolis, or City of the Dead, is the largest graveyard in the Empire. From Emperors to unknown commoners, most people in the Empire find their way to the Necropolis in the end.

Shen is alienated from the Imperial City because tradition demands he live in the graveyard in addition to working there. To add insult to injury, his backyard has recently been haunted by the ghost of Shen's mother-in-law.

Gravedigger Shen's House

This magnificent tomb is still under construction. It's intended to someday hold the remains of the current Emperor, Sun Hai. Fading Moon, a fugitive arsonist, is found hiding here if you're on the **Bounty Hunter** side quest.

The Unfinished Tomb

The Nature of the Spirit, Vol. 4: Some monks can summon the power of spirits by tapping into their deepest desires.

Tomb of the Masses

The Imperial City's numberless poor can't afford to construct individual family tombs, so they're interred in a huge mausoleum set aside just for them. You meet three ghosts here that you can lay to rest in the **Ghosts in the Graveyard** side quest.

The Pagoda

This beautiful tomb conceals a secret tunnel that leads to the Lotus Assassin fortress. This path is open only after you've gained the approval of a Lotus Assassin recruiter in the Imperial City.

The Nature of the Spirit, Vol. 5: These scrolls warn that to a spirit, the lives of others have no meaning.

You find Mad Wen Zhi and his daughter here in this shadowy underground chamber. Speak with them to embark on **The Scientist** side quest.

Tomb of the Forgotten Scholar

The Nature of the Spirit, Vol. 2: A spirit hunter tells of his search for a ghost that haunted an abandoned mine.

Ji Xin was an extremely corrupt nobleman in life, and his greed and dishonesty have followed him to the grave in the form of a curse. His decomposing mummy stalks the tomb and slays all who enter.

Tomb of Ji Xin

The Nature of the Spirit, Vol. 3: Continues the spirit hunter's tale of his contact with the ghost in the old mine.

Tomb of the Dignified Collector

The largest tomb in the Necropolis belongs to one of the city's wealthiest families. It's crawling with mummies and powerful ghosts that guard valuable gems and other treasure. You can only enter this tomb if you're on the **Jinlin** side quest.

CHARACTERS

Gravedigger Shen

① Gravedigger Shen's job is unpleasant enough, but as more spirits lose their way to the next world he begins to fear for his own life. He rewards you well if you can help him lay these ghosts to rest.

GRAVEDIGGER SHEN

Item (Number Available)	Cost (SP)
Inferior Monk Gem (1)	1,500
Inferior Charm Gem (1)	150
Charm Gem (1)	900
Superior Charm Gem (1)	2,500
Monk Gem (1)	3,800

Miss Chan

② Grief stricken over being separated from her baby's resting place, Miss Chan hasn't been able to find peace. You can ease her sadness by helping her find her way to her son's grave in the **Mournful Ghost** side quest.

Merchant Bai

③ Merchant Bai's ghost is tormented by the spirits of the two brothers who ended his life. You can help him in the **Fearful Ghost** side quest.

Mister Ren

4 Mister Ren, another restless spirit that lingers in the Necropolis, can't rest until he's taken vengeance on his wife Ren Feng for poisoning him. Undertake the **Vengeful Ghost** side quest if you want to help him out.

Wen Zhi

5 Wen Zhi, also known as Mad Wen, is a mad scientist trying to use transplanted organs to heal his dying daughter. You can help him find a donor liver in the **Mad Wen** side quest.

Ji Xin

6 Ji Xin is a corrupt nobleman who was recently buried in the Necropolis. Like many other poor souls in the Jade Empire, however, he can't move on to the next world. Mad Wen sends you to harvest Ji Xin's liver; even though he doesn't need it any more, the selfish noble isn't disposed to donate it to you.

Fading Moon

7 An accused arsonist, Fading Moon has fled into the Necropolis to hide from the authorities. The desperate (and insane) fugitive attacks you no matter what you do, leaving you little choice but to kill him; at least this allows you to claim the bounty Captain Sen has put on his head.

LOTUS ASSASSIN FORTRESS

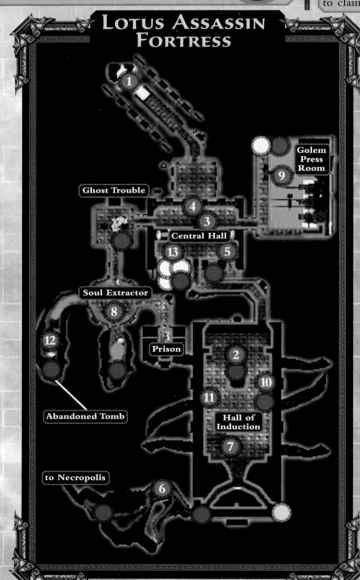

MAP LEGEND

●	*Container*
○	*Focus Shrine*
○	*Scrollstand*
●	*Spirit Font*
●	*Trapped Container*
1	*Grand Inquisitor Jia*
2	*Master Shin*
3	*Master Gang*
4	*Attendant Cohong, Attendant Kitan, Attendant Kai Feng, and Attendant Teng*
5	*Acolyte Trainer Guang*
6	*The Watcher*
7	*Lotus Acolyte Jin Tao*
8	*Lotus Acolyte Go Rin*
9	*Lotus Acolyte Shi*
10	*Merchant Kia Jong*
11	*Mold Master Gi and Mold Master Soto*
12	*Horselord Zeng Sai*
13	*Keeper of the Archive*

Deep within a secret cavern beyond the Necropolis lies the Lotus Assassin fortress, a place of dread and despair. It was originally built to be the future tomb of Emperor Sun Hai, but Death's Hand has converted it into a golem factory and training ground for new Assassin recruits.

Hall of Induction

New arrivals are ushered through a hall dominated by several colossal statues of the Emperor. New recruits must also face a harsh reception from other Lotus Acolytes before they may meet the master of the fortress.

Since a spirit shard was broken, several ghosts have haunted this room and have been killing slaves and acolytes. Master Gang's first assignment is to purge this room of spirits.

Ghost trouble

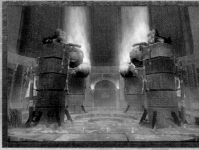

Soul Extractor

This huge device converts the bodies of the dead into spirit shards used to give life to the golems. The entire room is actually an elevator that lets you access different sub-levels of the fortress.

Abandoned tomb

The most evil and corrupted of spirits linger here, in the lowest level of the tombs. The powerful ghost of Horselord Zeng Sai guards his final resting place from grave robbers.

Golem press room

The inert clay bodies of the golems are formed here in gigantic molds. Frequent accidents make working the press one of the more dangerous jobs in a place that already bristles with danger. Lotus Acolyte Shi runs the machinery here.

Jade Empire Bestiary, Vol. 2: These scrolls give advice on the best way to effectively battle golems.

CHARACTERS

Grand Inquisitor Jia

1 This masked woman commands respect as the second-highest-ranking Lotus Assassin next to Death's Hand himself. Your first meeting with her takes place in the heart of the fortress, but deadly interruptions cut your questioning short.

Master Shin

2 The Lotus Assassin fortress is governed by Master Shin, one of the most ruthless and evil men in the Death's Hand's service. With Master Gang's encouragement, you can slay Master Shin and bring his fortress crumbling to the ground.

Master Gang

3 Master Gang is in charge of training new Lotus Acolytes. Impressed with your skill, he gives you a series of tests that that will let you penetrate deeper into the leadership of the Lotus Assassins and bring you one step closer to Death's Hand.

Attendant Cohong

4 Attendant Cohong is one of Master Shin's most ardent servants. He helps his master keep a watchful eye on Master Gang for any sign of betrayal.

Attendant Kitan
4 After you've become an acolyte trainer, Attendant Kitan challenges you to a duel to insure that you're up the job. She can then learn first-hand just how skilled you really are.

Attendant Kai Feng
4 Another of Master Shin's lackeys, Attendant Kai Feng's task is to make examples of Gang's acolytes who show too much skill.

Attendant Teng
4 Attendant Teng has been instilled with unquestioning loyalty. This level of dedication leads him to lay down his life to protect his patron, Master Shin.

Acolyte Trainer Guang
5 After you defeat Guang in combat, Master Gang gives you her job. Guang gladly retires to the sidelines, where her life expectancy will be much longer. Only then will she sell you her potent Techniques.

ACOLYTE TRAINER GUANG
Item (Number Available)	Cost (SP)
Inferior Monk Gem (1)	1,500
Gem of Mastery (1)	8,100
Eye of Inner Darkness (1)	5,000
Window to the Abyss (1)	3,500
Deadened Nerves (1)	3,500
Fearsome Visage (1)	3,000

The Watcher
6 The Watcher, hooded and masked, hides near the entrance to the Lotus Assassin fortress and challenges all who approach. He lets you pass if you've obtained a token from one of the recruiters in the Imperial City.

Lotus Acolyte Jin Tao
7 Jin Tao is ambitious, and he hopes to clear away rival acolytes by trying to kill any new recruits that arrive at the fortress. The last mistake he ever makes is trying this tactic on you.

Lotus Acolyte Go Rin
8 Acolyte Go Rin works in the Soul Extractor room, where the souls of the newly dead are condensed into spirit shards that are used to animate golems.

Lotus Acolyte Shi
9 Acolyte Shi operates the gigantic machines that form and transport the inert clay golems, but he'd much rather work with the Soul Extractor so he can watch people get killed by it.

Merchant Kia Jong
10 Kia Jong is the uncle of Kia Min, your fellow student back at Two Rivers. You can earn a 10 percent discount from Kia Jong if you tell him you knew her.

MERCHANT KIA JONG
Item (Number Available)	Cost (SP)
Inferior Warrior Gem	1,500
Inferior Intimidation Gem	150
Intimidation Gem	900
Superior Intimidation Gem	2,500
Intuition Gem	900
Gem of Struggle	3,800

Mold Master Gi
11 Mold Master Gi is one of two Lotus Assassins responsible for maintaining the golem press. He's a specialized engineer who doesn't dirty his hands with common labor; he visits the golem press only if there's a serious malfunction.

Mold Master Soto
11 The other machinery expert is Mold Master Soto. Find her talking with her colleague in the Hall of Induction. Both Gi and Soto must be cleared from the hall before you can attempt to kill Master Shin.

Horselord Zeng Sai
12 Zeng Sai the Tree that Defies the Fire was once a mighty Horselord. His chaotic soul can be used to make a spirit shard that will cripple the Assassins' Jade Golem and those that it commands.

Keeper of the Archive
13 Loyalty is inculcated among the Lotus Assassins by indoctrinating them in the history and tenets of their order. The Keeper of the Archive is responsible for maintaining the records, many of which are found with him in a cloister off the Central Hall.

CRITICAL PATH

At last you've arrived at the Imperial City, teeming capital of the Jade Empire. Pursuing the Lotus Assassins here won't be easy; they are masters of subtlety and stealth, always operating unseen. With the help of Silk Fox, who is revealed to be Princess Sun Lian, you must seek out the Lotus Assassins' hidden fortress and find a way to infiltrate it to the core.

THE EMPEROR AND THE ASSASSINS

ARRIVAL AT THE IMPERIAL CITY

The Marvelous Dragonfly drops you off at your base camp in the Market District. Imperial guards, under orders from Death's Hand, detain you with questions as you climb down from the boarding tower. Just when things begin to

We are questioning everyone who has arrived in the city recently. You... bear a resemblance to someone we are looking for.

look awkward, you are saved by the arrival of Princess Sun Lian, the Emperor's daughter.

Here, friend. Take this, with my compliments. I've never seen such a thing.

Though she was veiled the last time you met, her eyes and voice are unmistakable: Princess Lian is actually Silk Fox! She makes no pretense at concealing her alter ego from you, and she boldly proposes that the two of you reconvene in private after she's slipped into something more comfortable. She departs, leaving with you a **Note from Princess Lian** telling you to meet her at the Scholars' Garden. An attendant stays behind to deliver a more valuable gift on her mistress's behalf: the **Imperial Favor** gem (Spirit +3, Charm +1, Intuition +1, increased chance of power-ups during battle).

TIP

Whenever you're given a chance to say something to the princess, choose the last (and most impudent) reply from the list. Each blunt comment you utter causes one of Princess Lian's attendants to swoon with embarrassment. If you get all five attendants to drop (100 XP), an onlooker approaches you after the princess leaves and gives you a new Technique: Loutish Approval (Health +2). This is considered a display of courage rather than chaos, and therefore doesn't affect your alignment.

IMPERIAL CITY TOUR

Be on the lookout for the Scourge of the South. It is your duty as citizens of the Empire to report anyone who matches this description.

As you proceed through the Imperial City to the Scholars' Garden, talk to everyone you meet to learn more about the city and to trigger side quests. A Lotus Assassin warns citizens to keep an eye out for the "Scourge of the South" (as they're calling you), but fortunately your enemy doesn't have a reliable description to share. In fact, you can walk right up to the Lotus Assassin and chat with her; she won't recognize you.

SIDE QUEST

One side quest is available immediately: the Bounty Hunter missions. Talk to Captain Sen by the city gates to learn about the Empire's most wanted criminals (besides yourself, that is).

Well, no matter... if you're looking for weapons, I have quite a good selection and reasonable rates. Would you like to see what I have for sale?

Continue around the Market District, scouring the area for incidental treasure. Smash a jar outside the door to the Imperial Arena (56 SP), then go south across the bridge and find the blacksmith's shop. Two fighting styles are sold here: **Storm Dragon**, a Support style that damages enemies over time, and **Dragon Sword**, an artifact long sword that's 25 percent stronger than Fortune's Favorite. They are expensive, so if you don't have enough silver, come back later, after you've earned more cash. You should be able to buy the entire inventory before you leave the Imperial City.

SIDE QUEST

*Exit the Market District through a gate near the blacksmith to begin the **Black Leopard School** side quest. Visiting the school is completely optional, but don't miss this chance to learn new combat styles and Techniques.*

Your breath is like the wind of an ox. Your last meal was of suspect quality.

Leave the Market District through the southeast gate and bask in the opulence of the Golden Way, the city's wealthiest district. Encounter Servant Ji as you cross the large plaza; his master, the Minister of Culture, has ordered him to shout insults at passersby in the hope of luring out someone who commands respect. When you stand up to Ji's barbs, the minister is impressed and asks you to bring your nerve to the Scholars' Garden and challenge the Outlander, an arrogant visitor from the Mysterious East, to a gentlemanly debate.

HOSTEL

As you continue along the Golden Way, look for a small jar by the entrance to the Ministry Hostel (100 SP). The Theatre Pavilion is empty for now; pass it by and ascend the stairs to the Scholars' Garden.

SILK FOX'S PLAN

But it doesn't matter who your Master is. I could take you to the palace, but Death's Hand controls what my father hears. He must be discredited for you to succeed.

Construction on the Wall has stopped for the first time in generations. The workers now toil in factories, building powerful creatures of stone and clay called golems.

Princess Lian, now in the guise of Silk Fox, is waiting at the garden's entrance. She is convinced that her father is oblivious to the secret golem army being constructed by the Lotus Assassins, under orders from Death's Hand. She proposes that the best way for you to strike at the Assassins is to find evidence of their plot and present it to the Emperor, forcing Death's Hand to face justice. According to Silk Fox, the Lotus Assassins have a golem factory in the depths of their hidden fortress; this is where you must go to find the proof you seek. Getting into the fortress isn't going to be easy, as its location is a well-kept secret. Your only hope is to find a Lotus Assassin recruiter in the Imperial City and earn an invitation into their guild. Then you can just walk right into their fortress and see the golem army for yourself.

There are guilds within the Lotus Assassins. Executioners look for fearsome warriors. Inquisitors are more subversive, and they look for cunning.

There are two main guilds within the Lotus Assassins: the Executioners and the Inquisitors. The Executioners specialize in brute force and are typically drawn from among the champions in the Imperial Arena. The Inquisitors are masters of manipulation, secrecy, and sabotage; their agent looks for candidates who embody these subtle qualities. Each guild offers you a path to recruitment. You need to get an offer from only one recruiter to proceed to the Lotus Assassin fortress, but take the time to impress both the Executioners *and* the Inquisitors. Each guild offers the chance to earn XP, silver, and rare items.

Unless you want me with you, I will wait at your flying machine. You travel with such interesting peasants. I'm sure I'll be entertained for hours.

After discussing her plan, Silk Fox officially becomes your Follower. You can bring her with you or tell her to wait for you at the base camp. Silk Fox is more than an impressive fighter; her Support ability gives you a damage boost to all Martial styles. Because martial attacks affect almost every type of enemy, this makes her especially nice to have along.

Silk Fox Profile

Attack Style: Long Sword
Support Ability: Increase Martial Damage
Health: ~468
Chi: ~368

Nobody here suspects me to be anything but an overzealous scholar, and I'd like to keep it that way. So, you want to know about the recruiter?

Scholar Dongow is a spy looking for bright, impressionable minds he can recommend to his Lotus Assassin employers.

Go into the shelter by the garden entrance and talk to Scholar Dongow. Ask him about meeting the Inquisitor recruiter. Urging you to keep your voice down, Dongow admits that he works for the Assassins. He informs you that the recruiter will meet you back at your base camp in the Market District.

SIDE QUEST

*After you've spoken with Dongow, everything else in the garden is optional. If you stay and explore the area, however, you can complete the **Outlander** side quest and defend your people's honor against the bigoted foreigner. If you've accepted the **Bounty Hunter** side quest, one of the fugitives is hiding here disguised as Scholar Kongyu.*

As you leave Scholars' Garden, the two guards that questioned you back in the Market District appear. They've been following you all this time, waiting for a chance to grab you when Princess Lian wasn't around to interfere. This time you have no choice but to teach them a lesson.

Well, look who we have here. There's no Princess to save you this time.

CAUTION

Now that you've reached Chapter Three, even average foes such as these guards are much tougher than they were before. You have become stronger as well, but you can still find your adventure cut short if you aren't careful. Retreat out of range of the guards' spears and blast them with Magic and Support styles from a safe distance.

IMPERIAL GUARD BATTLE:
~242 XP, ~160 SP

Enemy	Style	Health	Chi
Imperial Guard	Spear	200	200

After defeating the guards, head back through the city. You must now choose which Assassin guild you want to get invited into first. To meet the Executioner recruiter, enter the Imperial Arena. To gain the Inquisitor's approval, return to your base camp.

SIDE QUEST

*Three new side quests become available upon your return from Scholars' Garden. Incisive Chorus appears on the Golden Way's northwest end. Talk to him if you want to take on a dramatic role in **The Play's the Thing**. To get involved in the case of the **Slave Traders**, find Prefect Jitong in the Market District by the entrance to Black Leopard School and ask him about the two men he has in custody. Finally, **Hin Goo** has arrived at the base camp; he has a trio of **Marvelous Dragonfly** missions for you.*

THE EXECUTIONERS
ENTER THE LISTS

Guess my spot in the roster's yours if you want it. Go find Qui the Promoter if you think you can fill my shoes.

When you enter the betting floor, you see a beaten gladiator getting thrown out by Lucky Cho. The humiliated fighter staggers out, commenting that his "retirement" means there's a new space open on the tournament roster.

Take a look around, then go upstairs and enter the Heart of the Empire tavern. The Lotus Executioner comes right up to you and proposes a test: defeat Iron Soldier to become the new Silver Division champion, and you'll be formally invited to join the Lotus Assassins.

If you were to knock Iron Soldier from his perch as Silver Division champion, I would be impressed.

Explore the kitchen to find a jar (100 SP) and a scrollstand, then continue around the upper story to meet Qui the Promoter. Under pressure from Lucky Cho (whom you saw earlier throwing out a washed-up fighter),

Qui eagerly helps you sign up for combat and explains the rules. You then get to choose a nickname for yourself: Raging Dragon, Silver Phoenix, or Tiger Lifts the Mountain.

Imperial Arena Tournaments

There are four levels of competition: Qualifying Division, Bronze Division, Silver Division, and Gold Division. Each division offers a series of battles against increasingly tougher opponents and culminates with a title match against the reigning champion.

Combat in the arena is slightly different from the life-or-death struggles you're used to. Arena battles are non-lethal, meaning your game won't end if you lose a fight. You can retry battles as much as you like at no cost. Instead of collecting silver and XP from your defeated enemies, you receive these rewards from Qui after each win. You are free to use any of your combat styles; the only restriction is that you can't bring any of your Followers into the ring, so you must manage your Chi and Focus carefully. If you need to replenish, rely on Spirit Thief. After each battle, your Health, Chi, and Focus are fully refilled.

The first thing to know is that this arena was founded under the auspices of Sagacious Tien himself. The Emperor's blessings rest upon this place as the one true test of martial skill in the Empire.

QUALIFYING DIVISION

Round	Opponent(s)	XP	SP
1	Ogre	300	300
2	Black Leopard Student x4	325	400
3	Stone Statue	350	500
Final	Hapless Han	400	500

BRONZE DIVISION

Round	Opponent(s)	XP	SP
1	Cannibal x5	450	400
2	Pit of Pain	480	500
3	Toad Demon	500	600
Final	Crimson Khana	1,050	700

SILVER DIVISION

Round	Opponent(s)	XP	SP
1	Elephant Demon	600	600
2	Guild Assassin x4	650	700
3	Golem x3	700	800
Final	Iron Soldier	750	1,000

GOLD DIVISION

Round	Opponent(s)	XP	SP
1	Phoenix Unity	850	1,000
2	Sung Brothers	1,000	1,250
3	Imperial Engagement	1,300	1,500
Final	Ravager	1,800	2,500

THE EXECUTIONERS: QUALIFYING DIVISION

Begin your climb through the ranks of the Qualifying Division with an inaugural battle versus a single ogre. Score an effortless win by leaping over the brute's head and attacking from behind. As the ogre helplessly attempts to track you, keep leaping back and forth to score more combos. For complete overkill, use Chi Strikes with your strongest weapon style.

Everyone has beaten the ogre, even Hapless Han.

QUALIFYING DIVISION, ROUND 1: 300 XP, 300 SP

Enemy	Style	Health	Chi	
Ogre	Ogre	250	250	

Send the Black Leopard cubs back to their den.

The second battle in the Qualifying Division pits you against four students from the Black Leopard School. Each one uses a different style, but none possesses any ranged attacks. Keep your distance and pelt them with Magic styles; they won't be able to retaliate.

QUALIFYING DIVISION, ROUND 2: 325 XP, 400 SP

Enemy	Style	Health	Chi	
Student	Basic	62	62	
Student	Legendary Strike	62	62	
Student	Iron Palm	62	62	
Student	Storm Dragon	200	200	

Your next battle is the only event that poses no risk to you. In fact, it's not really a battle at all. Qui has placed a big statue in the ring; all you have to do is pulverize it to dust within 25 seconds. Use a Weapon or Martial style, enhanced with Chi Strikes, to do the job. Toad Demon style also works very well.

Live out the art critic's dream.

QUALIFYING DIVISION, ROUND 3: 350 XP, 500 SP

Enemy	Style	Health	Chi
Statue	—	—	—

Hapless Han's bruised and scarred face betrays his lack of skill.

After three rounds, Qui finally offers you a chance to earn a Qualifying Division championship by facing off against Hapless Han. Han is a good-natured fighter with a terrible record; he's perfectly happy being a top Qualifying Division contender rather than just another victim in one of the upper brackets. His favored style, Legendary Strike, is terribly outmatched by any of your Magic or Transformation attacks.

QUALIFYING DIVISION, CHAMPIONSHIP ROUND: 400 XP, 500 SP

Enemy	Style	Health	Chi
Hapless Han	Legendary Strike	250	250

THE EXECUTIONERS: BRONZE DIVISION

You have earned the right to battle in the Bronze Division, which offers greater risks and rewards. Your meteoric rise

through the qualifying stage has turned some heads; Lucky Cho appears with compliments from his boss, Kai Lan the Serpent. Kai Lan is a former arena champ who now runs a criminal syndicate known as the Guild (not to be confused with the Lotus Assassin guilds). You get to meet him soon.

Some of the Black Whirlwind's past is revealed when he's recognized by Qui the Promoter. It's hinted that your burly Follower once plied his trade on the arena floor, but the circumstances of his departure remain a mystery for now. The Black Whirlwind doesn't need to be your active Follower for this scene to occur.

Begin your career in the Bronze Division with a battle against five cannibals. You honed your styles on these wretched creatures back in the Great Forest. The same strategies you used then are still effective. Unleash area attacks to send the ghouls flying and target the leader first. Once he's out of the picture, mopping up the rest is child's play.

The cannibals are going home hungry after this fight.

BRONZE DIVISION, ROUND 1: 450 XP, 400 SP

Enemy	Style	Health	Chi
Cannibal x4	Cannibal	150	150
Cannibal	Tempest	250	250

Qui's advice for surviving the Pit of Pain: try dodging. Thanks, Qui!

The next event is called the Pit of Pain. A ring of enchanted statues has been set up on the arena floor. These magical devices try to blast you with Dire Flame and Ice Shard bolts; you must survive their onslaught for one minute to pass the round. You can't harm the statues, so concentrate solely on evasion. Stay on the nearest side of the ring, where there are no statues. Save all your Focus for the last 10–15 seconds, when fireballs come whizzing toward you from every direction in a constant barrage.

Bronze Division, Round 2: 480 XP, 500 SP

Enemy	Style	Health	Chi
Statue Trap x8	Dire Flame, Ice Shard	—	—

The toad demon's enormous power does him no good if he can't hit you.

Lucky Cho stops by again to wish you victory in your next match; the Guild has a lot of money riding on your success. After he leaves, dive back into battle and face your next opponent. Kai Lan the Serpent has arranged a real spectacle for the crowd by pitting you against a toad demon. The demon is tougher than others you've seen, but he still shares their fatal weakness: he's slow. Using Free Target mode and evasion, get behind the demon and attack his exposed backside. Continue running circles around him until the beast falls.

Bronze Division, Round 3: 500 XP, 600 SP

Enemy	Style	Health	Chi
Toad Demon	Toad Demon	687	687

It should be a simple matter to slip a slow-acting, but extremely deadly, poison into Khana's drink before the match.

Guild agents try to talk you into cheating in the arena.

SIDE QUEST

*Before you can begin the championship match against Crimson Khana, you must have a word with Lucky Cho. Enter his office (which is now unlocked) and listen to his proposal; he wants Crimson Khana out of the picture and, to ensure your victory, offers to have your opponent poisoned before the fight. See the **Bronzed Opportunity** side quest for full details*

After you've accepted or refused Cho's offer, tell Qui you're ready for your next fight. If you had Crimson Khana poisoned,

she is much weaker and the fight becomes effortless. Even at her full strength, however, Khana is hampered by her lack of ranged attacks. Leap away from her and lob a few bolts using your favorite Magic style as she closes in. Keep this up and you can beat the sword mistress without a scratch.

The Crimson Khana wields an exotic Technique she learned back home in the Prosperous East.

Bronze Division, Championship Round: 1,050 (550 if poisoned) XP, 700 SP

Enemy	Style	Health	Chi
Crimson Khana	Crimson Tears	875 (50 if poisoned)	875

When Crimson Khana is defeated, you can try to increase your winnings by 200 SP with conversation skills (60 XP). If you didn't poison Crimson Khana (and revealed the plot against her), speak with her to learn the **Crimson Tears** Weapon style. If you defeat Crimson Khana without poisoning her, but you did not tell her about the poisoning plot (and you didn't piss her off and make her refuse to talk to you before), then she will still teach you the basic double saber style **Eyes of the Dragon**.

SIDE QUEST

Now that you have access to Lucky Cho's office, the Gambler's Favor side quest becomes available. Talk to Gambler Doshen near the Heart of the Empire tavern to look into it.

NOTE

Wondering what to do with all that silver you've been earning in the arena? Talk to Sweet Poison Lyn and Dr. An to browse their selection of useful Techniques and buy as many of them as you can afford.

The Executioners: Silver Division

In the Silver Division, the stakes are higher than ever. Not only do you face tougher opponents, but interference from the Guild also becomes a serious problem. The first round is a straightforward one-on-one battle against an elephant demon.

Use your better mobility to sidestep his attacks and unload combos on him from the back or flanks, similar to the way you fought the toad demon.

The elephant demon's frustration shows as you nimbly avoid his cumbersome attacks.

SILVER DIVISION, ROUND 1: ~600 XP, ~600 SP			
Enemy	Style	Health	Chi
Elephant Demon	Elephant Demon	687	687

Before you can advance to the next round, Qui tells you that Kai Lan wants to see you in his office, and that you are to go there alone. The guards by the office door make sure nobody follows you in. During the conversation, Kai Lan reveals that the Black Whirlwind was once an arena combatant, but he was thrown out in disgrace while his brother, Raging Ox, stayed on to claim the Imperial Championship.

The meeting is interrupted when the Black Whirlwind storms into the office and abruptly drags you down to the creature pens for a quick chat. Your Follower begins to explain that Kai Lan is a crook who can't be trusted, when another interruption occurs, this time thanks to Lucky Cho. The ruthless enforcer has a score to settle with the Black Whirlwind. Despite his incredible toughness, Lucky Cho is in serious trouble. With the Black Whirlwind's help, you can knock Cho into a corner and use your fastest attacks to interrupt his action when he tries to attack or escape. If you time your moves right, Cho will never be able to step out of the corner you trapped him in.

LUCKY CHO BATTLE: ~1,000 XP, ~3,000 SP			
Enemy	Style	Health	Chi
Lucky Cho	Thousand Cuts	1,250	1,250

NOTE
After this encounter, talk to the Black Whirlwind to learn the full story of his banishment from the arena.

You gain a **Strong Arm** (Intimidation +8, Charm -3, Intuition -3) gem after the battle. Go back upstairs and talk to Qui to get back into the tournament. Kai Lan has discovered Lucky Cho's body and, guessing you were the killer, arranges for your opponents in the next battle to use poison

Strike down the assassins from long range to avoid their venomous touch.

attacks. Use Magic styles to obliterate them as they close in. If you're surrounded, switch to a Martial or Weapon style and knock the assassins away with an area attack, then retreat to a better position.

SILVER DIVISION, ROUND 2: ~650 XP, ~700 SP			
Enemy	Style	Health	Chi
Guild Assassins x2	Sword	437	437
Guild Assassins x2	Viper	437	437

The next round pits you against a trio of golems provided by the Imperial Army. Before the fight, equip gems that boost your Mind to give yourself as much Focus as possible; you need to rely on weapons to defeat the golems. Using Chi Strikes maximizes damage and helps your Focus last

If you obtained Mirabelle from the Outlander, golem slaying is effortless.

longer. Wait for the golem to begin swinging before launching your own attack from a safe angle.

SILVER DIVISION, ROUND 3: ~700 XP, ~800 SP			
Enemy	Style	Health	Chi
Golem x3	Dual Axes	317	317

You're finally ready to challenge Iron Soldier for the Silver Division championship. This opponent is a tough arena veteran who relies on Leaping Tiger to tear his enemies to shreds. As with your fight against Crimson Khana, ranged attacks give you a huge advantage. Stay well away from Iron Soldier's rakes and pelt him with magic from afar.

Stay out of reach of Iron Soldier's claws.

SIDE QUEST

If you poisoned Crimson Khana during the Bronze Division championship, Iron Soldier has an underhanded deal for you. He's willing to throw the fight, but only if you do a favor for him first. See the Soldier's Offer side quest for full details.

SILVER DIVISION, CHAMPIONSHIP ROUND: ~750 XP, ~1,000 SP			
Enemy	Style	Health	Chi
Iron Soldier	Leaping Tiger	678	678

After the fight, you have another one-time chance to persuade Qui to give you a 200 SP bonus (60 SP). With the Silver Division title under your belt, the Lotus Executioner recruiter congratulates you on your victory and gives you the **Lotus Executioner's Seal** as a sign that you've been officially invited to join their order.

When you leave the arena, you're taken straight back to the base camp where your Followers chime in on your progress. Sagacious Zu, even more secretive and brooding than usual, slips away during the conversation and disappears (you'll meet

him again soon). Finally, Silk Fox asks if you're ready to head for the Assassins' fortress, or if you want to stay and try to earn a second recruitment offer from the Lotus Inquisitors. Resourceful players should choose the latter option.

SIDE QUEST

To trigger a new sidequest, look for Jinlin across the bridge from your base camp and agree to help her explore the Necropolis.

THE EXECUTIONERS: GOLD DIVISION

NOTE

Although technically a side quest, you can now optionally conquer the Gold Division for fun and profit.

Before you bid farewell to the arena, take a stab at claiming the arena's highest honor by winning the Gold Division championship. The top division offers the toughest battles to be found anywhere in the Empire, but offers enormous pay-offs to those who claw their way up to the very top.

Phoenix Unity is a powerful style that allows users to make duplicates of themselves.

Qui has your first Gold Division battle arranged, so speak with him when you're ready to begin. The phoenix assassin you face in this match relies on two styles: Viper and Twin Swords. During the first phase of the battle, conserve Chi and Focus while you wear down your opponent with quick combat moves. When your opponent is about to drop, the deadly power of Phoenix Unity style is revealed as the assassin splits into six identical copies, each with full health. Now is the time to use the Chi and Focus you saved before. Fire off volleys of magic as you retreat from the advancing mob to whittle down their numbers, then use Focus mode to dive in and finish them off cleanly with your strongest physical attacks.

GOLD DIVISION, ROUND 1: ~850 XP, ~1,000 SP

Enemy	Style	Health	Chi
Phoenix Assassin	Viper, Twin Swords, Phoenix Unity	437	437
Phoenix Assassin x6	Viper, Twin Sword	437	437

Each of the Sung brothers specializes in a different type of combat.

The second round pits you against the three Sung brothers. Their combined talents form an opposition that is very difficult to beat. Your first target should be Sung Sui, the magic specialist. Move around him in a wide circle while blasting him with your own magic, keeping well away from Sung Bo and Sung Bu. Keep this up until Sung Sui falls. Eliminate Sung Bo next; his Monkey Paw style gives him great mobility, but you can eliminate his advantage by now making use of Focus mode. When Sung Bu is the only brother left, use him to replenish your abilities with Spirit Thief and then dispose of him while you're at full strength.

GOLD DIVISION, ROUND 2: ~1,000 XP, ~1,250 SP

Enemy	Style	Health	Chi
Sung Bo	Monkey's Paw	500	500
Sung Bu	Twin Swords	500	500
Sung Sui	Dire Flame, Spear	500	500

After defeating the Sung brothers, you have another opportunity to squeeze an extra 200 SP from Qui with conversation skills (60 XP). Make sure you're fully healed and save your game before your next round, known as the Imperial Engagement. This battle is one of the most difficult of all; you must survive a severe test of endurance and defeat all the strongest champions you've faced before in a single battle, with a couple of demons thrown in for good measure.

The one saving grace you have in this battle is that the enemies don't appear all at once; instead, they are let into the arena at ten second intervals, in the order shown on the battle

table below. You should be able to defeat the ogre and Hapless Han without using Chi or Focus before the next opponents enter. A toad demon appears next. Use a weapon to finish it quickly with repeated combos from the rear. The final group of enemies requires a much more careful

The Imperial Engagement is a supreme test of endurance, skill, and tactics.

strategy. Instead of finishing off Iron Soldier, use your remaining resources to eliminate the elephant demon. Then use Spirit Thief on Sung Sui to replenish yourself and at the same time deplete his capacity to use magic. Finish the battle by dealing with the remaining Sung brothers the same way you did in Round 2.

GOLD DIVISION, ROUND 3: ~1,300 XP, ~1,500 SP

Enemy	Style	Health	Chi
Ogre	Ogre	250	250
Hapless Han	Legendary Strike	250	250
Toad Demon	Toad Demon	687	687
Iron Soldier	Leaping Tiger	687	687
Elephant Demon	Elephant Demon	687	687
Sung Bo	Monkey Paw	500	500
Sung Bo	Twin Swords	500	500
Sung Sui	Dire Flame, Spear	500	500

To win the Gold Division championship, there is one more combatant you must test yourself against: the Ravager. While he is much stronger than any other fighter you've seen in the arena, this battle appears much easier than the Imperial Engagement since you only have to worry

The Ravager wields twin axes of deadly keenness.

about a single enemy. However, Ravager has a hidden supernatural side, and Magic, Weapon, and Support styles are ineffective. A good strategy is to whittle him down as much as possible with your best Martial style, making sparse use of Focus to avoid his blades. Save your Chi for the final stretch and use Toad Demon form to stand toe-to-toe with the Imperial Champion. The Ravager is fond of using area attacks; the toad demon's bulk makes this Technique useless.

GOLD DIVISION, CHAMPIONSHIP ROUND: ~1,600 XP, ~2,000 SP

Enemy	Style	Health	Chi
Ravager	Tang's Vengeance	1,750	1,750

As the Ravager falls in defeat, his mask slips off to reveal his true identity: Raging Ox, the Black Whirlwind's lost brother. You've heard tales that Raging Ox was slain, but through foul arts Kai Lan has kept him chained to this world. The Black Whirlwind arrives to land the final blow on the twisted form of his former brother, after which you receive the Ravager's powerful weapon style, **Tang's Vengeance**.

To walk away with the title, you must put down a final challenge by Kai Lan himself.

Just when you thought your victory was complete, Kai Lan uses his influence to demand one last contest with you. You can opt to fight this battle yourself or let the Black Whirlwind stand in for you. Your muscle-bound follower performs well here, and we recommend using him. (However, you should also base your choice on which players you're used to fighting with and the difficulty setting.) The Black Whirlwind's axes have tremendous range, power, and speed which more than make up for his lack of Focus mode. In addition, he has enough health to absorb extreme amounts of punishment. On the other hand, so does Kai Lan. Stay close to the Serpent and keep interrupting his attacks with combo after combo.

When Kai Lan reaches zero health, he pulls a new trick out of his sleeve with Channeling style. He vanishes and causes two horse demons to appear in his place. The Black Whirlwind's axes once again are ideal and can carve the fiends to

shreds, but since there are two of them be careful you aren't surrounded. When the horse demons are defeated, Kai Lan re-appears, this time with twice as much Health and Chi as he had at the start. Continue laying into him with a constant sweep of fast axe attacks; even though you have a lot of Health, monitor it closely as the match concludes, and use Chi Heal whenever needed.

KAI LAN THE SERPENT BATTLE: ~1,800 XP, ~2,500 SP

Enemy	Style	Health	Chi
Kai Lan the Serpent	Viper, Sword, Ice Shard, Dire Flame, Channeling	1,250 (2,500)	1,250 (2,500)
Horse Demon x2	Horse Demon	1,250	1,250

Ransack Kai Lan's office for some valuable treasure.

After the ultimate battle is concluded, Qui the Promoter offers his deepest congratulations and gives you a **Superior Warrior Gem** (Body +6). Sweet Poison Lyn approaches next with a peace offering from the Guild; you can extort 200 SP from her with conversation skills (60 XP). As a final reward, search Kai Lan's office at the back of the arena. Behind his desks are four chests; three are trapped, but the fourth chest contains the unique gem **Absolute Dedication** (more XP and no power-ups from human enemies) and a Technique called **Scales of the Serpent** (Health +7, Intimidation +1).

If you make it through the entire arena undefeated, Sweet Poison Lyn will give you a special reward, the **Perfected Warrior Technique** (Health +15, Focus +150).

THE INQUISITORS

A DELICATE SITUATION

After you make arrangements with Scholar Dongow, the Lotus Inquisitor meets you at the base camp. He asks you to find a way to stop Minister Sheng (the inept governor of Tien's Landing) from delivering his official report on the Lotus Assassins' activities to Judge Fang. How you accomplish this is up to you, and you have several options to choose from. The Inquisitor, however, is judging you on your subtlety and style. If either Minister Sheng or Judge Fang is killed, you will not be invited to join the Lotus Assassins even though you've technically succeeded in your mission.

Would you want us to kill Fang and his guards too? Slaughter everyone? Not only does it seem excessive, but I don't think that's how Inquisitors operate.

For suggestions on how to proceed, talk the matter over with your Followers. Four possible plans are discussed:

Choice 1 Dawn Star has heard rumors that Judge Fang is one of the most corrupt officials in the government. She thinks you could easily find evidence that could be used as leverage to orchestrate his downfall.

Choice 2 Henpecked Hou recommends disgracing Minister Sheng by replacing his honor gift to Judge Fang with turtle eggs (a blatantly crude gesture, in terms of court etiquette). The wily chef even has a jar of the offensive ova right there in his pack.

Choice 3 The Black Whirlwind wonders why you don't simply kill Minister Sheng. Then again, when all you have is a pair of axes, everything looks like a tree.

Choice 4 Sagacious Zu also favors a blunt approach, but at least has the honor to target Judge Fang, who deserves death, instead of the helpless Minister of Harmony. If you have the Lotus Executioner's Seal, then Sagacious Zu isn't around to suggest this course of action. It nevertheless remains an option.

Only the first two choices lead to an invitation from the Lotus Inquisitor. If either of the remaining choices still seems like a good idea, you can still get recruited by the Lotus Executioner in the Imperial Arena, where brute strength is the only qualification. The details of each choice are covered under the next four headings below:

TIP

Before you embark on this quest, equip gems that enhance your conversation skills (such as the Bronze Tongue). To accomplish your goals with subtlety, you'll need to be at your most persuasive.

DISGRACE JUDGE FANG

Forget it! I won't go into details about what Fang did to the last guard he caught taking bribes, but restraints, starving dogs, and gravy on certain parts of the body were involved.

Find Judge Fang at the arena. He spends most of his time on a catwalk suspended above the ring so he can have a clear view of each blow striking home. His guards won't let you approach him unless you have a good reason, so you need to find one.

The key lies with Gentle Breezes, Fang's favorite courtesan. You can find her near the judge's catwalk. Tell her you want her to help you get Judge Fang thrown out of office. She's reluctant, but you can persuade her to conspire with you using conversation skills. It may seem cruel, but angry threats (using Intimidation) work best for this, and this course of action at least ensures that nobody gets hurt.

[Success] Don't... don't hurt me. Fang's already hurt me too many times and I won't let him hurt me again!

After you convince Gentle Breezes to help, she lures Judge Fang away to his private room and, during their tryst, steals his Imperial ring. She then returns and gives you **Judge Fang's Ring**. Show the ring to Fang's guards, who now let you pass.

Here's the ring. Fang will do anything to keep people from finding out he lost it to a whore... even if it means resigning his post.

Judge Fang is angered to be interrupted during a match, but his rage quickly turns to acceptance when you reveal the ring. Realizing that the Lotus Assassins want him out of the way, and happy to have escaped with his life, he departs. Take

Are you proud of yourself? Bowing and scraping at the feet of your Lotus Assassin masters? Helping them to bring me down?

Fang's Resignation to the base camp and show it to the Lotus Inquisitor to complete your mission.

DISGRACE MINISTER SHENG

Henpecked Hou gives you the **Turtle Eggs** during your conversation in the base camp. Take them to the Ministry Hostel, which is next to the Theatre Pavilion on the Golden Way. Minister Sheng is extremely anxious to curry Judge Fang's favor

with the expensive honor gift he brought. Use Sheng's anxiety to your advantage and use Charm or Intuition to persuade him to let you guard the honor gift overnight (30 XP).

The next morning, Judge Fang arrives to receive his honor gift. The sight of the turtle eggs makes him furious. Poor Minister Sheng, utterly devastated, cringes in despair as Judge Fang boils over with rage and condemns the minister to a life sentence in the provinces. Judge Fang then storms out, having forgotten all about the minister's report. Minister Sheng is ruined, but you accomplished your mission with tact; the Lotus Inquisitor is sure to be impressed (750 XP, 800 SP).

NOTE

*While you're in the Ministry Hostel, search the corners for a chest. It contains the **Configuration of the Horse**, a formula that you can use later on at Lord Lao's Furnace.*

KILL MINISTER SHENG

The only person who will be happy with the outcome of this plan is the Black Whirlwind, who suggested it. Go to the Ministry Hostel and tell Sheng you've come to kill him. The minister has never been in a fight in his life, and he can do little but cower in terror

as his guards rush in to protect him. Unarmed and untrained, the guards pose almost no threat. After everyone's dead (750 XP), return to the Lotus Inquisitor to learn that you failed his test.

MINISTER SHENG BATTLE: ~242 XP, ~180 SP			
Enemy	Style	Health	Chi
Guard x2	Basic	200	200

KILL JUDGE FANG

Judge Fang is so horribly cruel and depraved that you can kill him with a clean conscience, but you won't impress the Lotus Inquisitor this way. If you still want to go through with it, talk to Gentle Breezes and tell her you want to kill Fang. As in Choice 1, you must use conversation skills to convince her to betray the judge.

After you've made your case to Gentle Breezes, tell her you want to kill the judge. She lures him into the creature pens below the arena, where you can ambush him. Judge Fang won't give up without a fight. He uses White Demon, which can inflict serious damage, and calls on his two

Judge Fang, lured by uncontrollable depravity, walks right into your trap.

guards for backup. Use Harmonic Combos to eliminate the guards quickly, then strike down Judge Fang with Magic attacks. After the judge is dead (750 XP), head back to base camp to hear a stern lecture from the Lotus Inquisitor.

JUDGE FANG BATTLE: ~532 XP, ~500 SP			
Enemy	Style	Health	Chi
Judge Fang	White Demon	375	375
Fang Guard x2	Spear	250	250

TIP

During your talk with Gentle Breezes after the battle, you can make a strong Closed Fist gesture by deciding to kill her, too.

THE INQUISITOR'S APPROVAL

If you disgraced either Minister Sheng or Judge Fang, the Lotus Inquisitor meets you at the base camp to express his admiration for your fine work. He gives you the **Lotus Inquisitor's Seal**, which you can use to open the secret door in the Necropolis that leads to the Lotus Assassin fortress (1,850 XP).

I have been waiting for you to return. My sources tell me the problem of Minister Sheng and his report to Judge Fang is... no longer a problem.

INFILTRATE THE LOTUS ASSASSIN FORTRESS

THE NECROPOLIS

Ghosts have been rising up everywhere in the Empire, I've heard. So many have come up in the Necropolis that it just isn't safe anymore.

Bid farewell to the Imperial City for awhile and head southwest from the Golden Way to enter the Necropolis. Be prepared for frequent battles against lost spirits in this area by having your most potent Magic style at the ready. Ascend the stairs to the first intersection, where two lost spirits materialize in ambush. Blast them with Tempest or Stone Immortal, using Focus mode to give yourself time for extra attacks. Take a break from your onslaught to block any incoming fire from the enemy; evasive moves are of no avail against the lost spirit's homing shots.

NECROPOLIS BATTLE: ~290 XP, 0 SP

Enemy	Style	Health	Chi	
Lost Spirit x2	Lost Spirit	200	200	

Look for a red, yellow, and blue sign and follow the path beside it to enter an enclosed memorial dominated by a pair of colossal statues. A single lost spirit attacks you here. Disperse it quickly. Three exits lead from the memorial; take the one marked with a yellow and red sign to proceed.

WILD FLOWER

NECROPOLIS BATTLE: ~145 XP, 0 SP

Enemy	Style	Health	Chi	
Lost Spirit	Lost Spirit	200	200	

When you pass by the Tomb of the Masses, two more lost spirits manifest themselves. Deal with them as you have the others, then exit through the eastern archway. Keep a sharp eye out for headstones and scrollstands as you move between the tombs; check the map at the beginning of this chapter to see where everything's hidden.

NECROPOLIS BATTLE: ~290 XP, 0 SP				
Enemy	Style	Health	Chi	
Lost Spirit x2	Lost Spirit	200	200	

Cross the weedy courtyard, ignoring the ghosts that haunt the area unless you're on a Gravedigger's Ghost side quest. Find one more knot of lost spirits by entering the round chamber with a blue sign hung in the entrance. This time there are three of them to contend with. Finish them from a distance with Magic styles, as you did the others.

NECROPOLIS BATTLE: ~435 XP, 0 SP				
Enemy	Style	Health	Chi	
Lost Spirit x3	Lost Spirit	200	200	

Sagacious Zu was a Lotus Assassin once, and he still seems to know his way around.

Return to the courtyard and follow the red signs to find the pagoda. As you approach, you catch a glimpse of Sagacious Zu sneaking into the pagoda ahead of you. Follow him inside to find a massive trap door, but no trace of your former Follower. Examine the blessing board nearby and insert the token you got from either the Inquisitors or the Executioners. This causes the trap door to swing open. Descend the stairs to enter the Lotus Assassin fortress.

THE WATCHER

When you step into the tunnel leading to the fortress, the Watcher confronts you. Hidden behind mask and hood, he nonetheless has keen senses and maintains a vigil over the fortress's entrance. Word has already reached the Assassins that a new recruit was arriving, so he was expecting you. He tells you to pass through the Hall of Induction to find Master Gang, who is in charge of putting new recruits through basic training.

Among the Lotus Assassins, hazing takes on a murderous import.

Before doing as you were told, retrace your path to find a pile of bones by door to the Necropolis (120 SP). Then enter the fortress itself and descend the majestic staircase to meet four Lotus acolytes. They converge on you like a gang of territorial predators. After setting the mood with a few taunts, one of them (Jin Tao) attacks while the other three stand back and watch. For Jin Tao, attacking you is suicidal. While your Follower keeps the acolyte busy, stand back and hurl Magic attacks into the fray.

LOTUS ACOLYTE JIN TAO BATTLE: ~152 XP, ~150 SP				
Enemy	Style	Health	Chi	
Lotus Acolyte Jin Tao	Basic	250	250	

With Jin Tao defeated, the other acolytes sulk away, promising you that they will get revenge. Sagacious Zu appears from out of nowhere with a few words of encouragement and warning, then just as abruptly he disappears. If you follow the Closed Fist, locate Merchant Kia Jong up ahead and buy the **Gem of Purpose** (Body +2, Spirit +2, Mind +2, Closed Fist only); then look for a ceramic urn nearby that holds 263 SP.

MEET MASTER GANG

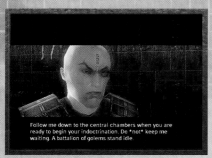

Follow me down to the central chambers when you are ready to begin your indoctrination. Do *not* keep me waiting. A battalion of golems stand idle.

At the Hall of Induction's far end, Master Gang gives you a cold reception. Follow him through the red door and down the stairs to the central hall. On arriving, you're just in time to see a terrified slave not quite manage to escape from an attacking ghost.

Following Master Gang's orders, go through the east door to disperse the ghosts. Target the spirit that uses Ice Shard and eliminate that one first, then deal with the others. Afterward, smash the jar by the south door for 37 SP and

The old scorpion had one of his followers shatter a spirit shard during training. There are ghosts everywhere! I've lost eight slaves and three acolytes to them.

return to Master Gang to report your accomplishment.

GHOST BATTLE: ~580 XP, 0 SP

Enemy	Style	Health	Chi
Ghost x3	Spear	200	200
Ghost	Ice Shard	200	200

You... you live. And the ghosts are gone? Well, I did not expect this. It would seem that I have a competent acolyte for once. Interesting.

Impressed with your battle prowess, Master Gang decides to make you his protégé. He gives you two main tasks to perform, both of which must be completed to gain access to the inner sanctum of the fortress. The first task is to kill Gang's superior, Master Shin. For your second task, you must harvest a soul from the tunnels below the fortress and use it to create a spirit shard, a mystical power source used to animate golems.

NOTE

The Lotus Assassins' archives are kept in a cloister off the central hall where Master Gang waits. Stop by to browse the literature and to find the Configuration of the Rabbit, which is used in Lord Lao's Furnace.

SLAYING MASTER SHIN

PROVE YOUR METTLE

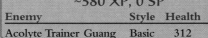

Before taking up these tasks for Master Gang, talk to Acolyte Trainer Guang in the central hall. Before you can buy any of her Techniques, you must defeat her in a non-lethal sparring match. Afterward you can look at her inventory. Those following the Closed Fist should buy the **Gem of Mastery** (Body +3, Mind +3, Spirit +3, Closed Fist only). The **Eye of Inner Darkness** (Chi +15, Focus +5) is also a great buy, whatever your philosophy.

ACOLYTE TRAINER GUANG BATTLE: ~580 XP, 0 SP

Enemy	Style	Health	Chi
Acolyte Trainer Guang	Basic	312	312

After defeating the acolyte trainer, you are promoted to her job. Master Shin's attendants, gathered in the central hall, resent your rapid rise and eagerly jump at the chance to take you down a peg. Talk to them to begin a duel with the weakest of their group, Attendant Kitan. Stay clear of Kitan's poisonous Viper style and batter her from long range with Magic.

ATTENDANT KITAN BATTLE: ~151 XP, ~150 SP

Enemy	Style	Health	Chi
Attendant Kitan	Viper	200	200

Return to the central hall and speak with the group of attendants again. Another of their group, Attendant Kai Feng, challenges you with the intent of taking revenge for Attendant Kitan. This battle is exactly the same as the last, except Kitan has almost twice as much health. A little extra perseverance on your part is all that's needed to win.

ATTENDANT KAI FENG BATTLE: ~225 XP, ~215 SP

Enemy	Style	Health	Chi
Attendant Kai Feng	Viper	375	375

But Kai Feng was a full Assassin. How could he have fallen?

The attendants fight to the death in defense of Master Shin's honor.

After the battle, the remaining two attendants appear and reveal that Kai Feng was no mere attendant, but actually a full-fledged Lotus Assassin. They depart in a rage. Follow them back to the central hall, where they and two acolytes challenge you for the honor of their master, whom you have insulted by killing his attendants. During this battle, use area attacks to give yourself room while you take down the attendants one by one. The remaining acolytes are too unskilled to pose a threat after that.

ATTENDANT BATTLE: ~470 XP, ~415 SP

Enemy	Style	Health	Chi
Attendant Cohong	Viper	200	200
Attendant Teng	Viper	200	200
Lotus Acolyte x2	Basic	62	62

THE GOLEM PRESS

Be careful, fool! One distraction and I could have been crushed!

After dealing with the attendants, exit the central hall by the west door to have a look at the golem press. As you enter, a mishap occurs and a Lotus Assassin is nearly killed when an inert golem falls mere inches from him. Head into the room and look for a trapped chest next to a scrollstand. Check them out, then climb the nearby scaffold and talk to Lotus Acolyte Shi for a lesson on how to operate the golem press and a warning about frequent accidents.

Take a moment to tinker with the golem press; this helps you set up an easy way to get rid of Master Gang later on. Examine the golem press to pour raw materials into the mold, then use the crane operation lever to retrieve the golem.

GOLEM PRESS

Move the crane right, positioning it over the walkway below. Now the trap is laid, and you can return to the central hall.

REMOVE THE PRESS OPERATOR

You may as well try and drop one of the golems on him. He would never be so distracted as to enter the press. We are Lotus *Assassins,* after all.

Now that you've seen the golem press in action, talk to Master Gang and suggest using the press as a means of eliminating Master Shin. Master Shin is far too wary to be lured back into the golem press, so you must kill him yourself and then set up the scene so that it looks like an "accident." This is no easy job, and a great deal of preparation is required.

I see. The ways of the order are mysterious and brutal. If an... opening is created away from witnesses, all of us under him will benefit. I understand.

First, go back to the golem press room and talk to Shi. When you insinuate that you're planning to take down Master Shin, Shi takes the hint and leaves the golem press (200 XP).

Assassins are loyal to strength. If they sense that a master is weakening, they run for cover.

CLEAR THE HALL OF INDUCTION

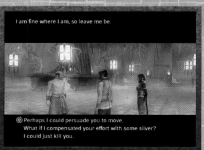

I am fine where I am, so leave me be.

Perhaps I could persuade you to move.
What if I compensated your effort with some silver?
I could just kill you.

Continue your preparations by clearing all the assassins out of the Hall of Induction, where you will eventually ambush Master Shin. First, talk to Merchant Kia Jong. There are two ways to convince him to move his shop into the central hall:

Choice 1 Use conversation skills to persuade Kia Jong to move somewhere else. If you have the Black Whirlwind, Henpecked Hou, or Silk Fox with you, they step up and make the case if your attempt at persuasion fails (260 XP).

Choice 2 Pay Kia Jong 1,000 SP for the inconvenience (200 XP).

Next, look for Mold Masters Gi and Soto on the Hall of Induction's west side. Again, there are two ways to get them to vacate the Hall of Induction:

Lotus Assassins aren't known for backing down from a challenge.

We are not acolytes of your petty master. You have no authority over us. Unless you are challenging two full Lotus Assassins to combat, you should step back.

Choice 1  The simplest way to get rid of the mold masters is to kill them; it's easy to trigger a fight by talking to them and choosing the most aggressive replies. As with many Assassins, they use the Viper style. Despite their arrogant boasts, they don't fare any better against you than the other Assassins you've faced.

MOLD MASTER BATTLE: ~380 XP, ~340 SP

Enemy	Style	Health	Chi
Mold Master Gi	Viper	312	312
Mold Master Soto	Viper	312	312

[There is an opening in the side that looks like it accepts clay containers of some kind. Other than that, it seems quite simple.]

◉ [Insert Phoenix Oil container.]
[Make a clay golem.]
[Leave the machine.]

Create a maintenance crisis by pouring Phoenix Oil into the golem press.

Choice 2 If you want to avoid showing the Closed Fist, there is an alternative. You can avoid a cold-blooded battle by talking to the mold masters and asking them about the golem press. They mention a volatile substance called Phoenix Oil that can sometimes cause the machinery to break down. Locate Merchant Kia Jong (he's in the central hall if you got him to move already) and ask him for the **Phoenix Oil**. Take this to the golem press room and insert it into the machinery (200 XP).

Golems are immune to Magic, Martial, and Support styles, so either unsheathe a weapon or transform into a toad demon or horse demon to damage them. If you obtained Mirabelle from the Outlander, this is the ideal style to use. If you retreat up the scaffold, the golems crowd together in an attempt to pursue you. This makes it easier for you to hit several of them with each of your attacks.

GOLEM PRESS BATTLE: ~888 XP, ~780 SP

Enemy	Style	Health	Chi
Clay Golem x3	Clay Golem	375	375

After defeating the golems, return to the Hall of Induction and break the news of the broken press to the mold masters. They immediately depart to try to repair the damage you caused.

To rid the Induction Hall of its last witnesses, locate the Lotus Assassin Sorcerer in the southeast corner. He attempts to show off his demon-summoning skills, but his spell goes awry and causes two acolytes to become wreathed in flame. The poor victims, berserk with pain and fury, must now be killed. Avoid their wreath of flames by attacking from a safe distance with Magic styles.

Uhkir sitakawuwir wosair yoof, praawun!

LOTUS ACOLYTE BATTLE: ~242 XP, ~190 SP

Enemy	Style	Health	Chi
Lotus Acolyte x2	Basic	200	200

When the acolytes are put out of their misery, the sorcerer flees in shame. With the Hall of Induction now empty, the only task remaining is to lure Master Shin out into the open.

Stop the Slave Shipment

> ### TIP
> When you encounter Slave Driver Rong, you can simplify matters greatly by using conversation skills. Rong isn't easily persuaded, however, so if you plan to sway her, equip gems that enhance your Charm, Intimidation, or Intuition before venturing onward.

These prisoners must be delivered to the fortress to be inspected by Master Shin. I will not allow you to make me late.

Leave the Lotus Assassin fortress and return to the Necropolis. Exit the pagoda and look for the arriving slave shipment by the unfinished bridge, led by Slave Driver Rong. There are several ways this confrontation can end:

Choice 1 Those following the Open Palm can display compassion by setting the captured slaves free without shedding one drop of blood. Lie to Rong for a chance to persuade her into turning the shipment over to you. If this works, you can then tell the slaves the good news and watch in satisfaction as they escape their terrible fate (400 XP).

Choice 2 If your argument doesn't sway Rong, she attacks. The best way to deal with her Thousand Cuts style is with ranged Magic attacks; the extra reach provided by any of your Weapon styles provides a similar advantage if you prefer to battle in closer quarters. After the slave drivers are dead, you can then set their captives free (600 XP).

Slave Driver Battle: ~349 XP, ~300 SP

Enemy	Style	Health	Chi	
Slave Driver Rong	Thousand Cuts	375	375	
Slave Driver	Basic	200	200	

Choice 3 You can convince Rong to kill the slaves for you (360 XP), providing by far the shortest and easiest solution to the problem.

Choice 4 One way to ensure things are done right is to do it yourself. First, kill the slave drivers as in Choice 1. Then turn on the slaves. They are desperate for freedom and won't give up without a struggle. Untrained and outmatched, they have no hope of defeating you; complete butchery is the final result (300 XP).

Slave Battle: ~380 XP, ~290 SP

Enemy	Style	Health	Chi	
Slave x5	Basic	62	62	

The Assassination

You... you are Gang's new acolyte. I see what is happening here. You think to promote your master by threatening me. You are bold, but foolish.

With the slave shipment interrupted, return to the pagoda and examine the Blessing Board to return to the Lotus Assassin fortress. If you've completed all the tasks outlined above, Master Shin appears as you cross the Hall of Induction. He realizes what Master Gang is planning and doesn't hesitate to attack. If you didn't defeat Shin's four attendants earlier, they join in the battle, making things much more difficult. Master Shin should be your first target, whether he's alone or not. When he's lost half of his Health, two nearby golems animate and join the fracas. Because they move so slowly, you can safely ignore them until all other threats have been disposed of.

Master Shin Battle: ~804 XP, ~658 SP

Enemy	Style	Health	Chi	
Master Shin	Tempest, Storm Dragon, Legendary Strike	875	875	
Golem x2	Clay Golem	100	10	

How unfortunate. I will make certain he is dead, but not from too close. I don't want to share his tragically foolish fate.

Because you have eliminated all his servants and allies, there is no one to mourn Master Shin.

After the battle, the scene shifts to the golem press, where you planned for Master Shin's body to be found. Master Gang verifies that Shin is dead. If you loaded up the crane with a golem earlier and positioned it over the walkway, step up to the crane control lever and yank it as Master Gang walks beneath. The golem falls, crushing Gang to a pulp (300 XP). Killing Gang in this way is optional, but if you don't get rid of him now, you'll have to face him in battle later.

CREATE A SPIRIT SHARD

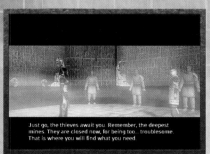

Just go, the thieves await you. Remember, the deepest mines. They are closed now, for being too... troublesome. That is where you will find what you need.

Whether you've slain Gang or not, you must still complete his second task: creating a spirit shard. Enter the room where you fought the ghosts earlier for a surprise meeting with Sagacious Zu. He explains that the souls used to make spirit shards are harvested from tortured slaves, but if you were to use the spirit of a chaotic being, you could sabotage the golem factory. Your enigmatic Follower then departs once more.

Head through the south door to the Soul Extractor room. Tell Lotus Acolyte Go Rin that you've come to make a spirit shard; she offers some advice and gives you permission to use the equipment. The entire room is actually an elevator that allows you to access three sub-floors: the prison, the upper mines, and the lower mines.

It is mounted on an elevator that reaches deep into the Necropolis. Until recently we excavated bodies to extract spirits that lingered near their graves.

Make the prison floor your first destination; you can release the slaves to throw a further kink into the Assassins' plans. To unlock the cell door, you must defeat the Assassin guarding it. He uses the rare Iron Palm style, which is capable of fast, powerful strikes. Use your full arsenal of skills, including Focus mode and Chi Strikes, to slay him quickly.

[There are three sub-surface levels accessible. Select the floor you wish to visit.]

◎ [Prison level.]
[Near-surface mine level.]
[Abandoned deep-level mine.]

PRISON BATTLE: ~228 XP, ~195 SP				
Enemy	Style	Health	Chi	
Guard	Iron Palm	375	375	

Then you can open the prison door and talk to the slaves. They ask if the escape route is safe, leading to different outcomes:

Thank you again for your help. We await your signal that it is safe to make our way to the mine. It is our only hope.

Unless you clear a safe path out of the fortress, most released prisoners won't make it.

Choice 1  Return to the Soul Extractor and tell Go Rin you've set the slaves free. Obviously, she can't let you get away with this and the fight begins. Without any real combat skills, Go Rin is hardly a challenge. After defeating her, return to the prison and tell the slaves the coast is clear (500 XP).

PRISON BATTLE: ~152 XP, ~125 SP			
Enemy	Style	Health	Chi
Lotus Acolyte Go Rin	Basic	250	250

Choice 2 Tell the slaves that if they want freedom, they'll have to fight for it. They escape into the Soul Extractor room, where all but one of them are slain by Go Rin (who is also killed). The lone survivor departs after stopping to take back all the nice things he said about you when you opened the prison door (100 XP).

Choice 3 If you tell Go Rin that the slaves escaped after promising to help them, she enters the prison and kills them all; this choice leads to no reward at all.

Use the elevator controls to access the upper mine level next. Enter the mine and locate a skeleton, which yields a random gem and a jar containing a **Iron Skin Gem** (Body +3, no damage from traps). Return to the elevator controls and descend to the deepest mine level.

OBTAIN ZENG SAI'S SOUL

The mighty ghost of Zeng Sai appears when you enter the deep mine chamber. In life, he was a leader of the Horselords from the Plain of Barren Hope. Death has corrupted his already twisted soul into an apparition of ghastly strength. There are several ways to take him down quickly. With your Follower in

Attack mode, you can hang back and use Stone Immortal or Tempest while Zeng Sai is kept occupied. If the ghost switches to Ice Shard, evade and get behind him to attack while he recovers.

Zeng Sai feels you... feels the pain again. So close. So close to perfect chaos, and you ended it all!

ZENG SAI BATTLE: ~501 XP, 0 SP			
Enemy	Style	Health	Chi
Zeng Sai	Twin Hammers, Ice Shard	675	675

After you defeat the ghost, Sagacious Zu makes another appearance. Search the coffins in back of the mine after he's gone to claim Zeng Sai's body and place it in the Soul Extractor. The Horselord's chaotic spirit causes the machinery to go haywire; if you haven't killed Go Rin already, she attacks you now. Then take the **Golem Spirit Shard** and return the elevator to the top floor.

GRAND INQUISITOR JIA AND ESCAPE

SAGACIOUS ZU RETURNS

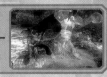

There you are. Remember me? I "welcomed" you in the hall when you first arrived. Well, I said I wasn't through with you. I've got numbers on my side, now.

As you return to the central hall, the three Lotus Acolytes you met when you first arrived show up to make good on the threats they made. Evade and use area attacks to avoid being surrounded, and take out the acolytes one by one. Take advantage of the many shrines here, and make liberal use of Chi and Focus to get the job done.

LOTUS ACOLYTE BATTLE: ~494 XP, ~407 SP			
Enemy	Style	Health	Chi
Lotus Acolyte	Spear	250	250
Lotus Acolyte	Basic	250	250
Lotus Acolyte	Basic	312	312

When you enter the central hall, Sagacious Zu appears yet again. This time, he reveals much of his secret past, but he may still hold some things back if you didn't talk to him frequently back in Chapters One and Two. The Appendix has full details on Sagacious Zu's personal demons if you want to know more.

It wasn't always like this. Fear used to be the primary tactic. Destroy the family of one to ensure the loyalty of all. It caused chaos, uprisings. Close allies turning on each other.

You have the spirit shard? Very good, acolyte; you are on the verge of being welcomed into the heart of the fortress. Have you completed all other business?

> **NOTE**
>
> *If you killed Master Gang earlier in the golem press room, he obviously won't be present in any of the following parts of your quest. His absence makes the next battle you must fight much easier but otherwise has no other effects.*

And you... hidden in plain sight, like your master. You caught us unsuspecting, but not unprepared. Who are you, to think you could enter our lair so easily?

Grand Inquisitor Jia is finally unmasked.

Enter the Ritual Chamber north of the central hall. If Master Gang is still alive, talk to him and show the spirit shard to gain access. When the corrupt spirit shard you made is inserted into the massive Jade Golem, chaos ensues as the corruption spreads and other golems around the fortress go on a rampage, slaying Lotus Assassins left and right. Grand Inquisitor Jia arrives to find out what went wrong, and quickly figures it out after recognizing your Dragon Amulet. She reveals that the Assassins were using the amulet's third piece (which the Water Dragon told you of back in Tien's Landing) as the bait for whoever was opposing them.

Jia then leaves, but you must defeat her guardians before you can begin pursuit. Some of the golems remain under her command, and she orders two of them to attack you. Executioner Zogu and Master Gang (if he's still alive) join the battle as well. Gang is the deadliest of the four enemies, so concentrate on eliminating him first. The Black Whirlwind is a good Follower to have with you here, as he can hold off the Jade Golems for a while so you can deal with the master Assassin. Save all your Focus for weapon attacks against Jade Golems; Horse Demon's fireball attack is also effective if you have lots of Chi. Keep Executioner Zogu around so you can tap him for Chi with Spirit Thief.

RITUAL CHAMBER BATTLE: ~1,729 XP, ~1,100 SP

Enemy	Style	Health	Chi	
Jade Golem x2	Jade Golem	437	437	
Executioner Zogu	Viper	200	200	
Master Gang	Viper, Twin Axes	678	678	

The incredible power of the **Jade Golem** Transformation style is yours after the battle. Not only does it provide a golem's immunity to Magic, Martial, and Support styles, but its mighty axes deal out enormous damage. Make a priority of spending style points on Jade Golem the next time you gain a level.

> ## NOTE
> *Be sure to search the Ritual Chamber carefully. If you've read all of the literature in the Lotus Assassin fortress, this final document bestows a new Technique: Legacy of Death's Hand (Chi +10) (1,000 XP). On the other side of the chamber, a chest contains 1,000 SP and a random gem.*

DEFEAT INQUISITOR JIA

> You are strong, but you do not know real power. *Our* strength lies in preparation.

Make sure you're at full strength before continuing north from the Ritual Chamber. In the next hall, Grand Inquisitor Jia finally confronts you in battle. She is a smart and tough opponent who can slay you quickly if you find yourself on the sharp end of her sword. Fortunately, she is human, making her vulnerable to every style in your arsenal. There are several viable strategies for defeating her. Jia occasionally activates a damage shield that can be brutal to anyone using melee attacks on her (especially Thousand Cuts). Keep an eye on your health when attacking her. If you get hurt just by touching her, jump back and use ranged attacks. Having a Follower in Attack mode gives you time to use ranged attacks while Jia is kept occupied, though this guarantees your Follower gets knocked out. The powerful Jade Golem style you just learned is also useful; get as close as you can before transforming, unleash a couple of attacks, then quickly switch to another style so you can escape her deadly sword. Slowing or paralyzing her first gives you time for extra attacks with this strategy.

GRAND INQUISITOR JIA BATTLE: ~720 XP, ~760 SP

Enemy	Style	Health	Chi	
Grand Inquisitor Jia	Tempest, Sword	1,250	1,250	

When Grand Inquisitor Jia is finally slain, you receive the **Gem of Storm's Rage** (Wind Shield damages enemies that touch you, Closed Fist only) and another gem of random type (1,000 XP). You can then retrieve the next piece of your **Dragon Amulet**. As you turn to leave, Death's Hand leaps out in ambush, but Sagacious Zu reveals himself one last time and, making the ultimate sacrifice, gives you the chance you need to escape.

ESCAPE THE IMPERIAL CITY

The chaos of the last battle has triggered a collapse, and the fortress begins to crumble to pieces. You're not out of danger yet! Return to the central hall, where a group of Lotus Assassins do their best to stop you. Most of these foes are weak; ignore the acolytes at first and go after the Assassin. The acolytes have very little Health and easily fall after taking one or two blows.

LOTUS ASSASSIN BATTLE: ~349 XP, ~300 SP

Enemy	Style	Health	Chi
Lotus Acolyte x3	Basic	50	10
Lotus Assassin	Basic	200	200

Another group of enemies assail you on the other side of the central hall. Deal with them in the same way, targeting the strongest foe (who uses Tempest style) first.

LOTUS ASSASSIN BATTLE: ~1,729 XP, ~1,100 SP

Enemy	Style	Health	Chi
Lotus Acolyte x2	Basic	50	10
Lotus Assassin	Basic	250	250
Lotus Assassin	Tempest	250	250

Climb up to the Hall of Induction to face more enemies. This time, three clay golems bar your passage; two attack at the north end of the hall, while the third (and weakest) puts up a feeble last resistance at the south end. Compared to the Jade Golems you faced earlier, these three are child's play. Unsheathe your weapon and destroy them, then climb the final stairs and exit the fortress.

The Lotus Assassin fortress is crumbling into ruin.

CLAY GOLEM BATTLE: ~254 XP, ~280 SP

Enemy	Style	Health	Chi
Clay Golem x2	Clay Golem	100	10
Clay Golem	Clay Golem	50	10

The exit tunnel opens into the back of the Unfinished Tomb in the Necropolis, where the Watcher (remember him?) and a large group of Assassins make a final stand. As none of these foes have any weapons, Jade Golem style is completely immune to all their attacks. Use this form to deal with the Watcher first. If you still have enough Chi, continue using the same style to mop up the remaining Assassins, starting with the one using Ice Shard. If not, area Support attacks and Focus can give you the time needed to even the odds.

UNFINISHED TOMB BATTLE: ~803 XP, ~691 SP

Enemy	Style	Health	Chi
Lotus Assassin x2	Thousand Cuts	200	200
Lotus Assassin	Ice Shard	150	150
The Watcher	Tempest	375	375

You've eliminated all the Assassins in this area (1,000 XP), but more battles remain before you can complete your escape, so use the Chi Shrines here to heal up before moving on. Two lost spirits, roused by the collapse of the fortress, attack as you approach the tomb door. With full Health and Chi, you should have no problem dispersing the apparitions.

The collapse of the Lotus Assassin fortress has stirred ghosts from their graves.

UNFINISHED TOMB BATTLE: ~290 XP, 0 SP

Enemy	Style	Health	Chi
Masked Spirit	Masked Spirit	200	200

When you exit the tomb, more undead shamble toward you. The two lost spirits are accompanied by a mummy, an enemy you're familiar with if you explored the Necropolis thoroughly. The lost spirits pose the greatest threat, so eliminate them first, using Focus mode to evade their Magic attacks. The mummy, unlike the incorporeal ghosts, is not immune to Weapon or Support styles, giving you more attack options. Beware the creature's diseased touch, which causes an affliction that damages you over time (similar to poisoning). Mummies are, thankfully, easy to defeat because they move very slowly.

UNFINISHED TOMB BATTLE: ~480 XP, ~167 SP

Enemy	Style	Health	Chi
Lost Spirit x2	Lost Spirit	200	200
Mummy	Mummy	312	312

Proceed through the Necropolis toward the Imperial City. Recurring lost spirit battles (described earlier) can still slow you down, so be ready for a spiritual ambush. A last mummy who hasn't appeared before stands at the final bit of road; without any back-up, he quickly crumbles under your assault.

MUMMY BATTLE: ~190 XP, ~163 SP

Enemy	Style	Health	Chi
Mummy	Mummy	312	312

As you exit the Necropolis, the scene shifts to your base camp, where you and your Followers discuss Sagacious Zu's sacrifice and the import of what you've learned from Grand Inquisitor Jia. Silk Fox remains adamant that her father, the Emperor, couldn't be behind such terrible evil. All are determined to voyage to the palace and find out.

This has been... troubling. We should return to the flyer as soon as possible so everyone can discuss what we have learned.

By the Water Dragon's mercy, they are enslaved until they die... and then trapped within the golems. I have seen the proof... but how can it be true?

After taking time to complete any loose ends left in the city, speak with Kang to board the Marvelous Dragonfly and wing your way to the floating Imperial Palace.

> **NOTE**
>
> *If you wish to take manual control of the trip to the Imperial Palace, learn more about the course hazards in "To the Palace" under the Marvelous Dragonfly Missions section of Kang's profile.*

SIDE QUESTS
THE OUTLANDER

A DUEL OF WITS

But, I will acknowledge that I am likely to disagree just because I know you are... lacking. We will need educated men to judge the merits of our arguments.

Arguments? What kind of contest are you looking for? Some sort of debate? Are you afraid to face me in battle?

Is this a five-minute argument, or the full half hour?

When you're exploring the Scholars' Garden, it's impossible to miss the Outlander. His full name is Sir Roderick Ponce von Fontlebottom the Magnificent Bastard, and he's taken center stage with his loud voice, extreme rudeness, and overwhelming arrogance. He's openly contemptuous of your people, whose culture he deems far inferior to his own. Approach him and accept his challenge of open debate in defense of the Empire's honor.

The debate consists of six rounds. In each, Roderick opens with an insulting criticism about the Empire. You then have a chance for rebuttal by choosing from several styles of counterargument. The winner is decided by a panel of five judges whose majority opinion decides the winner. Raised hands count as a vote for you. Each judge declares himself or herself to be completely impartial but confides to you the style of argument favored by his colleagues. All this information is summarized in the following table:

Are you implying that I am predisposed to be weak in certain areas? I can't accept that. Some of my fellows, however, are another story.

Talk to the judges before the debate to learn what kinds of arguments sway them the most.

PANEL OF JUDGES	
Name	Favored Argument Style
Minister of Culture	Sympathetic, Raging
Scholar Heng	Factual
Scholar Zou	Sympathetic, Dismissive, Factual
Scholar Cai	Mocking, Dismissive
Scholar Gu	Mocking, Sympathetic

The judges respond only to the type of argument they favor, and each time you use that argument type, they switch their opinion to further debate. The debate ends after all topics are done, or if there is ever a unanimous vote in your favor (1,000 XP). The next table shows how to do this in three rounds.

A show of hands decides the contest in your favor.

WINNING THE DEBATE

Round	Choose This Reply
1	Sympathetic
2	Dismissive
3	Factual

A DUEL OF WEAPONS

Sir Roderick concedes the debate, but his arrogance is undiminished. He declares that true honor can be won only in battle. Talk to him again when you're ready to accept the challenge. The duel takes place in the entrance to the Scholars' Garden. Sir Roderick wields Mirabelle, a blunderbuss of incredible power: one shot can knock off more than half your Health. Fortunately, the gun's rate of fire is very slow. As he raises the gun to his shoulder, enter Focus mode and dodge behind him as he fires. Once you're in close, it's all over. Use your fastest and strongest Martial or Weapon style to begin a chain of fast attacks that can prevent the Outlander from firing another shot.

DUEL WITH THE OUTLANDER: ~304 XP, ~250 SP

Enemy	Style	Health	Chi
Sir Roderick/ Outlander	Mirabelle	500	500

After you win the duel (2,100 XP), the Outlander graciously offers you a choice of items from among his spoils (per the dueling customs of the Mysterious East). The item you get depends on your reply. The reward you take is up to you, but Mirabelle is strongly recommended. It's the only Weapon style that works at long range, making it very effective against golems or even Death's Hand.

Mirabelle (Weapon Style): "I prefer something useful. Your weapon, for example."

Fitness for the Upright Gentleman (Body +3): "Physical strength is the quality I am interested in."

Duchess of Ulmsbottom's Rules of Engagement (Mind +3): "I am interested in improving my mind."

Manual of Trepanation (Spirit +3): "I am concerned with spiritual matters."

The Silver Tongue (Charm +6, Intimidation +6, Intuition +6): "Have you encountered any interesting gems?"

NOTE

The scholars and philosophers offer their thanks after you humble the Outlander. If you won the debate, won the combat, and successfully argued for a larger reward, the Minister of Culture also has a few odd (and hilarious) admissions to make. Another notable conversation takes place with Philosopher Shendao, who replies to your every question with a condescending insult. Earn 60 XP by using Intimidation to make the old man cower in silence.

THE PLAY'S THE THING

After Silk Fox has joined you, look for Incisive Chorus the Playwright on the Golden Way. His latest play is intended to tell, with honorable majesty, of how Sagacious Tien and his army founded the Jade Empire, but a rich nobleman with republican sentiments has paid the actors to insert satirical revisions. Incisive Chorus fears the embarrassment this would cause him, not to mention the risk of being targeted by the Lotus Assassins. He begs you to step into the role of Lady Fourteen Flowers (which requires a costuming miracle if you're male) and recite the original lines, and of course offers you the standard acting fee. After you agree to this, he gives you **Incisive Chorus's Original Script**.

Head for the Theatre Pavilion on the other end of the Golden Way. When Thespian Phong stops you, tell him you're the replacement actor he's been waiting for. He checks your script and then gives you the **Edited Script** to use instead. You now have a chance to check your lines and prepare for the scene. Stand next to the pavilion to compare the scripts. In the original version you have six lines; in the edited version two of them have been changed into disguised barbs against the Lotus Assassins, referring to them as "flower guardians." Look over the scripts carefully; during the play you must recite three of the six lines correctly or you won't get paid.

Talk to Thespian Phong when you're ready to begin. During each of your six cues, choose the line you want to speak from the list. After the play, you discover that your choice of dialog resulted in one of the following outcomes:

Tread the boards to take a dramatic pause from your quest.

Choice 1 (icon) Recite Incisive Chorus's original script as shown (1,000 XP). After the performance, Phong hands over your pay: 1,000 SP. Then head back to Incisive Chorus (who was too nervous to actually attend in person) and to receive an additional reward of 1,000 XP and 1,500 SP.

Scene 1: "White banners fly"

Scene 2: "Was it reached, or did the heavens guide it to him? Either way, the dusk was slipping into night."

Scene 3: "He stood at the edge of a vast plain, the ground covered in snow."

Scene 4: "Heaven's reach is wide. Weather is not the same in all places, Puzzle."

Scene 5: "He turned to the heavens themselves, as they had already turned to him."

Scene 6: "A shooting star traced the border of our lands."

Choice 2 (icon) Recite the subversive, edited script (1,000 XP). The lines used are the same as in Choice 1 except for the second and fourth (see below). Phong delivers your fee afterward (1,000 SP) and is then arrested by the Lotus Assassins as he leaves the pavilion. If you speak with Incisive Chorus, he angrily refuses to pay you anything.

Scene 2: "Tien's decision was made over the mid-day meal. The Flower Guardians would allow nothing else."

Scene 4: "The Flower Guardians may blossom but the warmth of spring can hide an icy heart."

Choice 3 All other outcomes carry diminished rewards. If three or more of the lines don't match any of the ones listed in either choice above, Thespian Phong and Incisive Chorus pay you nothing (100 XP). If you use only one of the two edited lines your alignment doesn't shift, Thespian Phong doesn't get arrested, and Incisive Chorus rewards you with only 500 XP and 500 SP.

MECHANIC HIN GOO

Mechanic Hin Goo appears at the base camp after you've met Silk Fox. He offers three challenging flying missions that earn you silver, XP, and the chance to buy some new Marvelous Dragonfly upgrades. Hin Goo has nothing for sale at first, but as you complete missions, his inventory expands as shown in the following table. Each upgrade costs 3,000 SP.

TIP
Save your game before doing the Escorting the Prefect mission. If you let his ship get destroyed, you can't repeat the mission, and you'll have to restore from a previous save.

Requirement	Upgrade
Complete "A Test for Hin Goo"	Tremor
Complete "Escorting the Prefect"	Reverse Tides
Complete "Rescue"	Dragon's Breath, Firestorm

A Test for Hin Goo

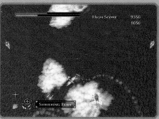

During the first half of this mission, dozens of small ships swoop in from the sides and circle around behind you, making them almost impossible to hit with your forward cannon. Shrieking Fury's homing missiles are the key to racking up kills. Stay near the center, between the arcs described by the incoming enemies. Hold your fire until many targets surround you; this way every missile you launch can score multiple strikes. Watch for Weapon orbs that appear during the densest waves.

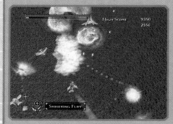

After a short lull around the halfway point, a steady stream of heavy planes come angling in from the flanks. Stay low and concentrate on the left or right formations; if you remain in the center, the targets will either collide with you or slip by unharmed. Use this time to replenish your Chi for the final stretch. Then two large gunships appear. Watch out for a small, sneaky black plane that tries to collide with you as you blast the gunships; it has a lot more Health than most planes its size. Finally, the sky empties of smaller crafts and three gunships slide in one after another. Slip between them as they fly past each other, guns blazing at all times.

When the mission is complete, Hin Goo uses the supplies you recovered to construct the **Tremor** upgrade, which damages all visible enemies at the cost of half your Chi. Depending on how many of the 162 enemies you destroy, you're awarded up to 1,000 XP and 4,500 SP maximum.

Escorting the Prefect

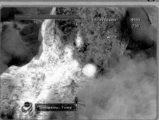

The second mission requires you to safely escort a government official's private aircraft through dangerous bandit country. Your escort keeps a steady position a little below center, giving you just barely enough room to strafe back and forth behind it and shoot down the enemy planes gliding in from the left and right. Fortunately, your weapons pass harmlessly through the prefect's ship. Stay behind your escort and keep scanning back and forth to blanket the sky with gunfire. Most incoming ships can be destroyed in one or two hits; save missiles for the slow armored ships that drift in occasionally. Grab the first Weapon orb you see, as wide shots allow you to coast easily through much of the onslaught. A pair of solo gunships heralds the end of the mission.

By striking down all 79 enemy ships, you can earn the maximum reward of 2,000 XP and 4,500 SP. Completing the mission causes a new upgrade, **Reverse Tides**, to appear in Hin Goo's inventory. This upgrade slows all enemy ships with an effect similar to Focus mode.

Rescue

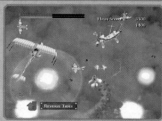

Hin Goo's final challenging mission is a frantic dogfight through extremely dangerous airspace. For most of the mission, a steady wave of mine-dropping dirigibles pass slowly in front of you. The shield provided by Radiant Aura is the best defense against the mines. They are well-armored and can take even more damage than a gunship. Try to destroy as many as you can, but don't get lured into the path of the smaller incoming planes if the dirigible starts to drift away from you—just let it go. The waves of smaller fighters become stronger and stronger as the mission proceeds; this forces you to pilot more and more defensively until near the end of the mission you should be concentrating primarily on evasion. Look for the safe spot in each formation of planes and stick to it. At the end of the mission, two gunships appear. This is a perfect time to use Tremor if you've managed to save enough Chi for it.

Rescue (cont'd)

A total of 78 enemies appear in this mission. The more you destroy, the closer you can get to the maximum reward of 2,500 XP and 4,500 SP. After you've survived the mission, Hin Goo offers two final upgrades for sale: **Firestorm** blankets the sky with sheets of flame, causing damage over time to all enemies; **Dragon's Wrath** unleashes a very powerful blast of energy that can destroy everything in its path.

> ### NOTE
> *Each of Hin Goo's missions becomes available directly from the main menu after you finish them for the first time.*

THE GAMBLER'S FAVOR

After you've gained access to the Lucky Cho's office in the arena, Gambler Daoshen has a favor to ask you. He needs you to deliver a 500 SP pay-off to Sweet Poison Lyn to expand his maximum bets from 5 SP to 25 SP without incurring the wrath of the Guild. There are several ways this can unravel:

Gambler Daoshen will never expand beyond his small-time operation unless he pays off the Guild.

Those on the Way of the Closed Fist can ruin Daoshen and keep all his winnings.

Choice 1 Tell Daoshen you're happy to help, and no cash advance is needed. Then talk to Sweet Poison Lyn and give her 500 SP. Return to Daoshen and, when he offers to pay you back, tell him to keep his money (500 XP). He gives you a **Superior Warrior Gem** (Body +6) in thanks.

Choice 2 Daoshen is reluctant to entrust you with the money beforehand, so use conversation skills to talk him into giving you his **Winnings Purse** (30 XP). Talk to Daoshen again and tell him you plan on keeping the money, earning an easy 500 SP.

Choice 3 Persuade Daoshen to give you his Winnings Purse as in Choice 2 (30 XP). Then take it Sweet Poison Lyn and tell her you won all of Daoshen's money on one roll of the dice, leading her to believe the gambler is taking high-stakes bets without Guild consent. In thanks for the bogus tip, Lyn knocks 10 percent off her prices for you. Gambler Daoshen is driven from the arena in ruin, while you get to keep his 500 SP.

Choice 4 If you pay Sweet Poison Lyn on Daoshen's behalf and then accept repayment, or if he gives you the money ahead of time and you deliver it without incident, there is no alignment shift and you still get the Superior Warrior Gem (500 XP).

> ### NOTE
> *If you want to try your luck with Daoshen, don't expect to make a vast profit. He plays a simple high-low dice game. Place a wager, then declare whether your roll will be higher or lower than Daoshen's; the house advantage comes from the fact that Daoshen wins all ties. If you guessed right, you win back double your bet. If you guessed wrong, you lose your bet. The only guaranteed winning strategy is to save your game before each bet and restore it if you lose. If, using this method, you sustain a 20-roll winning streak, the gods of fortune restore the balance by causing Daoshen to explode, and you can no longer use him.*

A BRONZED OPPORTUNITY

Before you can try for the Bronze Division championship, you must first meet with Lucky Cho and either accept or reject his offer to have your opponent, Crimson Khana, poisoned before the fight. The details of each choice are shown below; information on the battle itself is found in the Critical Path section of this chapter.

With the Guild preying on everyone, most fighters have learned to watch each other's backs.

We should warn the sword mistress. They're trying very hard to kill her.

Choice 1 🖐️🖐️ Refuse to dishonor yourself by cheating. Lucky Cho seems not to care, as long as you win. Return to the fight office and tell Crimson Khana of the Guild's vendetta against her. In exchange for your honesty, she teaches you her weapon style, **Crimson Tears** after you win the Bronze Championship.

Choice 2 🖐️ Refuse to poison Crimson Khana, but don't tell her of the Guild's plot. After the battle, speak with her to learn the basic double saber style, **Eyes of the Dragon**. Be warned, though: If you've angered her before your match with repeated insults and insolence, she'll storm off without teaching you anything.

Choice 3 ✊ Lucky Cho is happy to arrange the poisoning, but he expects you to pay for it by giving half your winnings to the Guild (330 XP). You can negotiate this down to only a quarter of your winnings with conversation skills (30 XP).

Soldier's Offer

This side quest is available only if you poisoned Crimson Khana before the Bronze Division title match. Iron Soldier, the Silver Division champion, suspects you were involved in foul play. Suspecting that if you cheated once, you'd be willing to cheat again, he asks you to meet him in the creature pens before your match against him.

Soldier's adamantly refused to face you, and until I hear otherwise from him, the fight seems stalled.

Iron Soldier is ready to retire from the arena, but he wants to strike it rich before he does and he has a plan to accomplish this. His partner, Pretty Li-Li, will place a huge bet on you. Then, Iron Soldier will throw the fight and leave the arena for good, taking Pretty Li-Li and their winnings with him. If you refuse his offer, the battle takes place normally, as described in the critical path. If you agree, however, then things start to get more complicated.

Here's the deal. I like you. The way you "dealt" with Khana showed me that you have the will to do what it takes to win. I know a way you and I can both win in this upcoming fight.

The blunt veteran knows you're taking a risk and offers to cut you in on a quarter of the money Li-Li wins. With the offer of silver and an effortless title match win, Iron Soldier knows you're getting the better end of the bargain and asks that you do a favor for him, kill an old rival of his,

When you find him, challenge him to a duel to the death. The old fool's too proud to decline, even though his skills have over the years.

General Stone Kao. Agree, then meet the general in the Market District by the city gate. After listening to his story, you can either fight him to death as you originally intended or you can decide to let General Stone Kao live (effectively quitting the sidequest). You can still spar with the general for fun if you take the latter course.

General Stone Kao is a war veteran who uses multiple styles. The main difficulty in this battle is the confining space. With your Follower in Attack mode, turn this into an advantage by ganging up on the general, trapping him in a corner. If he leaps away, follow closely and keep attacking until he drops permanently.

GENERAL STONE KAO BATTLE: ~228 XP, ~160 SP			
Enemy	Style	Health	Chi
General Stone Kao	Sword, White Demon	375	375

After you've slain Kao, return to the arena and talk to Qui to begin the match as usual. During the fight, Iron Soldier won't attack or block, making your victory a breeze. When the duel is over, Li-Li hands over one quarter of her winnings (1,000 SP), as promised.

BOUNTY HUNT

You can undertake two bounty hunting missions for Captain Sen, who is found by the city gate in the Market District. After you find both fugitives, a third mission involving Captain Sen himself completes the quest.

FADING MOON

You'll scream like a demon when Fading Moon puts the light inside of you.

The first and simplest bounty is for infor-mation on a wanted arsonist called Fading Moon. To find her, head for the door to the Unfinished Tomb in the Necropolis. Fading Moon is completely homicidal and attacks no matter what you say to deter her. She's an arsonist, so it's no surprise that she prefers Dire Flame. Assuming toad demon or horse demon form provides total immunity. Fading Moon's attacks are very swift; Support styles and Focus mode can slow her to a manageable speed. After defeating her, claim the **Gem of Pure Flame** (Mind +3, Spirit +3, Open Palm only), then return to Captain Sen to collect your reward (300 XP, 2,000 SP).

FADING MOON BATTLE: ~152 XP, ~150 SP

Enemy	Style	Health	Chi
Fading Moon	Dire Flame, Legendary Strike	250	250

CREATIVE YUKONG

According to Captain Sen, Creative Yukong is a master of disguise wanted for bilking silver from a rich nobleman. To find him, head for Scholars' Garden and locate Scholar Kongyu. If you question the scholar, he tries to discourage you with jargon-laden replies. Keep probing, however, and the scholar's facade eventually crumbles.

How did he get past me? He couldn't access a flyer. What *is* that man doing? Are you *certain* he's gone? Would a bit of silver jog your memory?

You'll need plenty of patience to help Yukong get through the city gate to freedom.

With his true identity revealed, Creative Yukong drops his charade. He claims that the money he's accused of stealing was an endowment from Lady Rento, but when her husband found out he flew into a rage and declared it a theft. With knowledge of Yukong's innocence, you now have several options:

Choice 1 Agree to help Yukong escape the city for free. Yukong, disguised as a mercenary, will sneak out of the Imperial City while you keep Captain Sen busy with conversation.

The scene then shifts to the city gate so you can put the plan in to action. Captain Sen seems unwilling to believe that Yukong has left, and suspecting that you're angling for a higher reward, offers to raise the bounty. Stick to your story while Yukong dallies around behind you until eventually he manages to get through the gate unnoticed (1,000 XP).

Choice 2 This outcome is the same as above, with one exception. When you agree to help Yukong, ask for compensation; he reluctantly pays you 250 SP.

Choice 3 Claim Yukong's life and his bounty. After unmasking his true identity, tell him you've come to collect his head to initiate battle (250 XP). Resigned to his fate, the fugitive fights for his life. He has a mercenary's disguise, but that doesn't mean he has a mercenary's skill. Your array of fighting styles and ability to use Focus mode leave Yukong little hope of survival. After the skirmish, return to Captain Sen for the reward (2,000 SP, 300 XP).

CREATIVE YUKONG BATTLE: ~76 XP, ~70 SP

Enemy	Style	Health	Chi
Creative Yukong	Twin Hammers	250	250

Lay a trap for Yukong by falsely promising to help him escape, then turn him in to Captain Sen.

Here's the expanded bounty. In light of his successful capture, I'll overlook that the man almost made it out of the city.

Choice 4 Pretend to go along with Yukong's plan as in Choice 1 (and take the 250 SP he gives you). At any point in the conversation with Captain Sen, you can betray Yukong and collect the bounty. Maximize your earnings by waiting for Sen to up the bounty a few times, but if you're too greedy, Yukong can escape. The safest plan that earns the best reward is to turn Yukong in after Sen has raised the bounty two times, earning you 2,500 SP (300 XP).

AISHI THE MOURNFUL BLADE

With both fugitives taken care of, you're approached by an old man as you leave the city gate. He tells you of a third bounty: Aishi the Mournful Blade, a notorious killer who can be found in the Black Leopard School's garden; if you've already

My daughter's life was nothing but pain. Her crimes were a way to forget, for a while.

been to the school and been banned by Master Smiling Hawk, then this bounty won't be offered. Equip gems that enhance your conversation skills before talking with her. There are several outcomes to your dialogue:

It is all to easy to lose your conscience once you have denied it. I was not always like this, but I remember all too well how my descent began.

If you're persuasive enough, you can convince Aishi to tell you her story and help her attain closure.

Choice 1 Use conversation skills and Aishi tells her tale (100 XP). She admits to being a killer, plunderer, and worse, and tells how it all began when Captain Sen led her along the first steps of the Way of the Closed Fist. She's regretted it ever since and agrees to return with you to the city gate so she can end her sorrow by putting

Captain Sen to the sword. Ignore Sen's pleas for help and allow Aishi to take her revenge (500 XP). After Sen dies at her hand, she asks you to indulge her in a final battle so that she can find ultimate peace (800 XP). Use Focus mode to evade the scythe of her twin swords and enhance your counterattacks with Chi Strikes. In the confining space before the city gate, it's hard to find the space to use Chi Heal. Don't take the risk of absorbing too much damage. Instead, unleash your full power to end the fight quickly.

AISHI THE MOURNFUL BLADE BATTLE: ~418 XP, ~360 SP

Enemy	Style	Health	Chi
Aishi the Mournful Blade	Twin Swords	687	687

After the battle, the old man who first set you on this path reveals that he's actually the ghost of Aishi's father. Satisfied that his troubled daughter has at last ceased to mourn, he rewards you with 2,500 SP and the **Gem of Unity** (Body +3, Spirit +3, Mind +3, Open Palm only) (1,500 XP).

No, I *was* weak, otherwise I would have ignored you by the river. I'm going to pay for my crimes, but there's one thing I have to do first. I have to kill you.

Aishi's need to confront her past is a weakness that you can use to exploit both her and Captain Sen.

Choice 2 Convince Aishi to tell her story and accompany you back to Captain Sen (100 XP). Instead of allowing her to kill Sen, however, intervene and fight her to the death (1,000 XP). This battle is exactly the same as in Choice 1. Afterward, Captain Sen rewards your deeds and buys your future silence with 5,000 SP and a **Gem of Mastery** (Body +3, Spirit +3, Mind +3, Closed Fist only). Aishi's father does not appear again if you opt for this outcome.

Choice 3 If you fail to convince Aishi to relate her tale, she attacks. Defeat her, then talk to Captain Sen to claim the reward: 2,500 SP and the Gem of Mastery (500 XP).

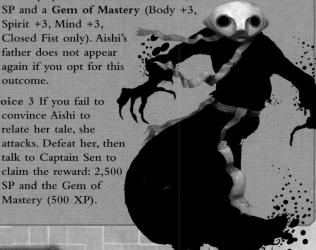

THE SLAVE TRADERS

After you meet Silk Fox in the Scholars' Garden, Prefect Jitong appears in the Market District. He has two men in custody who are both accused of the same crime: slave trading. Chandler Ling, a rich merchant, is truly guilty, but his wealthy friends are trying to pull some strings to get him acquitted. Scholar Songtao is completely innocent, but without proof he is doomed to be sentenced in Changler Ling's place.

To get to the bottom of the matter, you need to get in direct contact with the slavers. Following Jitong's advice, seek out Zi Bao in the arena and ask him to set up a meeting with them. You must either pay a hefty bribe (2,000 SP) or use conversation skills (30 XP) to convince him to do this; save your game before trying as you only get once chance. If Zin Bao gets nervous and runs off, you can follow him. If you let him go, you've blown your chance to complete the quest.

The meeting takes place in the creature pens. No matter what you say at first, Slaver Cao Zeng commands his men to attack you. Zi Bao and three spear-wielding slavers close in. Back out of the cell where your meeting takes place so you have more room, then use Magic attacks to safely strike down the slavers from a distance. Harmonic Combos in Focus mode are also very effective.

SLAVER BATTLE: ~515 XP, ~400 SP

Enemy	Style	Health	Chi
Slaver x3	Spear	200	200
Zi Bao	Basic	250	250

Slay the slaver to get the evidence needed to have Scholar Songtao set free.

The ensuing conversation with Cao Zeng can end in several different ways:

Choice 1  Slaver Cao Zeng does his best to recruit you to his cause. Refuse every offer until he has no choice but to fight. Cao Zeng uses Storm Dragon exclusively, and like all tough enemies, he's immune to Harmonic Combos. If you depleted your abilities in the last battle, use Spirit Thief to recharge before meeting Cao Zeng's challenge. After beating him, take the **Slaver's Documents** back to Prefect Jitong and hand them over to see Scholar Songtao go free (800 XP). In thanks, you're given an **Aura of Calm Gem** (Body +2, Intimidation +2).

SLAVER CAO ZENG BATTLE: ~304 XP, ~240 SP

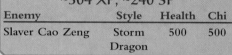

Enemy	Style	Health	Chi
Slaver Cao Zeng	Storm Dragon	500	500

If you ally with the slavers, an innocent man is sent to the Wall.

Choice 2  After defeating Zi Bao and the others, tell Cao Zeng you want in on his operation. He gives you the **Forged Slaver Documents**; deliver them to Prefect Jitong to clinch a conviction for Scholar Songtao while the *real* slaver, Chandler Ling, goes free (800 XP). Chandler Ling gives you a **Gem of Seductive Power** (Spirit +2, Charm +2, Closed Fist only). Meet him later on the Golden Way for a further reward of 500 SP and a chance to browse his selection of gems.

TIP

When you hand in the evidence, you can use conversation skills to milk Prefect Jitong for payment. If successful, he reluctantly hands over 1,000 SP for your services (60 XP).

THE BLACK LEOPARD SCHOOL

The Black Leopard School south of the Market District is in a leadership crisis as two rival masters divide the students' loyalty. Master Smiling Hawk follows the Closed Fist and currently controls the majority; Master Radiant of the Open Palm, who is still nominally in charge, has secluded himself in his chambers and hasn't been seen by even his most loyal students. This gives you a chance to intervene and support those who agree with your chosen philosophy.

The chaos that's descended on the school is immediately evident when you enter, as four acolytes brazenly attack without provocation. These junior students are the weakest in the school, but facing four at once can be tricky. Target Novice Han Tao,

Oh, and Master Radiant's ways are better? I don't think so. Brute force *is* the only way to get what you want, and I can prove it.

the strongest of the group, and defeat him first. Use area attacks to give yourself breathing room if things get crowded. Liberal use of Magic and Support styles help seal your victory.

BLACK LEOPARD NOVICE BATTLE: ~76 XP, ~70 SP

Enemy	Style	Health	Chi
Novice Shen	Leaping Tiger	250	250
Novice Bo	Leaping Tiger	250	250
Novice Feng	Iron Palm	250	250
Novice Han Tao	Iron Palm	437	437

After you best the novices, First Brother Kai approaches with an offer to join the school. If you accept (700 XP), he informs you that in order to meet Master Radiant, you must first prove yourself by defeating the "Brothers," Black Leopard School's top students.

I'm Sixth Brother Gaoshan. If you think you can defeat a disciple of Master Smiling Hawk, challenge *me*. I assure you, I'm much tougher than the novices.

Your first opponent is Sixth Brother Gaoshan. Locate him in the school garden to initiate a fight. Gaoshan uses Iron Palm and Heavenly Wave; if you become slowed, switch briefly to any Transformation style to dispel the effect. Your Follower doesn't help you when dueling the Brothers or fighting the Masters.

SIXTH BROTHER GAOSHAN BATTLE: ~300 XP, 0 SP

Enemy	Style	Health	Chi
Sixth Brother Gaoshan	Iron Palm, Heavenly Wave	437	437

Enter the school, where you find a small jar with 22 SP and a scrollstand. Locate Fifth Brother Shangjin, one of Master Radiant's few supporters. He knows why you've sought him out and politely agrees to duel with you. His staff makes close combat difficult, so use Magic style attacks from range to avoid being skewered.

FIFTH BROTHER SHANGJIN BATTLE: ~400 XP, 0 SP

Enemy	Style	Health	Chi
Fifth Brother Shangjin	Spear	437	437

Note that your health, Chi, and Focus are replenished after each Brother fight. Seek out Fourth Brother Yu to proceed to the next battle. Defeat him using the same strategy you used on Shangjin and Gaoshan.

FOURTH BROTHER YU BATTLE: ~500 XP, 0 SP

Enemy	Style	Health	Chi
Fourth Brother Yu	Storm Dragon, Legendary Strike	437	437

After the fight, you're summoned to an audience with Master Smiling Hawk. He explains in blunt terms that he intends to wrest complete control of the school away from Master Radiant, but he needs you to clear his path. This leaves you two main options:

You can place the school back on the Way of the Open Palm by defeating Master Smiling Hawk.

Choice 1 Refuse to help Master Smiling Hawk, who dismisses you in anger. Head into the dining hall to find Third Brother Renshan and challenge him to a fight to continue your way through the gauntlet of students. Renshan is eager to show off the fighting styles he learned from Master Smiling Hawk. Use short bursts of Focus mode to evade his attacks and keep pounding him until he finally concedes defeat.

THIRD BROTHER RENSHAN BATTLE: ~750 XP, 0 SP

Enemy	Style	Health	Chi
Third Brother Renshan	Leaping Tiger, Hidden Fist	625	625

First Brother Kai knows that you refused to help Master Smiling Hawk and takes you directly to Master Radiant's room after the battle with Renshan. The reason for Master Radiant's reclusiveness is now obvious: he's a ghost! He was murdered by Master Smiling Hawk, but the ruthless Assassin wasn't able to face the ghost that remained. After sharing his tale, Master Radiant urges you to defeat Master Smiling Hawk before he can corrupt any more students.

Master Smiling Hawk gives you one last chance to join him; if you accept, the quest plays out as in Choice 2. If you refuse, then prepare to defend yourself. After Smiling Hawk kicks you through the wall into the dining area, battle begins.

The brutal master is a deadly combatant who executes attacks with lightning speed. Slip into Focus mode to evade, but do so only as long as needed to get out of the way. Switch styles to choose an effective foil against Smiling Hawk's varied tactics. If he uses Ice Shard and Hidden Fist, Toad Demon and Horse Demon forms render these attacks harmless against you. When he employs White Demon, choose a more maneuverable style and take evasive action. When Smiling Hawk loses all his Health, he absorbs Third Brother Renshan's soul to fully restore himself, meaning that you essentially have to defeat Smiling Hawk twice. Spirit Thief helps you last the full duration of the battle.

MASTER SMILING HAWK BATTLE: ~418 XP, ~383 SP

Enemy	Style	Health	Chi
Master Smiling Hawk	White Demon, Hidden Fist, Ice Shard	687 (+687)	687 (+687)

With Master Smiling Hawk slain, Master Radiant ensures you're well-rewarded. He gives you a **Heaven's Blessing Gem** (Wind shield, Open Palm only) and teaches you a new Support style, **Paralyzing Palm** (2,000 XP). As the name implies, this potent style can paralyze enemies, rendering them helpless.

Help Master Smiling Hawk cement his grip on the school, and you'll be well-rewarded.

You receive two further gifts from First Brother Kai: the **Rote of the Endless Mind** (Focus +5, Chi +5) and a **Gem of Inner Genius** (Mind +10, Body –5, Spirit –5).

Choice 2 Agree to help Master Smiling Hawk consolidate his power. Third Brother Renshan voluntarily concedes his duel, allowing you to move directly on to a duel First Brother Kai (because the Second Brother has vanished). Try to conserve Chi and Focus, because you'll need as many resources as possible to handle the ensuing battles. A useful technique against Kai's staff is to block, goading Kai into using a strong attack. As he does so, drop your guard and sidestep out of harm's way to take advantage of the opening with a strong attack or combo of your own.

FIRST BROTHER KAI BATTLE: ~330 XP, ~360 SP

Enemy	Style	Health	Chi
First Brother Kai	Heavenly Wave, Spear	625	625

When Kai is defeated, Masters Radiant and Smiling Hawk emerge into the courtyard for an open confrontation (800 XP). With your intent to destroy Master Radiant made plain, his two most devoted students join forces to try to prevent you. You've faced both of these trainees before. Defeat each of the accomplices once, then fight Radiant himself.

BLACK LEOPARD SCHOOL BATTLE: ~532 XP, ~380 SP			
Enemy	Style	Health	Chi
Novice Han To	Iron Palm	437	437
Fourth Brother Yu	Storm Dragon, Legendary Strike	437	437

Finally, Master Radiant realizes he must face you personally. Thousand Cuts, his favored Martial style, may have short range but Master Radiant has honed it to deadly quickness. Use Focus mode to safely dodge when he attacks, then make an attack of your own. Master Radiant tends to use a lot of area attacks; it's safer to simply block during this fight than to try evading.

MASTER RADIANT BATTLE: ~501 XP, 0 SP			
Enemy	Style	Health	Chi
Master Radiant	Thousand Cuts, Storm Dragon	687	687

Master Smiling Hawk meets you in his cloister after your victory (2,000 XP). To thank you for helping him, he gives you 800 SP and a **Gem of Black Flame** (Closed Fist only). This gem boosts your attributes. His most valuable gift is the support style **Hidden Fist**, which renders foes disoriented and unable to attack or defend. He then refuses to speak with you any further. Before you leave the school, check Master Radiant's room for an urn containing 800 SP and a Technique: **Warrior of the Inner Eye** (Focus +7, Intuition +1).

JINLIN

Jinlin appears in the Market District after you've been formally invited to join the Lotus Assassins. She's only a little girl, but she's burdened with the responsibility of buying her mother back from slavery. To do this, she must obtain a valuable bowl from a tomb in the Necropolis. Agree to help, and she departs with instructions to meet her at the Tomb of the Dignified Collector.

EXPLORE THE TOMB

Follow the blue signs in the Necropolis to find Jinlin and the tomb. Before you enter, scour the area within the tomb's outer wall to find four headstones; one is trapped, while the other three yield 154 SP and a random gem.

Without Jinlin to open the door for you, you'll never see the inside of this tomb.

Jinlin slips inside the tomb through a small crack and unlocks the door from the inside (100 XP). Now it's your turn; the tomb is crawling with undead that you must defeat so Jinlin can recover the bowl she was sent to find. Head inside to trigger the first battle against a trio of mummies. Unlike spirits and other undead, mummies are solid beings and can be affected by Support and Weapon styles. Their slow attacks can inflict disease (similar to poisoning) but are easy to avoid. After defeating them, continue on to smash three more mummies into dust.

MUMMY BATTLE (x2): ~684 XP, ~530 SP			
Enemy	Style	Health	Chi
Mummy x3	Mummy	375	375

With the tomb's main hall finally cleared, look in the corners for some loot. The urn on the left is trapped, while the urn on the right contains 1,000 SP and a gem: **Spirit Harvest** (more XP and no power-ups from ghosts). Proceed into the Inner Sanctum for a final challenging battle.

> ### TIP
> *Equip the Spirit Harvest Gem right away so you can take advantage of its effects while you defeat the remainder of the tomb's spirits.*

BATTLE THE INSANE EMPEROR'S GHOST

Four aggressive spirits guard Jinlin's bowl. This battle is tough; the three lost spirits launch a constant stream of magic bolts that home in on you, while the Insane Emperor's Ghost weakens you with draining attacks. Immobilize as many as you can with an Ice Shard or Tempest area attack, casting the spell in Focus mode to ensure you're not interrupted. Then quickly attack any spirits that escaped the spell while the others are held in stasis. Continue this strategy until the lost spirits are defeated, then turn your attention to the Emperor and give him a taste of his own medicine with Spirit Thief. After recharging yourself, finish off the insane ghost with Chi Strikes in your strongest style.

More death, more intruders... My tomb has lain sacrosanct for centuries and now mortals tread on my very ashes.

INNER SANCTUM BATTLE: ~891 XP, 0 SP			
Enemy	Style	Health	Chi
Lost Spirit x3	Lost Spirit	200	200
Insane Emperor's Ghost	Red Minister	625	625

ESCAPE WITH JINLIN

The Wanderer's Jewel (Body +3, Spirit +3, Mind -5) is yours after the battle. Jinlin arrives to claim the bowl she seeks, but two mummies follow close behind. Before fighting them, meditate at the Focus Shrine and open the trapped container near it for more silver. Then descend the steps and pulverize the mummies.

INNER SANCTUM BATTLE: ~456 XP, ~380 SP			
Enemy	Style	Health	Chi
Mummy x2	Mummy	375	375

A ghost and mummy ambush you when you return to the main chamber. Avoid the ice blasts and answer with your own Magic attacks or simply close in and disperse him in a flurry of fists and feet, saving the ponderous mummy for last.

GHOST BATTLE: ~501 XP, ~200 SP			
Enemy	Style	Health	Chi
Ghost	Ice Shard	375	375
Mummy	Mummy	375	375

More undead stand between you and escape. This time, two ghosts with Magic styles attack from opposite sides; the one on the left is accompanied by a mummy. Escape the crossfire in Focus mode and take out the lone ghost on the right first, using a Transformation style so that you can shrug off attacks from the other ghost. A Follower in Attack mode helps a great deal in this battle.

UNDEAD BATTLE: ~501 XP, ~200 SP			
Enemy	Style	Health	Chi
Ghost x2	Dire Flame	375	375
Mummy	Mummy	375	375

Finally, you and Jinlin emerge into the daylight. Jinlin reads a puzzling inscription carved on the bowl; it turns out to be the **Configuration of the Tiger**, which you can use later at Lord Lao's Furnace. Then, eager to trade the bowl for her mother's freedom, she thanks you and departs (2,000 XP).

I wonder why Purveyor Shouji wants this bowl so badly. It looks so... ordinary, except for maybe this writing.

The writing on the bowl turns out to be the real treasure.

JADE EMPIRE

THE GRAVEDIGGER'S GHOSTS

After meeting Gravedigger Shen at the Necropolis entrance, visit his home to learn more about the ghosts plaguing the area. Shen first asks you to dispel the haunting in his own backyard. Go through Shen's house, stopping to claim 18 SP and a gem from the cabinet, and defeat the lone ghost out back. Open a trapped headstone by the fence before you go.

Help! One of those damn spirits came up right in my backyard! The stupid thing won't let anyone get by! It's got my tools and everything! Just kill the damn thing!

Shen's mother-in-law remains a thorn in his side.

GHOST BATTLE: ~145 XP, 0 SP

Enemy	Style	Health	Chi
Ghost	Dire Flame, Iron Palm	200	200

When you tell Shen the yard is now safe, he rewards you with 500 SP and a gem: **The Mournful Soul** (Mind +3, Spirit +3, Body –5) (400 XP). Question him to gain further information about three ghosts he needs you to take care of, then head back into the Necropolis to look for them.

THE SORROWFUL GHOST

Find Miss Chan drifting around the central courtyard. There are several ways to lay her spirit to rest:

Choice 1 Miss Chan can't rest because she's searching for her baby son. Sadly, she's unaware that he has died (and doesn't seem aware of her own death, either). You must prove that her son is dead so Miss Chan can give up the search and finally rest. Tell her you know where the grave is; a list then appears of the four markers on her family plot. Select Chan Tuo. As the truth dawns on Miss Chan, she slowly fades away.

Choice 2 Simply disperse Miss Chan by force. She was never a fighter and has no combat training. She's no match for your legendary powers.

GHOST OF MISS CHAN BATTLE: ~145 XP, 0 SP

Enemy	Style	Health	Chi
Ghost of Miss Chan	Basic	200	200

Choice 3 If you show Miss Chan the wrong grave, her sorrow deepens to angry despair and she attacks. You must then defeat her as in Choice 2.

After Miss Chan is gone, return to Gravedigger Shen to claim your reward of 400 SP (600 XP).

THE FEARFUL GHOST

My spirit cannot rest quiet with them here. Even now, in death, they mock me and torment me as they did in my final moments of life. They drive me mad!

The ghosts of Merchant Bai's murderers continue to stalk him.

Find the second ghost, Merchant Bai, in the central courtyard. He was killed by a pair of brothers who, now ghosts themselves, stand between Bai and his tomb. There are two ways to solve Bai's problem:

Choice 1 Help Bai get to his coffin safely by defeating the ghosts who stand in his way. Enter the nearby Tomb of the Masses (which was previously sealed) to find the ghosts of Si Tsu and Si Ran; like most spirits, the pain of undeath has corrupted them to pure malevolence. Each brother has poor combat skill limited to Basic style. Evade their clumsy attacks and strike blows from the back or flank.

TOMB OF THE MASSES BATTLE: ~418 XP, 0 SP

Enemy	Style	Health	Chi
Ghost of Si Tsu	Basic	315	315
Ghost of Si Ran	Basic	315	315

Afterward, search the tomb for treasure. The three smallest containers are all trapped. The large chest opens safely, and contains 800 SP and a **Gem: Sixth Sense** (Intuition +8, Charm −3, Intimidation −3). Return to the surface and tell Bai the good news. In thanks, he gives you one piece of silver and a **Cow Bezoar** (used in Lord Lao's Furnace).

Choice 2  Disperse Bai's ghost through combat. Though he's clearly terrified of Si Tsu and Si Ran, Bai is not afraid of the living. He does his best to fight against you, but like Miss Chan, has no combat skills to defend himself with. You can still go into the Tomb of the Masses to kill the other two ghosts and grab the treasure as in Choice 1.

GHOST OF MERCHANT BAI BATTLE: ~145 XP, 0 SP

Enemy	Style	Health	Chi
Ghost of Merchant Bai	Basic	200	200

With Merchant Bai's ghost exorcized, collect your 400 SP reward from Gravedigger Shen (600 XP).

THE VENGEFUL GHOST

The third ghost, Mister Ren, lies on the path that connects Shen's house with the Tomb of the Masses. He's seething with hatred for his widow, who he believes murdered him by poisoning his food. There are two ways to get rid of him:

Choice 1 Look for Ren Feng outside the couple's home in the Market District. Ask about her husband to hear the whole story. Ren Feng *did* poison her husband, but the ingredients she bought were to blame, not her. It was a terrible accident that she has mourned every day since. Agree to escort her to the Necropolis so she can explain this to her husband's ghost. When Mister Ren realizes the depth of his wife's love and sorrow, he melts away.

Choice 2 Meet Ren Feng in the Market District, and tell her you've come to kill her on her dead husband's behalf. Poor Ren Feng doesn't even try to put up a fight. Return and tell Ren Ming that his wife has joined him in the spirit world. He thanks you with a gift of 350 SP and then vanishes.

Choice 3 Dispel Ren Ming's ghost in combat. He lacks the skills to enforce his threats.

GHOST OF REN MING BATTLE: ~418 XP, ~383 SP

Enemy	Style	Health	Chi
Ghost of Ren Ming	Basic	200	200

Talk with Gravedigger Shen after Ren Ming disappears to collect 400 SP (600 XP).

TANNER FONG

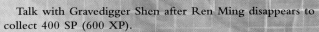
One spirit didn't stay here at all, though! Took up his body and left! Moved in with his son, I heard, and the son isn't pleased. He even asked me for a refund!

After you've taken care of all three spirits, Gravedigger Shen has one last job for you. One of his tenants, Elder Tanner Fong, was mistakenly buried alive; after Fong awoke inside his tomb, he escaped and returned home. Now his family wants a refund on the burial, and that's against Gravedigger Shen's policy.

Return to the Market District and locate the Fongs' house next to the blacksmith's. Because of the spate of recent hauntings, Younger Tanner Fong assumes his father is a ghost and asks you to go inside and deal with him. This leads to many potential outcomes:

Choice 1 Ask Elder Tanner Fong about his family. After talking about them, his anger cools and he asks you to help him convince his son that he's not dead. He offers to pay you for your service, and you can wring maximum silver from him using conversation skills (60 XP). As father and son begin talking, more conversation skills from you ease their reconciliation (60 XP). When they finally stop wishing each other dead, they reward you with 500 SP.

The Fong family's going to need a bigger plot in the Necropolis after this.

Choice 2 Convince father and son to talk, as in Choice 1. When a chance to use a conversation skill appears, ignore it and instead declare that you'd rather just kill them both than listen to them argue. Neither Fong resists if you opt for this outcome, and you receive no reward.

Choice 3 Elder Tanner Fong protests that he's not a ghost, but you don't have to listen to him. If you choose to kill him, Younger Tanner Fong rewards you with 500 SP.

Choice 4 If you tell Elder Tanner Fong that you've come to kill him once and for all, he offers to pay more than whatever you've been offered to leave and slay Younger Tanner Fong instead. Take his money, using Intimidation to extort every last penny (60 SP). Finally, change your mind one more time when Younger Tanner Fong makes his own counteroffer and kill Elder Tanner Fong after all (750 SP).

If Gravedigger Shen dies, who buries him?

Choice 5 Accept Elder Tanner Fong's offer as in Choice 4, but instead of killing anyone (yet) take the old man back to Gravedigger Shen. While the two of them keep arguing about how to solve the problem, solve it for them by killing them both. Gravedigger Shen is the weakest opponent in the whole Empire; slay him with one kick, then turn your attention to Elder Tanner Fong. The sick old man, while tougher than the gravedigger, has no hope of survival.

Choice 6 While talking to the Fongs, you can decide to just bring Tanner Fong back to Gravedigger Shen (as in Choice 5) and have Shen give Fong a job. There is no alignment for this choice, and it involves no killing.

NECROPOLIS BATTLE: ~152 XP, ~127 SP

Enemy	Style	Health	Chi
Gravedigger Shen	Basic	10	0
Elder Tanner Fong	Basic	250	250

If you followed any path except Choice 5, return to the Necropolis to claim a final reward from Gravedigger Shen (600 SP, 1260 XP). If you killed either of the Fongs, you can Intimidate Shen into handing over an extra 200 SP(60 XP).

THE SCIENTIST

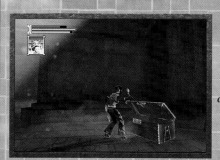

Find 200 SP in a chest buried within the Tomb of the Forgotten Scholar.

While exploring the Necropolis, look for the Tomb of the Forgotten Scholar. Enter it to meet Mad Wen Zhi, a physician. His daughter is deathly ill and, in a desperate attempt to save her life, Wen Zhi plans to attempt a liver transplant. But so far, he hasn't found a liver well-preserved enough to use. There are several ways you can help:

Dr. An in the arena has the medical expertise to help perform Wen Zhi's controversial operation.

Choice 1 Wen Zhi would gladly give his own liver, but he can't very well operate on himself. Return to the arena and explain the situation to Dr. An. When she understands that a young girl's life is at stake, she agrees to follow you back to the Necropolis to help. Wen Zhi makes the ultimate sacrifice, and his daughter goes on to make a full recovery as Dr. An's new apprentice (500 XP).

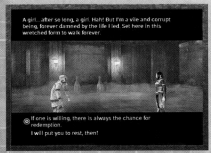

If Ji Xin gives up his liver voluntarily, it won't be tainted with the curse of his undeath.

Choice 2 Following Wen Zhi's advice, head back into the Necropolis and look for the tomb of Ji Xin. He was a rich and corrupt nobleman, now doomed to walk earth in torment as a mummy. Use conversation skills to convince Ji Xin that he has one last chance at redemption by donating his liver to save the dying girl (60 XP). Your words stir some echo of remorse in the old villain's soul, and he willingly gives you his **Preserved Liver** (100 XP). Give the organ to Wen Zhi, who successfully performs the transplant. After the operation, Ji Xin's spirit appears one final time to give you his thanks and 500 SP.

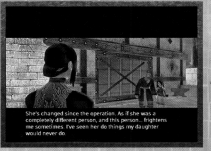

Using a rotten liver is temporarily successful, but Wen Zhi's daughter is tainted with evil.

Choice 3 Find Ji Xin's tomb as in Choice 2, and simply take the **Preserved Liver** from his motionless corpse. Like all mummies, Ji Xin is very slow, making it easy for you to run circles around him. Be wary if he switches to Tempest, however; if you're trapped in a whirlwind, switch to a Transformation style to escape.

NECROPOLIS BATTLE: ~152 XP, ~130 SP

Enemy	Style	Health	Chi
Ji Xin	Mummy, Tempest	250	250

If you convince Ji Xin to willingly give up his liver, the operation is a success, and Wen Zhi gives you 275 SP. If you kill him for it, the operation results in the daughter being tainted by the tainted liver. If you meet up with him later on in the Imperial City, you can learn the ultimate fate of Wen Zi's daughter.

CHAPTER FOUR

OVERVIEW

Don't lecture me. Master Li's student brought me evidence from the Lotus Assassin fortress. You allowed Death's Hand to corrupt the Empire.

Your defiance grows tiresome, student of Li. You must learn your place in the order of things.

Wherein the palace keeps its secrets,   *An Emperor is met in battle,*   *And a Master shows his gratitude.*

You infiltrated and destroyed the Lotus Assassin fortress and learned that the Emperor had full knowledge of what was held there. It was a costly endeavor, and the loss of one of your fellows casts a pall across your coming confrontation in the palace of the mighty Emperor Sun Hai.

IMPERIAL PALACE

Great Spire — to Throne Room

Grand Staircase

Dragonfly Gate

MAP LEGEND

- ⬤ *Container*
- ⬤ *Focus Shrine*
- ⬤ *Scrollstand*

Chapter Four is very brief and showcases your infiltration of the Emperor's palace. From a dangerous landing at the Dragonfly Gate, where Wild Flower's inner demons erupt in conflict, you battle through hordes of soldiers and assassins to the Throne Room for a decisive confrontation with Emperor Sun Hai. Only by putting an end to the Emperor's evil can you finally reunite with Master Li.

One of the Empire's greatest achievements, the Imperial Palace hovers in the sky thanks to the Sprightly Stones from which it was constructed. Strong aerial defense patrols protect the airspace around the palace, so this small section is the only available entrance.

The Great Spire is a massive hollow tower in the center of the Imperial Palace. Its moveable floor functions as an elevator, raising you from the level of the Dragonfly Gate to the Throne Room.

The Great Spire

Dragonfly Gate

Silk Fox's personal landing pad is one of the few places in the palace that isn't completely overrun with Lotus Assassins, making it the only place where your flyer can alight safely.

A four-aisled staircase leads from the Dragonfly Gate into the heart of the palace. A full squad of Imperial guards and Lotus Assassins patrol here to keep out intruders.

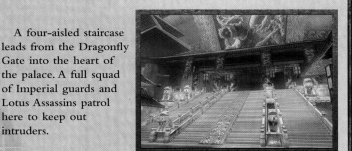

Grand Staircase

The Celestial Order, Vol. 2: Tells the story of the dawning of the age of Man.

The Lotus Monks: These records describe what the Lotus Monks were like before they became the Lotus Assassins.

THRONE ROOM

Throne Room

Tomb Entrance

to Palace

Audience Chamber

MAP LEGEND

- Container
- Focus Shrine
- Scrollstand
- Spirit Font
- Trapped Container
- **1** Emperor Sun Hai
- **2** Master Li

The Empire's most notable leaders are entombed here: Seng Si the Broken Bough, Khor Miah the Swift Arrow, and even Sagacious Tien himself.

Tomb entrance

The southern portion of the Throne Room is a massive hall completely open to the sky at one end. Pairs of alcoves conceal elite guards who can rush forth at a moment's notice to protect the Emperor.

Audience chamber

The Righteous Siege: This is a vague account of the attack on the Spirit Monks that hints at the actions that tormented Sagacious Zu.

Emperor Sun Hai rules the Empire from the highest level of the Throne Room, which is dominated by a gigantic replica of your Dragon Amulet. The Emperor keeps the Water Dragon's heart here so that he might be close to it at all times.

Throne Room

CHARACTERS

Emperor Sun Hai

1 Emperor Sun Hai wields supreme power, a responsibility that has corrupted even the loftiest and noblest souls. The only way to learn just how the Emperor has been affected is to confront him personally.

Master Li

2 Master Li reveals how he earned the name of Glorious Strategist when you finally meet up with him again in the Emperor's Throne Room.

CRITICAL PATH

THE HEIGHT OF POWER

WILD FLOWER'S DEMONS

NOTE

The following battle automatically occurs at this point, but only after you have talked at length to Wild Flower about her demonic alter egos prior to arriving at this point.

Ya Zhen: The time has come, mortal. I won't share this shell anymore! I'll destroy you, Chai Ka, and her mind, as well, if I have to!
FPS: 29.985008   MEM: 62.06 MB ACTUAL: 50.66 MB

With help from Silk Fox, your group alights at the Dragonfly Gate. If you have spoken regularly with Wild Flower up to this point, the two demons struggling inside her begin to break free as soon as you've landed. Both Chai Ka, the Guardian, and Ya Zhen, the Other, ask you to enter Wild Flower's mind to help them win the struggle. If Chai Ka wins, he remains to watch over both you and the girl while the Other is forever banished. If you support Ya Zhen on the other hand, the evil demon claims supremacy and dooms Wild Flower to a lifetime of torment. You must now choose which demon you wish to aid:

A war between demons rages in Wild Flower's mind.

Choice 1 ✋ Agree to help Chai Ka. The demon draws you into a psychic battlefield where the Guardian and the Other are already engaged in a life-or-death struggle. Ya Zhen, your foe, has taken the form of a powerful toad demon. Your many prior battles with this type of fiend give you a useful advantage: practice. There is a catch, however. Not only must you slay Ya Zhen, but you must also protect Chai Ka. If Chai Ka is killed, you'll be trapped forever in the stormy turmoil of Wild Flower's subconscious.

If you obtained Mirabelle from the Outlander, fire off as many shots as you can from range before you close in. Transformation styles are also very effective, especially Jade Golem. If you prefer close martial or weapon combat, stay behind the toad demon, where his flailing claws can't reach you. Fight the temptation to hang back and watch Chai Ka fight the battle for you; the Guardian will be slaughtered. After the battle, you receive a new technique: **Guardian's Strength** (Health +5, Chi +5).

YA ZHEN BATTLE: ~897 XP, 0 SP

Enemy	Style	Health	Chi
Ya Zhen	Toad Demon	1,500	1,500

Choice 2 ✊ Agree to help Ya Zhen. As in Choice 1, you must not only slay your enemy but also preserve your ally. Chai Ka is a much tougher foe thanks to his deadly area attack, which he uses incessantly. If you have Mirabelle, use it to weaken Chai Ka before you approach, but save enough Focus to make a quick escape if needed. Once you've closed in, switch to Jade Golem style and cleave the demon with your gigantic axes. If you use any other type of close combat, be ready to block to defend against the area attack waves that *will* be flung against you. When Chai Ka is slain, a new technique is yours: **Mastered Evil** (Health +5, Focus +5).

CHAI KA BATTLE: ~516 XP, 0 SP

Enemy	Style	Health	Chi
Chai Ka	Chai Ka	1,500	1,500

Wild Flower is still host to a demonic soul, but at least she's only got one now (2,000 XP). You can now proceed into the palace.

STORM THE PALACE

In the next room, search the corners to find some jars; each contains 5 SP and might yield a gem as well. Meditate at the Focus Shrines if needed; numerous foes teem just beyond the next door. Four Imperial soldiers close in when you enter the Grand Staircase. As you battle through the ranks

of guards, soldiers, and Assassins that stand between you and Emperor Sun Hai, Harmonic Combos are your best weapon. Rely on them and you'll save yourself a lot of expended Chi, Focus, and Health.

Smashing these jars won't make you rich, but every useful gem is a welcome addition to your inventory.

GRAND STAIRCASE BATTLE: ~910 XP, ~635 SP

Enemy	Style	Health	Chi
Imperial Soldier	Twin Hammers	300	300
Imperial Soldier x3	Legendary Strike	240	240

At the top of the stairs, a horde of enemies comes pouring in from the Grand Spire beyond. Unleash area attacks as they rush toward you, then pick off the troops one by one with Harmonic Combos. Focus mode gives you time to complete the combos when you're surrounded by enemies.

GRAND STAIRCASE BATTLE: ~1,384 XP, ~900 SP

Enemy	Style	Health	Chi
Imperial Soldier	Sword	300	300
Imperial Soldier	Viper	240	240
Imperial Guard x2	Viper	240	240
Lotus Assassin	Twin Swords	300	300
Lotus Assassin	Viper	240	240

The Black Whirlwind

Before moving on, open the urns that flank the door to find a total of 1,000 SP; each urn might contain a gem, as well. Finally, read both scrollstands and then head into the Grand Spire. Your group gathers here with you as the floor rises, lifting you to the upper level of the palace and the Emperor's Throne Room.

Two more guards rush to meet you as you advance down the winding path. Without any real combat styles to use against you, they have no hope of even slowing you down.

Imperial Soldier

IMPERIAL SOLDIER BATTLE: ~436 XP, ~320 SP

Enemy	Style	Health	Chi
Imperial Soldier x2	Basic	240	240

Continue along the path; as you pass the gate to the Imperial Tombs, Silk Fox steps up to tell you of some of the great men and women entombed there. Across from the door, look for a scrollstand and two jars; each jar holds 5 SP (and possibly a gem, too). Three more low-ranking guards emerge and put up a feeble resistance. Knock them out and keep moving.

IMPERIAL SOLDIER BATTLE: ~654 XP, ~440 SP

Enemy	Style	Health	Chi
Imperial Soldier x2	Spear	240	240
Lotus Assassin	Basic	240	240

As you move down the final corridor, one of your Followers steps forward to offer you **Friends in High Places** (Chi +5, Intuition +2).

See the Romance Plots section of this guide for complete details on matters of the heart.

THE AUDIENCE CHAMBER

You arrive in the Audience Chamber, where Emperor Sun Hai greets you with sneering contempt. Silk Fox demands that her father explain why he's fostered so much chaos and suffering throughout the Empire, but he loses patience with the questioning and evokes a wave of power that flattens all your Followers—and reveals that the Emperor is nearly god-like with power! Rather than fighting you himself, he summons his elite guards and commands them to attack.

I am the eldest and, therefore, the Emperor! I have you at a disadvantage, and yet you toy with me. What do you know, Glorious Strategist? Where is the Spirit Monk amulet?

ENOUGH!

There are 18 foes in this attack wave, more than you've ever had to face at one time. Fortunately, they attack you six at a time; as you defeat each one, a replacement emerges from one of the four alcoves on either side of the Audience Chamber. Because none of these guards can use ranged attacks, back away as they sidle closer and hammer them with attacks in your strongest Magic style (either Stone Immortal or Tempest, most likely.) When you're down to the last few enemies, use Harmonic Combos to create Health, Chi, or Focus orbs, or use Spirit Thief, to ensure that you're in top condition for the next battle.

AUDIENCE CHAMBER BATTLE: ~3,924 XP, ~2,650 SP

Enemy	Style	Health	Chi
Lotus Assassin x3	Viper, Sword	240	240
Imperial Guard x14	Viper, Sword	240	240
Lotus Inquisitor	Viper, Sword	240	240

Ascend to the next landing to fight the Emperor's final protectors. Four Lotus Assassin Masters attack with Viper and Tempest styles. Use Support styles to incapacitate them and area attacks to scatter them, then target one Assassin at a time to defeat them sequentially. If you can eliminate just one Assassin very quickly, the rest of the battle becomes a lot more manageable.

IMPERIAL SOLDIER BATTLE: ~654 XP, ~440 SP

Enemy	Style	Health	Chi
Lotus Assassin Master x4	Viper, Tempest	525	525

Help yourself to a few thousand SP from the Emperor's hoard.

There are three hidden treasures on this landing. A chest in the southeast corner contains a technique: **Warrior of the Infinite Spirit** (Chi +7, Charm +1) and 1 SP. Two urns on the west side hold 5,000 SP between them. There's also a trapped chest here. Your showdown with the Emperor awaits at the top of the next staircase. Use the Focus Shrines and Spirit Fonts before climbing up to meet him.

Apart from incredible stamina, speed, and attacking power, the Emperor has one more trait that makes him tough to defeat: variable immunity. When he switches to Tempest, he can't be hurt by magic; when he employs White Demon, he is invulnerable to Martial style; and when he uses Viper, he can't be harmed by Support styles.

To ensure that your attacks are effective, watch the Emperor carefully to see what style he's using; he likes to switch often, especially after you've damaged him. When he uses Tempest, counterattack with Martial styles; when he uses White Demon, unleash Magic. There is another and much better way, however: Jade Golem. Not only is your golem form immune to all of Emperor Sun Hai's attacks, but the twin axes of the colossal construct can slay the Emperor in just a few blows if you've invested plenty of Style Points into this form. Use Focus mode and evasion to get into a close position, then quickly switch to Jade Golem and start swinging! While Jade Golem is the most effective, any of your Transformation styles can bypass the Emperor's immunities.

When the Emperor is finally defeated, Master Li collects the Water Dragon's heart...and claims it for himself! Master Li, who rescued you from Dirge and raised you at his school, has planned every step of your quest all along so that he might take ultimate power for himself. Fast as lightning, his hands reach through the flaws he built into your technique, slaying you before you can react. With this final act of betrayal, the chapter closes.

Master Li has one more lesson to teach you.

EMPEROR SUN HAI BATTLE: 0 XP, 0 SP			
Enemy	Style	Health	Chi
Emperor Sun Hai	Staff, Tempest, Viper	1,500	1,500

CHAPTER FIVE

OVERVIEW

Your Master, Sun Li the Glorious Strategist, betrayed you. He killed you to claim the power of the Emperor--my power--as his own. You... are dead.

Wherein the Water Dragon intervenes,

I can only imagine what lies and distortions he told you about Dirge, your heritage, and his own role in events here. But now, you deserve to hear the truth.

True history is revealed,

Binding the living condemns them to a fate worse than death. It forces the subject to obey and robs them of their free will. As a Spirit Monk, you must never do such a thing.

And the Spirit Monk legacy is reclaimed.

The defeat of Emperor Sun Hai was supposed to set things right, but with one careful blow, Master Li left you crumpled on the floor, a pawn in his carefully plotted revenge. The spirit realm stretches before you, but a beacon in the distance calls. You are not yet lost to the living.

THE SPIRIT PLAIN

Barren Plain

1

The Beacon

Spiritual Transformation

Furious Ming

Lu the Prodigy

Monk Zeng

Radiant Jen Xi

Scholar Ling

Tiger Shen

Wu the Lotus Blossom

Your character's appearance changes drastically during your sojourn in the spirit world.

MAP LEGEND

1 *Water Dragon's Spirit*

The Spirit Plain is a vast, bleak battlefield where you first awaken after being slain by Sun Li. The ghostly remains of the dead and their equipment still dot the landscape.

This desolate field, wreathed in eternal shadow, is the first place you visit in the Spirit Realm. Countless lost spirits make exploration hazardous.

Spirit Plain

The beacon

To guide you out of the plain, the Water Dragon's Spirit illuminates the sky to the south with a brilliant beacon.

Characters

Water Dragon's Spirit

1 Now that Master Li has the Dragon Amulet, the Water Dragon's Spirit is weaker than ever. She transports you into the spiritual aspect of Dirge, the Spirit Monks' monastery.

Outer Courtyard

to Inner Courtyard

Courtyard Gate

Bridge

Dirge Fountain

Map Legend

⬤ Containers		**1** Abbot Song	
⬤ Scrollstand		**2** Xian Wu the Betrayer	

The temple of Dirge is surrounded by a series of terraced courtyards. The Outer Courtyard is the first sight to greet visitors to the monastery. It now lies in ruins, haunted by the spirits of those who died in the great battle two decades ago.

Bridge

Scrollstand

The Ritual of Binding: One of the greatest powers of the Spirit Monks is their ability to bind departed souls to themselves.

Dirge fountain

While Dirge stood, sacred fountains channeled the Water Dragon's energy, creating a protective barrier around the monastery. The Emperor's spies destroyed their sanctity by defiling them with human blood.

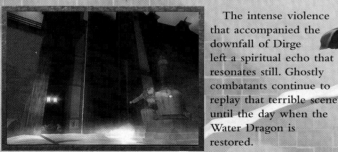

Courtyard gate

The intense violence that accompanied the downfall of Dirge left a spiritual echo that resonates still. Ghostly combatants continue to replay that terrible scene until the day when the Water Dragon is restored.

CHARACTERS

Abbot Song

1 Abbot Song was once the head of the Spirit Monk order. Even though he's a ghost, he still intends to fulfill his responsibilities by guiding you through the ruins of Dirge.

Xian Wu the Betrayer

2 Xian Wu was once a Spirit Monk who guarded the sacred fountain in the Outer Courtyard. Tempted by false promises from the Emperor, she betrayed her order by contaminating the fountain.

INNER COURTYARD

to Temple

to Dirge Cave

Treasury

Dirge Fountain

Path of Demons

to Outer Courtyard

MAP LEGEND

Container

Focus Shrine

The inner courtyard, once a place of quiet contemplation, is now a shattered ruin. Wide, elegant stairs and paved colonnades lead from the valley to the temple high above. Frequent demon attacks make exploration of this area quite dangerous.

The sacred fountain was not only defiled by the Emperor's troops, but the seal that contained its power was stolen by the Minion of Suffering.

Dirge fountain

Abbot Song's Journal: These notes reveal that many evil omens heralded the fall of the Water Dragon.

Path of Demons

A winding, undulating path, lined with the elegant cloisters of the Spirit Monks, leads east from the fountain to a an ancient cave. As the name suggests, the Path of Demons does not offer you a friendly welcome.

The treasury

The strongest gem in Dirge is kept in the treasury, and it has remained safe only thanks to a protective seal placed around it by the Water Dragon. Several ghosts linger here, drawn by the gem's power but unable to touch it.

DIRGE CAVE

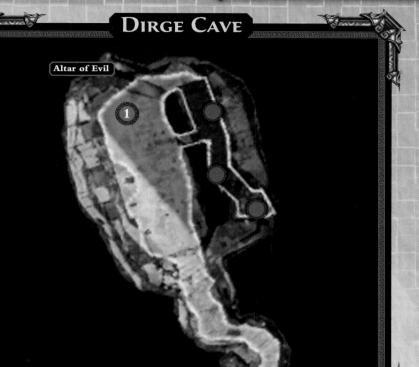

Altar of Evil

to Inner Courtyard

MAP LEGEND

- ◯ Container
- ◯ Trapped container
- ① Minion of Suffering

This cave lies at the end of the Path of Demons in the Outer Courtyard. It's actually a high, narrow cleft with a strip of open sky showing high above. Even the ghosts seem to avoid this area, which is now the lair of demons.

Altar of Evil

The Minion of Suffering is strong, but even he serves a greater master: a nameless being of pure darkness and evil. A sickly green orb adorns a pedestal where this malevolent force first contacts you.

CHARACTERS

The Minion of Suffering

① Few creatures are more terrible to behold than the Minion of Suffering. This powerful bull demon has stolen one of the Dirge Fountain Seals; you must defeat him to get it back.

TEMPLE COURTYARD

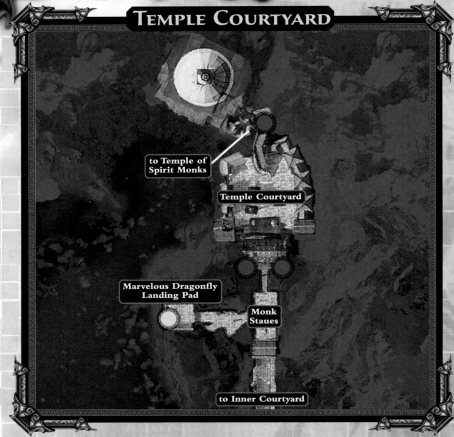

to Temple of
Spirit Monks

Temple Courtyard

Marvelous Dragonfly
Landing Pad

Monk Staues

to Inner Courtyard

MAP LEGEND

- ○ *Focus Shrine*
- ● *Spirit Font*

A final courtyard leads up to the mountain peak. The Inner Courtyard lies to the south, while the temple of Dirge towers to the north.

A small platform to the west makes a perfect landing pad for incoming flyers, though in the spirit world it's simply another lair for ghosts. If you cleanse the area of spirits, you can use the Focus Shrine here to prepare for your battle in the temple.

Marvelous Dragonfly Landing Pad

The path is lined with statues honoring the first 13 monks of Dirge. When they died long ago, the Water Dragon rewarded their service by allowing them to become one with her.

Monk statues

Temple courtyard

Battle still rages on in the courtyard, where ghostly combatants continue the fight that ended with the fall of Dirge. Abbot Song remains here to join his brothers, while you proceed into the temple alone.

TEMPLE OF THE SPIRIT MONKS

to Temple Courtyard

The temple was once the Water Dragon's home, but an alien force of pure evil from beyond the natural world has settled here to feed on the chaotic reverberations caused by the siege. You must defeat it before the Water Dragon can restore your life.

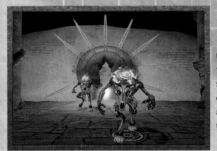

Portal

This portal connects the physical and spiritual worlds, but it's now sealed. The Water Dragon can open it briefly, allowing you to return to the mortal realm.

CRITICAL PATH

NOTE

Because you are a ghost, no SP are awarded, either from battles or from containers, during Chapter Five.

THE LAND OF SPIRITS

After your death at the hands of Master Li, your spirit awakens on a shadowy plain. Move toward the beacon shining upward in the distance. As you journey toward it, lost spirits begin a relentless assault. They tend to appear at a great distance, sometimes too far away for you to target them. They can easily wear you down with energy bolts if you simply try to run up to them; instead, launch Magic attacks as soon possible. After each fight, the Water Dragon's Spirit speaks in your mind and urges you to hurry across the plain so that she might transport you someplace safer. You must defeat seven lost spirits over the course of five battles to reach the Water Dragon.

Ghostly artillery litters this ancient battlefield.

SPIRIT PLAIN BATTLE: ~2,506 XP, 0 SP

Enemy	Style	Health	Chi
Lost Spirit x7	Lost Spirit	280	280

When you reach the beacon, the Water Dragon explains some of the motives behind Sun Li's actions. Your former master is using your Dragon Amulet to siphon away her power, and she has little time left. Using her last ounce of strength, she transports you to Dirge so that you might cleanse it of spiritual corruption.

THE MINION OF SUFFERING

ABBOT SONG

You arrive at the Outer Courtyard of Dirge, home of your lost people. A flaming glyph blocks the path you entered from, so there's no going back. Stride forward and open the urn to find a **Gem of Premonition** (Mind +1, -50 percent trap evade Focus cost). Two demons attack when you approach the flight of steps leading onward. Break out a weapon and start with the horse demon, slaying him first. Then mop up the rodent.

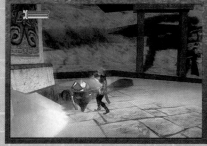

DEMON BATTLE: ~1,233 XP, 0 SP

Enemy	Style	Health	Chi
Rat Demon	Rat Demon	437	437
Horse Demon	Horse Demon	525	525

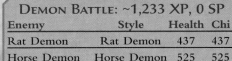

Continue across a wooden bridge to meet the ghost of Abbot Song, former head of the Spirit Monks. He tells you the *true* story of what happened the day Dirge fell, and his tale reveals the depth of evil to which Master Li sank in his treachery. Because you are now the last of the order, Abbot Song is devoted to helping you and becomes your new Follower. In Support mode, he recovers all three of your abilities; an essential service in this unsafe realm.

Abbot Song Profile

Attack Style: Monk's Spade
Support Ability: Recover Health, Chi, and Focus
Health: ~618
Chi: ~468

THE SACRED FOUNTAINS

Once across the bridge, bear left to find a scrollstand. Continue beyond it to the first fountain. Three vicious ghosts attack when you get near. One of them, Xian Wu, was once the guardian of the fountain, but lured by the promise of power offered by Sun Li, she betrayed the Spirit Monks by contaminating the fountain with human blood. In this difficult battle, all three enemies make liberal use of Magic attacks. Use Focus mode and blocking to avoid damage, or use a Transformation style to make yourself immune to their attacks. To ensure that your Chi and Focus last throughout the battle, use Abbot Song in Support mode; in a long fight, his regenerative powers come in handy.

XIAN WU BATTLE: ~1,071 XP, 0 SP

Enemy	Style	Health	Chi
Betrayer x2	Thousand Cuts, Dire Flame	1,225	1,225
Xian Wu	Thousand Cuts, Ice Shard	1,225	1,225

[Power surges through the fountain as the seal is restored.]

When the battle is over, Abbot Song tells you the full story of Xian Wu and explains how spirit binding can be used to enslave ghosts to your will. You then receive the **Dirge Fountain Seal** (5,000 XP). Examine the fountain and use the seal you just obtained to cleanse it. The fountain springs back to life, opening the door to the next area.

Head for the gate that just opened. There are still many spirits here, trapped in an endless re-enactment of the battle that destroyed your people. After Abbot Song takes more time to answer your questions, go through the gate. The Water Dragon's Spirit appears and encourages you and Abbot Song to continue restoring the fountains.

THE ABBOT

As you approach the second fountain, you learn that its seal has been stolen by a powerful demon known as the Minion of Suffering. You must find and defeat him to reclaim the seal and restore the fountain.

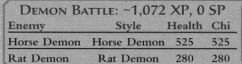

I am the Minion of Suffering. It was I who devoured the guardian bound to this fountain and claimed the seal for my Master.

SIDE QUEST

Abbot Song tells you of a powerful gem, still hidden somewhere nearby, that can help you defeat the Minion of Suffering; but he warns that the spirits drawn by the gem's power may be just as difficult to defeat. For full details, see the Gem of Power side quest.

Go north from the fountain to confront a pair of demons. Eliminate the horse demon first with weapons, then finish off his companion. Because horse demons damage you every time you touch them, monitor your Health closely and take a break to use Chi Heal if needed. There are numerous Spirit Fonts and Focus Shrines here, so don't hesitate to use all your resources to emerge victorious.

DEMON BATTLE: ~1,072 XP, 0 SP

Enemy	Style	Health	Chi
Horse Demon	Horse Demon	525	525
Rat Demon	Rat Demon	280	280

Continue your ascent. After a wide curve in the stairs, a lone rat demon challenges you. Without help from any tougher demons, however, his fate is sealed. Destroy him and climb the remaining flight of stairs.

DEMON BATTLE: ~411 XP, 0 SP

Enemy	Style	Health	Chi
Rat Demon	Rat Demon	280	280

At the top, another demon group appears in ambush. As usual with this combination of fiends, eliminate the biggest threat first. After the horse demon falls, the rat demons pose almost no trouble.

DEMON BATTLE: ~1,483 XP, 0 SP

Enemy	Style	Health	Chi
Rat Demon x2	Rat Demon	280	280
Horse Demon	Horse Demon	525	525

A trapped container lies in the northeast corner. Open it, then move into the cave to the north where the Minion of Suffering awaits. Before you can challenge him, you must face a few more demons. The first, a horse demon, appears as you head inside. Your extensive experience with battling these creatures allows you to cinch an easy victory.

HORSE DEMON BATTLE: ~661 XP, 0 SP

Enemy	Style	Health	Chi
Horse Demon	Horse Demon	525	525

Two more of the equine fiends appear next. Finish them efficiently with strong attacks such as Jade Golem or Toad Demon; this also ensures that you won't get singed by the horse demons' flaming manes. After defeating them, proceed to the back of the cave.

HORSE DEMON BATTLE: ~1,322 XP, 0 SP

Enemy	Style	Health	Chi
Horse Demon x2	Horse Demon	525	525

DEFEAT THE MINION OF SUFFERING

The Minion of Suffering lurks in the very back of the cave. After the obligatory taunts, the battle is joined. Because Magic styles have no effect on him, you must conduct the fight in close quarters unless you use Mirabelle or Horse Demon. The best strategy, however, is to use a quick Martial or Weapon style. The Minion of Suffering attacks with blasts of electricity that can shock you, exactly as if you'd been struck by Storm Dragon. Dodge or block these attacks and quickly close with the demon, then use evasive maneuvers to leap over him and attack from behind with a Chi Strike–enhanced combo. As he slowly turns to face you, leap over again and repeat your attack. Using this pattern, you can defeat the Minion of Suffering with ease.

MINION OF SUFFERING BATTLE: ~2,055 XP, 0 SP			
Enemy	Style	Health	Chi
Minion of Suffering	Bull Demon	1,225	1,225

The **Dirge Fountain Seal** is yours after defeating the Minion. Explore the catwalks that line the east side of the cavern before you return to the Outer Courtyard. The ceramic urn might contain a random gem, while the other cask and urn farther on are trapped.

After claiming everything, leave the cave and head back to the fountain. As you approach the end of the Path of Demons, two horse demons appear and begin launching fireballs in your direction. Dodge using Focus mode, and with Abbot Song in Attack mode, quickly move in and destroy them.

CERAMIC URN

HORSE DEMON

HORSE DEMON BATTLE: ~1,322 XP, 0 SP			
Enemy	Style	Health	Chi
Horse Demon x2	Horse Demon	525	525

DIRGE FOUNTAIN

The fountain's seal restores its former beauty.

Approach the fountain and use the seal you got from the Minion of Suffering to reactivate it (3,000 XP). This causes the temple doors to open. Climb the stairs to the north and enter the Temple Courtyard. When you enter, three lost spirits attack. Reply to their bolts with your own Magic attacks.

LOST SPIRIT BATTLE: ~1,074 XP, 0 SP			
Enemy	Style	Health	Chi
Lost Spirit x3	Lost Spirit	280	280

RED MINISTER

A pair of sinister ministers attack in deadly combination.

Another tough battle awaits at the end of the Dragonfly Landing Pad. There are *two* red ministers to contend with here in addition to a lost spirit. Place Abbot Song in Attack mode to help take some of the heat, or you can be quickly overwhelmed. Use Focus mode to retard your foes' movements and, with your strongest attacks, defeat one of the ministers first. Target the second minister next, leaving the lost spirit for last. Don't worry about conserving Focus; you can use a shrine here when the skirmish is won.

SPIRIT BATTLE: ~1,668 XP, 0 SP			
Enemy	Style	Health	Chi
Red Minister x2	Red Minister	612	612
Lost Spirit	Lost Spirit	280	280

When you approach the temple entrance, the Water Dragon appears to thank you for restoring the two fountains. She tells you that you must accomplish the rest of your tasks in Dirge alone and sends Abbot Song on his way. If you destroy the abomination that has settled in the temple, feeding on the lingering power, the Water Dragon promises to restore you to life.

ATTACKING THE ASPECTS

Three dopplegangers stand between you and rebirth.

ASPECT OF DESPAIR

The evil force manifests in the form of three mirror images of yourself that reflect the darkest aspects of your character. This can be a very challenging fight, but there is a sure path to victory: Jade Golem. Combined with Focus mode, this colossus can carve a swath of destruction through the aspects in no time. If you lack the Chi and Focus reserves to use this technique, then supplement yourself with Spirit Thief. If you prefer to use conventional styles, target the aspects one by one. Eliminate the Aspects of Rage and Suffering first so you can face the Aspect of Despair without getting frozen or immolated.

ASPECTS BATTLE: ~2,418 XP, 0 SP				
Enemy	Style	Health	Chi	
Aspect of Rage	Ice Shard, Basic	962	962	
Aspect of Sorrow	Dire Flame, Basic	962	962	
Aspect of Despair	Twin Swords, Basic	962	962	

With the nameless evil dispelled, the Water Dragon recovers enough of her power to open the portal that takes you back to the physical world. Once reborn, you can begin your final journey to confront your former master and bring him to justice.

SIDE QUESTS

THE GEM OF POWER

Ceramic Urn

To claim the gem Abbot Song told you about, follow the west path from the Dirge Fountain. A ceramic urn before the red gate contains the **Brilliant Gem of Balance** (Body +4, Spirit +4, Mind +4).

Pass through the gate and look for a narrow stairway on the left. Follow it to find a Focus Shrine and urn on a secluded balcony. The urn contains the **Gem of the Infinite Spirit** (Spirit +10, Body -5, Mind -5). Meditate at the shrine if needed, then return and follow the main road to the treasury.

The Abbot

Two lost spirits attack as you ascend the wide stairs. Use Focus mode to evade their attacks and eliminate them with Chi Strikes in your strongest style. If you're badly hurt during this fight, retrace your steps to replenish at the Focus Shrine and Spirit Font so that you're in perfect health for the tougher battle ahead.

LOST SPIRIT BATTLE: ~716 XP, 0 SP				
Enemy	Style	Health	Chi	
Lost Spirit x2	Lost Spirit	280	280	

The red minister, a spirit very similar to Bladed Thesis (who you may have met in the Great Forest) attacks all who try to claim the gem stored here. With two lost spirits providing backup, this battle is very difficult without relying on Focus mode to avoid their barrage. Eliminate the lost spirits first so you can concentrate on the red minister without distractions. With attacks that drain your Health and Chi, the red minister can restore himself while weakening you at the same time. Use the same tactic against him with Spirit Thief style.

RED MINISTER BATTLE: ~1,137 XP, 0 SP				
Enemy	Style	Health	Chi	
Lost Spirit x2	Lost Spirit	280	280	
Red Minister	Red Minister	350	350	

The gem you get as a reward for the Gem of Power quest depends on your alignment. If you're mostly Closed Fist, you can claim the **Eye of the Demon** (Body +6, Spirit +6, Mind +6, Demon Skin: 5 percent chance of draining Health from your attacker, Closed Fist only) (3,000 XP). If you meet the alignment requirements, equip this incredibly powerful gem immediately! If you're Open Palm, you get the **Eye of the Dragon** (Body +6, Spirit +6, Mind +6, Celestial Aura: 5 percent chance of a shockwave knocking down an attacker). You also learn a new Transformation style, **Red Minister**. This ghostly form allows you to restore your Health and Chi with every strike against your enemies.

To earn further experience, continue your ascent and confront two more lost spirits. Then enter the narrow passage, which leads back down to the fountain area to continue your quest.

LOST SPIRIT BATTLE: ~716 XP, 0 SP				
Enemy	Style	Health	Chi	
Lost Spirit x2	Lost Spirit	280	280	

CHAPTER SIX

OVERVIEW

Dawn Star guided us to this place, but I expected a ghost, not flesh and blood.

⊗ Skip

You know nothing about me, about what I endure. Your fists will not defeat me. Not while I must obey.

Wherein a friend is returned to the living,   *Dirge is under siege once more,*   *And the fate of Death's Hand is sealed.*

Restoring the fountains of Dirge has allowed the Water Dragon to grant you a second chance at life. Your Followers now rush to be at your side, but Sun Li also moves. He knows the threat a Spirit Monk poses. Here, at the ruins of Dirge, history will repeat itself in spectacular fashion.

TEMPLE

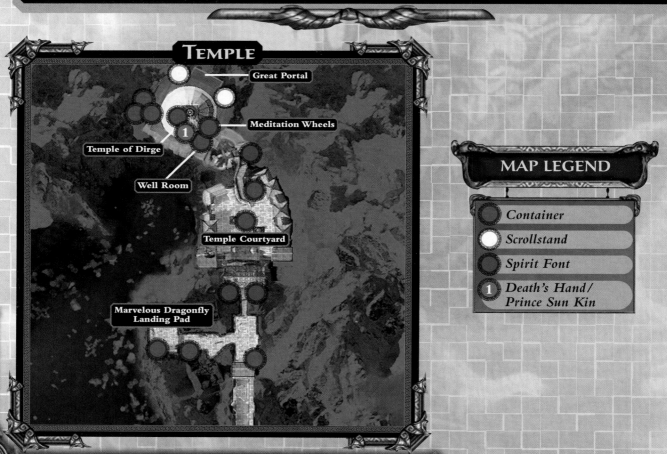

Great Portal

Meditation Wheels

Temple of Dirge

1

Well Room

Temple Courtyard

Marvelous Dragonfly
Landing Pad

MAP LEGEND

⬤	*Container*
⚪	*Scrollstand*
⬤	*Spirit Font*
①	*Death's Hand / Prince Sun Kin*

The Great Portal

The portal that connects the spiritual and material worlds is still active, but without the Water Dragon's power it remains impassable.

A dry well below the temple served as a secret passage for the Spirit Monks and Imperial spies that conspired to overthrow Dirge. Unfortunately, the secret of how it opened was lost along with the last of the Spirit Monks.

Well Room

The Temple of Dirge

Even though you cleansed the evil from the temple in the spiritual world, echoes of chaos still linger. Numerous corpses and skeletons testify to the tragic siege that ended the prosperity of your people.

The Journal of Abbot Song: Before Dirge fell, Abbot Song saw troubling signs begin to surface among some of the acolytes.

Mantra of Inspiration: This ancient text teaches you how to properly use the meditation wheels at the temple's entrance.

Meditation wheels

Within the temple entrance stand a series of meditation wheels, heavy stone drums carved with spiritual intonements and prayers. Some of them have broken, but you can find the parts to fix them and benefit from the insight they provide.

Temple courtyard

The ghosts of Imperial soldiers, trapped in the material world, linger in the courtyard where they fell in battle. They blame their suffering on the Spirit Monks and attack you without hesitation.

Your Followers, guided by the Water Dragon's spirit, have come to Dirge and made a hasty camp south of the temple on this wide platform. It may be a little exposed, but thick-walled tents provide adequate shelter.

The Marvelous Dragonfly Landing Pad

CHARACTERS

Death's Hand/Prince Sun Kin

1 Prince Sun Kin, bound to Sun Li's old armor and transformed into Death's Hand, meets you in the temple of Dirge for a decisive battle. After wresting control of him from Sun Li, you can either enslave him to your own will, making him your Follower, or you can allow the Prince's soul to finally be rid of the curse that binds him to this world.

OUTER COURTYARD

Bridge

MAP LEGEND

◎ Container

Bridge

A slender but sturdy bridge provides the only path into Dirge capable of supporting Sun Li's heavy troops. You can blow up the bridge to slow down the enemy's forces in defense of the monastery.

CRITICAL PATH
THE RETURN TO DIRGE

You awaken in the physical world. The portal you came through remains ajar as demons rend their way through it after you. There are two courses of action for this battle. For a quick and painless victory, destroy the glowing disturbance to close the portal (though no Experience Points are earned this way). A shockwave from the disturbance sends you flying if you touch it, so use Magic or other ranged attacks to avoid this. A more challenging alternative carries greater rewards. One of the horse demons is an ancient scion of his breed, and much stronger than the others. Concentrate strictly on evasion until he appears, as the lesser horse demons give no XP and continually respawn each time they're destroyed. When the ancient horse demon appears, target and destroy him to instantly end the battle and receive a new technique: **Bone Splinter** (Health +15).

HORSE DEMON BATTLE: ~1,942 XP, 0 SP

Enemy	Style	Health	Chi
Horse Demon x?	Horse Demon	280	280
Ancient Horse Demon	Horse Demon	380	380

NOTE

It might seem like a clever idea to wait for the ancient horse demon to appear and then destroy the portal, but unless you slay him personally you won't gain either the technique or any XP.

So many are gone, but not all. What did we do to deserve this curse? Must we fight for all eternity?

There is much to discover in the temple ruins, but before you investigate further, make a pass through the courtyard to clear out the ghosts and to meet your Followers, who await you on the Marvelous Dragonfly Landing Pad. Leave the temple (ignoring the meditation wheels for now) and descend the stairs to the courtyard, where the angry ghosts of Imperial soldiers who died in the siege confront you. Despite the ghosts' unimpressive stamina, the long reach of their spears demands respect. Fortunately, there's a Spirit Font at the top of the stairs; make liberal use of ranged Magic attacks to nullify their threat, then replenish yourself at the font before moving on.

GHOST BATTLE: ~1,140 XP, 0 SP

Enemy	Style	Health	Chi
Imperial Soldier Ghost x4	Spear	100	100

Move into the center of the courtyard to trigger another battle with three more ghosts identical to the ones you just fought. Disperse them in the same manner.

GHOST BATTLE: ~855 XP, 0 SP

Enemy	Style	Health	Chi
Imperial Soldier Ghost x3	Spear	100	100

Exit the courtyard to the south, pausing at the Spirit Fonts flanking the gate if needed. Pass by the abbot statues and approach the gate to the Inner Courtyard at the end of the path, where another three ghosts lie in wait. After they rise from the cold ground, back away and disperse them with a volley of Magical energies.

GHOST BATTLE: ~855 XP, 0 SP

Enemy	Style	Health	Chi
Imperial Soldier Ghost x3	Spear	100	100

Venture onto the Marvelous Dragonfly Landing Pad, where your Followers have already set up a pair of tents against the frigid mountain air. Your loyal friends are overjoyed to see you returned to life, but the happy reunion is darkened by news that Master Li (now Emperor Sun Li) has activated his golem army and is marching them inexorably toward Dirge. Take time to chat with everyone and catch up on events, then return to finish your exploration of the temple before turning in for the night.

Your former master, my uncle, has taken the Jade Empire as his own. Emperor Sun Li has set the whole of his forces against us, and we are trapped here in Dirge.

You can perform two ceremonies here to further purify (or desecrate) the area and increase your abilities. The first requires an artifact called the Tome of Release; which must be assembled from the five scattered pieces strewn around the temple. The second ceremony is a prayer exercise that uses the heavy stone meditation wheels at the temple entrance; maximize the benefits from this by learning the correct mantra and fixing the broken meditation wheels before you pray. Read on to discover where to find all the needed components for both rituals.

THE TOME OF RELEASE

As you leave the camp, a final ghost confronts you. This spirit was a captain, and his rank is reflected in his extra strength and fighting prowess. As with the other undead soldiers you've faced here, ranged Magic attacks are the best way to circumvent his weapon slashes.

GHOST BATTLE: ~621 XP, 0 SP

Enemy	Style	Health	Chi
Imperial Captain Ghost	Sword	600	600

To perform the ritual of release, first gather the torn pages from scattered sites on the temple grounds. There are five pieces to collect; the following images show where they are found.

Pages from the Tome of Release (1/5): In front of one of the giant abbot statues.

Pages from the Tome of Release (2/5): By the Focus Shrine on the Marvelous Dragonfly Landing Pad.

Pages from the Tome of Release (3/5): Center of the courtyard.

Pages from the Tome of Release (4/5): Base of the stairs leading into the temple.

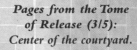

Pages from the Tome of Release (5/5): By the statue of the Heavenly Gate Guardian.

Search diligently inside to find more incidental treasure: a skeleton and chest in the corner hold 256 SP between them. Rummage through the pile of decaying bodies by the massive dragon fountain to obtain a new technique: **Replenishment of the Mind** (Focus +7, Chi +7). After collecting everything and assembling the complete Tome of Release, you can now use it to perform a ritual. There are two ways to do this:

[You start the mental preparation for the ritual to release the spirits of the cursed imperial guards and allow them to find peace.]

Perform the ritual of release under the auspices of Mah Tsung to end the dead soldiers' suffering.

Choice 1 Complete the ritual at the statue of Mah Tsung (1,000 XP). This grants relief to all the soldiers whose ghosts still linger in Dirge, earning you a new technique: **The Turning Wheel** (Focus +7, Chi +7).

[You start your mental preparation for the ritual that will sever the spirits of the cursed imperial soldiers from the Wheel of Life.]

The Heavenly Gate Guardian's influence exorcises the temple by permanently destroying the ghosts that haunt it.

Choice 2 Complete the ritual at the statue of the Heavenly Gate Guardian (1,000 XP). This rids the monastery of lingering ghosts by tearing their souls to shreds, and bestows a new technique: **The Broken Wheel** (Health +7, Chi +7).

THE MANTRA OF INSPIRATION

The Beveled Cogs are located near the gate to the Inner Courtyard.

Search the Well Room to find the Machined Cogs.

This scrollstand in the temple teaches you the Mantra of Inspiration.

go back upstairs. Finally, peruse the scrollstand in the temple's east corner to learn the **Mantra of Inspiration**.

To gain maximum reward from meditation in the temple, first locate the **Beveled Cogs**, found on the skeleton just outside the Marvelous Dragonfly Landing Pad, and the **Machined Cogs**, found in a chest in the Well Room. While in the Well Room, smash open the vase for 200 SP, then

To complete the ceremony, find the meditation wheels just inside the temple entrance. Repair the wheels using the cogs you scavenged (the cylinders will glow blue), spin the wheels, then meditate upon the mantra. You receive enlightenment in the form of a new technique, the **Communion of the Dragon** (Health +5, Chi +15).

NOTE

*If you meditate upon the mantra after repairing only one of the broken wheels, you receive the technique **Communion of the Ocean** (Chi +10) instead.*

FEARLESS FOLLOWERS

After finishing your duties within the temple, return to your Followers' camp. When you enter the tent, any romantic interests you've pursued with one (or more) of your companions culminates in a tender moment (or, if you have neglected your Followers, you end up sleeping alone). For complete details on the possible outcomes, see Appendix II: Character Romances.

Memories of Two Rivers come flooding back to you in the night.

During the night, Sun Li contacts you through a dream. In a half-real vision tinged in sepia tones, he conjures nightmarish versions of your former classmates and forces you to battle them. The blurriness of memory makes visibility difficult, so rely on targeting to help you aim your attacks. Ranged assault with Magic styles is a preferred tactic, but any strong combination of physical attacks is also effective. Despite being only shadows in your mind, your foes are vulnerable to any type of assault; use Support styles to give yourself an extra edge.

DREAM BATTLE: ~855 XP, 0 SP

Enemy	Style	Health	Chi
Jing Woo	Basic	1,100	1,100
Student Wen	Thousand Cuts	400	400
Student Lin	Spear	400	400

But what about the rest of us? Why just send them? Why are we sitting here holding our... Ohhh, I get it. They're coming here, too, aren't they?

The next morning finds you assembled in the Outer Courtyard with your followers. Sky reports that siege golems, gargantuan constructs that tower dozens of feet high, are closing in on Dirge. While the rest of the group spreads out to fight in defense of the monastery, Dawn Star, Silk Fox, and Kang stay behind to plant explosives on the nearby bridge, thus denying the siege golem a route up the mountain.

Before everyone splits up, Kang suggests taking a brief trip in the Marvelous Dragonfly to see if an aerial assault might tilt the odds in your favor. This is optional, but if you succeed, there are fewer troops to fight in the upcoming battles. For full information on this flying mission, see the Flying Missions section of Chapter Three.

A short run in the flyer to take the brunt of their advance. It might be a worthwhile mission. Or it might be suicide.

DEMOLISH THE BRIDGE

DAWN STAR

Next, choose either Dawn Star or Silk Fox to lead the team that's responsible for blowing up the bridge. These two haven't always seen eye to eye, but the threat of imminent attack unites them now. As you approach the bridge, Dawn Star receives a message from a helpful spirit that a powerful weapon is hidden nearby. To claim it, leave the bridge area and look for a chest hidden behind the fountain that you restored earlier. Inside is the weapon, which makes the upcoming battle much easier. Then return to the bridge.

Here they come! Hold them off! I only need a minute!

Imperial troops storm the far side as you step onto the bridge. Your goal is to protect Kang at all costs so he can complete the job of rigging the bridge with explosives. The enemies that swarm toward you are supported by an endless supply of reinforcements, so it's not possible to destroy them all. Instead, use area attacks liberally to keep the enemies from nearing Kang. The mad inventor's health is displayed at the bottom of the screen: if he dies, your quest ends. After one minute, the first attack wave ends.

BRIDGE BATTLE: 0 XP, 0 SP

Enemy	Style	Health	Chi
Imperial Soldier x∞	Spear	75	10

A second surge of enemies follows on the heels of the first. This time, stronger enemies are mixed in with the low-ranking soldiers. Target any who use Magic styles first and keep them distracted while Kang does his work. After another minute, Kang finally completes his sabotage and the bridge falls into the chasm below, stranding the siege golem on the far side. With this line of defense secure, return through the gate to the Inner Courtyard.

BRIDGE BATTLE: 0 XP, 0 SP

Enemy	Style	Health	Chi
Imperial Soldier x∞	Basic	75	10
Lotus Assassin x∞	Basic	320	320
Lotus Assassin x∞	Dire Flame	400	400

KANG'S HEALTH: 50%

THE BLACK WHIRLWIND STRIKES

Meanwhile, the Black Whirlwind and Henpecked Hou mount a desperate struggle against Imperial forces in the temple courtyard. This battle has a few unusual features. You take control of the Black Whirlwind, and your primary goal is to destroy the golem. You can't eliminate all of the Lotus Assassins, because reinforcements arrive as fast as you can pile up bodies. Henpecked Hou scampers around the fringe of battle, dropping his usual wine casks; grab these to refill your Health. **Maker's Bane and Placid Guiju** are hidden in this courtyard. You can find them during the big fight. After the golem is demolished, you can finally leave the courtyard.

> ## NOTE
>
> *Avoiding the jade golem can enable an interesting minor easter egg: For every 20 Assassins you kill, you hear a voice shouting out in bloodthirsty celebration. You get this voice for 20, 40, 60, 80, and 100 kills. The voice for 100 kills is only there if you still haven't killed the jade golem yet by then. There is not stat bonus or reward for this other than the voice, which might be Whirlwind's internal voices celebrating the slaughter.*

COURTYARD BATTLE: 0 XP, 0 SP			
Enemy	Style	Health	Chi
Lotus Assassin x∞	Viper	50	0
Golem	Golem	1,100	1,100

Return to the Marvelous Dragonfly Landing Pad, carving a swath through another squad of Assassins. Return to the courtyard, then climb the steps and enter the temple, relinquishing control of the Black Whirlwind.

DEFEATING DEATH'S HAND

Within the temple, Sky reveals that the Lotus Assassins tried to recruit him to their side, and that he agreed! But he's been planning to double-cross Death's Hand the entire time, and when the Assassins' leader strides into the temple, Sky sets off the trap he laid during the night. A huge portion of the ceiling collapses, crushing the Assassins under a pile of rubble.

Death's Hand, now revealed to be Prince Sun Kin, is not so easily defeated, however, and he rises to face you, seemingly unscathed. After swapping boasts, you begin the battle! Death's Hand is, by far, the most powerful foe that you have ever faced. One swipe of his black sword can slice more than 100 points from your Health. Your main advantage lies in the fact that your nemesis is vulnerable to all styles of attack.

There are a number of ways to increase your odds of survival. While in Focus mode, use strong Magic or Support style attacks to immobilize and debilitate the Assassin lord, then attack while he's less of a threat. Under no circumstances should you try to face Death's Hand without hobbling him first. Jade Golem is powerful, but too slow to avoid being shattered to dust by his cruel swords. Mirabelle offers a very potent ranged attack option. If you need to replenish your abilities, use Spirit Thief with extreme caution; Death's Hand can lunge out of the draining effect to strike you with his strongest attack unless you're at a comfortably safe distance.

DEATH'S HAND BATTLE: 0 XP, 0 SP			
Enemy	Style	Health	Chi
Death's Hand	Twin Swords	2,000	2,000

When Death's Hand falls, an image of Sun Li appears. Your former master explains that Emperor Sun Hai bound Kin to his armor with the power of the Water Dragon, the power that Li now controls. At his word, Death's Hand is completely healed. You can only truly defeat Death's Hand by breaking Li's hold over him. You must counter Li with the Spirit Monk ability to bind spirits.

TIP

It is possible, using Intuition, to convince Sun Li that further combat is a waste of time (100 XP). He agrees and abandons Death's Hand to you without a fight. You get only one chance at persuasion; if it fails, then the combat proceeds as normal.

Contend with Sun Li for control over the Sun Kin's soul. Torn between the two of you, Prince Kin's spirit is wrested from the armor of Death's Hand.

Break Li's grip on Death's Hand by guiding Sun Kin in a battle against his own corrupted body. This battle is actually much easier than the last one thanks to Prince Kin's incredible speed. Rush into battle with repeated fast attack combos; Death's Hand is too slow to retaliate. Keep slashing with fast attacks to end the battle in no time.

DEATH'S HAND BATTLE: 0 XP, 0 SP			
Enemy	Style	Health	Chi
Death's Hand	Twin Swords	2,000	2,000

Losing won't end the game (Sun Kin is destroyed, not you), but you must win to get the choice of keeping Death's Hand.

If Prince Kin loses despite your guidance, Death's Hand ceases to exist.

Choice 1 After Prince Kin triumphs over Death's Hand, release his soul from bondage. Deeply grateful to finally rest, Sun Kin's spirit dissipates, bestowing you with a potent gem, **Way of the Open Palm** (Intuition +10, Spirit +5, Body −5).

Know this, Spirit Monk. You walk a path very near that of your Master. Both lead to power, but the cost cannot be avoided!

Prince Kin is free from Sun Li, but is still enslaved in the terrible black armor.

Choice 2 Bind the prince's soul to your will, forcing Death's Hand to become your Follower. This corrupted Assassin, subject to your every command, brings with him twin swords of deadly keenness. If you choose this dark path, you're rewarded with a potent gem: **The Way of the Closed Fist** (Intimidation +10, Body +5, Spirit −5).

Death's Hand Profile

Attack Style: Fallen Blades
Support Ability: None
Health: ~912
Chi: ~324

OVERVIEW

Well, I can't say my time with you has been boring... Dangerous, nerve-wracking, even exciting at times... but never boring.

Ah, there you are. I knew you would come, and I have grown very good at waiting. You are very different from the student I once taught. Death changed you, I imagine.

Wherein the cost of war is tallied,   *A Master is finally confronted,*   *And the fate of an Empire is decided.*

You have come far, from borderland school to the ruins of Dirge, and now the fate of the Empire depends on the decisions before you. Stung by the loss of Death's Hand and the defeat of his siege force, Emperor Sun Li readies for your inevitable confrontation in the palace.

IMPERIAL PALACE

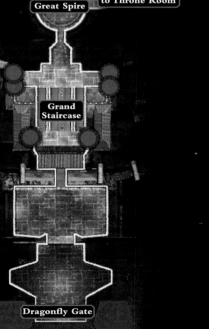

Great Spire — to Throne Room

Grand Staircase

Dragonfly Gate

CAUTION

SPOILER ALERT

This chapter details the final steps of your quest through the Jade Empire. All secrets divulged at the end of the story are revealed in detail. If you wish to discover this knowledge for yourself, glance ahead at your peril!

MAP LEGEND

Container

Trapped Container

In order to reach the Throne Room for your final confrontation with the Glorious Strategist, you must fight through an ornate wing of the palace.

The palace looks much as it did during your last visit, even down to the hordes of Lotus Assassin guards. Watch carefully for subtle differences, however, such as several newly stocked urns.

Grand Staircase

Your last flight ends at the Marvelous Dragonfly Gate, where your Followers gather to discuss one last time the chain of events that have led them this far.

Marvelous Dragonfly Gate

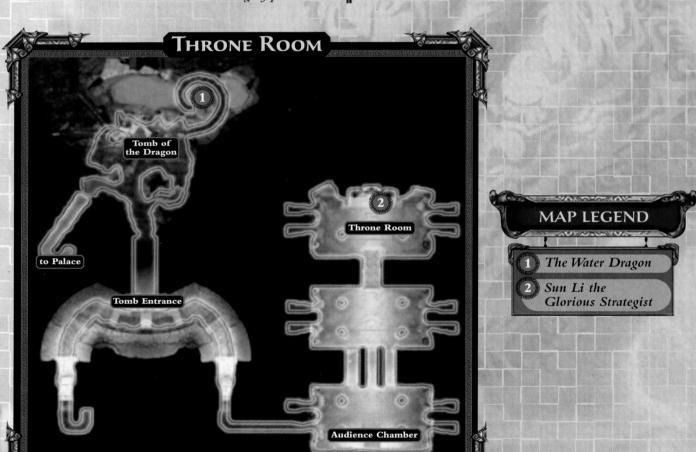

THRONE ROOM

1 — Tomb of the Dragon

to Palace

Tomb Entrance

2 — Throne Room

Audience Chamber

MAP LEGEND

1 *The Water Dragon*

2 *Sun Li the Glorious Strategist*

Tomb of the Dragon

The Water Dragon's body lies concealed in a deep chamber at the heart of the Imperial Palace. The gruesome secret of how endless water is extracted from her tortured body is finally made clear.

When you last came here, it was with the goal of rescuing Master Li, whom you had always trusted as the only guardian you had ever known. This time, however, you have come to slay him for his villainous treachery.

Throne Room

CHARACTERS

The Water Dragon

1 You've met the Water Dragon's spirit many times during your journey, but her ghostly form barely hints at her true shape.

Sun Li the Glorious Strategist

2 Despite your resilience, almost everything else has gone according to Sun Li's plan. He now reigns where his brother once sat, and prepares for your arrival.

CRITICAL PATH
THE WATER DRAGON'S DESTINY

FAREWELL TO DIRGE

After the battle in the temple, return to the courtyard to join your Followers (8,247 XP, 2,050 SP). If you chose to bring Death's Hand along, your Followers revolt in horror and plead with you to reconsider. There are two possible outcomes to this conflict:

Can you blame us? There is an unsettling new presence in the group.

It is not right. Such a torment to inflict.

Your Followers do not fear Death's Hand, they pity him.

Choice 1 Allow your Followers to change your mind about chaining Death's Hand to your will. They show visible relief when Prince Sun Kin's soul departs for good.

The Ritual of Binding compels your Followers to obey your commands.

Choice 2 Insist on absolute obedience by binding the dissenters in your group (Sky, Dawn Star, Silk Fox, and Henpecked Hou) in the same way you bound the Prince. Unable to resist, they unwillingly remain by you even though they now believe you are at least as bad as Sun Li himself. If you have turned a romantic interest (Sky, Dawn Star, or Silk Fox) "evil," that character will side with you on the Death's Hand issue.

Take time to speak with each of your friends (or slaves) to hear their reactions to the battle. When you're ready, speak with Kang at the Marvelous Dragonfly Landing Pad to travel to the floating palace and the fulfillment of your destiny.

STORMING THE PALACE

Your group gathers at the Marvelous Dragonfly Gate, eager to press onward and resolve the conflict once and for all. Pass through the door and take advantage of the Focus Shrines and Spirit Fonts to ensure that you're in top condition for the intense battle in the next room.

Ha! You thought that the last visit was easy? This should be more fun than even I could've hoped for.

LOTUS ELITE

The Lotus Elites form the strongest fighting force that Sun Li has at his command. Their speed and variety of styles make them even deadlier than a gang of golems. Because they are human, they have one severe weakness: vulnerability to Support styles. This means you can use Support attacks not only to hamper your foes, but also to set up deadly Harmonic Combos. Use area attacks and Focus mode to make some room, then target the Assassins one by one with your best Magic or Support attacks. Avoid slow styles such as Mirabelle or Toad Demon, or the Elites will cut you to pieces in a deadly swarm. Also avoid placing a Follower in Attack mode; you want all your allies (willing or not) to be in top shape.

GRAND STAIRCASE BATTLE: ~1,620 XP, ~934 SP			
Enemy	Style	Health	Chi
Lotus Elite x4	Viper	500	500
Lotus Elite	Sword, Hidden Fist	500	500
Lotus Elite x2	Sword, Viper	500	500

Trap sprung!

When the Assassins are slain, use the Spirit Font and Focus Shrine in the previous room to recharge. Then scour the Grand Staircase for treasure. At the lower landing, an urn on the west contains a random gem; the urn on the east is trapped.

Four more urns await on the upper landing. Three of them are simply traps, but the one on the northwest corner holds 5,000 SP! After claiming everything, return once more to the Spirit Font and Focus Shrine on the lower level to restore any damage you sustained from the traps. Once more in perfect Health, you can now enter the Great Spire.

CERAMIC URN

TIP

What could you possibly do with silver at this point in your quest? You might not be able to shop in the Imperial City, but Zin Bu the Magic Abacus is always ready to make a sale. Because your final confrontation looms very close, you can freely spend every last silver coin without hesitation.

The Water Dragon's spirit appears and urges you to follow her to the secret room where her physical body is kept. The spire's elevator rises to drop off most of your group, while you and a single Follower continue, to see for yourselves exactly how the Sun brothers have created the miracle of endless water.

You have come. Destiny set this moment in motion, but from here, your choices are your own to make.

The gruesome truth is finally revealed when you enter the Tomb of the Dragon. Before you have time to react to the sight, four Assassins launch a desperate attack. Each one wields a kit of styles, meaning there is no best foe to target first. As in the Grand Staircase, using Harmonic Combos is much easier than simply trying to wear each Assassin down. Use Focus mode to accomplish the first Harmonic Combos so that you're not interrupted by your target's allies; setting your Follower to Attack mode here can also help you execute your strongest moves without being caught off guard.

Behold. Words would not have sufficed. You had to see with your own eyes to truly know your fate. This cannot continue!

LOTUS ELITE BATTLE: ~1,220 XP, ~1,373 SP

Enemy	Style	Health	Chi
Lotus Elite x4	Spear, Viper, Tempest	750	750

This... this is not right. Gods... gods do not bleed!

When the Assassins are dead, your Followers pour into the cave and behold in horror the grim spectacle of the Water Dragon's broken body. Each expresses his or her sadness and outrage at the sight, imploring you to grant her request and destroy the foul machinery sustaining her so that she can truly die. At this juncture, you must make an important decision:

Then let it be so. Take hold of a blade, Spirit Monk, and let it strike true. Destroy the machine that maintains this abomination.

Choice 1 👊👊👊 With the full support of your Followers, destroy the Water Dragon's body so that her spirit might be free. A thrown spear jams the complex machinery, resulting in a massive explosion (1,000 XP). If you are aligned with the Closed Fist, this act converts you to Way of the Open Palm, as symbolized by the gem you receive afterward: **Open Palm** (Spirit +10, Mind +5, Open Palm only).

Chai Ka: If the decision is yours, so is the task of bringing the blood. Who of your fellows would you sacrifice for your gain? Whose blood will you use?

Petrified

Henpecked Hou

Choice 2 👊👊👊 Remembering the lessons you learned from Abbot Song in Dirge, suggest poisoning the Water Dragon's body with human blood in order to weaken Sun Li. Henpecked Hou and any romance characters whom you haven't turned to the Closed Fist resist this idea. If you insist on the plan and choose to sacrifice one of them to accomplish it, the four dissenters are left with no choice but to resist with every ounce of strength they have. This act automatically tilts your moral balance to the Closed Fist, even if you were Open Palm before.

If you made the second choice, a massive brawl ensues, with only the Black Whirlwind, Wild Flower's demon (both Chai Ka and Ya Zhen fight for you), and Death's Hand (if you bound him to you) on your side. Any Follower you've romanced and turned to the Closed Fist will fight alongside you, as well. The Health and Chi capacity of your Followers depends on your experience level, so the values shown on the table below are all approximate.

Of the possible opponents, Silk Fox poses the greatest threat. Her speed and constant use of area attacks can quickly overwhelm you, so use Focus mode and strong Magic or Support style attacks to immobilize her and the rest of the group. With most of your former allies hobbled by debilitating status effects, you can begin the actual slaughter. Target one Follower at a time, pausing to re-inflict status effects on your former friends when they recover. After the battle, you desecrate the Water Dragon's body with human blood, condemning her to a painful and lingering fate. A powerful chaotic gem, **Closed Fist** (Body +10, Spirit +5, Closed Fist only), is your reward.

BATTLE OF BETRAYAL: ~1,220 XP, ~1,373 SP

Enemy	Style	Health	Chi
Dawn Star	Sword	~416	~570
Silk Fox	Twin Swords	~558	~428
Sky	Twin Swords	~558	~428
Henpecked Hou	Iron Palm	~416	~570

MASTER LI'S FATE

THE DEMON CONSTRUCTS

Whichever choice you made, you find yourself in the Throne Room. Ascend to the middle level to face Sun Li. Your former master justifies his actions by declaring that order and stability are worth any price. He then summons forth his most powerful guardians: stone golems in demon form. These beasts combine the devastating attacks of their respective demon types with incredible toughness, but unlike true golems they are vulnerable to Martial styles. Your best attacking options are with Transformation or Weapon styles. Mirabelle and Horse Demon offer the only ranged attack choices, but they are severe drains on your resources. Spirit Thief and other styles with Support effects don't work, but you can still

Ah, there you are. I knew you would come, and I have grown very good at waiting. You are very different from the student I once taught. Death changed you, I imagine.

replenish yourself with Red Minister form. Jade Golem is powerful and immune to the shocking effects of the bull demons, but you can easily be crushed if enemies are too close; if you decide to use Jade Golem, do so only in short bursts. Chi Strikes with your most powerful weapon are effective because these styles (except Mirabelle) allow you to retain your full mobility while still causing respectable damage.

STONE CONSTRUCT BATTLE: ~3,052 XP, 0 SP

Enemy	Style	Health	Chi	
Elephant Construct x2	Elephant Demon	750	750	
Bull Construct x2	Bull Demon	750	750	

PERSISTENT DOUBTS

You and your followers are playthings. The rest are held just as you are. You are each too weak to match my power.

With the constructs disposed of, ascend to the highest level of the Throne Room. Sun Li has one more trick up his sleeve; he casts a spell and traps you within the stormy ether of your own mind. Four strange stone-like creatures bearing a resemblance to the Sun brothers rush toward you to attack. Formed from your own inner turmoil, they are deadly

combatants. The choices you made in the Tomb of the Dragon have a big impact on this battle:

You are not alone. We are also imprisoned, but if we do not resist in our own minds, we can lend our strength to you.

Choice 1 If you followed the Way of the Open Palm and stayed loyal to your allies, they appear to help even the odds. Up to three of them rush forward, canceling out an equal number of your opponents in a flash of annihilation. Now you only have to fight one of the Doubts.

Choice 2 Even if you tread the Way of the Closed Fist, at least two Followers remain with you: the Black Whirlwind and Chai Ka/Ya Zhen. Death's Hand also appears if you made him your Follower; in this case, the battle is exactly the same as in Choice 1.

Doubts are susceptible to all but Weapon styles. If you had three Followers with you, the resulting one-on-one battle shouldn't be too challenging as long as you don't neglect evasion and defense. Use Support styles such as Heavenly Wave instead of Focus mode to gain an advantage in speed. Those on the Way of the Closed Fist should try to conserve resources for the next wave, when you won't have any more Followers to help turn the tide of battle.

BATTLE OF THE DOUBTS: ~1,151 XP, 0 SP

Enemy	Style	Health	Chi	
Doubt	Sword	500	500	
Doubt	Leaping Tiger	500	500	

Sun Li's mocking laughter rings out as the last Doubt falls. Four more of the phantoms appear; just as before, any surviving Followers lead the way to help make things easier for you (if you stayed true to the Open Palm, you only have to fight one Doubt in this second battle as well). For those who have no friends left, this battle is a stiff challenge. The Doubts are very aggressive and intelligent; use quick, mobile styles against them so you can react in an instant to their feints, leaps, and charges. Use Focus mode to destroy one or two of them, greatly increasing your chances of survival. Avoid using slow attacks until you've eliminated some of the Doubts, or they will swarm all over you as you recover from executing your move. With no supporting Followers, monitor your Health closely and keep a reserve of Chi set aside for healing, should you need it.

BATTLE OF THE FOUR DOUBTS: ~1,220 XP, ~1,373 SP

Enemy	Style	Health	Chi
Doubt	Death's Hand	500	500
Doubt	Staff	500	500
Doubt	Sword, Leaping Tiger	500	500
Doubt	Thousand Cuts	500	500

THE FINAL LESSON

After all the Doubts are laid to rest, approach the obelisk that juts from the center of the void. Amazingly, Sagacious Zu appears! His ghost has followed you unseen ever since he fell to Death's Hand in the Lotus Assassin fortress. Now, for the second time, he shows up unexpectedly to save you. His spiritual power is strong enough to shatter the obelisk, releasing you from the spell.

Back in the Throne Room, a last conversation with Sun Li the Glorious Strategist begins. Your responses during this dialogue determine the final outcome of the story, so choose your words carefully:

I see now that the Water Dragon's power is the prize, not the means to victory. No matter what I expend, while you live you will resist. That is your role.

It is the Celestial Bureaucracy attempting to restore balance. We must bring the fight back down to earth. Unless... you are made to see reason.

○ There can be no deals. Let's end this. Master versus student.
I'm listening.

Sun Li reigns in triumph if you heed his advice and sacrifice yourself for the good of the Empire.

Choice 1 Don't listen to Sun Li. Just fight him. The details of the battle are described in the next section.

Choice 2 Sun Li knows that you will never cease fighting against him as long as you live, and he tries his best to convince you that his plan for order and peace is the best thing for the Jade Empire. To further this end, he encourages you to lay down your life in sacrifice as the only way to end your conflict. If you hear out his argument and ultimately agree, you can end your quest here. This choice leads to the **Sacrificial Ending** described below.

Final Battle: Sun Li the Glorious Strategist

Sun Li is an incredibly powerful, quick, and intelligent fighter with more styles at his disposal than any enemy you've faced so far. Prepare yourself by assembling your own kit of styles to match. Having Jade Golem at hand is a *must*, as this form not only inflicts huge damage but is also immune to every style Sun Li uses except the Twin Sabers. Be ready to transform if you become paralyzed or frozen.

Sun Li is fluent in all types of Magical attacks, including a variety of energy blast very similar to an attack from a Lost Spirit. Remember that against fast Magic attacks, it's often better to block than evade, as this allows you to recover a split second faster. All of your Transformation styles are immune to Magic (except Red Minister), so this offers another defense.

Surprisingly, your former master is at his most vulnerable when using Twin Sabers because they are his slowest attack. Use your fastest moves, such as Leaping Tiger or Thousand Cuts, to interrupt his swordplay with a series of combos. Be careful, however, that the Glorious Strategist doesn't change styles on you mid-swing, switching to Paralyzing Palm or Spirit Thief.

Final Battle: Sun Li the Glorious Strategist (cont'd)

These styles have never been wielded against you by any opponent you've faced before, so learning to avoid them can take a little practice. Transformations are the surest defense.

To top off this deadly arsenal of moves, Sun Li can also use Focus mode. He can't sustain it for extended durations, but it can take you by surprise if you aren't prepared. Use your Focus mode to counteract his Focus mode and return to Normal speed. All you can do is concentrate on evasion while you wait for the effect to lapse; do not try offensive moves during this time as your nemesis is quick to exploit any opening you present to him.

Your own attacking options are just as varied, thankfully. Despite the fact that Sun Li seems to know all your moves, there is one thing you can do that he can't: Transform. If you've invested plenty of

Style Points into Jade Golem, you can easily win the battle in less than 30 seconds by combining it with Chi Strikes and Focus mode. Spirit Thief also comes in handy, allowing you to turn the tables on your former master by matching him drain for drain. Avoid using all your Chi, however, and conserve some for Chi Heal.

Understanding the best way to react to each of his styles is the key to victory. If he uses Twin Saber, use ranged attacks or very fast close attacks. When he switches to Leaping Tiger, stay as far away as possible and answer with strong or area attacks with Magic and Support styles. Use Focus mode in short bursts to aid evasion, especially if he's just leapt over your head to attack you from behind. His Magic attacks are best countered by moving in close and using fast Support styles as he recovers, creating an

Final Battle: Sun Li the Glorious Strategist (cont'd)

opening to more combos from you; if you're frozen, immolated, petrified, or trapped in a whirlwind, transform into a demon or golem to break free.

Sun Li is a crafty and deadly opponent, but as his student, you've learned everything he knows and a little more to boot. With carefully chosen tactics, judicious Transformations, and controlled aggression, you will triumph over your former master.

SUN LI THE GLORIOUS STRATEGIST
BATTLE: ~1,220 XP, ~1,373 SP

Enemy	Style	Health	Chi
Sun Li the Glorious Strategist	Leaping Tiger, Spirit Thief, Paralyzing Palm, Magic Master, Twin Saber	2,500	2,500

ENDING IT ALL

You've triumphed over Sun Li in epic battle, but your story isn't finished yet. Now you can sit back and enjoy the ending you've worked so hard to see. There are three possible resolutions. The Sacrificial Ending is shown if you allowed Sun Li to convince you give up without a fight. Otherwise, you see either the Open Palm or Closed Fist ending, depending on how you dealt with the Water Dragon's body. Will the Jade Empire be free of tyranny? Or will you take Sun Li's place as the Empire's new overlord?

SACRIFICIAL ENDING

In which the Golden Hero is unveiled,   *Harsh lessons are learned,*   *And Sun Li has the last laugh.*

A new generation is indoctrinated with the virtues of unquestioning obedience and passive acceptance. With his power firmly consolidated, none dare challenge the supreme might of Emperor Sun Li.

OPEN PALM ENDING

In which the Water Dragon's soul is released,   *Your labors come to an end,*   *And the citizens celebrate your victory.*

When Sun Li falls, the Water Dragon's power is released, and her spirit departs, free now to be born anew as the great Wheel of Life begins to turn. You emerge from the Palace, where your Followers and crowds of rejoicing citizens greet you with thunderous applause.

CLOSED FIST ENDING

In which untold power is absorbed,   *A new Emperor claims rulership,*   *And the Lotus Assassins vow allegiance.*

Using the techniques of the Spirit Monks, you claim the Water Dragon's power and emerge from the palace to cast down Sun Li's broken body before the gathered Lotus Assassins. Recognizing that you are the most powerful being in the land, they bow before you and your rulership begins.

GEMS, ITEMS, AND TECHNIQUES

The following checklist shows all of the Dragon Amulet gems, items necessary for quest advancement, and Techniques available (in a roughly chronological order) during your adventures throughout the Jade Empire. The icon for each is shown, along with a brief description, to help you decide which commodities you should imbue your character with.

GEMS FOR YOUR MIND, BODY, AND DRAGON AMULET

Flawed Warrior Gem

Body +1

This flawed gem provides minor bonus to your Body.

Inferior Warrior Gem

Body +2

This inferior-quality gem provides a small bonus to your Body.

Warrior Gem

Body +4

This average-quality gem provides a good bonus to your Body.

Flawed Monk Gem

Spirit +1

This gem, while flawed, provides a minor boost to your Spirit.

Inferior Monk Gem

Spirit +2

This gem, while of inferior quality, provides a small boost to your Spirit.

Monk Gem

Spirit +4

This average-quality gem provides a sizeable boost to your Spirit.

Flawed Scholar Gem

Mind +1

This flawed gem provides a minor boost to your Mind.

Inferior Scholar Gem

Mind +2

This gem is of inferior quality and provides a small boost to your Mind.

Scholar Gem

Mind +4

This average-quality gem provides a sizeable boost to your Mind.

The Eye of the Dragon

Body +6	Mind +6	Spirit +6

Celestial Aura: 5 percent chance a shockwave will knock attackers down when you are struck. Only followers of the Way of the Open Palm may use this gem. The Eye of the Dragon is a gem of heroes and figures of legend.

The Eye of the Demon

Body +6	Mind +6	Spirit +6

Demon Skin: When damaged, the wielder has a 5 percent chance of draining a small amount of the attacker's Health. Only followers of the Way of the Closed Fist may equip this gem. Rumored to be the eye of a great demon lord.

The Bronze Tongue

Charm +4	Intimidation +4	Intuition +4

Often used by magicians and charlatans, this gem gives the wielder persuasive skills that could make a man sell the shirt off his back for a pittance.

Gems can be found in the unlikliest places.
Search everywhere!

The Silver Tongue

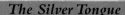

Charm +6	Intimidation +6	Intuition +6

Many famous and influential members of the Imperial Court have a gem like the Silver Tongue, which lends power to their lies and bargains in their games of power and influence.

The Golden Tongue

Charm +8	Intimidation +8	Intuition +8

The treacherous advisor to the great Emperor Sun Jin ordered the Order of the Lotus to construct this gem. The gem gave the advisor nearly unparalleled manipulative power.

The Jade Tongue

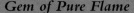

Charm +10	Intimidation +10	Intuition +10

Legends of the fabled Jade Tongue, also known as "the tongue of the gods," say that anyone lucky enough to possess it can control the minds of others.

Gem of Pure Flame

Mind +3	Spirit +3

Only followers of the Way of the Open Palm may use this gem. Flame can destroy, but it can also purify. Burning with inner fire and zeal, users of this gem find themselves more focused in battle.

Guarding Gem of Stone

Body +5

Only followers of the Way of the Open Palm may use this gem. The earth cradles those who follow the Way of the Open Palm, lending the strength and endurance of mountains themselves to users of this gem.

Heaven's Blessing Gem

Damage Shield

Only followers of the Way of the Open Palm may use this gem. This gem surrounds you in an aura of wind that damages any who attack you. Its effect is constant while the gem is equipped.

Superior Warrior Gem

Body +6

This gem is of superior quality and provides an excellent bonus to your Body.

Flawless Warrior Gem

Body +10

This flawless gem provides a great bonus to your Body.

Superior Monk Gem

Spirit +6

This gem is of superior quality and provides an excellent bonus to your Spirit.

Trapped containers may be dangerous, but they always give you a chance to earn a free gem.

Flawless Monk Gem

Spirit +10

This flawless gem provides a powerful bonus to your Spirit.

Superior Scholar Gem

Mind +6

This gem is of superior quality and provides an excellent bonus to your Mind.

Flawless Scholar Gem

Mind +10

This flawless gem provides a powerful bonus to your Mind.

Gem of Order

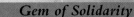

Body +1	Mind +1	Spirit +1

Only followers of the Way of the Open Palm can use this gem. Knowing one's proper place in the order of creation is a step toward enlightenment. Accept one's place and fulfill one's own purpose.

Gem of Solidarity

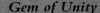

Body +2	Mind +2	Spirit +2

Only followers of the Way of the Open Palm can use this gem. Some realize that to be a productive member of society one must set aside one's own selfishness and greed. One must band with others of a like mind.

Gem of Unity

Body +3	Mind +3	Spirit +3

Only followers of the Way of the Open Palm can use this gem. To find true unity, one must set aside one's egotism and know that all are one. The shared fate of the entire Empire matters, not that of the individual.

Brilliant Gem of Balance

Body +4	Mind +4	Spirit +4

No matter what a person's path in life, fate, destiny, and human desire decide how far one goes. Whether on a path of peace or of power, the will must exist in balance with the needs of the body, the mind, and the spirit.

Scintillating Gem of Power

Body +5	Mind +5	Spirit +5

When one is at peace, one can achieve a form of transcendence. The goal of every true master and every true scholar is to surpass the physical form and unite with one's own spirit.

Gem of Unyielding Strength

Body +10	Mind −5	Spirit −5

This gem makes its wielder capable of great physical feats that are normally possible only with years of training. The sudden improvement to the user's physical abilities disrupts inner balance.

Gem of the Infinite Spirit

Spirit +10	Body −5	Mind −5

A powerful Spirit usually takes decades to attain, but this gem offers ambitious seekers a shortcut to that lofty goal. The gem empowers its wearer's spiritual energy by unbalancing the user's physical and mental abilities.

Gem of Inner Genius

Mind +10	Body −5	Spirit −5

This gem imparts great wisdom and mental abilities to its wearer, but it teaches a lesson of its own: that great and sudden power is only available at a great price. The wielder's mental capacity is greatly strengthened.

The Hero's Prize

Body +3	Mind +3	Spirit −5

The first victor of the Imperial Arena was the supremely cunning and vicious Gao Mahn. Undefeated for 15 years, he earned the lasting favor of the people and the Emperor himself. In recognition of his deeds, he was given this.

The Wanderer's Jewel

Body +3	Spirit +3	Mind −5

A musician who traveled the breadth of the Empire was once the owner of this gem. He carried it with him for years. His fame spread ahead of him, and he was welcomed in all corners of the Empire. No one knows what became of him.

The Mournful Soul

Mind +3	Spirit +3	Body −5

The Grandfather River flows through the Empire, taking with it a tale of years too long for human memory. Sailors of merchant vessels on the river speak of the ghost of a woman crying out in agony.

The Soft Petal

Charm +5	Body +1	Mind +1

In the reign of the Empress Sun Lin, arts flourished, especially dancing and poetry. The Empress surrounded herself with beautiful young women, masters in their respective art forms.

Good Fortune

Intuition +5	Mind +1	Spirit +1

Master Gambler Wu Pin was the scourge of betting houses across the Empire. Rumor has it that one would never know he was present until it was too late, because he would always lose every single game until the very end.

Gentle Persuasion

Intimidation +5	Body +1	Spirit +1

The Yung family was well respected in the Imperial City and had a tradition of dedicating their lives to public service. They served as town guards and city officials for many generations.

Strong Arm

Intimidation +8	Charm −3	Intuition −3

Protector Lo Wan was an enforcer for an openly secret society that offered "protection" to merchants and citizens throughout the Empire, in return for regular payments.

Divine Radiance

Charm +8	Intimidation −3	Intuition −3

One of the reasons behind the formation of the Order of the Lotus was the potential influence of a rising priesthood. The personal magnetism and radiance of the Priestess Wu Lin made her an object of desire.

Sixth Sense

Intuition +8	Charm −3	Intimidation −3

Never has a man or woman had greater fortune than a lowly farmer named Jun Bin. His mother gave him an amulet on the day of his birth, and he removed it only at the end of his life.

Inferior Charm Gem

Charm +2

This gem surrounds the user in an aura of vitality that people find irresistible. This gem is of inferior quality.

Charm Gem

Charm +3

This gem surrounds the user in an aura of vitality that people find irresistible. This gem is of average quality.

Superior Charm Gem

Charm +5

This gem surrounds the user in an aura of vitality that people find irresistible. This gem is of superior quality.

Inferior Intimidation Gem

Intimidation +2

This gem surrounds the user in an aura of menace that people find intimidating. This gem is of inferior quality.

Intimidation Gem

Intimidation +3

This gem surrounds the user in an aura of menace that people find intimidating. This gem is of inferior quality.

Superior Intimidation Gem

Intimidation +5

This gem surrounds the user in an aura of menace that people find intimidating. This gem is of superior quality.

Inferior Intuition Gem

Intuition +2

This gem enhances the user's perception and intuition, enabling the wearer to feel out the lines of fate connecting each thing in the world. This gem is of inferior quality.

Intuition Gem

Intuition +3

This gem enhances the user's perception and intuition, enabling the wearer to feel out the lines of fate connecting each thing in the world. This gem is of average quality.

Superior Intuition Gem

Intuition +5

This gem enhances the user's perception and intuition, enabling the wearer to feel out the lines of fate connecting each thing in the world. This gem is of superior quality.

Gem of Evil Thought

Mind +2	Intuition +2

Only followers of the Way of the Closed Fist may use this gem. The evil energies that resonate in this gem speak of its previous owners, dark and evil men and women driven beyond the boundaries that society imposes on them.

Gem of Gentle Mind

Mind +2	Intuition +2

Only followers of the Way of the Open Palm may use this gem. This gem radiates peace and serenity, reflecting the past owners, who imprinted fragments of their own thoughts on it. This is a gem of enlightened scholars and philosophers.

Aura of Malice Gem

Body +2	Intimidation +2

Only followers of the Way of the Closed Fist can use this gem. Legends tell of bandits and warlords so evil that their mere presence in a room could cow people into submission. This gem is part of that legend.

Aura of Calm Gem

Body +2	Intimidation +2

Only followers of the Way of the Open Palm can use this gem. Some of the wisest masters and sages radiate such a sense of peace and understanding that their uncanny calm almost seems threatening.

Gem of Seductive Power

Spirit +2	Charm +2

Only followers of the Way of the Closed Fist can use this gem. People of negotiable virtue can often be overwhelming in their advances. No small thanks for that go to this gem, nicknamed "a Woman's Best Friend."

Gem of Irresistible Spirit

Spirit +2	Charm +2

Only followers of the Way of the Open Palm can use this gem. This gem is a tool of inner reflection for the wielder and, unwittingly, those around him. This gem exposes the inner strength and virtue of the user to all.

Warrior's Gem of Fate

Increased chance of Health power-ups
Body –1

The wearer of this gem gambles away some of his physical ability for the chance that fate will favor him in combat. Some warriors prefer a second wind in combat over a strong opening volley.

Greater Warrior's Gem of Fate

Greatly increased chance of Health power-ups
Body –5

Warriors who revel in the chaos of combat find comfort in this gem's machinations of fate. The gem feeds on the warrior's physical capabilities, but it also increases the chances of that warrior getting Health power-ups.

Scholar's Gem of Fate

Increased chance of Focus power-ups
Mind –1

It behooves one who seeks to strengthen one's mind to consider the vagaries of fate in one's actions. This gem aids in this experiment by tapping its wielder's mental capacities in return for a greater chance of Focus power-ups.

Greater Scholar's Gem of Fate

Greatly increased chance of Focus power-ups
Mind –5

There are times in which raw mental power is not as important as the ability to summon reserves of such power when the time is right. This gem enables the user to trade innate mental ability for a greater chance of Focus power-ups.

Monk's Gem of Fate

Increased chance of Chi power-ups
Spirit -1

While it may not seem wise for one to sacrifice one's spiritual nature for a gamble on fate's table, one must certainly see the wisdom in entering a card game with a stacked deck.

Greater Monk's Gem of Fate

Greatly increased chance of Chi power-ups
Spirit -5

One who is content with water every day may never enjoy the taste of wine. Not every master finds wisdom in caution, and those willing to compromise their spiritual abilities with this gem often find Chi power-ups.

Slick Gem

-10 percent Focus cost for evading traps

The surface of this gem is oddly slick, making it difficult to hold. Prized by thieves, it makes one move with less resistance, making it much easier to avoid the unavoidable. It has saved many an inattentive burglar.

Gem of Black Flame

Mind +3	Spirit +3

Only followers of the Way of the Closed Fist may use this gem. Fury and rage will render a warrior helpless unless directed and turned to a purpose. This gem infuses the wearer's mind and spirit with the flame of their anger.

Gem of Earth Power

Body +5

Only followers of the Way of the Closed Fist may use this gem. Tearing winds and coursing waters test their strength, but the mountains endure. Wearers of this gem gain some of this strength, their bodies hardened by its magic.

Gem of Storm's Rage

Damage Shield

Only followers of the Way of the Closed Fist may use this gem. This gem wraps you in whirling winds that tear at any who attack you. Its effect is constant while the gem is equipped.

Quicksilver Gem

Mind +2
50 percent chance to evade traps

When they hold this gem up to the moonlight, some claim they can see in the center of this gem a single drop of quicksilver spinning endlessly. The wielder becomes as fast and as mercurial as quicksilver.

Key Items are needed to advance the story and to gain access to new areas.

Lightning Gem

Mind +3
100 percent chance to evade traps

Named not for its appearance, but for the speed at which its owner acts, this gem sharpens the mind and senses by orders of magnitude. The wearer becomes smarter and quicker, more easily anticipating or evading attacks.

Gem of Premonition

Mind +1
-50 percent trap evade Focus cost

This gem's inner structure does not appear similar to any other essence gem, and there are no records of it ever having been created. Its origin is a mystery, as is the nature of its power.

Gem of Foresight

Mind +2
Evading traps costs no Focus

This object has been called an essence gem by the few who know of its existence, but none of those who speculate on it have ever truly held it in their hand. It gives the wielder a flash of insight into the future.

Thick Skin Gem

Body +1
50 percent damage from traps

This gem thickens a warrior's skin, strengthening it against damage. This makes the warrior resistant to sudden damage from an undirected source, but it will likely not protect as well against an opponent already aiming.

Iron Skin Gem

Body +3
0 percent damage from traps

The power of this gem toughens the skin until it as strong as iron. Traps and other undirected attacks have no effect at all upon the wielder. Calculated, cunning strikes from an intelligent opponent will still harm the wearer.

Gem of the Clumsy Ox

Body +3
Cannot evade traps

There is much to be said for strength, but strength often comes at the expense of agility, and the users of this gem prize strength and stamina over any attempts at subtlety.

Gem of the Frail Scholar

Mind +1	Body -3
+100 percent experience from books	

This gem has passed through the hands of many great scholars and men and women of learning. Their dedication and experience has been passed on into this essence gem. The gem expands its wielder's mind.

Gem of the Barbarian

Body +2
Gain no experience from books

Time and again, the Horselords descended from the plains and laid waste to the Empire. Each time they were eventually driven back, but their repeated forays into the Empire began to imprint true culture upon them.

Way of the Closed Fist

Intimidation +10	Body +5	Spirit -5

Only followers of the Way of the Closed Fist may use this gem. The Way of the Closed Fist is the way of violence and personal power. Take the world in your grasp and make it yours.

Way of the Open Palm

Intuition +10	Spirit +5	Body -5

Only followers of the Way of the Open Palm may use this gem. Life brings many challenges, and one must learn to flow and adapt to them, to yield and be firm at the same time.

The Closed Fist

Body +10	Spirit +5

Only followers of the Way of the Closed Fist may use this gem. A master of the Closed Fist is a force that changes the face of destiny to suit his will. Those who seek the ways of power will always remember such strength of purpose.

The Open Palm

Spirit +10	Mind +5

Only followers of the Way of the Open Palm may use this gem. In accordance with one's own spirit and the way of the Heavens, the Open Palm is at peace with nature. This ultimate harmony gives mastery over one's self and attunement.

Imperial Favor

Spirit +3	Charm +1	Intuition +1

Increased chance for getting power-ups from fallen enemies. The emperors of the Sun dynasty have long been famed for their magical aptitude, but they also enjoy the adulation of the people of the Jade Empire.

Gem of Thief's Sense

Spirit +1

Allows the wielder to detect traps. The past users of this gem did not always live by the law, but they always lived on the edge. That edge and their fates on either side of it are imprinted on this gem.

Gem of Purpose

Body +1	Mind +1	Spirit +1

Only followers of the Way of the Closed Fist may use this gem. The key to getting what one wants is to first know what it is and what it takes to get it. This sense of purpose empowers the truly strong.

Gem of Struggle

Body +2	Mind +2	Spirit +2

Only followers of the Way of the Closed Fist may use this gem. Every worthwhile goal requires hardship and struggle. A victory gained with ease means nothing. The struggle defines the worth of a goal.

Gem of Mastery

Body +3	Mind +3	Spirit +3

Only followers of the Way of the Closed Fist can use this essence gem. The goal of every struggle, no matter what its initial justification, is dominance. Power over others and over fate will determine the true outcome.

Absolute Dedication

More experience from human enemies
No power-ups from human enemies

With proper focus on the techniques of your human enemies, you pick up lessons and moves that help you develop your own style. Your dedication to learning in combat is absolute.

Warrior's Gem of Forethought

Body +2

Lesser chance of Health power-ups

A battlefield is chaotic enough without leaving one's successes to chance. Some warriors prefer to rely upon solid and predictable strengths rather than the random chance of respite during battle.

Scholar's Gem of Forethought

Mind +2

Lesser chance of Focus power-ups

The concepts of mental focus and of distraction are mutually exclusive. Many believe that one cannot succeed in a mental capacity by always relying on the subtle whims of fate to fuel one's success.

Monk's Gem of Forethought

Spirit +2

Lesser chance of Chi power-ups

To some, being prepared for any situation is the very essence of wisdom. While the world rewards those who excel, many warriors find that relying upon these rewards can lead to laziness and recklessness in battle.

Lucky Hand

More silver from human enemies

When properly prepared, this gem plucks the silken strands of fate, gently placing small amounts of local currency in the pockets of the people within a certain distance of the wielder.

Burning Essence

Mind +3	Spirit +3

Burning Essence channels elemental flame to sharpen the mind of its wearer and to strengthen the ability to channel Chi. Unlike similar gems that channel elemental fire, this essence gem burns with all aspects of the flame.

Cyclone Gem

Damage Shield

Among the first monks who developed the Tempest style, there was one who began to question the Closed Fist tenets of his order. Ostracized from his ruthless order, the monk sought new ways to harness the wind without relying upon Closed-Fist maneuvers.

Spirit Harvest

More XP from killing ghosts

No power-ups from killing ghosts

Those who hunt ghosts and wayward spirits often find that the knowledge gained from defeating ephemeral foes is more useful than the recuperative pockets of essence that they leave behind.

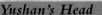

ITEMS FOR YOUR CRITICAL QUESTING ADVANCEMENT

Ruins Key

Given to you by Minister Sheng of Tien's Landing, this key unlocks the gate west of the town that leads to the ruins of the flooded town.

Yushan's Head

All that remains of Kindly Yushan. His face now in rigor, it will forever reflect the terror that Yushan felt when he died at your hands.

Cameo Portrait

A small portrait of a beautiful young woman, carved into a gemstone in layers of contrasting colors. An inscription on the back reads, "To my beloved husband, Wei. Yours forever."

Wind Map

A copy of a wind map that clearly shows the air currents and passages that lead from Tien's Landing to the Imperial City.

Dirge Fountain Seal 1

The small seal is made of ancient stone and carved with intricate designs. Though it appears lifeless, you can sense a powerful energy contained within.

Dirge Fountain Seal 2

The small seal is made of ancient stone and carved with intricate designs. Though it appears lifeless, you can sense a powerful energy contained within.

Red Lion Figurine

Lacquered a bright red, this stone figurine is a replica of the lion statue found in Master Li's house.

Yellow Lion Figurine

Coated in a yellow lacquer, this lion figurine is a replica of the large statue in Master Li's house.

Blue Lion Figurine

Carved from simple rock and coated in a blue lacquer, this figurine is a miniature replica of the lion statue in Master Li's house.

Jade Heart

This magical gem provides the means to allow the dam to be opened and closed. By removing this gem you can ensure that the dam remains open and merchant Jiang's business continues to thrive.

Inscrutable Power Source

It should come as no surprise that you can't figure out how this device functions, or even what it really does. A complicated collection of gears, pistons, and various projecting apertures befuddles the mind but still speaks of virtually limitless power.

Preserved Liver

This liver has been preserved by special medical and arcane means. It's so well preserved that it almost looks alive.

Dragon Powder

A small canister of the volatile black substance called dragon powder. The Lotus Assassins were clearly using this substance to excavate in the lower ruins of Tien's Landing, but this charge doesn't look sufficient for blasting anything.

Temple Crystal

This large gem isn't made of a valuable material, but it was cut in a very specific way, as if designed for a particular setting. The edges of the crystal are slightly discolored and smell vaguely of moss.

Red Silk Grass Poultice

A medicinal poultice designed to accelerate the healing of wounds. This poultice is infused with extract of red silk grass, a powerful herb that hastens recovery by binding the wounded flesh together.

Bearded Tongue Grass Poultice

A medicinal poultice designed to accelerate the healing of wounds. This poultice is infused with bearded tongue grass, a medicinal herb used to dull pain. Its medical value is somewhat questionable.

Judge Fang's Ring

An imperial signet ring given as a token of office to the Chief Minister of Harmony, Judge Fang. It is Fang's official seal of office, procured for you by Gentle Breezes.

Fang's Resignation

This is Judge Fang's letter of resignation from his post as the head of the Ministry of Harmony. It is stamped with his Imperial signet ring.

Note from Princess Lian

A carefully folded piece of paper, given to you by Princess Lian. The note reads, "Meet me in the pavilion at the entrance to the Scholars' Garden."

Slaver Documents

Several pages detailing the actions and transactions of the slave traders in the Imperial City. These documents clearly indicate that Chandler Ling is involved with the slave traders.

Forged Slaver Documents

Several pages detailing the actions and transactions of the Slave Traders in the Imperial City. These documents are cleverly doctored to falsely indicate Scholar Songtao's involvement with the slave traders.

Winnings Purse

This small satchel is marked to make it identifiable as one of Gambler Daoshen's winnings purses. It contains the silver he plans to offer to the Guild in return for permission to increase the limits on his wagers.

Turtle Eggs

There are few greater ways to insult a person than a gift of turtle eggs. The difficulty of their acquisition tells the tale of a person willing to put forth a serious effort in their desire to say, "I hate you." This group of eggs is particularly ripe.

Lion Head Token

A small stone token from the grave of the Old Master, acquired after a humble tribute of silver. Made of simple granite, and thus essentially valueless, the token is in the shape of a lion's head.

Incisive Chorus's Original Script

The original script for your scene as Lady Fourteen Flowers. In this version of the play, your character explains that the end of the Jade Empire's expansion occurred because Sagacious Tien listened to the will of the heavens.

Edited Script

A script for your scene as Lady Fourteen Flowers in Incisive Chorus's play. This version of the script has been edited from the original text so that two of the lines satirize the Lotus Assassins by referring to them as "flower guardians."

Clay Figure

A small, virtually worthless clay figurine. Despite its lack of material value, the figurine is exquisite and strangely comforting to gaze upon.

Phoenix Oil

A sturdy clay vessel containing a volatile oil that burns at a very high temperature. The shape of the container allows you to pour the contents into the mixing controls in the golem press room with relative safety.

Golem Spirit Shard

Normally these shards are made from the concentrated spirit of an unfortunate victim of the Lotus Assassins and are used to power golems. This one is made from the chaotic spirit of an ancient Horselord. It will corrupt the Jade Golem for which it is intended.

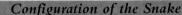

A Vial of Sulfurous Water

The yellow-tinged water in this vial has a strong stench, similar to that of a rotten egg.

Eyes of the Void

Kang called these gems the Eyes of the Void. They don't appear to have any conventional value, but they may produce something extraordinary if used in Lord Lao's Furnace.

A Bar of Nickeled Iron

This bar is made of iron alloyed with nickel, producing a far stronger metal referred to by some smiths as "steeled iron" or simply "steel."

Cow Bezoar

Used to treat conditions of the blood and circulation, a cow bezoar forms only in the stomach of very ill cattle. Cow bezoars are extremely rare, but many seek them for their curative nature.

Configuration of the Rat

This wrinkled sheet of paper is filled with diagrams doodled in the corners and along the margins. The majority of the page, however, is taken up by the following text: "The dual eyes of fire can fuel greatness, but only if all save the conductor work."

Configuration of the Ox

This strange schematic has had better days, the paper ragged at the corners. While the page is filled with doodled diagrams, including one for a device that seems designed to colorize rice for easy sorting.

Configuration of the Tiger

You found this obscure set of instructions and copied them down on a hunch. "Iron is made stronger through the alloy, and nickel binds well to make a sharp blade. It can also be a reactive fuel, but certain configurations must be preserved."

Configuration of the Rabbit

You stumbled across an obscure diagram that seems to indicate a configuration for a machine. A small stone with medical runes surrounding it seems to be a key component.

Configuration of the Dragon

Something about this strange poem made it stick in your mind. "Configurations guided by the tiger burn bright, as the cauldron bubbles in the night. The cogs whirl their graceful dances, but they grow tired unless they drink of the water infused."

Configuration of the Snake

You found this academic leaflet and kept it. The crux of the argument reads, "To think that any machine could be designed around the principles of starting motion with a tiger, of all things, is to dally with utter madness."

Configuration of the Horse

You found this strange excerpt from a diary; the pages were torn from the book but kept together as if they were an important secret. "...in his ravings, my husband talked of madmen with eyes of metal and of a strange island in the skies..."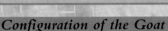

Configuration of the Goat

A note, probably written to the author as a reminder. "It will likely break the machine, but with a pair of flawless rubies, and care to leave the clappers and cauldron out of the process, the tiger might be able to manage a reconfiguration of the user..."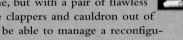

Lotus Inquisitor's Seal

A small stone marked with a rune that must hold some meaning to the Lotus Assassin Inquisitors. The stone feels heavy and warmer than the surrounding air.

Lotus Executioner's Seal

A stone engraved with a rune that must hold some meaning to the Lotus Assassin Executioners. The stone is unnaturally heavy, and it feels cold in your hand no matter how long you hold it.

Silk Strings

These strings are carefully woven and made of the finest silk. They look as if they were made for a musical instrument.

Zither Case

This box is obviously the main case for a type of musical instrument called a zither. Designed to be played across a lap or at a table, a zither normally has strings stretched atop the soundboard and a bridge to hold the strings off the case.

Zither Bridge

This small piece of wood is a finely crafted bridge for a musical instrument.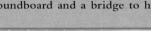

Boathouse Key

From the markings on the head of the key, it looks like it would unlock the gate leading to the upper office in the Tien's Landing boathouse.

Interpreted Furnace Movement

A note scribbled by Kang after he noticed an odd pattern in the movements of Lord Lao's Furnace. It suggests that one of the machine's configurations is in "a fortress of the dark handed ones" within the city.

Transcribed Leaf Note

A note scribbled by Kang that he copied off of a leaf floating around Lord Lao's Furnace. It suggests that one of the machine's configurations may be found in a chest in "the cages of animals kept for sport."

Patched Together Note

A note Kang found in pieces in Lord Lao's Furnace. It suggests that one of the machine's configurations is near "the archivist of the Order."

Scrap Paper Note

A note found near one of the devices in Lord Lao's Furnace. It suggests that one of the machine's configurations is secreted away in "a dock house ministry."

Transcribed Post Carving

A note scribbled by Kang after he translated the carvings on a post near the controls of Lord Lao's Furnace. It suggests that one of the machine's configurations is in "a garden of ineffectual intellectuals."

Transcribed Gear Etchings

A note scribbled by Kang after he translated some of the markings on the larger gears of Lord Lao's Furnace. It suggests that one of the machine's configurations is in a chest somewhere in "the place of all dead."

Found Furnace Note

A note found in Lord Lao's Furnace. It suggests that one of the machine's configurations may be found near the machine. "They can't all be secreted across the Empire. Who has the time?"

Pages from the Tome of Release (1/5)

So many of the pages from this tome are missing that it's impossible to tell what purpose it served, or what mysteries it held, when it was complete.

Pages from the Tome of Release (2/5)

From the scattered pages you have recovered, this tome seems to outline some sort of ritual. While the ritual deals with curses of some sort, it's hard to make out exactly what effect it might have if performed.

Pages from the Tome of Release (3/5)

You seem to have roughly half of the missing sections from this ancient book. From what you can piece together, the Tome of Release details a ritual that can free spirits bound to a place by a curse or other magic.

When you gain a new technique, your body resonates with power.

Pages from the Tome of Release (4/5)

You almost have all of the missing sections of the Tome of Release, and except for a few key elements, you could almost perform the ritual outlined within. Doing so would clearly free the spirits of the last few Imperial Army soldiers who haunt Dirge.

Pages from the Tome of Release (5/5)

Now that you have read the fully assembled Tome of Release, you know how to perform a ritual that would lift the curse from the spirits of the last few Imperial Army soldiers who still haunt Dirge.

Mantra of Inspiration

An ancient text penned by some of the first Spirit Monks, this book has taught you how to properly focus upon the Mantra of Inspiration. "Understanding the totality of being is the only goal worth achieving, and yet it is a goal that cannot be fulfilled..."

Beveled Cogs

These cogs are carefully engineered and made of a strange, and likely valuable, material. The gears still have traces of oil, suggesting that they were used, but signs of wear are visible.

Machined Cogs

These cogs are carefully engineered and made of a strange, and likely valuable, material. The gears still have traces of oil, suggesting that they were used, but signs of wear are visible.

TECHNIQUES FOR CHARACTER IMPROVEMENT

Belly of Iron

Health +3	Chi -1

A series of exercises developed by Smiling Mountain. Those who learn and use his Belly of Iron Techniques learn to take blows better, giving them more stamina in combat.

Heart of Gold

Chi +3	Focus -1

Heart of Gold is a set of meditative techniques developed by Smiling Mountain to help his students learn to master their Chi. By remembering specific mantras in battle, it is possible to channel slightly more Chi than normal.

Mind of Steel

Focus +3	Health -1

Mental exercises that test the memory and quickness of thought, Smiling Mountain's Mind of Steel Techniques can help warriors better focus in battle. The time spent honing the mind can have the side effect of slightly weakening oneself.

Balance of Nature

Focus +15	Chi +3

To be one with your art, it must be your entire world, your only focus. But to lose yourself in that world is also a serious failing. If you balance the needs of your art with the needs of your inner self, you can achieve true transcendence.

Hawk's Elegance

Focus +7	Health -3

As brittle and as elegant as it may be, a bird must have a keen mind to adapt and make use of its surroundings. This constant attention to detail is a sign of one who focuses more on one's mind than on one's body.

Conditioning of the Body

Health +7	Chi -3

The lithe grace of any serious physical artist, be they dancer or martial artist, belies the strength of their body. Through their arts, all fat and useless muscle is burned away, leaving only the hard muscle beneath.

Swallow's Grace

Charm +3	Intuition -1

A dancer must learn to glide as softly and as delicately as a small bird, flitting from here to there. Many people find this behavior fascinating but mysterious.

Hunter's Spirit

Chi +15	Focus +3

Know yourself, and you can know your prey. By knowing your own limitations, you can surpass yourself, see the limitations in others, and gain true power flowing from your own spirit outward into the world.

Boar's Strength

Health +7	Chi -3

The boar is a surprisingly cunning and resourceful opponent when encountered in the wild. Even the most experienced hunter can fall prey to it if he does not watch himself. The boar uses its natural strength and weight in battle.

Tracking Eye

Focus +7	Charm -1

To track a beast in the forest, one must have keen eyes that catch every movement and track it undeterred by distraction. The Tracking Eye is that Technique. Following it, one can gain much greater Focus.

Predatory Intuition

Intuition +3	Chi -5

To find a beast, one must understand the beast and how it thinks. This applies to humans just as with the lesser animals. Learning this makes a warrior more intuitive, but it lessens inner harmony.

Cleansed Body and Mind

Health +15	Focus +5

Once a body has been purified in the correct manner, with all the forces and pressures of the body in proper balance, one will find one's strength greatly increased and more able to resist the hardships of life.

Vigorous Body

Health +10	Chi -2

The body is a harbor for many poisons and toxins that accumulate within. Without the proper steps to release these poisons, the body can become slow and sluggish. Clear these and allow the blood to flow more freely.

Clear Mind

Focus +10	Intimidation -1

A clear mind can see truly where a clouded one cannot. Removing the imbalances from the body that distract the mind can greatly increase one's clarity and focus.

Porcelain Skin

Charm +2	Chi -4

A clear complexion is the hallmark of a healthy and attractive individual. By correctly balancing the forces within one's body, one can improve one's outward appearance. Such vanity does true enlightenment no favors.

Eye of Inner Darkness

Chi +15	Focus +5

Looking out from the void inside, the place in which the spirit resides, is a person's inner eye. A person at peace with their inner self gains great power and strength of mind from this eye.

Window to the Abyss

Chi +10	Focus –3

The spirit is endless. The depths one can sink to is limitless. If one looks inside, they will see nothing but themselves. Inner strength, the strength of the spirit, comes from this limitless inner void.

Deadened Nerves

Health +10	Chi –3

Lotus Assassins often use a technique common to many martial arts, but in their fanaticism, they take it to an extreme. They beat their body continuously, first with ropes, then with wooden sticks, then finally with iron rods.

Fearsome Visage

Intimidation +3	Charm –1

Training as a Lotus Assassin takes its toll. A Lotus Assassin sometimes deliberately deforms himself to present a more disturbing visage to his opponents and instill fear in his foes.

Strength of Wood

Health +2
Literary: Granted by studying "The History of Flight."

An ancient technique that strengthens a warrior's body until his skin becomes as tough as wood. While the skin looks unchanged, it is tougher and more resilient than normal.

Inner Peace

Chi +4
Literary: Granted by studying "The Celestial Order."

Contemplation on the inner mysteries of one's own mind is a path many try to take to true enlightenment. Few succeed, for many make the mistake of neglecting the physical world.

Legacy of Master Li

Focus +7
Literary: Granted by studying the books in Two Rivers.

Master Li's training techniques have been passed down to all of his students. Some learn better than others and see the greater pattern present within each of his smaller teachings.

Legacy of Death's Hand

Chi +10
Literary: Granted by studying the tomes in the Lotus Assassin fortress.

Death's Hand's training is incessant and brutal. It admits no failure, and no one who fails will survive it. But at its core, its aim is to improve the student.

Scales of the Serpent

Health +7	Intimidation +1

Your study of carefully kept notes penned by Kai Lan the Serpent has led you to an understanding of his techniques. His notes outline a series of postures and forms designed to make the user tougher and more intimidating.

Theories of Medicine

Focus +7	Intuition +1

Mad Wen Zhi learned much in his quest to save his daughter. While his medical knowledge may not be directly applicable, the genius that went into his researches has not been lost on you.

Chaotic Strains

Health +5	Chi +5

Played by skilled hands, the Zither of Discord can attune the chaos in a person's soul, making one stronger and better able to walk the Way of the Closed Fist. Every so often you catch a hint of music carried on the breeze.

Alloyed Body

Health +5	Focus +5

The Alloyed Body is Smiling Mountain's ultimate series of exercises, designed to offset some of the weaknesses the corpulent trainer saw in the exercises he developed earlier in his career.

Gaze of the Lion

Health +2	Focus +2

A masterful hunter, the lion must always be aware of the totality of its domain and be ready to protect it. You feel a kinship with the mighty predator after solving the riddle left by the old master of Two Rivers.

Replenishment of the Body

Health +7	Chi +7

These techniques of the ancient Spirit Monks teach how to strengthen the spirit, and through it, the body. By controlling the flow of Chi through one's body, one can refine his control of Chi and use it to harden one's body.

Replenishment of the Mind

Focus +7	Chi +7

These techniques of the ancient Spirit Monks teach how to enhance the mind by focusing one's Chi. By focusing on the ebb and flow of one's Chi, one can strengthen one's mind and gain greater mastery over one's Chi.

Strength of the Bull

Damage Increase

After correctly configuring the furnace, you learn the Strength of the Bull Technique. With the power of the mighty bull behind you, your martial attacks inflict more harm on your opponents.

Spirit of the Master
Increased Magical Damage

After selecting an appropriate configuration in Lord Lao's Furnace, you learn the Spirit of the Master Technique. With the help of the master's spirit, you find that your Magical attacks are far more effective.

The Quieted Mind
Focus +30

A successful configuration of Lord Lao's Furnace has taught you to enter a state the legends call "the quieted mind." This meditative combat technique provides incredible focus.

A Mountain Within
Body +5

The correct configuration in Lord Lao's Furnace produces A Mountain Within. This Technique provides an increase to your Body.

Calm as the Morning Breeze
Mind +5

Lord Lao's Furnace generates Calm as the Morning Breeze when a correct configuration was used. This technique provides a +5 increase to Mind.

The Song of the Spirit
Spirit +5

A proper configuration of Lord Lao's Furnace creates the Song of the Spirit. This technique provides an increase to Spirit.

Harmony and Balance
| Body +3 | Mind +3 | Spirit +3 |

Using the uncut ruby and the correct configuration in Lord Lao's Furnace generates Harmony and Balance. This technique provides an increase to Body, Mind, and Spirit.

Viper's Wit
| Focus +2 | Charm +1 |

A sharp wit and mind are key to winning the hearts of people. Too many believe that looks and strength alone rule the day, and they neglect to realize that a mind will always triumph. One's wit and skill must strike like a snake.

Structured Body
| Health +3 | Intimidation +1 |

Intense training can result in more than a healthy physique. With an understanding of the body's subtleties, one also realizes that slight shifts of weight and changes of stance can give one's arguments more force.

The River of Time
| Chi +5 | Intuition +1 |

Life is made of many details, many facets of being. A person in tune with his surroundings may feel the subtle vibrations each thing makes as its fate passes nearby.

Dragon Mantra
| Health +5 | Chi +5 |

The dragon is a creature of mystery and power. It is among the most powerful of all symbols. Strong in both body and spirit, it is a relentless, irresistible force. Followers of this path are overwhelming in both body and spirit.

Snake Mantra
| Focus +5 | Chi +5 |

The snake is a creature of cunning and intelligence. It is not large or powerful as the others are, but when it strikes, it is no less deadly. The way of the snake is the way of inner power. Followers strengthen their minds and wits.

Tiger Mantra
| Health +5 | Focus +5 |

The tiger relies on strength and speed. It is a symbol of passion and power. In the tiger lies the utmost physical ability of an individual. By dedicating yourself to the tiger, you strengthen your body along with your mind.

Warrior of the Inner Eye
| Focus +7 | Intuition +1 |

The inner eye, the eye within the mind, sees much. There is nothing that cannot be understood by a clear mind and a pure spirit. Warriors of this path seek to rid themselves of all distraction, and focus on their arts.

Warrior of the Infinite Spirit
| Chi +7 | Charm +1 |

The spirit knows no bounds. One who is great in spirit is destined to achieve great things. One who knows his own spirit and uses it accordingly can often shape the world around him to his desires.

Warrior of the Unyielding Heart
Health +7

The body is the final arbiter of any choice. Our destinies are made in this world, and warriors of this path seek to strengthen their bodies by any means, usually through courage and strength.

Heaven Mantra
Chi +10

This meditative technique was once the exclusive possession of the Spirit Monk order. They taught their monks its secret, giving them uncompromising power over spirits and lesser creatures through their arts.

Rote of the Endless Mind

Focus +5	Chi +5

The Rote is a method of cleansing the mind and body, focusing the power of the inner self through your thoughts and actions. One who practices this technique frequently gains inner strength and clarity of purpose.

Guardian's Strength

Health +5	Chi +5

The Guardian, Chai Ka, regains control over Wild Flower from the demon Ya Zhen. He is grateful for all that you have done for both him and the girl, and he lends his strength and wisdom against the troubles to come.

Mastered Evil

Health +5	Focus +5

You have freed Ya Zhen from his imprisonment, and now the power of that demon is yours. He not only aids you physically, but his power insinuates itself into your being, as well, bringing out an aspect of him within you.

Dawn's Gift

Chi +10

Your lifelong friendship with Dawn Star has had a strong effect on the way you think and feel. In these troubled times, this friendship has strengthened your spirituality as some of her esoteric power has rubbed off on you.

Sharpened Mind

Focus +5	Charm +2

Sky is unlike anyone you have ever met: strong, cunning, and charming. Simply speaking with him and learning about his way of life have opened your mind to new possibilities and new ways of dealing with people.

White Lotus

Health +5	Chi +5

You may have had reason to distrust him, but Sagacious Zu's secret shows the strength and integrity that lies within this conflicted man. His tale of sacrifice strengthens your spirit.

A Mercenary's Life

Health +5	Intimidation +2

It's hard to know for sure where the truth ends and the foggy memories of a wild and careless drunk begins, but one thing is for sure: The Black Whirlwind has led an extremely diverse life.

Henpecked Indeed

Focus +5	Intuition +2

How any man could survive a life, or a marriage, like Henpecked Hou's is a mystery. Though seemingly small and insignificant, this fierce bunmaster teaches you a great deal about persistence and surviving.

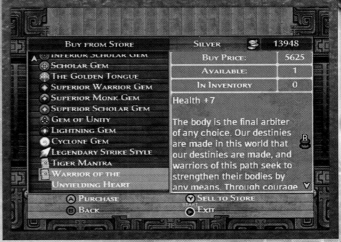

Don't forget to check in with Zin Bu the Magic Abacus from time to time to see what new items he has in stock!

Fitness for the Upright Gentleman

Body +3

A worn copy of Fitness for the Upright Gentleman, a manual of regimented conditioning. This small leather-bound book with the outline of a man in some strange fighting style on the cover contains radical exercises that offer alternate training.

Duchess of Ulmsbottom's Rules of Engagement

Mind +3

A worn copy of The Duchess of Ulmsbottom's Rules of Engagement. A leather-bound book, its cover emblazoned with two silhouettes of musketeers aiming large blunderbusses at each other in an upright stance. Virtually incomprehensible.

Manual of Trepanation

Spirit +3

This manual outlines the step-by-step process for drilling a small hole in the skull that will, in theory, release pressure on the brain, allowing the mind to expand and work more efficiently.

Lessons of the Forge

Health +2

Smiling Mountain's training sessions in Two Rivers can teach valuable lessons. Standing one's ground against increasing numbers of students helps young warriors learn to pace themselves and last longer in battles.

Loutish Approval

Health +2

Few possess the nerve to stand up to a member of the Imperial family. Fewer still survive such impertinence. The fierce determination you showed when dealing with the Princess and her delicate entourage will serve you just as well in the battles to come.

Mother's Touch

Health +5	Chi +5

Despite their tiny stature, the cannibals of the Pilgrim's Rest Inn possess surprising strength and resilience. Their connection with the ancient beast known as The Mother has made them strong, and they have rewarded your aid.

Craftsman's Litany

Focus +5

Many craftsmen repeat litanies in their heads while they work, the repetition helping them focus. A warrior who has learned the power of such exercises can adapt their meditative nature to the battlefield with much the same results.

Friends in High Places

Chi +5	Intuition +2

You helped Princess Sun Lian see that her father is behind the Empire's troubles. Whatever happens, you will always have an ally in court, an asset that cannot help but buoy your spirit.

The Broken Wheel

Chi +7	Health +7

The last remnants of the Emperor's invading force have been torn from the cycle of rebirth, and their spirits are lost for all time. Regardless of whether these soldiers deserved such a cruel fate or not, you have harnessed the tatter.

The Turning Wheel

Focus +7	Chi +7

The last remnants of the Emperor's cursed army have dispersed from Dirge and yet you can still hear whispers of thanks on the winds. Far from a distraction, they serve as a reminder of the tasks ahead.

Bone Splinter

Health +15

In the battle against the elder horse demon that follows you out of the gateway in Dirge, a splinter off of its leering skull-like visage becomes lodged under the skin of your forearm. It causes you no pain or irritation.

Lesson's End

Focus +15

Is your battle against your fellow students just a dream, or is Master Li's growing power enough to summon something more real?

Spiritual Sacrifice

Chi -10

Your sacrifice for Mad Wen's daughter left a small hole in your spiritual potential, and you can feel the loss of energy whenever you exert yourself magically. Somewhere, a little girl walks free and alive because you were selfless.

The Perfected Warrior

Health +15	Focus +15

An ancient Technique taught only to the finest champions in the Empire, the Perfected Warrior Technique serves to focus an already razor-sharp mind and condition an already powerful body to the heights of perfection.

Communion of the Ocean

Chi +10

The Spirit Monks have long used the meditation wheels lining the entryway of Dirge's inner temple to aid their meditations. Three of the wheels spin freely during your meditations, and your spirit feels more in tune with your heritage.

Communion of the Dragon

Health +5	Chi +15

With five of the ancient meditation wheels of Dirge spinning as you meditated, you soon realized that, like the amulet, the wheels are merely a training tool. You feel closer to understanding the nature of the Water Dragon than before.

The Path of the Warrior

Health +50

There are those who test themselves with combat, and then there are those who walk the Path of the Warrior. Those who have practiced these ancient techniques—codified over millennia—are possessed of inhuman resilience.

The Path of the Monk

Chi +50

The road walked by the monk is one of outward tranquility and inward struggle. A warrior's life is a denial of peace by its very nature, and yet there are those who have found calm in the shifting tides of battle. A collection of ancient techniques.

The Path of the Scholar

Focus +50

The heavens smile upon those who pursue knowledge, but the battle also favors he of the quick mind. The Path of the Scholar is a codified—and cross indexed—series of meditations and exercises designed to hone one's thoughts.

ROMANCE PLOTS

CHARACTER ROMANCES

OVERVIEW

During your adventure, you can indulge in a number of romance quests. And the results can be surprising. These quests take the form of a series of conversations between you and your intended partner, and you must progress these talks before you leave a current chapter, or the romance will fail to blossom. Although not all combinations are viable, it is possible to romance more than one Follower.

The following shows the three characters that can be romanced:

CHARACTER ROMANCE

Dawn Star		
Available to Male Characters	**Available to Female Characters**	
Yes	No	

Silk Fox		
Available to Male Characters	**Available to Female Characters**	
Yes	Yes	

Sky		
Available to Male Characters	**Available to Female Characters**	
Yes	Yes	

NOTE
In Chapter Three, when romancing Dawn Star and/or Silk Fox, if you neglect their romance dialogue for too long, you will get different responses from the women and may end up either having to charm them (at increasing levels of difficulty) or risk losing the romance altogether.

ROMANCING DAWN STAR

Dawn Star has a fear of commitment due to her childhood as an orphan. Shunned because of her spiritual powers, she worries about losing control and is concerned that trusting someone too much is dangerous because they have the power to leave. There are two courses to take with Dawn Star: reassurance to show her that it is all right to trust, or reassurance that it is all right to blame those who hurt her. If you choose the latter, eventually Dawn Star can be changed into a bitter version of herself who won't object to evil actions (specifically the taking of the Water Dragon's power). She does not become intrinsically evil, but she accepts that the only way to make matters right is to force them to be right.

CHAPTER ONE

You may engage in various male-only responses with suggestive flirtatious language. This is purely optional and has no effect on the romance progression.

CHAPTER TWO

Dawn Star spends most of this chapter revealing her background rather than speaking about her feelings for you, although there are male-specific responses that can induce a more flirtatious response.

Once you have claimed the Dragonfly flyer in the pirate base, secured the wind map in the Forest, and taken the Inscrutable Power Source in the ruins, Dawn Star will, at each point, ask to speak to you about personal matters. When you speak to her, there is no right or wrong in these conversations, other than telling her you are not interested in what she thinks. If you do that, the romance is over.

CHAPTER THREE

The continuation of this romance plot is now possible only if your character is male. Conversations become available after the following quests are finished:

1. Upon arrival in the Imperial City. You can use conversation skills to try to toughen Dawn Star up, suggesting that she should lash out against those who hurt her instead of turning the other cheek.

2. Acquiring Silk Fox as a henchman. Again, you can use conversation skills to try to toughen Dawn Star up, suggesting that she should lash out against those who hurt her instead of turning the other cheek. If you succeed, Dawn Star becomes a more bitter version of herself, who will tolerate the Closed Fist decisions you can later make. The conversations that follow this are exclusive to the Open Palm or Closed Fist forms of Dawn Star.

3a. Completion of one of the Lotus Assassin quests with an Open Palm Dawn Star. You may then talk and build more familiarity between you both. Do not be too harsh, or the romance will end.

3b. Completion of one of the Lotus Assassin quests with a Closed Fist Dawn Star. She demonstrates a colder side than you have previously encountered, and if you are wavering in your path to darkness, you can attempt to turn her back to the ways of the Open Palm, although this is difficult to achieve. Fail, and the romance will end.

4. Arrival at the Lotus Assassin fortress. Before you enter the Lotus Assassin fortress, any characters you are actively romancing will interject a conversation or appear from the city's entrance. If you have been following the romance interludes mentioned above, the romance continues. Dawn Star uses this opportunity to express a tentative affection for you. If you rebuff her, the romance is over. If your libido is working overtime, and you are actively romancing both Silk Fox and Dawn Star, both will speak. You can then choose which romance to continue with, and the other ends.

However, if you choose the correct conversation paths and attempt to persuade both women that a double romance is a fine idea, Silk Fox will become intrigued, while Dawn Star is confused. Both romances continue.

5. Once you are ready to leave for the Palace, and Dawn Star is Open Palm or Closed Fist oriented. This isn't necessary to further the romance, as the talk involves her concerns about Sagacious Zu's sacrifice, but you can end the romance by being too harsh (Open Palm), or complaining about her new bitter attitude (Closed Fist).

CHAPTER FOUR

Before you enter the throne room in the Palace, Dawn Star confirms her feelings for you. If you are juggling romances with Silk Fox and Dawn Star, both characters speak up. You may either choose the romance to continue with (and the other ends), or once again convince both women that a double romance is a good idea.

CHAPTER SIX

After you return from the dead and reach your party, there is a discussion about what to do next. After this is over, the character you are romancing asks to speak to you privately.

With Dawn Star's romance only, the two of you kiss and share an intimate moment. Your romance is complete!

If Silk Fox is also part of your romancing plans, she is the Follower who speaks with you, asking you to choose between them.

If you choose Silk Fox or Dawn Star, contradicting your previous behavior, Silk Fox explains that the two of them became friends while mourning you while you were dead. After Silk Fox and Dawn Star learned you would return, they agreed that if you chose either one, the other would be hurt, and this was unacceptable now that they had shared such grief. Silk Fox now leaves and both romances end.

If you again say that you cannot choose between them, Silk Fox sympathizes, and then explains that she and Dawn Star grew close when they were mourning you. Dawn Star then arrives to complete your tryst....

And neither did I.

ENDGAME

The biography for Dawn Star changes depending on a successful romance, as well as if she turned bitter or not.

ROMANCING PRINCESS SUN LIAN THE SILK FOX

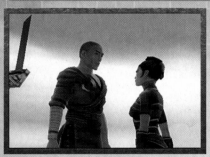

Silk Fox is a manipulator who enjoys toying with people. She doesn't open up to most people because she is sure they are only concerned with her position in the court, not her true self. You have a much more direct role in pursuing her. There are two courses to take with Silk Fox: reinforcing the Princess persona or the Silk Fox persona. If you choose the latter, eventually Silk Fox can be changed into a bitter version of herself who won't object to evil actions, specifically the taking of the Water Dragon's power. She does not become evil, but she accepts that the only way to make matters right is to force them to be right.

CHAPTER TWO

Silk Fox toys with you teasingly a little in your brief meeting. This doesn't affect your romance.

CHAPTER THREE

Although both male and female characters can attract Silk Fox, a female character must complete more dialog hurdles before Silk Fox is enamored with you. Conversations become available after the following quests are finished:

1. Silk Fox just arrived in the group, before you complete one of the Lotus Assassin missions. This is background interest and a little teasing, but a severe and gruff response will end the romance.

2. Once you begin one of the two Lotus Assassin quests, you can begin some direct flirting, which fails only if you are rude and unpleasant.

3. Once you complete one of the Lotus Assassin quests, before heading to the fortress. In this conversation, you can push her to being more selfish and less concerned about what is expected of her as a princess.

It is easier for your female character to romance her if she follows this path.

4. Arrival at the Lotus Assassin fortress. Before you enter the Lotus Assassin fortress, any characters you are actively romancing will interject a conversation or appear from the city entrance. If you have been following the romance interludes mentioned above, the romance continues. Silk Fox uses this opportunity to express a tentative affection for you. If you rebuff her, the romance is over. If you're actively romancing both Silk Fox and Dawn Star, both will speak. You can then choose which romance to continue with, and the other ends.

   However, if you choose correct conversation paths and attempt to persuade both women that a double romance is a fine idea, Silk Fox will become intrigued, while Dawn Star is confused. Both romances continue.

5. There is an aside just before you head to the Palace, but this does not affect the romance.

CHAPTER FOUR

Before you enter the throne room in the Palace, Silk Fox confirms her feelings for you. Also at this point, if you are juggling romances with Silk Fox and Dawn Star, both characters speak up. You may either choose the romance to continue with one (the other ends), or once again convince both women that a double romance is a good idea.

CHAPTER SIX

After you return from the dead and reach your party, there is a discussion about what to do next. After this is over, the character you are romancing asks to speak to you privately.

With Silk Fox's romance only, the two of you kiss and share an intimate moment. Your romance is complete!

If Dawn Star is also part of your romancing plans, Silk Fox speaks with you, asking you to choose between them.

If you choose Silk Fox or Dawn Star, contradicting your previous behavior, Silk Fox explains that the two of them became friends while mourning you while you were dead. After Silk Fox and Dawn Star learned you would return, they agreed that if you chose either one, the other would be hurt, and this was unacceptable now that they had shared such grief. Silk Fox now leaves and both romances end.

If you again say that you cannot choose between them, Silk Fox sympathizes, and then explains that she and Dawn Star grew close when they were mourning you. Dawn Star then arrives to complete your tryst....

ENDGAME

The biography for Silk Fox changes depending on a successful romance, as well as if she turned toward her Silk Fox or Princess personas, or not.

ROMANCING SKY

Sky's persona is a balance between the flippant and the serious, and much of that influences his romance. When you first meet him, Sky is set to avenge his daughter by eliminating the man responsible for her death. After the player eliminates Gao, Sky realizes that the slave trading he's determined to wipe out goes much higher than a crime lord. He allies himself with the player in the hopes of setting things right.

Sky is a romance option available mainly to female characters, but a male can start a romance with Sky if the conditions aid this type of rendezvous. A male character must have stopped both the Dawn Star and Silk Fox romances prior to the conclusion of Chapter Three. This gives Sky pause to wonder why you haven't shown any interest in the female Follower, and you can note that Sky is the reason.

CHAPTER TWO

You may flirt with Sky when you first meet him in the pirate base, and he returns the gestures to a female character. There is significantly more flirting if you are female, and this occurs when you talk about his life and how he tracked down Gao. This doesn't influence the romance at this point.

CHAPTER THREE

Although both male and female characters can attract Sky, a female character has many more conversational choices that result in flirting, while a male must complete more dialog

hurdles before Sky becomes interested in you. Conversations are available after the following quests are finished:

1. Initial arrival in the Imperial City. Sky talks about how thankful he is to be back in the Imperial City and reveals a little more about his past. He also resolves to look forward and bring closure to the terrible situation with his daughter, saying that he's done all he can.

2. Once Silk Fox is acquired. Sky talks more about his personal experiences with the Lotus Assassins and of former friends who were recruited into the order and twisted into mindless thugs. He expresses worry that the same thing might happen to you if you go through with the princess's plans.

3a. Completion of one of the Lotus Assassin quests. Sky talks about a story his father used to tell and applies it to the group's situation. The talk then turns serious and ends one of three ways: Sky tells your female character that he'll be there with her—a romantic gesture that's easy to spot. If you have a male character who's still pursuing a romance with Dawn Star or Silk Fox, Sky informs you that he's there to back you up, and you should worry less about him and more about your favored lady acquaintance. If you are male, and say you aren't interested in either Dawn Star or Silk Fox. Sky thinks about asking something, but backs away, letting you come to him, should you wish to.

3b. Completion of one of the Lotus Assassin quests. You must be a male character with no female romances. This is an additional talk that a female character never sees. Sky asks you why you've shown no interest in Dawn Star or Silk Fox, and your responses can unlock a male romance with Sky.

4. Arrival at the Lotus Assassin fortress. Before you enter the Lotus Assassin fortress, any characters you are actively romancing will interject a conversation or appear from the city entrance. If you have been following all the romance interludes mentioned above (and are either male or female), the romance continues. If not, the romance ends, and Sky requests you be safe and fight well.

5. Leaving for the Palace. Sky asks to speak to you before heading to the Palace, but only if the romance is active. Sky sounds harsher and less forgiving if you are following the Closed Fist. He's no less enamored with you, just edgier about matters than he would be otherwise. Regardless of Sky's mood, in this dialog, Sky asks you what you think will happen, and he remembers your reply.

Chapter Four

Before entering the throne room in the Palace, Sky senses an impending doom and attempts to tell you that he's fallen in love with you. He messes up this chance, but if you take the initiative and say you feel the same way, Sky remembers this later.

Chapter Six

After you return from the dead and reach your party, there is a discussion about what to do next. After this is over, the character you are romancing asks to speak to you privately. The romance concludes after a fairly straight-forward dialog. If you have followed a different alignment path since the Lotus Assassin fortress (which is rare, unless you left many side quests unfinished) you can persuade Sky to change to match your alignment.

Endgame

The biography for Sky changes depending on a successful romance, as well as if he turned toward the path of the Open Palm or the Closed Fist.

The Secrets of Sagacious Zu

This Follower has some interesting information to impart, as long as you follow the choices below:

Chapter One

It's fairly clear that Dawn Star's name causes a reaction in Zu.

Chapter Two

A conversation between Hui and Zu can occur when you first encounter Hui in Tien's Landing. A child is mentioned, but no details are provided. On the initial return to the camp area, a conversation occurs between Zu and Dawn Star, wherein he asks what she remembers about her childhood. You can try to shift focus to yourself, but Zu is only interested in Dawn Star. It is repeated that Dawn Star was named for a glow caused by the burning of Dirge, something she views as an ill omen. In the confrontation with Inquisitor Lim after all three side quests are completed, Zu is mentioned by name as a figure deserving of scrutiny. These are hints that you should speak with him.

Chapter Three

You must complete a series of conversations to advance the plot. They are generally impossible to fail unless you directly state that Zu should be quiet.

1. After defeating Inquisitor Lim, at the end of Chapter Two.

2. After defeating Inquisitor Lim. This is available once the first talk is completed. If the previous conversation occurred in Chapter Two, you must wait until Chapter Three to have this conversation.

3. After point 1, once Silk Fox joins.

If you complete the conversations *before* completing one of the Lotus Assassin quests, Zu advances the plot in the Lotus Assassin fortress later. Zu leaves the party when one of the Lotus Assassin quests is completed, so you must complete them beforehand.

Inside the Lotus Assassin fortress, Zu approaches you multiple times. As long as you do not tell him to be quiet, he continues.

At the completion of the Lotus Assassin fortress, Zu tells you his secret. What his secret is depends on how many conversations you got through.

If you didn't complete the three conversations earlier in the chapter, or told Zu to be quiet during one of his talks, Zu tells you only that he was one of the Assassins sent to kill Master Li's family.

If you completed the three talks earlier in the chapter and did not tell him to be quiet while in the fortress, Zu tells you that he was one of the assassins sent to kill Master Li's family, and that Master Li's child is still alive.

After the fortress, the other characters react to this information, generally agreeing that it is interesting but that it doesn't help them yet. They need to deal with the Emperor.

CHAPTER FIVE

During your final talk with the Water Dragon before being resurrected, you are told to exploit whatever advantage you have. The Water Dragon can sense what Sagacious Zu said about Master Li's child in your mind. You should say that you don't know how to find this child. The Water Dragon mentions Dawn Star was named for the burning of Dirge. She says Dirge is a secret place, unknown to most. The burning temple of Dirge was visible only from the Palace. Therefore, Dawn Star must have been born in the Palace, which means she is likely to be Master Li's child.

CHAPTER SIX

After your resurrection, speak with your group. The vision of the Water Dragon that led them to Dirge also revealed Dawn Star's status as Master Li's child. Comfort or quiet her as you see fit. After the Death's Hand battle, you can attempt to use the information to appeal to Master Li (to reach his honorable side), or use it against him (to weaken him so he can be attacked). Master Li first dismisses this, and then declares that it isn't important to him. If it ever was important, he would have died protecting her in the first place.

CHAPTER 7

In the final confrontation with Master Li, if Dawn Star is present, she asks whether she should speak to Master Li as a daughter.

(Open Palm) Dawn Star tries to appeal to his good side, his former honorable self.

(Closed Fist) Dawn Star, converted during your romance, tries to attack Master Li with this knowledge, hoping it makes him vulnerable.

Master Li again dismisses the significance of this, clarifying that he never really cared about his family, only the power he sought.